Bristol Rhode Island's Early Settlers

Dorothy Chapman Saunders, Ph.D.

HERITAGE BOOKS
2010

HERITAGE BOOKS
AN IMPRINT OF HERITAGE BOOKS, INC.

Books, CDs, and more—Worldwide

For our listing of thousands of titles see our website
at
www.HeritageBooks.com

Published 2010 by
HERITAGE BOOKS, INC.
Publishing Division
100 Railroad Ave. #104
Westminster, Maryland 21157

Copyright © 1992 Dorothy Chapman Saunders

All rights reserved. No part of this book may be reproduced or transmitted in any form or by any means, electronic or mechanical, including photocopying, recording or by any information storage and retrieval system without written permission from the author, except for the inclusion of brief quotations in a review.

International Standard Book Numbers
Paperbound: 978-1-55613-649-8
Clothbound: 978-0-7884-8548-0

PREFACE

The importance of primary sources in genealogical research is well known. But to make every later researcher search though public records, which have already been examined by others, is a duplication of time and effort. The author has examined the vital records of the town of Bristol, and of its two churches (Congregational and St Michael's Episcopal), and the Bristol County probate records, for each of the eighty-one settlers who attended the first town meeting of Bristol on 1 Sept. 1681, or who were the earlier original proprietors of the Mt Hope Lands which became Bristol. At the time of its organization, Bristol was in Plymouth Colony, then was in Mass., and on 22 Jan. 1746/47 it was annexed to R.I.

Many of these early Bristol settlers were the sons of original imigrants to Plymouth Colony in the Cape Cod area, or Lynn, Ipswich, and Boston in the Mass. Bay Colony. Some of these families stayed in Bristol for one or more generations before their children or grandchildren moved on to Conn. and N.Y. State. From there they expanded to the midwestern states. Present day midwestern descendants find it extremely difficult to trace their families back to New England, and often have no knowledge of their families' beginnings in R.I. The few R.I. primary sources available are not generally found in the smaller libraries of other parts of the country.

To aid such researchers, it seems worthwhile to bring together these data in this book. Each statement of birth, death, burial, marriage or parentage, where available, is followed by its primary source or other proof, given in brackets. Volumes 6 and 8 of James Arnold's Vital Records of R.I., have been searched and used. These references to the town of Bristol, Barrington or Warren, Bristol Co., are given as (6:page no) for Bristol; (Bar, 6:page no) for Barrington; and (War, 6:page no) for Warren. Primary references also include the series of wills, inventories and administrations of estates found in the R.I. Genealogical Register, and the two volumes of Bristol Co., Mass Probate Records, 1687-1762, by H.L. Peter Rounds. James Savage's four volumes, the NEHGS's Register, and C.A. Torrey's New England Marriages prior to 1700 were also examined. The dates of birth, death and marriage for each of the children of the early settlers have been included, if they continued to live in Bristol or nearby.

The town of Bristol became one of the most important ports in New England, and was the center of a major boatbuilding industry at one time.

THE EARLY SETTLERS

A. Proprietors of the Mount Hope Lands   Page
   1. Walley, John   1
   2. Burton, Stephen   2
   3. Oliver, Nathaniel   3
   4. Hayman, Capt Nathan   4
   5. Byfield, Nathaniel   6

B. The first white settler
   6. Gorham, Capt John   7

C. Settlers who signed Articles on 27 August 1680 to purchase land from the Proprietors
   7. Church, Col Benjamin   8
   8. Waldron, Dr Isaac   11
   9. Clarke, Timothy   12
   10. Ingraham, William   12
   11. Paine, Nathaniel   21
   12. Reynolds, Nathaniel   28
   13. Saunders, Christopher   37
   14. Wilkins, John   38
   15. Williams, Nathaniel   40
   16. Woodbury, Samuel   40
   17. Bosworth, Nathaniel   42
   18. Jones, Benjamin   50

D. Other settlers who were admitted as citizens at the first town meeting of Bristol, 1 Sept 1681
   19. Adams, Eliaship   51
   20. Atherton, Watching   53
   21. Baster, Joseph   53
   22. Bayley, John   54
   23. Birge, John   54
   24. Bletsoe, Thomas   55
   25. Bosworth, Benjamin   55
   26. Bosworth, Edward   56
   27. Brenton, William Jr   56
   28. Brown, William   57
   29. Burrill, James   58
   30. Burroughs, James   59
   31. Car(e)y, David   60
   32. Car(e)y, John   64
   33. Cobbett, Samuel   64
   34. Corps/Corpe, John   64
   35. Curtis, Solomon   66
   36. Curtis, Zechariah   66

		Page
37.	Daggett, Thomas Jr	66
38.	Davenport, Jonathan	67
39.	Dutch, Robert Jr	69
40.	Finney, Jeremiah	69
41.	Finney, John	74
42.	Finney, Jonathan	76
43.	Ford, Joseph	77
44.	Fry, Anthony	77
45.	Gallop/ Gallup, Samuel	79
46.	Gladding, John Jr	84
47.	Gorham, Jabez	91
48.	Hammond, Richard	95
49.	Hampton, Henry	96
50.	Hedge, William Jr	96
51.	Hoar, William	96
52.	Howland, Jabez	100
53.	Ingell/Ingalls, Benjamin	107
54.	Jacob(s), Joseph	107
55.	Landon/Langdon, Daniel	108
56.	Lewis, Thomas	109
57.	Martin, John Jr	110
58.	Mead, Nicholas	112
59.	Morey/Mowry, George	113
60.	Osborne, Jeremiah	114
61.	Papillon/Pampelion, Peter	115
62.	Penfield, Samuel	116
63.	Pope, John	117
64.	Ranger, Edmund	117
65.	Robinson, Increase	118
66.	Rogers, John Jr	119
67.	Saffin, John	120
68.	Sandy, Joseph	121
69.	Smith, John	121
70.	Smith, Richard	122
71.	Southard/Southworth, widow Elizabeth	133
72.	Taft, Robert	136
73.	Thompson, Major Robert	137
74.	Throope, William	137
75.	Thurston, John	150
76.	Waldron, George	150
77.	Walker, Thomas	162
78.	Wardwell, Uzell/Uzal	164
79.	White, Richard	170
80.	Wilson, John	170
81.	Woodbury, Hugh	170

ABBREVIATIONS

admin. administrator, administration
ae. age
aft. after
b. birth
Bar. Barrington, R.I.
bef. before
betw. between
bp. baptised
Br. Bristol, R.I.
bur. buried
ca. about
Ch. church
ch. child
co. company, county
Col. colonial, colony, Colonel
Congre. Congregational
d. died, death, day
dau. daughter
dcd, dec. deceased
desc. descent, descendant
div. division
dtd. dated
d.y. died young
est. estate
exec. executor
fam. family
fol. following
gch. grandchild
gdau. granddaughter
gen, geneal. genealogy, genealogical
gson. grandson
gt. great
hist. history, historical
ibid. the same
inv. inventory
kn. know(n)
LC. Little Compton, R.I.
m. married
Myflwr. Mayflower
mo. month
no. number
p. page
poss. possibly
prob. probate, probably
propr. proprietor
pvd. proved

Re. Rehoboth, Mass.
rec. record(ed)
rem. removed
sic. copied thus
unkn. unknown
unm. unmarried
unrec. unrecorded
vol. volume
VR. vital records
War. Warren, R.I.
wid. widow
wk. week
y, yr. year

PROPRIETOR NO 1. MAJOR JOHN WALLEY

The Hon John[2] Walley was b 1642 or 1644, prob in London, Eng, and d in Boston, Mass 11 Jan 1712, aged 68 (Sav, 4:400). His father was the Rev Thomas Walley, rector of St Mary's, White Chapel. John came to Boston bef his father, who arrived 24 May 1663 on the Society. He m, prob in Boston or Barnstable, Sarah ___, who d Br 2 Nov 1692 (6: 170). Major John was a member of the Ancient and Honorable Artillery Co in Boston in 1671, and for years was a member of the Council there and Judge of the Superior Court. His was the first signature on the Grand Deed of 27 Aug 1680 when he purchased an eighth part of the Mount Hope Lands which became Bristol (Munro, p 74, 96). In 1690 he commanded the land forces during Sir William Phip's unsuccessful expedition against Canada.

He was living in Br in 1684 when he was Representative from there to the General Court of Plymouth Col (Munro,) 384), and he had ch b Br betw 1685 and 1691 (6:110). The 1689 Census of Br listed Major Wally as living there with a wife, five children, and four servants (Geneals RI Fams, 1989, 2:402). He earned a fortune as a merchant. In his old age he developed a painful disease which caused him to return to Boston to live, and where he d. Sav (4:397-400) confused some of his ch with those of another John Walley. The will of Major John Walley named his son, John, to be exec; two unm daus, Elizabeth and Lydia, who were left L1500 each; and dau Sarah, widow of Charles Chauncey, and her four ch, Charles, Mary, Isaac and Walley.

CHILDREN:
1. ch[3], b 1677 prob Boston (Torrey, p 776); not named in father's will.
2. ch, b bef 1684 prob Boston (1689 Census of Br); not named in father's will.
3. Sarah, b 25 Aug 1684 Boston; m (1) Boston Charles CHAUNC(E)Y, b Eng, d 4 May 1711 Boston, son Rev Isaac Chauncey of London; m (2) Boston 11 Oct 1716 Francis WILLOUGHBY (Boston Mars 1700-1751, p 67), b 28 Sept 1672, son Nehemiah and Abigail (Bartholomew) Willoughby of Salem, Mass.
4. Elizabeth, b 1 Nov 1685 Br (6:110), bp 8 May 1687 Congre Ch, Br (Geneals RI Fams, 1989, 2:371); d 27 Oct 1756 (Sav, 4:54); m Boston 29 Oct 1713 Rev Joseph SEWALL (Boston Mars 1700-1751, p 47), bp 19 Aug 1688, d 27 June 1769, grad Harvard College 1707, son Samuel and Hannah (Hull) Sewall of Boston (Sav, 4:54).

5. Lydia, b 2 Sept 1688 Br (6:110); d aft father's will.
6. John, b 11 Sept 1691 Br (6:110); "perhaps d in a distant land" (Sav, 4:400) aft father's will. Sav also said that he m prob Elizabeth, dau of the second John Alden, and that she as his widow married (2) 30 Apr 1702 Simon Willard. Since John was b 1691, he cannot have been the John Walley she m (Bowman, p 8).

PROPRIETOR NO 2. STEPHEN BURTON

Stephen[1] Burton was the best educated of the Four Proprietors and was said to have attended Oxford. He signed the Grand Deed on 27 Aug 1680 to purchase an eighth part of the Mt Hope Lands which became Bristol (Munro, p 75-76, 96). His b date and place are unkn, and he d Br on 22 July 1693 (6:121). Munro (p 75-76, 384) said he was the first recording officer of the County as Clerk of the Peace, and he was a Representative of Br to the General Court in 1685, 1686, 1689, 1690 and 1692. He built a house in Br on Burton St which was burned by the British in 1778.

Stephen was a merchant in Boston, Mass where he m (1) aft 9 Feb 1673 (Myflwr Fams in Progress, Edward Winslow, p 1-4) Abigail BRENTON (Torrey, p 124) who was bur at Br 30 Mar 1684 (6:121), dau William and Martha Brenton of Boston and Newport, RI. William Brenton was Gov of RI from 1666-1668 (Sav, 1:242). Stephen m (2) 4 Sept 1684 Elizabeth WINSLOW (6:11), b 8 Apr 1664 Marshfield, and d Pembroke, Mass 11 July 1735 ae 72 (Torrey, p 124), dau Gov Josiah and Penelope (Pelham) Winslow of Marshfield. Josiah was the only surviving son of Gov Edward Winslow of the Plymouth Col, who came on the Myflwr in 1620 (Sav, 4: 598-600, 602-603). Stephen Burton d intestate and his heirs are identified by four deeds, two in Br Co and two in Middlesex Co, given in Myflwr Fams in Progress, Edward Winslow, p 3-4.

CHILDREN by first wife, Abigail, prob b Boston (Myflwr Fams in Progress, Edward Winslow, p 3):
1. Stephen[2].
2. Martha, b ca 1678 Boston; d Newport, RI 14 Apr 1750, 73 yr; m ca 1702 Edward CHURCH, a mariner, b 1680, d Br bef 19 Dec 1706, son Col Benjamin and Alice (Southworth) Church of Br and LC (LC Fams, p 167-168). Martha had two ch b Br, surname Church: Abigail, b 4 Mar 1702/03; and Benjamin, b 8 Oct 1704 (6:69). After Edward's d, Martha Church widow, lived in Newport, RI.
3. dau.

CHILDREN by second wife, Elizabeth, b Br (Myflwr Fams in

Progress, Edward Winslow, p 4):
  4. Penelope, b 8 Aug 1686; prob bur Br Mar 1687 (6:67).
  5. infant, bur Br 1687/88.
  6. Elizabeth, b aft 1687/88, living Duxbury, Mass, unm 6 Aug 1728.
  <u>7</u>. Thomas, b 19 Mar 1692/93 (6:67); d Pembroke, Mass 22 Oct 1779 ae 87.

Thomas^2 (Stephen^1) Burton was b Br 19 Mar 1692/93 and d Pembroke, Mass 22 Oct 1779 ae 87 (Myflwr Fams in Progress, Edward Winslow, p 4). He was only four mos old when his father d, and his mother prob returned to the Duxbury-Marshfield, Mass area with Elizabeth and Thomas, her two surviving ch. Thomas m Duxbury 10 May 1722 Alice WADSWORTH, b Duxbury 15 Apr 1697 and d Pembroke 9 June 1791 ae 95, dau Elisha and Elizabeth (Wiswall) Wadsworth. Alice was a desc of John Alden of the Myflwr, so all of her ch have a Myflwr line to him as well as to Edward Winslow (Ibid, p 6). Thomas was first a school teacher in Duxbury, as well as its Deputy Sheriff in 1722, but ca 1730 he rem to Pembroke, where he was a yeoman and d intestate.

CHILDREN, first three b Duxbury, fourth in Pembroke, where all were rec$_3$(Ibid, p 6):
  1. Martha^3, b 19 June 1723; d 15 Sept 1723.
  2. Penelope, b 27 Oct 1724; living 31 Mar 1788; m Pembroke 23 Oct 1751 Seth JACOB, b Bridgewater, Mass 6 Mar 1720/21, son Deacon Samuel and Susanna (Howard) Jacob. She had two ch b Pembroke, surname Jacob: Samuel and Penelope (Ibid, p 9).
  3. Eleanor, b 4 May 1728; d Pembroke 27 Oct 1751, 24 yr; m Pembroke 5 Feb 1746/47 Nathaniel BISHOP, bp Scituate, Mass 3 July 1715, son Hudson and Abigail (Keene) Bishop. She had two ch b Pembroke, surname Bishop: Nathaniel and Eliphalet (Ibid, p 9).
  4. Elizabeth, b 9 May 1737; d Pembroke 17 May 1807, 70 yrs; m Pembroke 15 May 1766 Daniel BONNEY, b Pembroke 2 July 1739, d there 13 Aug 1813, 74 yrs, son Elisha and Elizabeth (Lincoln) Bonney. She had one or two ch b Pembroke, surname Bonney: Seth? and Jonathan (Ibid, p 10).

PROPRIETOR NO 3. NATHANIEL OLIVER

Nathaniel^3 Oliver was b in Boston, Mass 8 Mar 1652, and d there 15 Apr 1704, son of Peter^2 (Thomas^1) and Sarah (Newgate) Oliver (Sav, 3:310). He m Boston 3 Jan 1677 Elizabeth BRATTLE, b Boston 30 Nov 1660 and d May 1719, dau Thomas and Elizabeth (Tyng) Brattle of Boston (Sav, 1:238-239; Torrey, p 544). Nathaniel was a wealthy merchant in Boston where he was on the Committee of Safety in 1689 after Gov Andros was overthrown, and he became a freeman in 1690. Although he signed the Articles of the Grand Deed to be a Proprietor and purchase an eighth part of the Mt Hope Lands, he never settled in Bristol, and sold his share to Capt Nathan Hayman (Munro, p 76). His interest in the town was great enough, however, for him to give a bell in 1684 to the Congre Church which had recently been formed there (Munro, p 76). He was replaced as one of the Four Proprietors by Capt Hayman bef the first town meeting was held in Br on 1 Sept 1681 (Ibid, p 79).

CHILDREN, all b Boston and none rem to Br (Sav, 3:310):
1. Elizabeth.
2. Capt Nathaniel, m Boston 30 Nov 1709 Mrs Martha HOBBS (Boston Mars 1700-1751, p 24).
3. Sarah, m Boston 11 Aug 1713 Richard JOHNSON (Ibid, p 52).
4. James, m Boston 31 Jan 1711 Rebecca LLOYD (Ibid, p 36).
5. Brattle, m Boston 11 Mar 1713/14 Anne GILLAM (Ibid, p 46).
6. Peter, m (1) Boston 8 Mar 1709/10 Jerusha MATHER (Ibid, p 24) who d 30 Dec 1710, dau Increase Mather; m (2) 1 Mar 1711/12 Hopestill WENSLEY/WINSLEY (Ibid, p 36).
7. Mary.

PROPRIETOR NO 4. CAPT NATHAN HAYMAN

Munro, p 76 said, "The name of Nathan Hayman appears in the records of the first town-meeting as one of the four proprietors." However, Munro, p 96 listed Nathaniel Byfield, John Walley, Nathaniel Oliver and Stephen Burton as the first four signers of the Articles on 27 Aug 1680, each of whom purchased an eighth part of the Mt Hope Lands which became Br. But (Ibid, p 79) he said that at the first town meeting of Br on 1 Sept 1681 the citizens were admitted by "John Walley, Nathaniel Byfield, Stephen Burton and Nathan Hayman (the four proprietors)." Capt Hayman had replaced Nathaniel Oliver as one of the Four Proprietors bef the first town meeting of Br was held.

Capt Nathan^2 Hayman prob came from England with his father, Major John^1 Hayman/Heyman, a ropemaker, who was in Boston in 1662 and became a freeman there in 1668. John$^1_2$ was called Mr and Major, and was m to Grace___. Nathan^2 lived in Charlestown, Mass and m 11 Mar 1673/74 Elizabeth ALLEN, b Boston, dau Capt John and Sarah Allen of Boston (Wyman, p 17). Nathan d Br 27 July 1689, and as his widow Elizabeth m (2) at Br 18 John 1690 Nathaniel BLA-

GROVE Esq (6:7; Torrey, p 75). Capt Hayman was a well-to-do sea captain and merchant of Boston, and at the time of his d in Br 27 July 1689, ae 38, he was still part owner of several ships. He lived in Charlestown until he rem to Br (Wyman, p 489), where he signed the Oath of Fidelity on 9 Aug 1686 (Munro, p 114). He was listed in the 1689 Census of Br with a wife, six ch, and two servants (Geneals RI Fams, 1989, 2:402). The inv of the est of Capt Nathan Hayman dcd, was taken 3 Feb 1689 by Jno Saffin and John Walley, It included among other things two house lots by Glading's, three lots by John Smith's, 2/3 of the Briganteen John and Mary, 1/6 of the Ketch Betty, ½ of the Pink Kathirine, 1/16 of another Pink, and 1/16 of the Ship Michael (Myflwr Source Recs, p 66). He was called marriner when the receipts of his est were signed and dtd 25 May 1696 by: Nathan Hayman Jr, mariner, for a double portion; Thomas Church for his wife, Sarah, dau of Nathan Hayman; John Hayman; William Brattle for the share of his wife (unnamed), dau of Nathan Hayman; Mary Hayman, dau; and Grace Hayman, dau (RIGR, 2:171).

CHILDREN (Sav, 2:388; 6:81):
1. Nathan Jr^3, b Charlestown 25 Jan 1675, bp 23 Apr 1675; m bef 1709 Priscilla WALDRON who was poss b 12 July 1681, dau Dr Isaac and Priscilla (Byfield) Waldron of Boston. Dr Isaac Waldron was made a citizen of Br at its first town meeting on 1 Sept 1681, but d in 1683 bef settling there (Munro, p 79, 96). There are no b's, m's, or d's for Nathan and Priscilla Hayman in the VR Br. Nathan Hayman, son of Nathan, mariner of Br, dtd his will 7 Jan 1709, pvd 13 July 1711, and named his wife, Priscilla, saying he was "being in good health...being called to hazard my frail life upon the Great waters" (RIGR, 2:17; Rounds, 1:52). Apparently he had no issue.
2. Elizabeth, b Charlestown 21 Feb 1677, bp 25 Feb 1677; d 28 July 1715; m 3 Nov 1697 Rev William BRATTLE of Cambridge, Mass, b Boston 22 Nov 1662, d Cambridge 15 Feb 1717, son Thomas and Elizabeth (Tyng) Brattle of Boston (Sav, 2:388). Rev William Brattle was graduated from Harvard College in 1680 and ordained 25 Nov 1696. Sav (1:239) said he was "a learned man and most valuable minister". Elizabeth had one ch, surname Brattle, b Cambridge: William Jr, who graduated from Harvard in 1722, m Boston 23 Nov 1727 Katherine SALTONSTALL (Boston Mars 1700-1751, p 136), and became a Brigadier.
3. Sarah, b Charlestown 22 Aug 1679, bp 15 May 1680; d bef 16 Apr 1712; m Br 21 Feb 1698 as his first wife, Thomas CHURCH (6:26), b 1673 Duxbury, Mass, d Little Compton, RI 12 Mar 1746, 73 yr, son Col Benjamin and Alice (Southworth) Church of Br and LC (6:69). She had four ch, surname Church, b Br (6:69): Sarah, b 15 Jan

1700/01, d 29 Aug 1701; Elizabeth, b 9 Sept 1702, d 27 Sept 1702; Thomas, b 20 Aug 1704, d LC 21 Aug 1718, 14 yr; and Alice, b 11 July 1696 (sic, prob 1706), d Br 10 July 1775, m Capt Paul UNIS of Newport, RI. All of Thomas Church's ch have a Myflwr desc.

4. Mary, bp Charlestown 18 June 1682; m Hull, Mass 25 May 1709 Rev Israel LORING of Sudbury, Mass (Wyman, p 489), b 15 Apr 1682 at Hull, d 9 Mar 1772, son John and Mary (Baker) Loring of Hull. Rev Israel graduated from Harvard College in 1701 and for 66 yrs was minister of the Church at Sudbury (Sav, 3:118). Mary had seven ch, surname Loring, b Sudbury (Ibid, p 118): John, b 27 Apr 1710; Elizabeth, b 16 Nov 1712; Mary, b 14 Sept 1716; Jonathan, b 29 Aug 1719; Nathan, b 27 Nov 1721; Susan, b 10 Nov 1724, twin; and Sarah, b 10 Nov 1724, twin.

5. Grace, b Br 31 Jan 1684/85, bp Charlestown 19 Apr 1695; m Richard OTIS of Charlestown, son Richard Otis of Dover. Grace d bef his second m 2 Nov 1714 at Watertown, Mass to Grace Smith. No issue (Wyman, p 489, 718).

6. John, b Br 22 Dec 1687; d betw 1709 and 1720, unm. The will of John Hayman of Br, brazier, was dtd 5 Jan 1709 and pvd 23 May 1720. He named his father-in-law (step-father) Nathaniel Balgrove (sic Blagrove) and unnamed brothers and sisters (RIGR, 3:89).

PROPRIETOR NO 5. HON NATHANIEL BYFIELD

The Hon Nathaniel Byfield was b 1653 in Long Ditton, co Surrey, England, son of Rev Richard Byfield, and he was the only person of this surname to be listed in early New England (Sav, 1:325-326). He d in Boston, Mass 6 June 1733 in his 80th yr (Torrey, p 129). He was in Boston by 1674 and m (1) Deborah CLARK, bp 9 June 1644 (Sav, 1:401), d 1717, dau Capt Thomas Clark, a merchant of Boston. He m (2) Boston 18 Apr 1718 Sarah LEVERETT (Boston Mars 1700-1751, p 74), bp 22 June 1673, d 21 Dec 1730, dau Gov John Leverett of Boston (Sav, 3:83). He had no issue by his second m. Nathaniel was a member of the Ancient and Honorable Artillery Co in Boston 1679. He signed the Articles on 27 Aug 1680 to purchase an eighth part of the Mt Hope Lands (Munro, p 96), and built one of the earliest houses in Br, on Byfield St. Soon he acquired almost all of the land on the penninsula of Poppasquash where he then built his homestead, and lived. The Byfield St house was then rented by the town for public use, and its first minister, the Rev Benjamin Woodbridge, lived in part of it.

Nathaniel was a Representative from Br in 1689 to the General Court of Plymouth Col, and again in 1693 (when he was Speaker), and 1694 in the General Court of Mass (Munro, p 384). He was also Judge of Probate, and of Common Pleas for the new Br Co, and later was a Judge in Suffolk Co, Mass, after he returned to Boston to live (Sav, 1:326). There are no b, bur, d or m recs for any Byfields in the VR Br. But 8:243 under the members of the Congre Ch of Br are given: Nathaniel Byfield received 3 May 1687 and rem 6 June 1733; and Deborah (wife) of Nathaniel, received 12 June 1695 and rem 1717. The 1689 Census of Br listed him as "Cap Nathl Byfield", living there with a wife, two ch, and ten servants (Geneals RI Fams, 1989, 2:402).

CHILDREN by first wife, Deborah, order unkn, prob b Boston (Sav, 1:325):
1. Nathaniel^2.
2, 3 and 4. ch who d.y.
5. Deborah, d 1708; m Boston 22 Oct 1696 Edward LYDE Jr, b betw 1661 and 1663, son Edward and Mary (Wheelwright) Lyde of Boston (Sav, 3:133; Torrey, p 480). She had one ch, b Boston, surname Lyde: Byfield, who graduated from Harvard College in 1722 (Sav, 3:133).

6. CAPT JOHN GORHAM

The General Court of Plymouth Col in 1669 granted to Capt John Gorham 100 acres of land (which were in the limits of what became Br), if it could be purchased from the Indians. It was north of the "Neck Burying-Ground" on the west side of the main road (Munro, p 77). He built a simple type of dwelling on this land, thereby becoming the first white settler in Br, although he did not stay there long.

Capt John^2 Gorham was bp 28 Jan 1621 in Benefield, Northamptonshire, England, and was bur 5 Feb 1675/76 in Swansea, Mass, son of Ralph^1 and Margaret (Stephenson) Gorham (Torrey, p 313). He came with his father to Duxbury, Mass bef 1637, and m 1643 Plymouth Desire HOWLAND, b Plymouth ca 1623 and d Barnstable, Mass 13 Oct 1683, dau John and Elizabeth (Tilley) Howland of the Myflwr (Geneals Myflwr Fams, 2:90-91; Torrey, p 313). John "of Barnstable" was Capt of the Second Co of the Plymouth Reg't in the Narraganset Campaign in King Philip's War. He rem from Plymouth to Marshfield, then to Yarmouth, and later to Barnstable. He d of fever at Swansea while still on service in the war (Bodge, p 183).

CHILDREN (Geneals Myflwr Fams, 2:91; Sav, 2:281):
1. Desire^3, b 2 Apr 1644 Plymouth; d 1700; m 7 Oct 1661 John HAWES of Yarmouth, b 1640, d 1701, son Edmund

Hawes (Sav, 2:380; Torrey, p 354).
2. Temperance, b 5 May 1646 Marshfield; d 1715; m (1) Edward STURGIS Jr who d 1678 Yarmouth, son Edward Sturgis Sr; m (2) 27 Jan 1679 Thomas BAXTER of Yarmouth (Torrey, p 54, 720).
3. Elizabeth, b 2 Apr 1648 Marshfield; m 1666 Joseph HALLETT of Sandwich (Torrey, p 337).
4. James, b 28 Apr 1650 Marshfield; d 1707; m 24 Feb 1673/74 Hannah HUCKINS (Torrey, p 313), bp 16 Oct 1653, dau Thomas and Rose Huckins of Barnstable (Sav, 2:487).
5. John, b 20 Feb 1651/52 Marshfield; d 1716; m 20 or 24 Feb 1674 Mary OTIS, b 1653 and d 1738 (Torrey, p 313), or b 14 Mar 1654 (Sav, 3:323), dau John Otis of Hingham.
6. Joseph, b 16 Feb 1653/54 Yarmouth; d 1726; m by 1678/79 Sarah STURGIS, poss b 1656 and d 1739, dau Edward Sturgis Sr of Yarmouth (Torrey, p 313, 720).
7. Jabez, b 3 Aug 1656 Barnstable; d Br betw 16 Mar and 18 May 1725; m Hannah (STURGIS) GRAY, b 1654? and d 1736, dau Edward Sturgis Sr and widow John Gray (Torrey, p 320). Rem to Br, RI. See No 47, this book.
8. Mercy, b 20 Jan 1658 Barnstable; d 24 Sept 1725, 67 yr; m ca 1677 George DENISON of Stonington, Conn, b 1653, d 27 Dec 1711, 59 yr, son Capt George and Ann (Borodell) Denison. Lived Westerly, RI. Mercy had eight ch, prob b Westerly, surname Denison (Wheeler, p 338, 340; Torrey, p 215).
9. Lydia, b 16 Nov 1661 Barnstable; d 1744; m as his second wife 1 Jan 1683/84 Capt John THACHER of Yarmouth, b 1639 and d 1713 (Torrey, p 733), son Anthony Thacher (Sav, 4:271).
10. Hannah, b 28 Nov 1663 Barnstable; m by 3 Aug 1683 Joseph WHEELDING of Yarmouth. Rem to Cape May, NJ (Torrey, p 802).
11. Shubael, b 21 Oct 1667 Barnstable; d bef 7 Aug 1750; m 1696 Puella HUSSEY, b 10 Oct 1677, d bef 23 Oct 1748, dau Stephen and Martha (Bunker) Hussey of Nantucket (Sav, 2:508; Torrey, p 313). Torrey called her Priscilla Hussey.

7. COL BENJAMIN CHURCH

Col Benjamin^2 Church was b ca 1639 in Plymouth, Mass and d 17 Jan 1717/18, 78th yr, in Little Compton, RI, son of Richard and Elizabeth (Warren) Church. Elizabeth was dau of Richard Warren of the Myflwr, so all of Benjamin Church's descs have a Myflwr line (LC Fams, p 166-168; Myflwr Fams in Progress, Richard Warren, p 17-18). He m, prob at Duxbury, Mass 26 Dec 1667 Alice SOUTHWORTH, b Duxbury ca 1646, d LC 5 Mar 1718/19, dau

Constant and Elizabeth (Collier) Southworth.

Benjamin settled first at LC in 1675, and became Capt of Plymouth Col's Army in King Philip's War. After the war he rem to Br where he was listed in the 11 Feb 1688/89 Census as living with a wife, six ch, and three servants (Geneals RI Fams, 1989, 2:402). In 1689 he was Commander-in-Chief of the several expeditions against the Indians in the "East". In 1696 he rem to Freetown, Mass, and in 1704 to LC where he d. An agreement for the div of his est was signed 6 Mar 1718 betw the widow, Alice, and her ch, namely: Thomas Church Esq of LC, Capt Constant Church of Freetown, Charles Church Esq of Br, Martha Church of RI widow of Edward Church dec, and John Sampson and Eliza his wife of Br (RIGR, 3:88-89).

CHILDREN (Myflwr Fams in Progress, Richard Warren, p 18):
1. Thomas^3, b 1673 Duxbury, d LC 12 Mar 1746, 73rd yr; m (1) Br 21 Feb 1698 Susan HAYMAN (6:13), b Charlestown, Mass 22 Aug 1679, d bef 16 Apr 1712, dau Nathaniel and Elizabeth (Allen) Hayman; m (2) LC 16 Apr 1712 Edith WOODMAN, b LC 7 Sept 1685, d LC 3 June 1718, 33rd yr, dau John and Hannah (Timberlake) Woodman; m (3) Hingham, Mass 10 Oct 1719 Sarah HORSEWELL (or m 10 Aug 1719 per VR Hingham, 1:180), b Hingham 11 Aug 1694, d LC 22 Apr 1768, 74 yr, dau Francis and Mary Horsewell. Thomas was a mariner. His will, he of LC, dtd 20 Feb 1745/46 and pvd 14 Apr 1746, named wife Sarah; sons Thomas and Benjamin Church; daus Alice Unis (wife of Paul), Elizabeth Lindsey (wife of Benjamin), Hannah Carey, Sarah Bailey, Mary and Mercy Church; and father Benjamin Church. He had four ch by his first m: Sarah, Elizabeth, Thomas and Alice; four ch by his second m: Elizabeth II, Hannah, Priscilla and Edith; and eight ch by his third m: Thomas II, Sarah II, Thomas III, Benjamin, Mary, Thomas IV, Benjamin II, and Mercy (LC Fams, p 174).
2. Capt Constant, b Portsmouth, RI 12 May 1676; d Freetown, Mass 9 Mar 1726/27 ae 49. He m Patience COOK who d Newport, RI 17 Jan 1764, dau John and Mary (Havens) Cook. Constant served in expeditions against the French and Indians, and he was the Coroner of Bristol Co in 1718. He had six ch, b Freetown: Edward, Benjamin, Mary, Martha, Constant and Nathaniel (Myflwr Fams, Richard Warren, p 73).
3. Capt Edward, b LC 1680; d Br bef 19 Dec 1706; m ca 1702 Martha BURTON, b Boston ca 1678, d Newport, RI 14 Apr 1750, 73 yr, dau Stephen and Abigail (Brenton) Burton. Edward was a mariner, and was a Capt when he served with his father against the French and Indians. After he d, Martha lived in Newport. He had two ch, b Br (6:69): Abigail, b 4 Mar 1702/03 who m George WANTON (Bowman, p

257); and Benjamin, b 8 Oct 1704 who m (1) (int) "of Newport" 26 Oct 1727 Elizabeth VIALL of Br (6:13), and m (2) Boston 6 Mar 1731 Madam Hannah DYER (Bowman, p 297; Boston Mars 1700-1751, p 170). He graduated from Harvard in 1727.
4. Col Charles, b Br 9 May 1692; d Br as Col Charles 31 Dec 1746, ae 64 (6:123); m by Rev John Sparhawk 20 May 1703 (6:13) or 20 May 1708 (6:41) Hannah PAINE, b Br 20 Apr 1685 (Myflwr Fams, Richard Warren, p 75; 6:96), d Br 16 Oct 1755 (6:123), dau Nathaniel and Dorothy (Rainsford) Paine of Br (6:96; Torrey, p 552). He prob m no earlier than 1708 as he was only 16 yrs old then. The will of Charles Church of Br, dtd 29 Nov 1746 and pvd 24 Feb 1747, named wife Hannah; dau-in-law Mary Church, widow of eldest son Constant, and her son, Peter; gson Charles, eldest son of Constant; gch Peter and Mary Church, ch of Constant; Hannah dau of Nathaniel; Charles Davis son of dau Hannah; dau Elizabeth wife of Major Thomas Greene; dau Hannah wife of Capt Simon Davis; dau Dorothy wife of Samuel Chandler Esq; dau Sarah James; dau Mary wife of John Chandler (Myflwr Fams, Richard Warren, p 75; RIGR, 3:134). The will of Hannah Church of Br, widow, dtd 28 May 1755 and pvd 10 Nov 1755, named brother-in-law Joseph Russell and son-in-law John Chandler Jr, execs; gson Charles Church; gch Peter and Mary Church; the ch of dau Elizabeth Greene, viz: Thomas, Nathaniel, Benjamin, Hannah and Mary; ch (unnamed) of Hannah Davis; daus Dorothy wife of Samuel Chandler of Woodstock, Sarah wife of Leonard James of Boston, and Mary wife of John Chandler Jr of Worcester; gdaus Ann Church, Hannah Davis, and Hannah Church dau of Nathaniel dec; mother Dorothy Paine (RIGR, 5:92-93; Myflwr Fams, Richard Warren, p 75).
Col Charles had seven ch, prob all b Br (6:69; Myflwr Fams, Richard Warren, p 75): 1. Capt Constant[4], b 12 Dec 1708, d 8 May 1740, 32 yr (6:123), m 25 Jan 1732 Mary REYNOLDS (6:14), bp 7 Jan 1710 Congre Ch Br, d 16 Apr 1722, dau Capt Peter and Mary (Giles/Gills) Reynolds of Br (Geneals RI Fams, 1989, 2:378); 2. Elizabeth, b 24 Dec 1710, d Woodstock 22 Apr 1774, 64 yr (6:137), m Br 9 Apr 1732 Major Thomas Greene of Newport, RI (6:14, 25); 3. Hannah/Anne, b 20 Feb 1712/13, m Br 30 Apr 1732 Capt Simeon DAVIS Jr of Br (6:13, 17); 4. Dorothy, b unrec, m (int) 11 Sept 1741 Samuel CHANDLER of Woodstock (6:14); 5. Nathaniel, b ca 1717 per d rec, d 26 Aug 1744, 27 yr (6:-123), m 21 May 1740 Ruth BOSWORTH (6:14) who m (2) 19 Apr 1747 Shearjashub BOURNE Sr of Br; 6. Sarah, b unrec, m 27 Aug 1741 Leonard JAMES of Boston (per her parents' wills), but 6:14, 29 call him Leonard JARVIS; and 7. Mary, b unrec, m 12 June 1746 John CHANDLER Jr of Worcester (6:14).
5. Elizabeth, b LC 26 Mar 1684; d Br 17 July 1757, ae 74; m (1) ca 1700 Joseph ROSBOTHAM who d bef 11 Sept 1717; m (2) Br 11 Sept 1717 John SAMPSON (Torrey, p 637

said James Sampson), mariner, who d Br 12 Jan 1734/35 (Myflwr Fams, Richard Warren, p 75-76); m (3) Br 18 June 1739 as his second wife Capt Samuel WOODBURY, b Br 30 Aug 1683 and d there 24 Mar 1757, son Benjamin and Mary Woodbury (Bowman, p 297). Elizabeth had four ch b Br, surname Rosbotham: Benjamin, Alice, Elizabeth and Hannah; and three ch, surname Sampson: John and Mary, twins, b Br, and John, b New Haven, Conn.
6. Nathaniel, b Br 1 July 1686; d 29 Feb 1687.

8. DR ISAAC WALDRON

Although Dr Isaac Waldron of Boston, Mass signed with the Proprietors for a sixteenth part of the Mt Hope Lands, he d in 1683 bef the time had expired within which he was to settle in Br with his family (Munro, p 96). He was present as a citizen at the first town meeting on 1 Sept 1681, as was his brother, George (Ibid, p 79). He m Priscilla BYFIELD of York, Me and Boston (Torrey, p 772), who m (2) Ebenezer BRENTON.

CHILDREN, b Boston (Appleton):
1. Isaac, b 23 June 1677 (p 143).
2. Priscilla, b 6 Dec 1678 (p 147).
3. Priscilla II, b 23 June 1680 (p 153).
4. Priscilla III, b 12 July 1681 (p 156).

Sav (4:389) listed Waldron (Walderne, Walrond, etc), Alexander, in Dover, NH 1664 who d without any family at Newcastle 7 June 1676, naming five brothers and one sister to have his property: Isaac, William, George, Samuel, Edward and Mary. Isaac, brother of this Alexander, was a physician in York, Me in 1670, rem to Boston in 1676, and was the purchaser of the Mt Hope Lands. George, the brother of Alexander, was in Dover, NH in 1661 and also rem to Boston (Sav, 4:389). Poss the William, brother of Alexander, was in Dover, NH in 1664 and was a gunsmith in Boston in 1672 (Sav, 4:391).

Torrey (p 772) gave the fol m's: Waldron, George, m Rachel BAKER, ch b 1676, of Boston and Br, RI; Waldron, Issac, d 1683, m Priscilla BYFIELD of York, Me and Boston; Waldron, Samuel, d 1728, m Hannah BRIGGS 17 Apr 1693, of Taunton. The will of Samuel Waldron of Dighton, Mass, yeoman, dtd 8 Aug 1727 and pvd 19 Aug 1729, named wife Hannah; sons Abraham (eldest), Samuel (2nd), and Benjamin (3rd) Waldron; daus Mary Waldron (oldest) and Abigail Waldron (2nd); and brother George Waldron of Br (Rounds, 1: 174-175). It is poss that the parents of the brothers George, Isaac and Samuel were George Walderne, b 1603 and d aft 1680 who m Bridget Rice at Alcester, Eng 21 May 1635, and came to Dover, NH (?) (Torrey, p 772).

9. TIMOTHY CLARK(E)

Capt Timothy^2 Clarke was b in Cambridge, Mass in 1657 and d 13 or 15 June 1737, ae 80 (Torrey, p 159; Sav, 1: 403; Paige, p 511), son of Elder Jonas and his second wife, Elizabeth (Clark) Clarke of Charlestown, Mass (Paige, p 511; Sav, 1:397). Capt Timothy m Sarah SPRAGUE, "sister of Richard Sprague" in Charlestown bef the b of their first ch on 11 Sept 1679. Richard Sprague of Charlestown, and therefore his sister, Sarah, were said to be ch of Ralph and Joan (Corbin) Sprague, prob of Upway in Devonshire, Eng, who came to Charlestown in 1629 "in the fleet with Higginson" (Sav, 4:154-155). However, with these dates, Sarah may have been a gdau of Ralph's, instead of his dau.

Capt Timothy's father, Jonas^1 Clarke, was in Cambridge by 1642 and was the Ruling Elder of the Cambridge Ch, and a noted navigator. Timothy was a sea captain, and he signed with the Proprietors on 27 Aug 1680 for a thirty-second part of the Mt Hope Lands. The 1689 Census of Br listed him there as head of a household of a wife, five ch, and two servants (Geneals RI Fams, 1989, 2:402). He then returned to Boston and Sav said that he became an important man there, being constable in 1693, a Representative in 1700, and a selectman for some years. Capt Timothy had one ch b in Br, Samuel, b 19 Apr 1688 (6:70).

KNOWN CHILDREN:
1. ch^3, b 11 Sept 1679 (Torrey, p 159).
2. ch, b betw 1680-1686. Br Census of 1689 says he had five ch.
3. Katharine, b 6 Apr 1687 Boston, twin (Appleton, p 173).
4. Sarah, b 6 Apr 1687 Boston, twin; prob d.y. (Ibid).
5. Samuel, b 19 Apr 1688 Br (6:70).
6. Jonas, b 8 Sept 1690 Boston (Appleton, p 189).
7. Sarah II, b 18 Oct 1691 Boston (Ibid, p 195).
8. Margaret, b 4 Apr 1697 Boston (Ibid, p 232).

10. WILLIAM INGRAHAM SR

William^2 Ingraham Sr signed with the Proprietors on 27 Aug 1680 for a thirty-second part of the Mt Hope Lands. The deed to this land was ratified and confirmed on 29 Sept 1680 by the General Court of New Plymouth, and at this time William Ingraham of Swansey, cooper, acted as the attorney for the settlers of Br (Munro, p 77-78). At the first town meeting on 1 Sept 1681, William was admitted as one of the citizens of Br. He m (1) at Boston 14 May 1656 Mary BARSTOW (TAG, 22:60), b Dedham, Mass 28 Dec 1641, dau William and Ann (Hubbard) Barstow (Sav, 1:129), and d 1708 (Torrey, p 411); m (2) Esther ___. William was son of Richard[1] Ingraham who was of Rehoboth and Northampton, Mass (Torrey, p 410). Although William bought land in Br while living in Swansea, he never lived on it himself, but rem to Groton, Conn. His will, dtd 1 May 1721 and pvd 15 July 1721 at Stonington, Conn, called him of Groton, and left land in Br to his son Timothy, and cooper's tools to two gsons, William and Jarrett, ch of son William Jr. Jacobus (TAG, 21:190-191) said that Richard[1] left land in Rehoboth to his two sons, William (Sr) and Jarrett, and that William Sr's son, Timothy[3], was the ancestor of the Br branch of the family. The VR Br show that both William Sr's sons, William Jr and Timothy, were in Br by 1690/91 and had ch b there. However, Timothy remained in Br, and William Jr rem elsewhere.

CHILDREN, first three, and poss all, b Boston (TAG, 21: 190-191; 22-60; Sav, 2:523):
1. William[3], b 9 Feb 1657. d. soon.
2. William Jr, b 27 Jan 1658/59; d Stonington, Conn 16 June 1708, ca 50 yr; m by 1689 Elizabeth CHESEBROUGH (Torrey, p 411).
3. Timothy, b unrec; d Br 22 Nov 1743; m by 1690 Sarah COWELL (Torrey, p 410).
4. Jeremiah, b 20 Jan 1664.
5. Mary, b 26 June 1666.
6. Elizabeth, b 1 Feb 1669.

William[3] Jr (William[2], Richard[1]) Ingraham was b Boston 27 Jan 1658/59 and d Stonington, Conn 16 June 1708, ca 50 yr (g.s.) (TAG, 22:60-61). He m by 1689 Elizabeth CHEESBROUGH (Torrey, p 411), who was b Stonington 6 Aug 1669, dau Samuel and Abigail (Ingraham) Cheesebrough of Stonington (Wheeler, p 292). William and Elizabeth had five ch b Br but aft the b of the last one in 1698 there are no other recs of them in Br, and they prob then rem to Conn. Their ch, b Br, were (6:83): William, b 17 Feb 1690; Mary, b 8 Dec 1692; Jeremiah, b 11 Feb 1694/95; Samuel, b 11 Apr 1697, d 25 May 1697; and Hezekiah, b 3 Oct 1698.

Timothy[3] (William[2], Richard[1]) Ingraham was b Boston, prob betw 1660 and 1662, and d in Br 22 Nov 1743 (6:140; 8:253). He m by 1690 Sarah COWELL, b 1660-69 poss in Boston (Torrey, p 410) and bur St Michael's Ch, Br, 2 Jan 1742/43 (8:228). Timothy was listed in the 1689 Census of Br with a wife and no ch, but his brother, William Jr, was not there as yet. Timothy was the only Ingraham on the list of tax payers of the town of Br on 20 Sept 1695, and he paid eight shillings (Geneals RI Fams, 1989, 2: 398, 401). Timothy and Sarah both joined the Congre Ch in

Br on 6 July 1696 (8:252).

CHILDREN, all₄b Br (6:83-84):
1. Timothy⁴ Jr, b 7 Jan 1691; poss the Timothy bur St Michael's 30 June 1748 (8:228) unless the latter was Timothy, son of Capt John⁴. No m rec Br, but under Ingraham b's is an entry which must refer to Timothy⁴ Jr: "Timothy, son of Margaret Maxfield and Timothy Ingraham, b Feb 1, 1712". Margaret was b Br 2 Apr 1695, dau Samuel and Christian Maxfield (6:90).
2. Sarah, b 23 Sept 1695.
3. Jeremiah, b 18 Jan 1697; m Br by Job Almy, JP, 10 July 1718 Mercy MUNRO (6:28, 37) who d 30 May 1743 (6:-140). Their only ch in the VR Br is the d of "Jer, child of, Sept 1732" (6:140). He was made the guardian of Mary Archer, minor over 14, dau John Archer of Br, on 23 Mar 1724/25 (Rounds, 1:116). It was prob Jeremiah's widow, Mercy, who was called "non Compus Mentis" when Joshua Bailey of Br, cooper, was made her guardian on 19 Sept 1738 (Rounds, 1:273).
4. Edward, b 2 Nov 1699 (6:83), bp Congre Ch, Br 25 Feb 1699/1700 (Geneals RI Fams, 1989, 2:374); d Sept 1745 at Cape Breton, Canada (6:140). He m (int) 1721 "Silence" MASON (6:29), although all of the bps of his ch at St Michael's Ch from 1726 to 1739 call them "of Edward and Salome". It is poss that aft Edward's d his widow with their ch left Br, as there are no further recs of this family in the VR Br. He had the fol ch, all bp St Michael's (8:160-161): Sarah, bp 10 May 1724; William, bp 13 Sept 1724 and bur St Michael's 20 July 1736 (8:228); Elizabeth, bp 31 July 1726; Eliza, bp 2 Mar 1727/28 and bur St Michael's 25 Nov 1726 (8:228); Mary, bp 18 July 1730, bur St Michael's 13 Jan 1734/35 (8:228); Nathaniel, bp 2 Apr 1732; Salome, bp 7 Apr 1734; Mary, bp 9 Feb 1736/37; and William II, bp 9 Aug 1739. The "Eliza" bur 25 Nov 1726 was prob Elizabeth, bp 31 July 1726, and an Eliza was bp 2 Mar 1727/28.
5. Capt John, b 8 Dec 1701; d 17 Feb 1786, 85 yr (6:-141; 8:375); m by Rev Nathaniel Cotton 12 Dec 1723 Mary FRY (6:22), b Br 24 July 1700, dau John and Deliverance Fry of Br (6:77).
6. Capt Joshua, b 12 Feb 1704/05 (6:84), bp Congre Ch 31 Mar 1706 (Geneals RI Fams, 1989, 2:376); d 1 Mar 1793, 89 yr (6:141; 8:375); m (1) 23 Oct 1729 Martha LAWTON (6:29), b 12 Sept 1712, d 24 Oct 1762 (6:140), bur St Michael's 26 Oct 1762 (8:228), dau Thomas and Margaret Lawton (6:86); m (2) St Michael's 23 Jan 1763 Mary RICHMOND (8:208).
7. Isaac, b 17 May 1706; m St Michael's 9 Nov 1725 (8:208) Eliza(beth) LINDSEY (6:29), b 19 Dec 1705, dau John and Elizabeth (Munro) Lindsey (6:87). He prob rem from Br aft Feb 1733/34 as there are no d recs for his

family. His ch were bp at St Michael's, all of "Isaac and Eliza" (8:161): Jeremiah, bp 19 Mar 1726/27; Elizabeth, bp 6 July 1729; Isaac, bp 25 June 1731; Lydia, bp 18 Feb 1732/33; and Samuel, bp 10 Feb 1733/34. A ch of Isaac's d 3 Mar 1733 (6:140).

Capt John[4] (Timothy[3], William[2], Richard[1]) Ingraham was b Br 8 Dec 1701 (6:83-84) and d there 17 Feb 1786, 85 yr (6:141; 8:375). He m Br by Rev Nathaniel Cotton 12 Dec 1723 Mary FRY (6:22), b 24 July 1700, dau John and Deliverance Fry of Br (6:77). He was made a freeman of RI from Br in 1751 (MacGunnigle, p 29). The 1774 Census of Br gave him as head of a household of 1 male above 16 and 1 female above 16 (Bartlett, p 180).

CHILDREN, b Br (6:84):
1. Timothy[5], b 20 Dec 1724; poss the Timothy bur St Michael's 30 June 1748 (8:228), unless the latter was Timothy[4], son of Timothy[3]. A Timothy was made freeman of RI from Br in 1747 and took the Oath of Bribery and Corruption at the town meeting of Br, held 10 Feb 1746/47 (Munro, p 161).
2. Mary, b 12 May 1726; m St Michael's 13 May 1742 James GIBBS (8:205, 208). She had five ch, bp St Michael's, surname Gibbs (8:157): James, bp 6 Mar 1742/43; Mary, bp 17 Feb 1744/45; Thomas, bp 6 Apr 1747; Nathaniel, bp 26 Mar 1749; and Ann, bp 9 June 1751.
3. John Jr, b 25 Jan 1727/28; d 3 Aug 1799, 72 yr (6:141; 8:375); m Br as John Jr by Rev John Burt 24 June 1750 Mary GLADDING, prob b 23 Aug 1732, d 19 Mar 1810, 78 yr (6:141; 8:375), dau John and Martha Gladding of Br.
4. Abigail, b 12 Jan 1729/30.
5. Capt Jeremiah, b 8 Dec 1731 (6:84); d 30 Sept 1807, 75 yr (6:141; 8:375); m (1) St Michael's 15 Sept 1754 Rebecca MUNRO (8:208), prob b 30 Apr 1736, d aft 19 Aug 1768; m (2) Abigail(DEWOLF) HOWE, b 11 Nov 1750, bur St Michael's 24 Feb 1833.
6. Rachel, b 24 Dec 1733; m St Michael's 30 Sept 1753 Daniel THORNTON (8:208). No issue in VR Br.
7. Thomas, b 17 Jan 1736/37.
8. Joseph, b 11 May 1738.
9. Samuel, b 17 Mar 1740.
10. Martha, b 14 Sept 1742; d 28 Mar 1824, 83 yr, widow (6:164); m John SPRINGER who d 27 May 1813, 85 or 86 yr (6:164). She had one ch rec in VR Br, surname Springer, she and John then being called of Newport (6:104): Joseph, b 24 Oct 1779 who m by Rev Alexander V. Griswold 10 July 1808 Mary VICKERY, dau Joseph and Susannah Vickery of Newport, he "son of John and Mary (sic) of Br" (6:51).

John[5] Jr (Capt John[4], Timothy[3], William[2], Richard[1]) Ingraham was b in Br 25 Jan 1727/28 and d there 3 Aug 1799, 72 yr (6:141; 8:375). He m, as John Jr, Br by Rev John Burt 24 June 1750 "Mrs" Mary GLADDING (6:29), prob b 23 Aug 1732 and d 19 Mar 1810, 78 yr (6:141), dau John and Martha Gladding of Br. John Jr was a Private from RI in the Rev War (Pat Index, p 361). The 1774 Census of Br showed him as head of a household of eleven persons: three males above 16, five males under 16, one female above 16, and two females under 16 (Bartlett, p 180).

CHILDREN, bp Congre Ch, Br (6:84; Geneals RI Fams, 1989, 2:388-396):
1. Jeremiah[6], "2d", b 4 June 1751, bp 8 July 1753; d 28 Aug 1811, 60 yr (6:84, 141; 8:375); m Priscilla ___, who d 20 or 22 Apr 1834, 85 yr, wid of Jeremiah (6:141). He had the fol ch, b Br (6:84): Lydia, b Dec 1778; Benjamin, b 20 Mar 1782 who d Africa Nov 1810 (8:375), and m 4 July 1803 Lois SANFORD, dau George and Elizabeth Sanford (8:338); Priscilla, b 14 Jan 1784 and m 2 Oct 1803 William DARLING (8:338); Mary, who d 30 Sept 1789, 16 mos (6:141); and Betsey, b 10 Oct 1790 (6:84).
2. William, b 25 Sept 1754, bp 13 Oct 1754 (6:84); not named in will of his brother, James Davis Ingraham, of 10 Sept 1796. (Note: A William Ingraham, b 7 Oct 1754, d 23 Feb 1810, m Louise DURKEE and was a Sgt from Conn in the Rev War, per Pat Index, p 361.)
3. John, bp 33 May 1757; not named in will of his brother, James Davis Ingraham, of 10 Sept 1796.
4. Samuel, bp 18 May 1760; not named in will of his brother, James Davis Ingraham, of 10 Sept 1796.
5. Benjamin, bp 6 Sept 1762; not named in will of his brother, James Davis Ingraham, of 10 Sept 1796, but was alive 3 Sept 1809 when he had three ch bp St Michael's Ch: Lydia, Ann Hammond, and Priscilla (8:162).
6. Capt Nathaniel, bp 4 Nov 1764 (8:279); d Br 18 Oct 1836, 72 yr (6:141); m Congre Ch, Br, 29 July 1789 Mary DIMAN, b 1764, d 12 Apr 1830, 66 yr (6:141; 8:375), dau Nathaniel and Ann (Gallup) Diman of Br (6:18, 22). Mary was bp Congre Ch 13 May 1804 (8:279). Nathaniel was named in his brother, James Davis Ingraham's will of 10 Sept 1796. He had eight ch, the last six of whom were bp Congre Ch, Br on 11 Aug 1805, "of Capt Nathaniel and Mary" (8:279): Lydia Pearce, d 29 Sept 1791, 20 mo (8:375); ch, d 30 Aug 1799, 1 mo (Ibid); Samuel; Melvin Diman; Ann; Mary; Hannah Luther; and Lydia French.
7. Lydia, bp 28 Sept 1766; m Timothy FRENCH, and named as his wife in her brother, James Davis Ingraham's will of 10 Sept 1796.
8. Capt Daniel, bp 23 July 1769; d 5 Nov 1841, 73 yr (6:141); m Congre Ch, Br 3 Feb 1793 Abigail MUNRO, b 30 July 1771 (6:92), d 16 Oct 1849, 79 yr "of Capt Daniel",

dau Nathaniel and Abigail (Gallup) Munro of Br (6:29, 92; 8:338). Nathaniel Munro's will is in RIGR, 7:169. Capt Daniel's kn ch were: Allen, b 27 Oct 1793 (6:84), m Congre Ch, Br 24 Jan 1816 Hannah EDDY who d 22 Nov 1822, 28 yr (8:375), dau Preserved and Lydia Eddy (8:-338); twin son, d 28 July 1812, aged 1 hr (8:375); twin son, d 10 Aug 1812, aged 12 d (8:375); Daniel, d 18 June 1817, 20 yr; Lydia, d 18 Oct 1817, 19 yr; and James Davis, who "of Daniel" m by Rev George W. Hathaway at Warren, RI, 25 Sept 1842 Elizabeth SMITH, dau Samuel C. Smith, both of Br (VR War 6:25).

9. James Davis, bp 23 June 1771; d 18 Sept 1796, 26 yr, unm (8:375). His will, dtd 10 Sept 1796 and pvd 3 Feb 1797, named: father, John Ingraham and unnamed mother, both living; brothers Nathaniel, Daniel and Jeremiah Ingraham; sisters Lydia wife of Timothy French, and Polly wife of Samuel Pitman; and James Davis Pitman, son of sister Polly (RIGR, 6:156-157).

10. Polly, bp 21 Aug 1774; d 2 May 1797, 25 yr (8:387); m Congre Ch, Br 29 Nov 1792 Capt Samuel PITMAN (8:338), son Peleg and Mary Pitman (8:346). He drowned from the sloop O.H. Perry in 1815 (8:387), having m (2) 30 Sept 1798 Sarah HOWLAND, dau John Esq and Elizabeth Howland (8:346). Polly had two kn ch, b Br, surname Pitman: James Davis, b 27 Aug 1793 (6:99) who m Congre Ch, Br 12 Apr 1818 Mary INGRAHAM (8:338); and Samuel, of Samuel, who d 7 Sept 1796, 11 mo (8:387).

Capt Jeremiah[5] (Capt John[4], Timothy[3], William[2], Richard[1]) Ingraham was b Br 8 Dec 1731 (6:84) and d there 30 Sept 1807, 75 yr (6:141). He m (1) at St Michael's Ch 15 Sept 1754 Rebecca MUNRO (8:208), prob b 30 Apr 1736, d aft 19 Aug 1768, dau Simeon and Rebecca (Wardwell) Munro of Br (6:37, 91); and m (2) Abigail (DEWOLF) HOWE, b 11 Nov 1750 (8:153), bur St Michael's as widow 24 Feb 1833 (8:228), dau Mark Anthony DeWolf of Guadeloupe, W.I. and Br, who m Abigail Potter of Br 26 Aug 1744. Abigail DeWolf's m to a Howe is not given in the VR Br, but one of her Howe sons was named Mark Anthony, and her mother was Abigail D'Wolf dec (6:29), per Capt Jeremiah Ingraham's will. The 1774 Census of Br listed Jeremiah as head of a household of eight people: two males above 16, two males under 16, one female above 16, two females under 16, and one black (Bartlett, p 180).

The will of Jeremiah Ingraham of Br, yeoman, dtd 8 Apr 1807 with a codicil dtd 21 May 1807, was pvd 5 Oct 1807 (RIGR, 7:164). He mentioned his unnamed former wife, now dcd, who was mother of the testator's dau Rebecca Greene; unnamed present wife, living; wife's mother Abigail D'-Wolf dcd; present wife's dcd sons: Mark Anthony, William and James Howe; sons George Ingraham, Thomas Ingraham, and Simeon Ingraham dcd, lving widow Sarah Ingraham and six unnamed ch; daus Rebecca wife of Joseph Whipple Greene of Pomfret, Conn, and Polly Ingraham who was under 21 at date of codicil and was to receive land which he had given to his present wife, after the latter's d; and his sister, Martha Springer.

CHILDREN by first wife, Rebecca, all b Br (6:84):
1. Simeon[6], b 12 Jan 1755; d bef father's will of 8 Apr 1807 leaving widow, Sarah, and six ch. No m or issue in VR Br. Simeon Ingraham and Sarah May "formerly of Bristol, RI, now of Rehoboth, were m Rehoboth by Rev Robert Rogers 31 Aug 1777" (VR Re, p 207). The 1790 Census of RI, p 11, gave Simeon Ingraham living in Br as head of a household of one male 16 and above, two males under 16, and five females, which agrees with his father's will.
2. Jeremiah, b 27 Jan 1758; not named in father's will of 8 Apr 1807.
3. Rebecca, b 14 Nov 1760; d 23 Sept 1821, 61 yr (6:-137); m Capt Joseph Whipple Greene, b 1761 per d rec, d 27 Apr 1829, 68 yr (6:137). They were called of Pomfret, Conn in her father's will. Rebecca had one ch b Br, surname Greene: Thomas Ingraham, b 20 Sept 1784 (6:80).
4. George, b 8 July 1764; not named in father's will of 8 Apr 1807; m Congre Ch, Br 21 May 1786 Sarah PECK (8:-338), prob b 28 Sept 1767, dau Jonathan and Mary (Throop) Peck (6:198). The VR Br name only two ch of his (6:141): infant ch of George d 29 Jan 1787, 12 d; and Henry, of George, d 4 Nov 1791, 3 yr. The 1790 US Census of RI, p 11, gave George Ingraham in Br as head of a household of eight persons, three males 16 and over, one male under 16, and four females. These can not be ch of this George since he m in 1786. It is either another George, or he had other people living with him. He poss later rem with his brother, Thomas, to Amenia, Dutchess Co, NY, as a George Ingraham was having ch m there in the early 1800's (Bowman, p 167).
5. Mary, b 20 Aug 1768; d 8 May 1793, 25 yr "of Jeremiah" (6:141).
6. Thomas, b 1771 per d rec and named in his father's will of 8 Oct 1807; d 12 May 1841, 70 yr, at Amenia, Dutchess Co, NY (6:141); m Congre Ch, Br 22 Dec 1793 (8:338) Peggy WARDWELL, bp as Peggy in Congre Ch, Br 25 Sept 1775, dau Capt John Jr and Hannah (Swan) Wardwell (6:56). No issue in VR Br, and he rem to Dutchess Co, NY.

CHILD by second wife, Abigail, b Br (8:279):
7. Molly/Polly, bp Congre Ch, Br 21 May 1797 "of Capt Jeremiah and Abigail".

Capt Joshua[4] (Timothy[3], William[2], Richard[1]) Ingraham was b in Br 12 Feb 1704/05 (6:84) and bp by Rev John Sparhawk in the Congre Ch 31 Mar 1706 (Geneals RI Fams, 1989, 2:376). He d in Br 1 Mar 1793, 89 yr (6:141; 8:375). He m (1) 23 Oct 1729 Martha LAWTON (6:29), b 12 Sept 1712, d 24 Oct 1762 (6:140) and bur St Michael's 26 Oct 1762 (8:228), dau Thomas and Margaret Lawton (6:86); and m (2) at St Michael's 23 Jan 1763 Mary RICHMOND (8:208) of LC, RI, who d aft Capt Joshua's will was pvd 1 Apr 1793 (RIGR, 6:157). Mary Richmond had a Myflwr desc from John Alden through her father, Rogers Richmond of LC, whose mother was Elizabeth Rogers, dau of John Rogers of Duxbury, Mass (LC Fams, p 514-515).

Joshua was made a freeman of RI from Br in 1747 (MacGunnigle, p 29), and he gave Public Service from RI during the Rev War (Pat Index, p 361). His will, pvd 1 Apr 1793 and rec 27 May 1799, named wife Mary Ingraham; sons Joshua and Simeon Ingraham; and four unnamed daus by his last wife (RIGR, 6:157). The 1774 Census of Br showed Capt Joshua Ingraham as head of a household of nine persons, one male above 16, two females above 16, four females under 16, and two blacks (Bartlett, p 180).

CHILDREN by first wife, Martha, b Br and bp St Michael's Ch (6:84; 8:161):
1. Joshua[5] Jr, b 13 Sept 1730, bp 4 Apr 1731; d aft father's will pvd 1 Apr 1793; m St Michael's 17 May 1752 Elizabeth GIBBS (8:208), b Br 12 Oct 1731 (6:77), d 7 Oct 1769, 38 yr (6:141) and bur St Michael's 9 Oct 1769 (8:228), dau John and Sarah (Jones) Gibbs of Br.
2. Lawton, b 23 Dec 1732, bp 31 Dec 1732. He was listed in the 1777 Military Census of RI from Providence, aged 16-50 and able to bear arms (p 70), but he was not mentioned in his father's will pvd 1 Apr 1793.
3. Margaret, b 4 Mar 1735, bp 9 Mar 1734/35; not mentioned in his father's will pvd 1 Apr 1793; m St Michael's 13 Nov 1757 Coomer HAILE/HALE (8:208) who d 22 Apr 1849, 84 yr, "a Revolutionary pensioner" (6:137). No issue in VR Br, although a Coomer Hale was listed in the 1790 US Census of RI in Bristol Town (p 10) with a family of one male 16 and upward, one male under 16, and two females. He was not in the 1774 Census of Br, however, so may have rem elsewhere for some yrs; or the 1790 US Census Coomer may have been his son.
4. Ruth, b 16 Apr 1737, bp 24 Apr 1737; d as widow 15 Oct 1791 (8:394); m St Michael's 8 Sept 1757 Mark Anthony VAN DOORN (8:208), b 1735 per d rec, d 1 Dec 1786, 51 yr (8:394). She had four kn ch b Br, surname Van Doorn: Moses, b 19 May 1758 (6:108), d 29 June 1805 (8:394) and m 27 May 1779 Lydia MUNRO; Martha, bp St Michael's 25 Apr 1762 (8:181); Anthony, b 4 May 1775 (6:108),

d 29 Sept 1803, 29 yr (8:394), and m 29 May 1796 Phebe MANCHESTER (6:54); and Hannah, b date unrec (6:108).
5. William, b 16 Dec 1738, bp 31 Dec 1738; bur St Michael's "of Joshua and Martha", 11 June 1743 (8:228).
6. Martha, b 31 Aug 1740; d 19 July 1762, 22 yr (6:-140), bur St Michael's 20 July 1762 (8:228).
7. Allen, b 9 July 1742, bp 11 July 1742; not named in father's will pvd 1 Apr 1793.
8. Sarah, b 7 July 1744, bp 15 July 1744; not named in father's will pvd 1 Apr 1793; m St Michael's 18 Nov 1764 James GIBBS (8:208).
9. Timothy, b 2 Mar 1745/46, bp 7 Mar 1745/46 (8:161); not named in father's will pvd 1 Apr 1793; m St Michael's 18 May 1769 Sarah MUNRO (8:208), poss b 16 Oct 1749, dau Simeon and Rebecca (Wardwell) Munro of Br (6:37, 91). The 1774 Census of Br listed Timothy with a family of one male above 16, one female below 16, and one female above 16 (Bartlett, p 180). He had three ch bp St Michael's (8:161): Martha, bp 1 July 1770 and bur St Michael's 19 Nov 1771 (8:228); Sarah, bp 3 May 1772; and Timothy, bp 13 Nov 1770 (sic?). A ch of Timothy's was bur St Michael's 8-1775 (8:228).
10. Elizabeth, bp 27 Sept 1747; bur St Michael's 11 Jan 1752 (8:228).
11. Simeon, b 24 Apr 1749, bp 14 May 1749; d aft father's will pvd 1 Apr 1793.
12. Thomas Lawton, bp 23 Oct 1751, twin (6:140; 8:161); bur St Michael's 7 Nov 1751 (8:228).
13. Mary, bp 23 Oct 1751, twin (6:140; 8:161); bur St Michael's 29 Oct 1751 (8:228).
14. Ann(a), b 14 Feb 1753, bp 14 Apr 1753; not named in father's will pvd 1 Apr 1793; m St Michael's 1 Aug 1773 John GRANGER (8:208).

CHILDREN by second wife, Mary, b Br (6:84):
15. Mary "of Joshua and Mary", bur St Michael's 26 Oct 1763 (8:228).
16. Hannah, b 11 June 1765.
17. Charlotte, b 2 July 1767; d 6 Nov 1836, 69 yr, "widow of Capt Samuel" (6:135); m St Michael's 20 Mar 1789 Capt Samuel GLADDING (8:206), b 4 Apr 1768, d 8 Dec 1813 (called "Samuel 2nd" in VR Br), son John and Lucretia (Smith) Gladding of Br. Capt Samuel was a ship owner and merchant-captain at Br. Charlotte had ten ch b Br, surname Gladding (6:79): Eunice, b 12 Oct 1789; Allen Ingraham, b 16 Aug 1791, d Dec 1811 in sloop Sally, from Havana (6:135); Samuel, b 22 Feb 1794 and d 22 Dec 1796 (6:134); Richard Smith, b 25 Feb 1796; John, b 8 May 1798; Edmund, b 8 Oct 1800 and d 17 Aug 1801 (6:134); Gilbert Richmond, b 4 Mar 1802; Samuel II, b 28 Feb 1804; Martha James, b 7 Sept 1806; and Mary Ingraham, b 14 Sept 1808.

18. Phebe, b 27 Nov 1768.
19. Molly/Mary, b 5 Sept 1771; d 11 Sept 1828, 57 yr, wife of Samuel (6:169); m St Michael's 23 Dec 1789 Samuel WALDRON, b 11 May 1772 (6:108), d 4 June 1840, 68 yr (6:169), son Nathaniel and Hannah (Throop) Waldron of Br (6:55). Molly's four kn ch b Br, surname Waldron were: Ambrose, bp Congre Ch 13 Sept 1798 and d 14 Sept 1798, 8 w (8:290, 394); Eliza, bp Congre Ch 13 July 1800 and m by Rev Wight 29 Oct or 29 Nov 1819 Nathaniel WALDRON, her first cousin (8:354); Mary Billings "of Samuel Waldron" d 13 Oct 1813, 18 m (8:395); and David, named in his uncle Billings Waldron's will of 1 June 1820 (RIGR, 9:59).
20. Martha, b 26 June 1774 (6:84).

Joshua[5] Jr (Capt Joshua[4], Timothy[3], William[2], Richard[1]) Ingraham was b in Br 13 Sept 1730 (6:84), and was bp at St Michael's Ch 4 Apr 1731 (8:161). He d aft his father's will was pvd 1 Apr 1793. He m at St Michael's 17 May 1752 Elizabeth GIBBS (8:208), b Br 12 Oct 1731 (6:77), d 7 Oct 1769, 38 yr (6:141) and bur St Michael's 9 Oct 1769 (8:-228), dau John and Sarah (Jones) Gibbs of Br. Eliza was bp as an adult at St Michael's 18 Apr 1753.

CHILDREN, bp St Michael's as "of Joshua Jr and Eliza" (8-161):
1. Eliza[6], bp 15 July 1753.
2. Lawton, bp 3 Aug 1755.
3. James, b 13 Feb 1758 (6:84), bp 16 June 1758; d Barrington, RI bef 30 Aug 1819 (Bar 6:12); prob m by Rev Solomon Townsend at Bar 16 Sept 1790 Anna HUMPHREY (Bar 6:12). He had the fol ch b Bar (Bar 6:29): Celinda/Selinda, b 27 Apr 1791 who m Bar 27 Sept 1812 Pearce BOSWORTH (Bar 6:12); Lawton, b 4 Feb 1793 and m Bar 30 Aug 1819 Polly Taylor BOSWORTH, dau Joseph dcd (Bar 6:12); Anna, b 18 Mar 1796 and d 15 Oct 1798; Sarah, b 20 Jan 1799; James, b 30 May 1802, twin; Nancy, b 30 May 1802, twin; and George Gibbs, b 5 Apr 1804.
4. Joshua, bp 29 June 1760; d.y.
5. Joshua II, bp 25 Apr 1762.
6. Thomas, bp 9 Sept 1764.
7. Sarah, bp 19 Sept 1767; bur St Michael's, Br, 20 Sept 1767 (8:228).
8. Daniel, bp 10 July 1768.

11. NATHANIEL PAINE JR

The Hon Colonel Nathaniel[3] Paine Jr was b 18 Oct 1661 in Rehoboth, Mass (VR Re, p 696; Sav, 3:334; NER, 143: 300), and d in Br in 1723/24 (Torrey, p 552). He was the only son of Nathaniel[2] and Elizabeth Paine Sr of Rehoboth. Nathaniel Sr was the son of Stephen[1] and Neele (Adcocke) Paine who came from Great Ellingham, co Norfolk, England to Hingham, Mass in the Diligent in 1638 (NER, 143:300-302; Sav, 3:334-335). Nathaniel Jr signed the Articles on 27 Aug 1680 to purchase a thirty-second part of the Proprietors' lands which became Br (Munro, p 96-97). Munro, p 92 said that he came from Swansey and succeeded Nathaniel Byfield as Judge of Probate in Br. The 1689 Census of Br listed Nathaniel Paine with a wife, four ch and two servants. Nathaniel m by 1681 Dorothy RAINSFORD, b 11 Sept 1663 in Boston, Mass, and d Br as Madame Dorothy 2 Jan 1755, 93 yr (6:153), dau Jonathan and Mary (Sutherland) Rainsford of Boston (Sav, 3:502). Nathaniel and Dorothy both joined the Congre Ch in Br on 6 July 1696 (8:259). Sav, 3:334 confused the ch of this Nathaniel and Dorothy Paine with those of another Nathaniel Paine, b 1667 and d 1718, who m 1 May 1694 Dorothy Chaffee of Rehoboth.

Madame Dorothy Paine, widow, and Nathaniel Paine, son, were appointed administrators of the est of their husband and father, Lt Col Nathaniel Paine, all of Br, on 17 Apr 1724 (Rounds, 1:99). The div of the real est of Nathaniel Paine of Br was dtd 17 Oct 1727. It was divided into nine shares betw his widow, Dorothey Paine, and his children: Nathaniel (eldest son); Stephen (2nd son); Samuel Varnum (sic, Vernon) in right of his wife Elizabeth; heirs of Mrs Mary Drown (dau) dcd; Lt Col Church in right of his wife Hannah; Timothy Failes in right of his wife Alathea; John Williams in right of his wife Dorothey; and to "Ms Sarah Paine one share" (Rounds, 1:154; RIGR, 3:89).

CHILDREN, b Br (6:96), bp Congre Ch, Br by Rev John Sparhawk (Geneals RI Fams, 1989, 2:373, 375):
1. Hannah[4], b 20 Apr 1685, bp 2 Aug 1696; d Br 16 Oct 1755; m Br 20 May 1703 Col Charles CHURCH, b 9 May 16-82, d Br 31 Dec 1746 ae 64 yr, son Col Benjamin and Alice (Southworth) Church of Br and Little Compton, RI. Hannah had seven ch b Br, surname Church, who have a Myflwr desc through Col Church who desc from Richard Warren (Myflwr Fams in Progress, Richard Warren, p 75): Capt Constant Church, b 12 Dec 1708, d 8 May 1740, 32 yr, m 25 Jan 1732 Mary REYNOLDS, dau Peter and Mary (Giles) Reynolds of Br (Torrey, p 619); Elizabeth, b 24 Dec 1710, d Woodstock 22 Apr 1774, 64 yr (6:137), m 9 Apr 1732 Major Thomas GREENE of Newport (6:25); Hannah, b 20 Feb 1712/13, m 30 Apr 1732 Capt Simeon DAVIS Jr of Br (6:13, 17); Dorothy, b unrec, m (int) 11 Sept 1741 Samuel CHANDLER (6:14) of Woodstock; Nathaniel, b ca 1717 per d rec, d 26 Aug 1744, 27 yr (6:123), m 21 May 1740 Ruth BOSWORTH (6:14); Sarah, b unrec, m 27 Aug 1741 Leonard JAMES of Boston, per father's will, altho

VR Br 6:14, 29 call him Leonard Jarvis; Mary, b unrec; m 12 June 1746 John CHANDLER Jr of Worcester, Mass (6:-14).
2. Col Nathaniel Jr, b 9 Mar 1688, bp 2 Aug 1696, d "about early 1730" (6:96), or poss as "Hon Col d 9 Dec 1729, 63 yr (sic) (6:153). He m by 1716 Sarah ___, who m (2) John CHANDLER Esq of Worcester, Mass.
3. Edward, b 7 Oct 1690, bp 2 Aug 1696; d bef div of est of father 17 Oct 1727.
4. Dorothy, b not rec, bp 2 Aug 1696; d 17 Feb 1699/1700 (6:153).
5. Jonathan, b 18 Apr 1695, bp 2 Aug 1696; d 26 Dec 1707 (6:153).
6. Alethea, b 28 Aug 1697, bp as Alitheah 5 Sept 1697; d Br 19 Sept 1747; m prob 1717 as his first wife Capt Timothy FALES, b 18 Aug 1690 Dedham, Mass, d 30 Apr 1777 Taunton, Mass, son James and Deborah (Fisher) Fales of Dedham. Timothy was first a schoolteacher in Br, and aft going to sea for some yrs, returned and became a J.P., and Judge of the Court of Common Pleas. He left Br for Taunton in early 1747 and m (2) Plymouth, Mass 11 July 1748 Mrs Elizabeth Gardner THOMAS (Fales Fam, p 33-34, 38, 42-44). Alethea had the fol ch b Br, surname Fales (Fales Fam, p 43-44): Timothy, b 14 Sept 1718 and d June 1739; Nathaniel, b 4 July 1720 who m Sarah LITTLE; Alethea, b 25 Aug 1722, prob d 20 July 1733; Mary, b 12 Sept 1724, m (int) 27 Feb 1744 William BOSWORTH; Jonathan, b 25 May 1727 and m Hannah PECK; Deborah, b 1 Aug 1731, d unm 22 Aug 1799, aged 68; Samuel, b 28 Sept 1733, d 8 Aug 1737; and a dau, b prob May 1739 and d 1 July 1740, aged 14 mo.
7. Sarah, b 5 May 1699, d 8 May 1699.
8. Col Stephen, b not rec, bp 14 June 1702; d 21 Sept 1749, 48 yr (6:153); m Priscilla ROYALL, b 1706 per d rec, d Br 24 Feb 1772, 66 yr (6:154), dau Samuel and Hannah (Reynolds) Royall. His kn ch named by his sister, Elizabeth Vernon in her will of May 1754 were: Stephen Royal, Hannah and Mary. No issue for him in VR Br.
9. Dorothy II, b 19 Mar 1706/07, twin, bp 23 Mar 1706/07; m (1) (int) 13 Oct 1726 John WILLIAMS of Boston (Boston Mars 1700-1751, p 161), per div of est of her father on 17 Oct 1727; m (2) ___ HUNTINGTON, per will of her sister, Elizabeth Vernon, of May 1754 (RIGR, 5:94). Dorothy's kn ch per sister's will were: John Williams, and Hannah Huntington. No issue in VR Br.
10. Sarah II, b 19 Mar 1706/07, twin, bp 23 Mar 1706/07; d 10 Jan 1764, 57 yr (6:160); m Br by Rev Barnabus Taylor 10 June 1733 (6:47) Hon Joseph RUSSELL Esq of Barnstable, Mass, who d 31 July 1789, 78 yr (6:160). Sarah had the fol ch, surname Russell, listed in the VR Br: Anna, b 10 May 1734 and d 7 Sept 1735 (6:160); Sarah, b 30 Aug 1735, d 22 Oct 1763 at Norwich (Ibid);

Jonathan, b 22 Mar 1736/37, d 17 July 1814, 78 yr (6:-160); Nathaniel, b 16 Nov 1738; Anna II, b 11 Dec 1747; and "younger daus" mentioned in will of Elizabeth Vernon dtd May 1754.

11. Elizabeth, b not rec, but named in div of est of father 17 Oct 1727 as wife of Samuel VARNUM (sic VERNON); m (1) ___ PRINCE (6:54); m (2) as Elizabeth Prince, Br by Rev Nathaniel Cotton 12 Jan 1724/25 Samuel VERNON of Newport, RI (6:54). No issue. The will of Elizabeth Vernon of Br, widow, dtd May 1754 and pvd 1st Mon of May 1759, named aged mother Dorothy Paine; brother Stephen Paine dec; sisters Dorothy Huntington and Sarah wife of Joseph Russell Esq; children of bro Stephen Paine dec, viz: Stephen Royal, Hannah and Mary; Jonathan, Nathaniel, Sarah, and Anna Russell under 18, and younger daus of brother-in-law Joseph Russell Esq; children of sister Dorothy Huntington, viz: John Williams, Elizabeth Williams, and Hannah Huntington under 18; Sarah Paine dau of my kinsman Nathaniel Paine dec. Kinsman Jonathan Fales and his sister Deborah Fales. Kinswoman Mary Bosworth wife of William Bosworth. Kinsmen Charles and Peter Church, sons of Constant Church dec, and Mary Church under 18 dau of Constant Church. Abigail Godfrey wife of Capt Caleb Godfrey. Sarah Paine, dau Edward Paine. Sarah Drown wife of Thomas Drown of Boston. Irene Drown. Hannah Church under 18 dau of Nathaniel Church dec. Mary Price wife of Francis Price of Dorchester. Jonathan Peck (RIGR, 5:94-95).

12. Mary, b not rec, but named in div of est of father 17 Oct 1727 as "Mrs Mary Drown, dau, dcd". Samuel Royal of Boston was appointed guardian of Alathea Drown, over 14, and Trenah? Drown, under 14, gch of Col Nathaniel Paine of Br, dtd 24 Feb 1726/27 (Rounds, 1:142).

Colonel Nathaniel[4] (Col Nathaniel[3]) Paine Jr was b Br 9 Mar 1688 (6:96), and was bp by Rev John Sparhawk in the Congre Ch there 2 Aug 1696. The VR Br (6:96) say he d bef the b of a ch on 8 July 1730. Poss he d 9 Dec 1729, 63 yr (sic), if his age is incorrectly given (6:153). He m bef 1716 Sarah ___, who m (2) bef May 1740 John CHANDLER, Esq of Worcester, Mass. John Chandler was b New London, Conn 10 Oct 1693, son John and Mary (Raymond) Chandler of New London, Woodstock, and Worcester, Mass. His father, aft rem to Worcester, was appointed the first Judge of Probate there (Sav, 1:357).

Nathaniel was Representative from Br in the General Court of Mass in 1724 to 1726, 1727, and 1728/29. The acct of Sarah Chandler, formerly Sarah Paine, adm of est of her former husband, Nathaniel Paine of Br, was dtd 2 May 1740 and included "Charges of Lying with a Posthumus Child"

(Rounds, 1:295). The div of the est of Col Nathaniel Paine, dcd, intestate, was dtd 12 May 1741 (RIGR, 3:90) or 16 June 1741 (Rounds, 1:309), and was betw his late widow, Madam Sarah Chandler, and his ch, viz: Edward Paine (eldest son), Nathaniel Paine (son), Sarah Drown (dau), Samuel Clark Paine (son), Timothy Paine (son), and Dorothy Chandler (dau). It included lands in Attleboro, Mass and Br (Rounds, 1:309).

CHILDREN, b Br except Edward (6:96):
1. Edward[5], b 18 Apr 1714 Boston; d Nov 1778, 65 yr at Worcester, Mass (6:154); m Br, St Michael's Ch 6 Mar 1739/40 Mary BOSWORTH, bur St Michael's as "wife of Edward" 25 May 1759 (8:233). He had two kn ch listed in the VR Br: Sarah, b 22 June 1743 (6:96), bp St Michael's 22 Nov 174_ (8:173); and Mary, bp St Michael's 10 Sept 1758 (Ibid).
2. Sarah, b 17 Aug 1716, bp Congre Ch, Br 26 Aug 1716 (Geneals RI Fams, 1989, 2:380); d aft May 1754; m Br by Rev Barnabus Taylor 24 Mar 1736/37 Thomas DROWN(E) of Boston (6:18, 41). She was named in the will of her aunt, Elizabeth Paine Vernon, dtd May 1754 (RIGR, 5:94-95).
3. Nathaniel, b 17 June 1719; d 15 Jan 1747 at Annapolis (prob Nova Scotia) (6:153); m Br St Michael's by Rev John Usher 13 June 1742 Mrs Eliza(beth) GALLUP (6:-41; 8:214), prob bp 9 June 1723 Trinity Ch, Newport, RI, dau William and Mary (Antill) Gallup of Br. She poss m (2) as Eliza Paine at St Michael's 2 Feb 1748/49 John COCKRAN (8:214). Nathaniel had two kn ch rec in the VR Br: Sarah, b 5 Jan 1742/43 (6:96), bp St Michael's 16 Jan 1742/43 (8:173); and Dorothy, bp 29 June 1746 (8:-173) bur St Michael's 10 Dec 1746 (8:233).
4. Dorothy, b 20 Jan 1723/24, bp Congre Ch by Rev Nathaniel Cotton 26 Jan 1723/24 (Geneals RI Fams, 1989, 2:-383); m ___ CHANDLER, prob son of John Chandler Esq of Worcester, Mass who was appted 17 Apr 1741 "to be guardian as chosen by Dorothy Paine now Dorothy Chandler (minor over 14), dau of Nathaniel Paine Esq of Bristol" (Rounds, 1:307).
5. Samuel, b 3 Sept 1725; d.y.
6. Samuel Clarke, b 11 Feb 1727/28, bp Congre Ch by Rev Nathaniel Cotton 17 Feb 1727/28 (Geneals RI Fams, 1989, 2:383). John Chandler Esq of Worcester was appted 17 Apr 1741 to be guardian of Samuel Clerk Paine, under 14, son of Nathaniel Paine Esq of Br, at the prayer of Madam Chandler (Rounds, 1:307).
7. Timothy, b 8 July 1730 posthumously; d 1793. John Chandler Esq of Worcester was appted 17 Apr 1741 to be guardian of Timothy Paine, under 14, son of Nathaniel Paine Esq of Br, at the prayer of Madam Chandler (Rounds, 1:307). Virkus, 4:557 said that Timothy was crown mayor of Worcester, Mass during the Rev War, and m Sarah CHANDLER. He had a son, Nathaniel, b 1759 and d 1840 who m

Elizabeth CHANDLER.
Note: the Sarah Paine who m St Michael's, Br, 1 Sept 1765 William CHRISTOPHER (8:214) was prob the dau of either Edward^5 and Mary (Bosworth) Paine, b 22 June 1743, or of Nathaniel^5 and Eliza (Gallup) Paine, b 5 Jan 1742/43.

Col Stephen^4 (Col Nathaniel^3) Paine was bp in the Congre Ch, Br, by Rev John Sparhawk 14 June 1702, and d 21 Sept 1749, 48 yr (6:153). He m Priscilla ROYALL, who was b in 1706 per her d rec, and d Br 24 Feb 1772, 66 yr (6:-154), dau Samuel and Hannah (Reynolds) Royall of Br. Col Stephen was Representative from Br in the General Court of Mass during 1737/40, 1741, 1742, and 1744/45 (Munro, p 384-385). The will of Stephen Paine Esq of Br, dtd 20 Sept 1749 and pvd 3 Jan 1749/50, mentioned unnamed living mother; sons Stephen, eldest, and Royall Paine; daus Hannah, Elizabeth and Mary Paine (RIGR, 3:136). The will of Samuel Royal of Br, dtd 10 Dec 1739 and pvd 27 July 1743, named wife Hannah; dau Priscilla Paine to have use of all real est until testator's gson, Royal Paine, turned 21; two gsons Stephen Paine and Royal Paine, both under 21 (RIGR, 3:263). The will of Priscilla Paine, widow of Br, dtd 6 Oct 1768 and pvd 4 May 1772, named dau Hannah wife of Capt Simeon Potter; gsons Stephen Paine, Royall Paine and Thomas Paine; and uncle John Reynolds (RIGR, 6:154).

CHILDREN, b Br (6:96):
1. Capt Stephen^5, b 14 Sept 1725; d 16 Mar 1762 at Berbeccia (6:153); m Br by Rev John Burt 18 Aug 1751 Mary BAILEY (6:41).
2. Royall, b 12 Mar 1730 or 1731; d 17 June 1764, 34 yr, at Boston, unm (6:153). Royall was a merchant in Br. His will, dtd 10 June 1764 and pvd 24 July 1764, named mother Mrs Priscilla Paine, living; brother Stephen Paine dec leaving widow Mary Paine; sister Hannah presumably wife of brother-in-law Capt Simeon Potter; three nephews, Stephen Paine, Samuel Royall Paine, and Thomas Paine (RIGR, 6:151).
3. Hannah, b 5 Jan 1732/33; d Br 14 Mar 1788, 56 yr (6:158); m 7 Mar 1754 Capt Simeon POTTER (6:41), b Br 1720 and d 21 Feb 1806, 86 yrs (6:158), son Hopestill and Lydia (Finney) Potter of Br (Munro, p 175). Simeon was a ship owner and sea captain, a vestryman at St Michael's Ch, and a Representative from Br in the General Assembly (Ibid, p 181, 184). They had no issue. By Simeon's will his est, which was valued at ca a quarter of a million dollars, was div among his nine sisters and their descs. For a time he rem to Swansea to live, although he still kept up a household in Br (Ibid, p 184-185). The 1774 Census of Br gave Simeon as head of a

household there of two males above 16, two females above 16, and eleven blacks (Ibid, p 190).
4. Elizabeth, b 5 Feb 1735/36; d bef brother Royall's will of 10 June 1764.
5. Mary, b 16 Feb 1738/39; d 9 July 1758, 20 yr (6:153).

Capt Stephen[5] (Col Stephen[4], Col Nathaniel[3]) Paine was b Br 14 Sept 1725 (6:96) and d 16 Mar 1762 at Berbeccia (6:153). He m Congre Ch, Br, 18 Aug 1751 Mrs Mary BAILEY (6:41), and was bp as an adult in the Ch on 21 Nov 1756 (8:283). He was a sea captain, and his will, dtd Br 16 Dec 1761 and pvd 1 Nov 1762, named wife Mary who received the furniture she had brought with her at their marriage; sons Stephen, Samuel Royall, and Thomas Paine all under 21; and brother Royall Paine (RIGR, 6:150-151).

CHILDREN, b Br (6:96), bp Congre Ch (Geneals RI Fams, 1989, 2:389, 390, 391):
1. Stephen[6], b 22 Dec 1754, bp 25 Apr 1756 (8:283). Did he m Elizabeth ___ who d "wife of Stephen" 1777, 23 yr (6:154)?
2. Samuel Royall (called Royall in some recs), b 23 Apr 1757, bp 5 June 1757 (8:283); d 26 Dec 1838, 82 yr "a Rev pensioner" (6:154); m (1) Olive ___; m (2) (int) 22 July 1787 Elizabeth/Betsey TORREY of Mendon, Mass (8:314), who d 12 Feb 1802 (6:154; 8:384); m (3) at St Michael's 1805 Mrs Abigail JOHNSON, b 1777 per d rec, d 14 Jan 1817, 40 yr (6:154; 8:385); m (4) by 1823 Bethia ___.
3. Thomas, b 16 Oct 1758, bp 31 Dec 1758 (8:283); d 2 Oct 1839; m Hulda VIGIL. There are no other VR Br recs for him. He was a Private and Matross from RI during the Rev War and he received a pension (Pat Index, p 512). There was only one Thomas Pain/Paine listed in the 1790 US Census of RI, p 33, who may have been he. This Thomas Pain lived in Providence Town and was head of a household of one male 16 or over, four males under 16, two females, and one other free person. The VR Providence have no entries under Thomas Paine.

Samuel Royall[6] (Capt Stephen[5], Col Stephen[4], Col Nathaniel[3]) Paine, sometimes called Royall, was b Br 23 Apr 1757 and bp 5 June 1757 (8:283). He d Br 26 Dec 1838, 82 yr "a Rev pensioner" (6:154). He m (1) Olive ___; m (2) (int) 22 July 1787 Elizabeth/Betsey TORREY of Mendon, Mass (8:314) who d 12 Feb 1802 (6:154; 8:384); m (3) at St Michael's 1805 Mrs Abigail JOHNSON, b 1777 per d rec, d 14 Jan 1817, 40 yr (6:154; 8:385); and m (4) by 1823 Bethia ___. He was a Private from RI in the Rev War and received a pension (Pat Index, p 512).

CHILDREN by first wife, Olive, b Br (6:96):
1. Mary⁷, b 5 May 1778; d 10 Oct 1779 (6:154).
2. Priscilla, b 17 June 1780.
3. Samuel Royall, d 6 July 1787, 4 yr, of Samuel R. (6:154; 8:384).

CHILDREN by second wife, Elizabeth/Betsey, b Br (6:96):
4. Samuel Royall II, b 2 Aug 1788; d 1 July 1804 (8:-385).
5. Nathaniel Terrey (Torrey?), b 8 May 1790; d Br 22 Mar 1838, 48 yr (6:154); m ___ and had three kn ch, b Br: Samuel Smith, d 16 Feb 1813, 17 mo (8:385); ch, d 12 Oct 1829, 18 mo (8:385); and William Henry Richmond, d 28 Aug 1834, 8 mo (6:154).
6. Stephen, b 15 Dec 1792.

CHILDREN by third wife, Abigail, b Br (6:96):
7. Betsey Torrey, b 4 Jan 1812.
8. Peter Torrey, bp St Michael's 24 May 1816 (8:173).

CHILD by fourth wife, Bethia, b Br (6:96):
9. Royal Luther, b 19 Oct 1823.

12. CAPT NATHANIEL REYNOLDS

Capt Nathaniel² Reynolds was b ca 1627 in England, and d "suddenly" 10 July 1708 in Br (6:159). He was the only son of Robert and Mary Reynolds who came with five young ch ca 1630/32 and settled in Boston, Mass (Reyn Gen, p 5; Sav, 3:526). Nathaniel m (1) 30 Dec 1657 (Reyn Gen, p 25) or 30 Nov 1657 (Bodge, p 279) Sarah DWIGHT, b 17 June 1638 and d 8 July 1663 Boston (Reyn Gen, p 44), dau John and Hannah (Close?) Dwight of Dedham, Mass; and m (2) aft 24 Jan 1664/65 Priscilla BRACKETT who prob d bef 1738, dau Peter and Priscilla Brackett of Boston and Braintree, Mass. Peter Brackett was a member of the Anc and Hon Artillery Co in 1648 (Sav, 1:229), as was Capt Nathaniel Reynolds in 1658. Nathaniel fought in King Philip's War in which he was a Lt in command of the garrison at Chelmsford, Mass during the fall and winter of 1675/76 (Bodge, p 279). He was a cordwainer, as was his father. At the 1655 town meeting in Boston he was chosen constable. His father's will (Reyn Gen, p 40) left him a large amount of property, and the family home on the corner of Washington and Milk Sts in Boston. He lived in Boston until ca 1681 when he and his family rem to Br where he built a home on the northeast corner of Bradford and Thames Sts (Reyn Gen, p 38-50).

Nathaniel had signed with the Proprietors on 27 Aug 1680 for a thirty-second part of the Mt Hope Lands, and was an original settler of Br (Munro, p 79, 96-97). He was one of the founders on 3 May 1687 of the Congre Ch at Br, and was elected grand juryman, sealer of leather, and selectman of Br. Capt Nathaniel Reynold's will (Reyn Gen, p 46-47; Rounds, 1:41-42) called him of Br, and it was dtd 7 Oct 1706 and pvd 3 Nov 1708. He mentioned no wife, but named five sons, Nathaniel (eldest) of Boston, John, Peter, Joseph and Benjamin (youngest) Reynolds; daus Sarah wife of John ffosdick of Boston, Mary Woodbery, Hannah wife of Samuel Royall of Boston, and Ruth Reynolds; his sister Mary Sanger of Watertown; his house in Boston, his farm and house in Br, and his 500 acres in "Quenepank" (Quinapaug). An inv of his est in Boston, located in the south end, was dtd Boston 3 Nov 1708; and the inv of his est in Br was dtd 28 Dec 1708 and totalled L794-05-06 (Reyn Gen, p 49-50).

CHILDREN by first wife, Sarah, b Boston (Reyn Gen, p 45-46; Bodge, p 279):
1. Sarah, b 26 July 1659, bp First Ch of Boston 26 Mar 1665; d Boston 1 Jan 1718; m (1) ca 1680 Thomas BLIGH Jr, a Quaker, b 1656, d 1683, son of Thomas and Sarah (Everton) Bligh Sr of Boston; m (2) ca 1683 John FOSDICK Jr, blacksmith, b 20 Feb 1658/59, son Sgt John and Anna (Shapleigh) (Branson) Fosdick of Charlestown, Mass. She had at least one ch, "John Blythe" by her first m, who became a weaver in Concord, Mass. John Fosdick Jr was given 27½ acres of land at Malden, Mass by a deed from his father, but he and Sarah lived in Boston near her brother, Nathaniel 2nd (Wyman, p 355).
2. Mary, b 20 Nov 1660; d Boston 8 Jan 1663, 2 yrs 2 mos.
3. Nathaniel 2nd, b 3 Mar 1662, bp First Ch Boston 26 Mar 1665; d Boston soon bef 31 May 1717; m ca 1685 Ruth LOWELL, b Scituate, Mass 11 July 1665, bur Boston 19 Sept 1716, dau John and Naomi (Torrey) Lowell of Boston.

Children by second wife, Priscilla, all but last two b Boston, and all of whom lived in Br (Bodge, p 279; Reyn Gen, p 45):
4. Mary II, b ca 1665 per Reyn Gen, p 45. Bodge, p 279 says she was ch #9, "b 1684?"; m Br 18 May 1694 Capt John WOODBURY of Br, mariner, who was dcd bef 3 Oct 1706 (Rounds, 1:36). No issue in VR Br.
5. John, b 4 Aug 1668; d Br 30 Jan 1757, 88 yrs, unm. His will, dtd 10 Mar 1749/50 and pvd 1 Mar 1757, named brothers Joseph and Benjamin Raynolds; cousin (nephew) John Raynolds son of brother Benjamin Raynolds; cousins (nieces) Anna and Sarah Raynolds, daus of brother Benjamin Raynolds; cousin (niece) Priscilla Paine widow of Stephen Paine Esq dec; cousin (nephew) Peter Raynold of

Enfield; cousin Mary Bradford of Br (RIGR, 5:93).
6. Capt Peter, b 26 Jan 1670; d Br betw 8 Dec 1726 and 28 June 1728; m ca 1699 Mary GILES/GILLS.
7. Philip, b 15 Sept 1674; d.y.
8. Ens Joseph, b 29 Dec 1676 (Reyn Gen) or 9 Jan 1677 (Bodge, p 279); d Br 16 Jan 1759, 82 yrs; m (int) 11 Aug 1718 Phebe LEONARD of Norton, Mass who d Br 18 Dec 1744, 49 yr.
9. Hannah, b 15 Jan 1681 (Reyn Gen) or 15 Jan 1682 (Bodge); d 10 Dec 1739; m 1704 Samuel ROYALL. The will of Samuel Royal, house carpenter of Br, dtd 10 Dec 1739 and pvd 27 July 1743, mentioned wife Hannah; dau Priscilla Paine (wife of Capt Stephen Paine) who was to use all of the testator's real est until the testator's gson, Royal Paine, turned 21; two gsons, Stephen Paine and Royal Paine, both under 21; wife to be exec (RIGR, 3:263; Rounds, 1:330).
10. Benjamin, b Br 10 May 1686, bp 8 May 1687 Congre Ch Br (Geneals RI Fams, 1989, 2:371); d Br 4 Aug 1770; m 1708/09 Susanna RAWSON, b 3 Oct 1686, d 11 Aug 1712 (8:-261), dau Rev Grindall and Susanna (Wilson) Rawson of Mendon, Mass.
11. Ruth, b 9 Dec 1688; d 3 July 1737; m Br 9 Nov 1710 Josiah CARY, b Br 6 May 1686, d bef 16 Feb 1730/31, son John and Abigail (Allen) Cary of Bridgewater, Mass and Br (6:12, 45). Reyn Gen, p 46 said that Ruth m Joseph CARY. The VR Br (6:68) rec two ch, b Br, of "Josiah and Ruth" Cary: Jemima, b 25 July 1711, and Nathaniel, b 6 Feb 1713/14. A Joseph, of Josiah, also d 9 Nov 1729 (6:-122). Ruth Cary of Br, widow, was named guardian of Nathaniel Cary, over 14, son of Josiah Cary of Br, dtd 16 Feb 1730/31 (Rounds, 1:191).

Nathaniel^3 Jr (Capt Nathaniel^2, Robert^1) Reynolds, also called Nathaniel 2nd in the recs, was b 3 Mar 1662/63 and bp in the First Ch of Boston 26 Mar 1665. He d Boston soon bef 31 May 1717 (Reyn Gen, p 58). When his father rem to Br, Nathaniel Jr remained in Boston and lived on part of his father's property. He m ca 1685 Ruth LOWELL of Boston. Nathaniel Jr left no will (Ibid, p 58-60). He had the following ch, all b Boston (Ibid, p 60): Sarah, b 23 Oct 1687, m (1) Robert YOUNG and m(2) Alexander HARPER; Ruth, b 11 Sept 1689 and d 16 Mar 1693/94; Mary, b 21 Aug 1691, m Edward MARION; Nathaniel 3rd, b 14 Jan 1693 and m Mary SNELL; John, b 29 Mar 1696, m Anna BLANCH; Ebenezer, bp 25 June 1679, bur 29 July 1701; Philip, b 12 May 1701, d Boston 27 Dec 1727, prob unm; Ruth II, b 1 Sept 1704, d 22 June 1721, aged 17; and Naomi, b 27 Oct 1706 and m Samuel RIDGEWAY.

Capt Peter[3] (Capt Nathaniel[2], Robert[1]) Reynolds was b 1670 in Boston and d Br by 28 June 1728. He m in Br ca 1699 Mary GILES/GILLS (6:100), who poss d Br 8 Jan 1740, 70 yr (6:169). The will of Peter Raynolds of Br, dtd 8 Dec 1726 and pvd 28 June 1728, named wife Mary; sons Peter (eldest), Eleazer and Nathaniel (under 21); dau Mary Raynolds under 18; wife Mary to be exec (Rounds, 1:162). The agreement of the div of the est of Peter by Mary Raynolds of Br, dcd intestate, betw her ch, was dtd 22 Feb 1739 and signed by her ch: Peter Raynolds, clerk of Infield, Hampshire Co, Mass; Eleazer Raynolds; Nathaniel Raynolds, cordwainer; and Mary Church and her husband, Constant Church, gentleman of Br. It mentioned Mary Raynold's real est in Br and in the "Colony of Conneticut" (Rounds, 1:291).

CHILDREN, all bp Congre Ch, Br (Geneals RI Fams, 1989, 2: 376-380; Reyn Gen, p 58-60):
1. Peter[4] Jr, b 26 Nov 1700 (6:100), bp 28 Oct 1705. He grad from Harvard College in 1720 and joined the Congre Ch of Br as Peter Jr on 3 Feb 1723. In 1738 he was the minister (clerk) of the Congre Ch in Infield, Hampshire Co, Mass when his father's est was div, and he was still there in 10 Mar 1749/50 when named in the will of his father's brother, John (RIGR, 5:93). The Reyn Gen, p 45, said he was minister at Enfield, Conn, which is not correct. The 1790 US Census of Adams Town, Berkshire Co, Mass, showed the family of a Peter Reynolds, the only one in the State of Mass, who was poss the son of Peter Jr.
2. Eleazer, b 12 Mar 1703/04 (6:100), bp 28 Oct 1705; d 1745 at Cape Breton, Canada; m Br 6 May 1733 Mercy THROOP(E), b 25 Jan 1712/13, d 23 Sept 1795, 83 yrs as "Mercy, widow", dau Thomas and Abigail Throope of Br. Eleazer had one ch rec in the VR Br (6:100): John, b Br 26 June 1744, bp 22 May 1748 Congre Ch "of Ebenezer dec and Mary". The will of Mercy's father, Thomas Throope, dtd 3 May 1754, mentioned two other ch of hers: Thomas and Mary Reynolds (RIGR, 5:93). The 1774 Census of RI listed Mercy Reynolds as living in Br, head of a household of two females above 16, and one female under 16 (Bartlett, p 182).
3. Mary, b unrec, bp 7 Jan 1710; d 16 Apr 1772; m Br 25 Jan 1732 Capt Constant CHURCH, b 12 Dec 1708, d 8 May 1740, 32 yr (6:123), son Col Charles and Hannah (Paine) Church of Br. The will of Charles Church of Br, dtd 29 1746 and pvd 24 Feb 1747, named his dau-in-law, Mary Church, widow of his eldest son, Constant, and his gch, the ch of Constant dec, Charles (eldest), Peter and Mary Church (RIGR, 3:134). On 20 May 1740 Mary Church, widow, was made admin of the est of Constant Church of Br. Mary

had four ch b Br, surname Church: Constant, b 5 Nov 17-33, twin, who d on a privateer as apprentice 21 Aug 17-45 (6:123); Charles, b 5 Nov 1733, twin d 14 Nov 1766, 33 yr, and m Mrs Eunice PECKHAM (6:14); Col Peter, b 1 Dec 1737, d 21 Oct 1821, 84 yr, m (1) Sarah FALES, and m (2) Hannah GAY; and Mary, b 2 Apr 1740 who m Benjamin BOSWORTH (6:14). Mary and Constant Church's ch have a Myflwr desc from Richard Warren (Myflwr Fams in Progress, Richard Warren, p 75).
4. Nathaniel, b unrec, bp 27 Oct 1717; poss d Sept 1746 at Jamaica (6:159). No issue in VR Br. The VR Br 6:45 give the m's of a Nathaniel Reynolds to: Mercy Pitts of Dighton, Mass on 12 Dec 1739; and Mary Little of Br on 13 June 1741. One or both may refer to Nathaniel^4, who was a cordwainer in Br, and alive on 22 Feb 1739.

Ens Joseph^3 (Capt Nathaniel^2, Robert^1) Reynolds was b 29 Dec 1676 in Boston (Reyn Gen, p 43), or b 9 Jan 1677 (Bodge, p 279), and d in Br 16 Jan 1759, 82 yr 0m 7d (6:159). He m 28 Aug 1718 in Norton, Mass Phebe LEONARD, b 1 Mar 1696 and d as "wife of Joseph" 18 Dec 1744, 49 yr, dau George and Anne (Tisdale) Leonard of Norton (Rounds, 1:219). Through her mother, Phebe Leonard had a Myflwr desc from Thomas Rogers (Myflwr Fams, 2:194, 278). Joseph Reynolds built the mansion called "Willowmere" on High St in Br which was still standing in 1926. He became a freeman of RI in 1747 (MacGunnigle, p 38), and on 10 Feb 1746/47 he took the Oath of Bribery and Corruption at a town meeting held in Br (Munro, p 160-161). He was bur in the old East Cemetery in Br under a stone carved with the Reynolds coat of arms which showed three foxes on the shield (Reyn Gen, p 43). The will of Joseph Reynolds of Br, "Inman", dtd 16 Feb 1757 and pvd 5 Feb 1759, mentioned: sons Joseph and Samuel Reynolds; daus Phebe wife of Daniel Waldron, and Elizabeth Watson of Plymouth dec; and two gch, John and Elizabeth Watson, ch of my dau Elizabeth Watson of Plymouth, dec (RIGR, 5:94). Joseph's will, as given in Myflwr Fams, 2:278, called him tanner of Br.

CHILDREN, b Br (6:100):
1. Capt Joseph^4 Jr, b 15 Nov 1719; d as Esq 11 Sept 1789, ae 70 (8:388); m 9 Aug 1744 Rehoboth, Mass by Rev John Greenwood (VR Re, p 166) Lydia GREENWOOD of Rehoboth, b 8 Feb 1723/24 (Ibid, p 629), d Br 1 May 1804, 80 yr, widow (1:159), dau Rev John and Lydia Greenwood of Rehoboth.
2. George, b 30 Apr 1721, bp 10 Oct 1721 Congre Ch, Br (Geneals RI Fams, 1989, 2:380); d 18 Oct 1745.
3. Elizabeth, b 15 Jan 1722/23; d bef father's will of 16 Feb 1757; m 1744 John WATSON of Plymouth, Mass, b 17-

16, son John and Sarah (Rogers) Watson. Sarah Rogers was dau of Daniel Rogers of Ipswich, Mass. Elizabeth had three ch b Plymouth, surname Watson (Gen Reg Plym Fams, p 278): Elizabeth, b 1745 and m Edward CLARK of Boston; John, b 1747 and m 1769 Lucia MARSTON; and Daniel, b 1749 and d bef gfather, Joseph Reynold's will of 16 Feb 1757.

4. Phebe, b 3 Aug 1725; d as widow 3 Mar 1789, 64 yr (6:-169); m Br 28 Sept 1746 (6:55) Capt Daniel WALDRON, b Br 14 Dec 1724, d on coast of Africa 27 Dec 1767, 44 yr (6:-169), son Joseph and Martha (Newton) (Toman) Waldron of Br. Phebe had ten ch b Br, surname Waldron, bp Congre Ch (6:109; 8:290): ch who d July 1747 (6:169); Daniel, bp 1 July 1750 and d 9 Mar 1775, 26 yr (Ibid); Newton, bp 16 Feb 1752, d 17 Mar 1827, 75 yr, and m Frances BOSWORTH (8:353); Capt George, bp 21 Apr 1754, d 9 Oct 1786, 33 yr at sea (6:169), m Sarah MARTINDALE; Samuel, bp 19 Oct 17-55 and d 4 Aug 1756 (Ibid); Leonard, bp 15 June 1760 and d aft father's will of 5 Sept 1761; Elizabeth, bp 30 May 1762, d 20 July 1834, 72 yr (6:128), m Thomas DIMAN; Molly, bp 8 Jan 1764 and m 15 Oct 1786 Benjamin REYNOLDS (8:-347); and Nancy/Mercy, b Dec 1767 and rec as Nancy (6:109) but bp 10 Jan 1768 as Mercy (8:290).

5. Samuel, b 14 July 1727; d 30 July 1727.
6. Samuel II, b 9 Jan 1728/29; alive when named in father's will of 16 Feb 1757. No m or d recs in VR Br.
7. Jonathan, b 28 Sept 1732; d 21 Jan 1753, 20 yr.

Capt Joseph[4] Jr (Ens Joseph[3], Capt Nathaniel[2], Robert[1]) Reynolds was b in Br 15 Nov 1719, and d there as Esq on 11 Sept 1789, ae 70 (8:388). He m Rehoboth, Mass by Rev John Greenwood 9 Aug 1744 Lydia GREENWOOD of Rehoboth (VR Re, p 166, 319), b Rehoboth 8 Feb 1723/24 (Ibid, p 629), d Br 1 May 1804, 80 yr (6:159; 8:388), dau Rev John and Lydia Greenwood of Rehoboth (VR Re, p 629). As Joseph Jr he became a freeman of RI from Br in 1747 (MacGunnigle, p 38), and on 10 Feb 1746/47, together with his father, he took the Oath of Bribery and Corruption in Br (Munro, p 161). In 1760 he was elected a Representative to the General Assembly of RI (Ibid, p 385). The 1774 Census of Br listed him as head of a household of fourteen people: two males above 16, two males under 16, five females above 16, one female under 16, and four blacks (Bartlett, p 182). He was called Joseph Sr in the Pat Index, p 565, for Civil Service from RI in the Rev War. His will, dtd 18 Feb 1789 and pvd Br 5 Oct 1789, named wife Lydia; sons Joseph (eldest), George, Samuel, and Jonathan Reynolds; daus Elizabeth Smith, Hannah Fales, Lydia and Mary Reynolds; and kinsman John Reynolds (RIGR, 6:156).

CHILDREN, all b Br, nine bp Congre Ch (6:100; 8:285):
1. Joseph[5] "2nd", b 20 Sept 1748, bp 25 Sept 1748; d 10 Oct 1818, 70 yr (6:159; 8:388); m Sarah COX, b ca 1745,

d 6 Sept 1838, 93 yr (6:159). Joseph 2nd was called Joseph Jr in the Pat Index, p 565 for his service as a Lt in Capt William Throop's Co of Br in the RI Militia during the Rev War (RIGR, 9:194-195). His will, dtd 11 Aug 1813 and pvd 2 Nov 1818, mentioned wife Sarah; sons William and Greenwood Reynolds; daus Sarah wife of Daniel Bradford, Ann wife of John Peck, Phebe Reynolds, Elizabeth wife of Samuel Bradford, and Hannah wife of James P. Burgess; gson Joseph son of Greenwood Reynolds; and his brother Samuel Reynolds (RIGR, 7:170-171).

2. Lydia, b 14 Nov 1749; d unm betw 27 Aug 1819 when she wrote her will, and 1 Jan 1821 when it was pvd. She was prob the Lydia who d Br 30 Nov 1820, 75 yrs, with her age given incorrectly (8:388). Her will named her father Joseph Reynolds Esq dec testate; brothers Jonathan, Samuel, Joseph dec leaving unnamed ch, and George Reynolds dec leaving unnamed ch; sisters Mary Reynolds, Elizabeth Smith dec, and Hannah Fales dec; niece Betsey Bourne widow of Allen Bourne dec and dau of my late sister Elizabeth Smith dec; two nieces Sarah Fales and Dorothy Wardwell wife of Nathaniel Wardwell, daus of my late sister Hannah Fales dec (RIGR, 7:172).

3. Elizabeth, b 21 Sept 1750, bp 23 Sept 1750; d 2 Oct 1797, 47 yr "wife of Josiah" (6:163); m 22 Aug 1776 Josiah SMITH (6:45), b 7 June 1742, d aft 26 Mar 1821, son Benjamin and Abigail (Howland) (Church) Smith (6:50, 103). Elizabeth's ch have a Myflwr line through Josiah's mother, Abigail, from John Howland of the Myflwr. Elizabeth had six ch, surname Smith, bp Congre Ch, Br, on 11 Sept 1788: Josiah Jr, George Reynolds, Jonathan, Elizabeth who m 7 June 1805 Allen BOURNE, Mary, and Eleanor. The will of Josiah Smith was given in RIGR, 10: 152-153).

4. Mary, b 11 Nov 1752; d 2 Dec 1836, 84 yr, unm (6:-159). Her will, she singlewoman of Br, aged 80 yrs and upward, was dtd 6 May 1836 and pvd 2 Jan 1837. She named her father Joseph Reynolds dec; only living brother Jonathan of Br, and dec brothers Samuel and George; nieces Sarah Fales and Elizabeth Bourne widow; George S. Bourne son of niece Elizabeth Bourne; gniece Rebecca S.B. Usher wife of George F. Usher of Br; and Dolly wife of Nathaniel Wardwell (no relation given) who received some clothes along with Mary's nieces (RIGR, 10:152).

5. Mercy, b 11 Nov 1752, twin; d bef father's will of 18 Feb 1789.

6. Phebe, b 18 Oct 1754, bp 20 Oct 1754 (Geneals RI Fams, 1989, 2:388); d 16 Oct 1779, 25 yr "of Capt" Reynolds (6:159).

7. George, b 7 Nov 1756, bp 14 Nov 1756; d Dutchess Co, NY betw 12 Apr 1795 and date of sister Mary's will of 6 May 1836; prob m Abigail PECK, b 14 Aug 1758 (6:-98), dau Capt Jonathan and Mary (Throop) Peck of Br.

George had the fol ch bp Congre Ch, Br, 12 Apr 1795 (8: 285-286): Jonathan, George, Joseph, Lydia and Abigail. George rem to Amenia, Dutchess Co, NY, where he d (Peck Gen, p 144).
8. Hannah,b 24 Dec 1758, bp 8 Apr 1759; d 1 Oct 1811, 53 yr (6:131; 8:369); m Timothy FALES, b 7 Feb 1745/46 (6:45), d bef father's will of 2 Feb 1800, son Nathaniel and Sarah (Little) Fales (6:20, 75; RIGR, 6:157). The ch of Timothy and Hannah have a Myflwr desc through his mother, Sarah Little, from James Chilton (Bowman, p 97, 294). Hannah had two kn ch surname Fales: Sarah, and Dorothy who m Nathaniel WARDWELL, named as nieces and daus of Hannah dec, in will of Hannah's sister, Lydia (RIGR, 7:172); and also by the will of Nathaniel Fales of Br, dtd 2 Feb 1800 and pvd 22 Dec 1801, in which he named Sally Fales and Dolly Fales, daus of my son, Timothy Fales dec (RIGR, 6:157).
9. Samuel, b 26 Dec 1760, bp 29 Mar 1761; d 28 Dec 18- 35, 75 yr (6:159). No m or issue in VR Br. However, 6: 158 gives the d of Hannah, wife of Capt Samuel Reynolds, 9 Sept 1830, who might be his wife.
10. Jonathan, b 29 Jan 1768 (sic), bp 26 June 1763 (Geneals RI Fams, 1989, 2:393); d Br 29 June 1845, 83 yr (6:159); m Congre Ch, Br 1 Jan 1789 Mary PECK (8:345), b 28 Sept 1767, dau Capt Jonathan and Mary (Throop) Peck of Br (6:98). The VR Br give no issue for them, but Rev Henry Wight's Deaths has that of Betsey Peck of Jonathan Reynolds on 8 Oct 1796, 3 yr (8:388).
11. Greenwood, bp 25 May 1766; d Br 21 Nov 1840, 64 yr; m Congre Ch, Br 8 Dec 1799 (6:12; 8:327) Mary CALDWELL, dau Robert and Elizabeth Caldwell. They had the fol ch bp St Michael's Ch (8:176): Mary, Samuel Godfrey, Robert Caldwell, Joseph, and John Greenwood, all on 9 Jan 1813, and Mary II "of Greenwood and Mary" on 24 May 1816. A ch of Greenwood d 7 Mar 1801 (8:388).

Benjamin[3] (Capt Nathaniel[2], Robert[1]) Reynolds was b 10 May 1686 at Br and d there 4 Aug 1770, 86 yr. He m 1708/ 09 Susannah RAWSON, b 3 Oct 1686 Mendon, Mass, and d 11 Aug 1762, dau Rev Grindall and Susanna (Wilson) Rawson of Mendon. The Rev Grindall Rawson graduated from Harvard College in 1678 and was the second minister of Mendon (Sav, 3:511). Both Benjamin and Susannah joined the Congre Ch of Br on 16 Sept 1722 (8:261). Benjamin Raynolds of Br, cordwainer, was appted 16 Feb 1730/31 as guardian of Thomas Rawson, over 14, son of Wilson Rawson of Uxbridge, Suffolk Co, Mass (Rounds, 1:191).

Benjamin became a freeman of RI from Br in 1747 (MacGunnigle, p 38), and on 10 Feb 1746/47 he took the Oath of Bribery and Corruption at the town meeting in Br, together with his father and brother, Joseph Jr (Munro, p 161). His will, he cordwainer of Br and far advanced in years, dtd 24 Oct 1769 and pvd 7 Jan 1771, named sons Benjamin, John and Grindall Reynolds; daus Mary Rawson, Sarah Weld and Ann Reynolds (RIGR, 6:153).

CHILDREN, b Br (6:100):
1. Priscilla^4, b 13 Apr 1711; poss d 24 Jan 1744, unm (6:159). Not named in father's will of 24 Oct 1769.
2. Ann(a), b 12 July 1715, twin, bp 31 July 1715 Congre Ch (Geneals RI Fams, 1989, 2:380); unm when father's will of 24 Oct 1769 was written.
3. Mary, b 12 July 1715, twin, bp 31 July 1715 Congre Ch (Ibid, 2:380); d.y.
4. Mary II, b 20 Nov 1716, bp 2 Dec 1716 Congre Ch; m ___ RAWSON per father's will. The VR Br (6:45) give the m (int) 17 May 1743 of Grindall Rawson of Mendon, Mass and Ann Raynolds of Br (6:45). Apparently he m Mary instead? Grindall Rawson Jr was b Mendon 6 Sept 1707 (Sav, 3:511).
5. John, b 1 Apr 1718; d aft father's will of 24 Oct 1769; m (1) (int) 11 Jan 1743/44 Susannah GILES of Salem, Mass (6:45); m (2) by 1753 Dorothy ___. The VR Br (6:100) call him John Jr, prob to distinguish him from his uncle, John Reynolds, of Br. As John Jr he had the fol ch rec in Br (6:100): by his first wife, Susannah: Priscilla, b 3 June 1745; by second wife, Dorothy: Samuel, b 3 Apr 1754; Grindall, b 12 Oct 1755; Benjamin, b 17 Mar 1757 who m 15 Oct 1786 Molly WALDRON, dau Capt Daniel and Phebe (Reynolds) Waldron (8:347); and John, bp 24 June 1759 Congre Ch Br (Geneals RI Fams, 1989, 2: 388-391).
6. Benjamin, b 15 Nov 1722; d aft father's will of 24 Oct 1769. The VR Br (6:159) give the d of a Sarah, wife of Benjamin Reynolds, in Br 11 Mar 1762, but no m or ch are rec for him there.
7. Lt Grindall, b 11 July 1726; d aft 1790; m 30 Jan 1758 Sarah SEARLES, b 28 Jan 1733, dau Hon Nathaniel and Elizabeth (Kinnicut) Searles of Little Compton, RI (LC Fams, p 550). Sarah's ch have a Myflwr line from John and Priscilla (Mullins) Alden through her gmother, Sarah Rogers, dau John and Elizabeth (Pabodie) Rogers (Ibid, p 549-550), and another Myflwr line through her father, who was son of Sarah Rogers, a desc of Thomas Rogers of the Myflwr (Myflwr Fams, 2:270-271).Grindall was listed in the Pat Index, p 564, as having served as Lt from Va during the Rev War. Since his son, Grindall Jr, was also listed there as a Rev War Private from Vt, the Va is prob a typographical error, and he was in Vt. The 1790 US Census of Vt showed in Putney Town of Windham Co (p 53) a Grindall Reynolds with one male 16 or over, and three females; and in So Hero Town of Chittenden Co (p

27) a Grinnel Reynolds with two males 16 or over, one male under 16 and one female. Lt Grindall joined the Congre Ch of Br on 6 May 1759 and had six ch bp there (8:-285): Nathaniel, bp 6 May 1759, Elizabeth, bp 5 Oct 1760, Benjamin, bp 17 July 1763, Grindall Jr, bp 23 Sept 1764, Constant, bp 21 Sept 1766, and Sarah, bp 14 Oct 1770. The Pat Index, p 564, said that Grindall Jr was b 1763 and d 29 Nov 1843 and m Dorcas LANDON. She was b 1774 and d 1811.
  8. Sarah, b unrec but named in father's will of 24 Oct 1769 as dau Sarah Weld; m Br 15 Apr 1752 Edmund WELD of Roxbury, Mass (6:57).

13. CHRISTOPHER SAUNDERS/SANDERS

Stiles, p 675, said that Mr Christopher[1] Sanders came to Windsor, Conn by 1671 and bought the property of Simon Wolcott on the Island. He was a merchant, in business with his brother, George, and in 1677 he bought Capt Marshall's warehouse at the ferry. His parentage, and place and date of b are not kn. He m, prob at Windsor, by early 1675 Elizabeth ___, and his last ch b in Windsor was in Apr 1681.

He signed the Articles on 27 Aug 1680 to purchase a thirty-second part of the land which became Br (Munro, p 97), and he was at the first town meeting on 1 Sept 1681 (Ibid, p 79). He was living in Br when other ch were b there. By 1688 he had rem to Rehoboth, Mass where he presumably lived for the rest of his life (Sav, 4:20). The list of the inhabitants and proprs of Rehoboth, dtd 7 Feb 1689, included Mr Christopher Sanders as an inhabitant (VR Re, p 915 Supplement; Bliss, p 128). He was Deputy from Rehoboth to the Plymouth Court in 1690, 1691 and 1692 (Bliss, p 169), and he witnessed the will of John Fitch of Rehoboth on 20 June 1693 (Rounds, 1:17).

CHILDREN (6:102; Sav, 4:20; Stiles, p 675):
  1. Daniel[2], d 22 Nov 1675 ae 11 days, Windsor (per Stiles) or d 22 Dec 1675 at 11 days (Sav).
  2. Susanna(h), b 20 Nov 1676, Windsor.
  3. Daniel II, b 27 Oct 1678, Windsor.
  4. Elizabeth, b 30 Apr 1681, Windsor; prob d.y.
  5. Elizabeth II, b 13 Oct 1684 (sic, 1682?), Br, "of Christian and Elizabeth" (6:102).
  6. Lovett, b 7 Mar 1683/84, Br "of Christian and Elizabeth (Ibid).
  7. Henry, b 4 Aug 1688 Rehoboth (VR Re, p 739) "of Christopher"; bur Rehoboth 6 May 1692 "of Capt ___". This is the only Sanders d in the VR Re.

14. JOHN WILKINS

John Wilkins signed the Articles on 27 Aug 1680 for a thirty-second part of the land which became the town of Br (Munro, p 96-97). His name was first on the list of those who took the Oath of Fidelity in Br on 20 June 1683 (Ibid, p 114). It is not kn who John's parents were, or where he was b. Torrey, p 816 said that John Wilkins m Anstis (GOLD) BISSETT, widow of Thomas, and had a ch b by 1671, and lived in Boston and Br, RI. Neither Torrey nor Sav listed the surname Bissett, and it was poss either Bassett or Bissell.

Sav, 4:551 mentioned only one John Wilkins of Boston, and said he was a freeman in 1673, might have come from Wiltshire, England, and had a dau, Abigail, b 1676 who m 30 July 1696 Benjamin Ellery. John had two ch b in Br (6:-112). Early Br horse descriptions list a horse of Mr Wilkins, described on 10 Apr 1701, which was prob his (TAG, 65:119). John Wilkins, and his wife, Anstis who d 31 Oct 1711 in 73rd yr, are both bur in the Common Bur Ground of Newport, RI (VR RI, Beaman, New Series, 11:453). On 1 Oct 1705 an acct of John's est was presented by Anstis and Samuel Wilkins, admins. The agreement of the div of his est, also dtd 1 Oct 1705, was among Anstis Wilkins, widow; son Samuel Wilkins to receive a double portion; dau Mary Jenkins; Benjamin Elleree and Abigail his wife, dau of the dcd; and youngest dau Mehettabell Wilkins (Rounds, 1:33).

CHILDREN (Torrey, p 816; 6:112):
1. Mary^2, b by 1671, poss Boston; m (1) ___ PEPPER, as she m (2) Br as Mrs Mary Peper, Richard JENKINS on 3 Feb 1701 (6:44). The inv of Richard Jenkins's est at Br was dtd 25 Feb 1703/04 by Mary Jenkins, widow, and included a "lengthy list of yard goods, thread, ribbons, buttons, etc" (Rounds, 1:31). Mary had one ch b Br, surname Jenkins: Anstis, of Richard and Mary, b 28 Oct 1702 (6:-85). She apparently m (3) ___ ROGERS, as she m (4) Br 26 July 1716 as "Mrs Mary Rogers of Br" Capt Stephen MUMFORD of Newport, RI (6:37). That Mary Wilkins m Capt Stephen Mumford is pvd by the agreement of the settlement of the est of her brother, Samuel Wilkins, which called, among his "brethren and sisters" Capt Stephen Mumford and Mary his wife of Newport, dtd 2 Mar 1720/21 (Rounds, 1:98). Mary, wife of Capt Stephen Mumford (Jr), d 2 Sept 1715 in 44rd yr; and Capt Stephen d 7 June 1731, age 65 yr. Both are bur in the Common Bur Ground of Newport (VR RI, Beaman, New Series, 11:285). Mary had the fol kn ch b Newport, surname Mumford (Ibid): Ann, d 28 Nov 1704 age 6 wks; John, d 22 Feb 1705 age 9 wks; Edward, d 3 Sept 1720 age 19 yr; and Elizabeth, d 11 June 1734 age 22 yr, and are bur with their parents.

2. Abigail, b 1676 Boston, d 15 Dec 1742, 65 yr (VR RI, Beaman, New Series, 11:147); m 30 July 1696 Hon Capt Benjamin ELLERY, b 1669 and d Newport, RI 26 July 1746, 76 yr, son William Ellery of Gloucester, Mass (Torrey, p 247). Her brother, Samuel's settlement of est, dtd 2 Mar 1720/21, called her and her husband, of Newport, RI. Benjamin Ellery was Deputy of Newport, Judge of the County Court, and an Assistant. He and Abigail are bur in the Common Bur Ground at Newport under slate platforms with his coat of arms on them. She had the fol kn ch b Newport, surname Ellery, all bur with their parents (VR RI, Beaman, New Series, 11:147-148): John of Capt Benjamin and Abigail d 2 Dec 1708 age 18 d; Hannah, d 16 Dec 1711 age near 2 yr; John II, d Mar 1713 age 11 mo; Samuel, d 1713; son stillborn d 20 June 1721; Abigail, 2nd dau Benjamin Ellery Esq and wife of George Wanton, merchant of Newport, d 12 May 1726 in 28 yr; Anstis, dau Benjamin and Abigail and widow of Thomas Coggeshall, d Newport 31 May 1769 age 70 yr. It is poss that she was also the mother of: Benjamin Ellery Esq who was b 1724 and d Newport 12 Dec 1797 in 73 yr and m Mehitable Redwood, dau Abraham Redwood (Ibid, p 148); and William Ellery Esq, d "Iles of Man" 1764 age 64 yr, a Deputy Gov., and of Harvard College (Ibid, 11:149).
3. Samuel, b 31 May 1683 Br. No m in VR Br and no issue named in the settlement of his est, dtd 2 Mar 1720/21, by his "brethren and sisters": Capt Stephen Mumford and Mary his wife, Capt Benjamin Ellery and Abigail his wife, and Mr Peter Treebe and Mehitabel his wife, all of Newport, RI (Rounds, 1:98).
4. Mehitable, b 2 May 1685 Br; m Peter TREBY/TREEBE of Newport, per the settlement of her brother, Samuel's est dtd 2 Mar 1720/21. Peter was prob Jr, son of Peter Treby Sr of Newport, and he d Newport 26 May 1734 in 47 yr (VR RI, Beaman, New Series, 11:415). Torrey, p 753 said that Peter Treby m Mehitable Shepard and they had a ch b 5 Apr 1714. It is poss that Mehitable Wilkins m (1) ___ Shepard, although Torrey did not give such a m. The VR Br (6:173) give the d in Br on July or Aug 1776, 92 yr, of Mehitable Wilkins "of John and Anstess", who prob refers to her, but oddly calls her by her maiden name instead of her married one. She had the fol kn ch b Newport, surname Treby, order unkn (VR RI, Beaman, New Series, 11:415; VR Newport, 4:72): Peter, prob b 5 Apr 1714, d 1 Oct 1717, 3 yr; Peter II, b 1720 per d rec, d 1 Nov 1759 39 yr, m Susannah___; Ruth, d 8 Apr 1725 age 9 m; Samuel who m Elizabeth ___; Mehitable who m 1752 (4:72); John who m 5 Sept 1754 Sarah RICHARDSON (Ibid); and Wilkins who m 15 Oct 1766 Honora SANFORD (Ibid). The Pat Index, p 687 called this name "Tribby (or Treby)" when they listed: John Sr, b 1725-30, d

1794, m Sarah Richardson, Pvt RI; and John Jr, b 1758, d 5__1819, m Abigail Hazard, Slr CT.

15. NATHANIEL WILLIAMS

Nathaniel[2] Williams was b Taunton, Mass 17 Nov 1639 and d there 16 Aug 1692, son of Richard and Frances (Deighton) Williams. Richard was an original propr of Taunton, and Nathaniel's ch have several royal lines through their mother who was the dau of Dr John and Jane (Bassett) Deighton of Gloucester, England (TAG, 1933, 9:212-222). Nathaniel m in Taunton 17 Nov 1668 Elizabeth ROGERS, b bef 1652 and d aft 7 Mar 1703, dau John and Ann(a) (Churchman) Rogers of Duxbury. Elizabeth's ch have a Myflwr desc through her gfather, Thomas Rogers, of the Myflwr (Myflwr Fams Thru 5 Gens, 2:158, 167-168).

Nathaniel signed the Articles on 27 Aug 1680 for a thirty-second part of the land which became Br, but it does not seem that he ever lived there. The VR Br do not contain any b, d, or m recs for his family. His wife, Elizabeth, was the sister of John Rogers who did live in Br for a time, and d there in 1691. The div of the est of Nathaniel Williams of Taunton, dtd 25 July 1698, named: wife Elizabeth; ch John (eldest son), Nathaniel (2nd son), and Elisabeth, only dau, under 18 (Rounds, 1:19).

CHILDREN, b Taunton (Myflwr Fams Thru 5 Gens, 2:167-168, 205-208):
 1. John[3], b 27 Aug 1675; d Taunton 18 Aug 1724, 49 yr; m ca 1701/02 Hannah ROBINSON (Bowman, p 242). 6 ch, b Taunton.
 2. Nathaniel, b 9 or 29 Apr 1679; d Taunton 24 Aug 1726, ae 47; m Lydia KING. 6 ch, b Taunton.
 3. Elizabeth, b 18 Apr 1686; d Taunton 2 May 1732, 47 yr; m 17 Mar 1707 John MACOMBER (Bowman, p 242). 10 ch, b Taunton, surname Macomber.

16. CAPT SAMUEL WOODBURY

Capt Samuel[3] Woodbury was bp 4 June 1654 at Salem, Mass, son of Hugh (William) and Mary (Dixey) Woodbury of Salem and Br, RI (Sav, 4:634). He m by 1684, place unkn, Mary ___, and he signed the Articles on 27 Aug 1680 for a thirty-second part of the land which became Br (Munro, p 97). It is rather unusual that he had the means to buy this amount of land when his father, Hugh, did not do so, but also moved to Br. Samuel took the Oath of Fidelity at Br on 21 May 1684 (Ibid, p 114). He appeared in the 1689 Census of Br as "Cap Sam Woodbry" with a wife, two ch and two servants, and he was the second man on the list after his father, Hugh (Geneals RI Fams, 1989, 2:401). His wife, Mary, became a member of the Congre Ch in Br on 24 July 1697 (8:269). Capt Samuel d Br bef 28 May 1706 when the est of Capt Samuel Woodbery of Br, mariner, was presented by Jonathan Woodbery, mariner, and eldest son (Rounds, 1:35). His widow, Mary, m (2) William FFULTON, "Chiriurgion" of Br (Rounds, 1:43). The agreement of the settlement of the est of Capt Samuel Woodbury, mariner of Br, was dtd 3 Mar 1708/09 and signed by: his widow, Mary ffulton, wid of Samuel Woodbury and now wife of William ffulton, Chirurgion of Br; and his ch, Jonathan Woodbery (son), mariner of Br; Samuel Woodbery (son), shipwright of Newport; Dr William ffulton as guardian of Sarah Woodbury (dau) (Rounds, 1:43). The inv of the est of Mrs Mary Fulton of Br, dtd 27 July 1732, was presented by Jonathan Woodbury, her son and admin (Ibid, 1:212).

CHILDREN, b Br$_4$(6:113):
1. Jonathan^4, b 5 May 1685; d as Esq 21 Jan 1766, 81 yr (6:174); m 24 May 1708 Katherine OSBORN (6:40, 60),b Br 12 Nov 1686, dau Jeremiah and Mercy (Davis) Osborn of Br. The VR Br 6:96 list the Osborn family under Osband, which is incorrect. Munro, p 79, called him Jeremiah Osborne, and he was an original settler of Br. No issue in the VR Br for Jonathan except for the d of an infant ch in June 1730 (6:174). Jonathan, mariner of Br, was guardian of Samuel and Sarah Woodbery, brother and sister of said Jonathan, all ch of Capt Samuel Woodbery, mariner dcd, mentioned 3 Oct 1706 in agreement of settlement of est of Hugh and Mary Woodbery of Br dcd (Rounds, 1:36-37).
2. Capt Samuel, b 5 Nov 1688; d 24 Mar 1757, 69 yr (6:-174); m (1) (int) 7 July 1721 Margaret OSBORN (6:60), b Br 27 May 1695, d Oct 1730, dau Jeremiah and Mercy (Davis) Osborn of Br (6:174); m (2) Br 18 June 1739 Elizabeth (CHURCH) (ROSBOTHAM) SAMPSON (6:60), b Little Compton, RI 26 Mar 1684, d Br 17 July 1757, 74 yr, as Mrs Woodbury, alias Sampson (6:174).
3. Sarah, b 18 Sept 1690.

Capt Samuel^4 (Capt Samuel^3, Hugh^2, William^1) Woodbury was b Br 5 Nov 1688 (6:113), and d there 24 Mar 1757, 69 yr (6:174).He m (1) (int) 7 July 1721 Margaret OSBORN(E), b Br 27 May 1695 and d Oct 1730 (6:95, 174), dau Jeremiah and Mercy (Davis) Osborne of Br; m (2) Br 18 June 1739 Elizabeth (CHURCH) (ROSBOTHAM) SAMPSON (6:60), b LC 26 Mar 1684 and d Br 17 July 1757, 74 yr (6:174), dau Col Benjamin and Alice (Southworth) Church, widow Joseph Rosbotham, and widow John Sampson, mariner of Br (Rounds, 1:235, 300; Bowman, p 297). He had no issue by his second m. Samuel was called Shipwright of Newport on 3 Mar 1708/09.

CHILDREN by first wife, Margaret, b Br (6:113):
1. Jonathan[3], "Jr", b 11 Apr 1722; d 1752 at Surinam (6:174); m by early 1752 Lydia ___, b 1729 per d rec, d Br as widow of Jonathan 28 July 1812, 83 yr (Ibid; 8: 398). Jonathan, b 1722, was called "Jr" to distinguish him from his uncle, Jonathan, b 1685, who also lived in Br. He had one ch b Br, Katherine "of Jonathan Jr and Lydia", b 11 Dec 1752 (6:113). The 1774 Census of Br included Lydia as the only head of a Woodbury household there, and she was living alone (Bartlett, p 183). She was still living there alone as Lydia Woodberry when the 1790 Census of RI was taken (p 10), and she was the only Woodbury/Woodberry living in RI at that time.
2. Sarah, b 16 Sept 1723; m 27 Oct 1745 John COY (6:60). She had five ch b Br, surname Coy (6:71): John, Samuel, William, Sarah and Jonathan Woodbury.
3. Margaret, b 30 Nov 1724.
4. Samuel, b 1 Nov 1726.

17. NATHANIEL BOSWORTH SR

Nathaniel[2] Bosworth Sr was b 4 Sept 1617 in England and came with his father, Edward, in 1634 to Mass on the ship Elizabeth and Dorcas. He d 31 Aug 1690 in Br (6:117). Ca 1645/46 he m in Hingham, Mass Bridget, prob widow of both Jeremiah Bellamy and Nicholas Lobdell. He was a cooper, fisherman, and Deacon of the Ch of Christ at Hull, Mass, where he and Bridget had nine ch b, but bp in Hingham. In 1683 he left three of his sons in Hull, and rem to Br with his wife and daus, and three unm sons, Jeremiah aged 34, Bellamy aged 29, and Edward aged ca 24. His son, John, came to Br later (Bosworth Gen, p 95, 112-113, 178, 195, 221, 224, 301-312, 368; NER, 142:270-278). He had bought two-thirds of a thirty-second part of the Mt Hope lands from the Proprietors.

In Br in the 1680's he built the first frame house in town on his land on the east side of Hope St, just north of the bridge across Silver Creek. His name appears on the Founders Tablet in Memorial Hall. Nathaniel became a prominent man in town, and was the first Deacon of the first Ch formed in Br, the Congre (Munro, p 79, 91-92, 103-104). The 1689 Census of Br listed him with a wife, 2 ch and 2 gch (Geneals RI Fams, 1989, 2:401). His will was dtd 15 Mar 1689/90 and pvd Br 20 Nov 1690. In it he, termed yeoman, named wife Bridget; sons Nathaniel (eldest), Joseph, John, Jeremy, Bellamy and Edward; daus Mary and Bridgett (no surnames), Hanah Jacob; also Mary, Sarah, John and Nathaniel Lobdell (prob his wife's ch by a former m); and cousin Benjamin Jones; land in Hull that he still owned

(Rounds, 1:2).

CHILDREN, all bp Hingham, Mass except John (Bosworth Gen, p 112):
1. Dau[3], b ca 1647; m 21 Feb 1664/65 John LOBDELL (per Bosworth Gen, but not in Torrey).
2. Nathaniel Jr, bp 29 July 1649; d Hull 25 Aug 1693; m(1) Plymouth, Mass 7 Dec 1670 Elizabeth MORTON, b 3 May 1652, d 6 Apr 1673, dau Nathaniel and Lydia (Cooper) Morton (Bosworth Gen, p 178); m (2) by 1676 Mary MORTON, dau John and Lettice Morton Sr of Middleboro, Mass. He had one ch by his first wife, Nathaniel, b 1673 who d unm; and nine ch by his second wife: Elizabeth, John, Samuel, Mary, Ephraim, Lemuel, Joseph, Bridget and Jeremiah (Ibid, p 301-312; Gen Reg Plym Fams, p 29-30).
3. Jeremiah, bp 29 July 1649; d Br 20 Mar 1717, unm.
4. Hannah, b 30 Apr 1650, bp 16 July 1650; d Br aft 17-22; m Hull ca 1670 Joseph JACOB(S), b Hingham 1 May 16-46, d Br 9 Feb 1708, son Nicholas and Mary (Gilman) Jacob(s) of Hingham (Torrey, p 414). Joseph and his family rem to Br soon aft 1683, where he was a carpenter. Hannah had six ch surname Jacob(s), all b Hingham: Joseph, Joseph II, Benjamin, Benjamin II, Nathaniel and Mary (6:84). The will of Joseph Jacob, carpenter of Br, dtd 26 May 1703 and pvd 22 Apr 1708, named wife Hannah, and Nathaniel Jacob, only surviving son (no other ch named) (Rounds, 1:40).
5. Capt Joseph, bp 6 June 1652; d at sea bef Jan 1710; m ca 1698 Mrs Elizabeth (DORBY) MILLER, wid Capt Paul Miller. He remained at Hull where he was a mariner. No kn issue.
6. Bellamy, bp 30 Nov 1654; d Br 16 Mar 1717/18 (6:117); m Rehoboth, Mass 11 Nov 1685 Mary SMITH (6:8; VR Re, p 52), b Rehoboth 13 Aug 1666, d 20 Apr 1740, 73 yr, dau Daniel and Esther (Chickering) Smith of Rehoboth (VR Re, p 343).

7. John, b ca 1656; d Br 20 Aug 1725; m Hull ca 1680 Sarah ___, b 1656, d Barrington, RI and bur Br 6 Apr 1735, 79 yr.
8. Mary, bp 4 Oct 1657; d Br 21 Apr 1735, aged 78 unm, where she had been a school mistress for many years. Her will, dtd 22 Mar 1734/35 and pvd 23 Apr 1735, mentioned: kinswoman Mercy wife of Richard Heart; kinswoman Susannah wife of Joseph Phillips; kinswoman Mercy wife of John Twing; kinsman Edward Bosworth of Barrington; kinsman Joseph Phillips of Br; and kinsmen Nathaniel Jacobs and Nathaniel Phillips; friend Samuel Howland to be exec (Rounds, 1:240).
9. Edward, bp 29 May 1659; d Br 22 Feb 1743 (6:117); m (1) by 1695 Mary/Merry ___; m (2) ca 1703/04 Elizabeth ESTABROOK/EASTERBROOK (Bosworth Gen, p 368), prob b 19

Dec 1673 Warren, RI, d Br 15 Jan 1750 (6:117), dau Ens Thomas and Sarah (Woodcock) Estabrook (Torrey, p 239; Bosworth Gen, p 221). Edward was admitted as a citizen of Br at its first town meeting, and his father's will dtd 15 Mar 1689/90 left him a farm there. The VR Br called him Edward Sr ca 1712/13, to separate him clearly from Edward[4] Jr, son of John[3] Bosworth. He had one ch b Br by first wife, Mary (6:63): Hannah, b 16 Mar 1696 who d.y.; and he had two ch by his second wife, Elizabeth (Ibid): Hannah II, bp 25 Mar 1705 Congre Ch, Br, who m Joshua CHASE of Swansea, Mass (6:8); and Sarah, b 4 Dec 1710, d Br 22 Mar 1801, 91 yr (6:142), who m 1728 Thomas KINNECUT (6:30).
10. Bridget, bp 19 Aug 1660; m by 1684 Joseph PHILLIPS of Boston (Torrey, p 578) as his second wife. She had three ch b Boston, surname Phillips (Bosworth Gen, p 224): Joseph, b 7 May 1684 who d Br 9 July 1753, 68 yr (6:157); Benjamin, b 18 Oct 1685; and Nathaniel, b 30 Mar 1689, who was living in Br in 1735.

Bellamy[3] (Nathaniel[2]) Bosworth was bp 30 Nov 1654 in Hingham, Mass and d Br 16 Mar 1717/18 (6:117). On 20 June 1683 he took the Oath of Fidelity at Br. He m at Rehoboth, Mass 11 Nov 1685 Mary SMITH (6:8), b 13 Aug 1666 Rehoboth (VR Re, p 343), and d Br 20 Apr 1740, 73 yr (6:117), dau Daniel and Esther (Chickering) Smith (Ibid). Bellamy and his family lived in Br in a large house which his father built for him on the corner of Hope and Oliver Sts. The 16-89 Census of Br listed him with a wife and two ch (Geneals RI Fams, 1989, 2:401). The will of Bellamy Bosworth of Br, yeoman, dtd 13 Mar 1717/18 and pvd 23 Apr 1718, named wife Mary; sons Benjamin (eldest) and Nathaniel; three daus Bridget, Hester and Mary (no surnames); and his brother "Jerom Bosworth" (sic, Jeremiah) (RIGR, 3:89). The will of his widow, Mary, she of Br, dtd 2 Apr 1735 and pvd 17 June 1740, named sons Nathaniel and Benjamin Bosworth; daus Bridget and Mary (no surnames), and Esther dcd wife of Obediah Papillion; gsons John, Samuel and Peter Papillion, sons of her dau Esther dcd; gdau Bridget Bosworth, dau of her son, Nathaniel; and he was to be exec (Rounds, 1:296-297).

CHILDREN, all b Br (6:63):
1. Bridget[4], b 29 Oct 1686; d by 29 Apr 1768 (inv of est taken in Boston); m (1) poss 7 June 1710 John PAPILLION/PAPILLON, mariner, b Br 20 July 1685, bp 13 May 1688 Congre Ch, d 1718 London, Eng, son Peter and Joan Papillion; m (2) Br 29 Nov 1722 James PECKER of Boston, wharfmaster, b 15 Nov 1684 Haverhill, Mass, d 28 Apr 1734; m (3) Boston 20 Feb 1734/35 Capt Edward EVELETH of Ipswich, Mass, b Ipswich 25 July 1679, d Ipswich as Col-

one1 5 Nov 1759. She had only one ch: Ebenezer Papillion, b Br 9 Apr 1712 who d at sea in late 1734 or early 1735 (E.W. Wait, Papillons of Boston and Br in NER, 124:161-182; Geneals RI Fams, 1989, 2:40-48). The will of Bridget Eveleth of Br, widow, dtd 1 Aug 1763 and pvd 6 Feb 1769, mentioned: brother Benjamin Bosworth dec; niece Esther Pappilion; nieces Ruth Bourn, Elizabeth Church, and the two (unnamed) ch of Bridget Phillips dec; my cousins (nephews?) Belomy Bosworth, Benjamin Bosworth, William Bosworth, Benjamin Bosworth son of Obediah, and the four ch of my cousin Samuel Bosworth dec; Rev John Burt of Br (RIGR, 6:152).

2. Benjamin, b 26 June 1689; d Br 13 Oct 1740 (6:117); m (int) 20 Dec 1718 Br Ruth LOWDER (6:18), who d Br as widow 19 June 1758 (6:117). In 1722 he was named as guardian of his nephew, Ebenezer Papillion (Geneals RI Fams, 1989, 2:42). In a deed of 13 Feb 1722 he was called Benjamin "Jr", yeoman. The inv of his est, taken 15 Nov 17-40, called him Mr Benjamin Bosworth, and totaled L6502, a large amount at that time (Bosworth Gen, p 315-316). He had three ch b Br (Geneals RI Fams, 1989, 2:381): Ruth, b 7 Sept 1721, d 28 Jan 1793, m (1) Nathaniel CHURCH, m (2) 1747 Shearjashub BOURNE Sr; Samuel, b 6 Jan 1722/23, d 8 Aug 1761, m 8 Oct 1752 Elizabeth PECK; and William,b 5 Sept 1724, d 15 Nov 1808, 86 yr (6:118); m (int) Br 27 Feb 1744 Mary FALES who d 30 July 1793, 68 yr (6:118).

3. Hester/Esther, b 7 Jan 1692/93, bp 4 Aug 1695 Congre Ch; d Br 20 Jan 1731/32 (Bosworth Gen, p 319); m by 1716 Obadiah PAPILLION, b Br 19 May 1692, d 13 Jan 1760 in So. Carolina, son Peter and Joan Papillion. He was a ship carpenter. Esther had five ch b Br, surname Papillion (Geneals RI Fams, 1989, 2:47-48): Hester/Esther, b 17 Oct 1717, bp 22 Oct 1721 Congre Ch, bur 27 June 1729 St Michael's Ch, Br (8:233), or d 20 Jan 1731/32 (Bosworth Gen, p 319); John, b 8 Apr 1719, bp 22 Oct 1721 Congre Ch Br, d 28 or 29 Oct 1740 Newport, RI, unm; Samuel, b 25 Nov 1721, d at Jamaica 24 Feb 1745, m 3 July 1743 St Michael's Rebecca BOSWORTH and had no kn issue; Mary, b 3 Nov 1724, bur 14 June 1727 St Michael's; and Peter, b 27 Mar 1727, d 1746 at sea.

4. Capt Nathaniel, b 3 Mar 1693/94, bp 4 Aug 1695 Congre Ch (Geneals RI Fams, 1989, 2:372); d 17 Aug 1745 "Capt at Attleboro" (6:117); m (1) Br 26 Oct 1716 Lydia CORNISH, d "suddenly" 11 May 1726 (8:124), or d 15 Mar 1726, 32 yr, dau James Cornish (Bosworth Gen, p 319); m (2) as "cooper of Bristol" at Newport 18 Aug 1727 (6:8) Elizabeth (LAYTON?) LINDSEY, widow Christopher of Newport. She d Br 7 Dec 1751.

5. Mary, b 29 July 1701; d aft 2 Apr 1735, date of her mother's will; m Boston 6 Sept 1727 Jeremiah WHEELWRIGHT, b Wells, Me 5 Mar 1697/98, d Portsmouth, NH 1768, son

Col John and Mary (Snell) Wheelwright. Mary had one kn ch, Jeremiah Jr, b Portsmouth, NH 13 June 1732, d 28 Jan 1778 (Bosworth Gen, p 329-330).
6. Bellamy, b 16 Jan 1703/04; d 20 Jan 1703/04.

Capt Nathaniel^4 (Bellamy^3, Nathaniel^2) Bosworth was b Br 3 Mar 1693/94, bp 4 Aug 1695 Congre Ch (Geneals RI Fams, 1989, 2:372), and d 17 Aug 1745 at Attleboro, Mass on his way home from the Expedition against Louisburg, Canada, in which he fought and became ill (6:117). He m (1) Br 6 Oct 1716 Lydia CORNISH who d 11 May 1726 (8:124) or d 15 Mar 1726, 32 yr (Bosworth Gen, p 319), dau James Cornish. He m (2) at Newport as "cooper of Bristol" 18 Aug 1727 Elizabeth (LAYTON?) LINDSEY (6:8), widow Christopher of Newport. She d Br 7 Dec 1751. In deeds Nathaniel was termed cooper, gentleman and Captain. On 9 June 1722 he was given land in Br on which to build the first wharf in town for the use of the public (Munro, p 158). Before leaving to fight at Cape Breton, Canada, he made his will in Br, dtd 5 Mar 1744/45. In it he called himself gentleman and named wife Elizabeth; sons Bellomy (eldest), Nathaniel, Daniel, Obadiah and Benjamin; daus Ann Bosworth and Bridget Phillips; son-in-law Michael Phillips; and friend Joseph Russell Esq of Br to be exec (RIGR, 3:263; Bosworth Gen, p 323-324).

CHILDREN by first wife, Lydia, all b Br and bp in Congre Ch Br (6:63; Bosworth Gen, p 327-328):
1. Bridget^5, b July 1715, bp 10 Oct 1721; d 2 July 1750 (6:157); m 30 Oct 1736 Michael PHILLIPS, b 8 Feb 1712/13, son Joseph and Susannah Phillips of Br. Bridget had four kn ch b Br, surname Phillips (6:99, 157): ch of Michael d 13 Sept 1741; ch of Michael d 2 July 1743; Bridget, b 25 May 1745; and Michael, b 16 Oct 1746.
2. Bellamy, b 26 Nov 1716, twin, bp 10 Oct 1721; d 12 Dec 1786, 70 yr (6:118); m (1) (int) 23 Feb 1744, he of Br, Elizabeth MAYHEW of Chilmark, Mass (6:44); m (2) Br 17 May 1750 Esther MAXFIELD. The bp recs of Rev John Burt in Br list two ch of his, by his second wife: Nathaniel of Belamy and Esther bp 16 Feb 1752; and Ebenezer, bp 20 Oct 1754 (6:64).
3. Dr Nathaniel, b 26 Nov 1716, twin, bp 10 Oct 1721; d in Hispaniola 10 Apr 1750, 33 yr, unm. He was a physician in Br (Bosworth Gen, p 326).
4. Anne, b 1 Mar 1720/21, bp 10 Oct 1721; d 21 Aug 1745, 24 yr, unm (6:117).
5. Ebenezer, b 9 Feb 1723/24, twin, bp 16 Feb 1723/24; d at "Surinam, Dutch Guiana" 26 Dec 1741, aged 18 (6:-117).
6. Lydia, b 9 Feb 1723/24, twin, bp 16 Feb 1723/24; d 14 Dec 1729, bur Granary Bur Ground, Boston (Bosworth Gen, p 328).

CHILDREN by second wife, Elizabeth, b Br (6:63; Bosworth Gen, p 328):
7. Elizabeth, b 10 Oct 1728; d 27 Jan 1770, 42 yr (6:-123); m Br 1 July 1746 Thomas CHURCH (6:8), b LC, RI 10 Sept 1722, d 22 Apr 1794, 72 yr, son Caleb and Deborah (Woodworth) Church of LC (LC Fams, p 175). Her ch have a Myflwr desc from Richard Warren of the Myflwr through her husband (Ibid, p 166). Elizabeth had the fol kn ch, surname Church, listed in the VR Br (6:69, 123): ch of Thomas d 26 Apr 1747; ch of Thomas d 16 May 1748; ch of Thomas d 7 Mar 1749; Deborah, b 1753; Elizabeth, b 1756; ch of Thomas d 1762; and Nathaniel who d 23 Jan 1823 at the asylum, 72 yr. Elizabeth and Thomas lived in LC.
8. Lydia II, b 26 May 1730; d 7 or 9 Dec 1738, 9 yr (6:117).
9. Daniel, b 26 Sept 1731, twin; d 25 Sept 1790 (6:-118); m 12 Oct 1752 (8:472) at Second Congre Ch of Newport, RI, Elizabeth PECKHAM (6:459). A deed of 6 July 1753 called Daniel "of Newport, Hatter". No issue in VR Newport, Vol 4.
10. Obadiah, b 26 Sept 1731, twin; d bef Dec 1767; m Br 8 Feb 1753 Mrs Ruth LAWTON (6:8). Obadiah was a mariner. No issue in VR Br.
11. Benjamin, b 9 Jan 1732/33; d 18 Oct 1810 (Bosworth Gen, p 328), or 7 Nov 1810 (Pat Index, p 73); m (1) Newport by Rev William Vinal 14 Feb 1757 Frances (BENNETT) NICHOLS, widow Benjamin of Newport (4:10), who d 5 Feb 1763, 36 yr and bur Common Bur Ground, Newport (VR RI, Beaman, New Series, 11:45). He m (2) Br by Rev John Burt 19 July 1764 Mary CHURCH of Br (6:69), prob b Br 2 Apr 1740, dau Constant and Mary (Reynolds) Church; m (3) Abigail (POTTER) MONROE. Benjamin was a Major from RI in the Rev War (Pat Index, p 73). He and his second wife, Mary Church, had six ch bp Congre Ch, Br, all of whose desc have a Myflwr line from Richard Warren of the Myflwr: Nathaniel, bp 13 Sept 1767; Frances, bp 25 June 1769; Mary Bradford, bp 30 Dec 1770; Alfred, bp 4 July 1773; Benjamin, bp 24 Sept 1775; and Elizabeth, bp 11 July 1779 (8:271).
12. Peleg, b 27 Sept 1734, bp Rehoboth, Mass Nov 1734; d 23 July 1736 (Bosworth Gen, p 328).
13. Peleg II, b 22 Oct 1737; d 10 Oct 1738 (Ibid).

John[3] (Nathaniel[2]) Bosworth was b ca 1656, prob in Hull, Mass, and d 20 Aug 1725 at Br. He m Sarah ___, b Hull ca 1662 and d Br 24 Oct 1754 (Bosworth Gen, p 43, 330; NER, 142:279; 6:117). John and his family lived on land given him by his father in Hull until ca 1708, when he rem to Br. At Hull he was a selectman, fence viewer, and tithingman, and in 1675 he fought in King Philip's War under Capt Isaac Johnson (Bodge, p 161-163). John's will was dtd 9 Apr 1716 and pvd 18 Jan 1725/26, he called yeoman of Br. He named wife Sarah; sons John, Nathaniel, Benjamin, Edward, Jeremiah and Jacob Bosworth; and he mentioned his lands in Conn. A codicil was dtd 17 Aug 1725, and said that his sons Edward, Benjamin, John and Jeremiah were so far without issue (RIGR, 3:90; Rounds, 1:130). This codicil is difficult to understand as both the VR Br and Bosworth Gen show that his sons Edward, Benjamin, and John were m and had issue bef the codicil was written on 17 Aug 1725. The VR Br, 6:63 give: Mehitable, b 24 May 1715 and Edward, b 28 Aug 1717 to Edward and Mehitable; Benjamin and Judeth had five ch b betw 1718 and 8 Oct 1724; and John and Elizabeth had John, Henry and Elizabeth b betw 1708 and 1713. Did all of these ten ch d bef 17 Aug 1725?

CHILDREN, all b Hull (NER, 142:279):
1. John^4 Jr, b ca 1682; d Br 24 Oct 1754 (6:117); m (1) 22 Sept 1707 Elizabeth CHAMBERLAIN, b ca 1684 and d Br 27 Nov 1716, 33rd yr (Ibid), dau Henry Chamberlain; m (2) 7 Oct 1818 "both of Boston" Anna/Hannah (WILLARD) LEFAVOUR (6:8), b Sudbury, Mass 5 May 1686, d Br 20 Aug 1747 (Ibid), dau David and Hannah (Cutter) Willard and widow of Timothy LeFavour Sr of Boston (Bosworth Gen, p 330-336).
   John Jr lived first in Hull, but by 6 May 1711 had rem to Br. The will of John Bosworth Jr of Br, yeoman, dtd 25 Apr 1752 and pvd 4 Dec 1754, named sons John and Henry Bosworth; gch (whom he was bringing up) Daniel, Anna and Elizabeth Lefavour, ch of his dcd dau who m their father, Timothy Lefavour dcd; gson Phinehas Rice, son of one of his (unnamed) daus who was also apparently dcd; and sons John and Henry Bosworth to be execs (RIGR, 3:137). John Jr had four ch by his first wife: John^5, who m Br Mary HAYWARD, dau Samuel, and had eight ch b and bp there (6:63); Sarah, who m Br Joseph RICE and had at least one son, Phinehas Rice; Elizabeth, who m Timothy LEFAVOUR Jr, mariner of Br, and had five ch b Br, surname LeFavour (6:86); and Henry, who m Br Phebe EDDY and had nine ch b there (6:64).
2. Benjamin, b ca 1685; d betw 30 Aug 1773 and 27 Jan 1774 at Ashford, Conn; m (1) Br ca 1717 Judith TORREY, b ca 1694, d Br 2 Feb 1725/26 (6:117), dau Angel and Hannah Torrey; m (2) (int) Br 15 Apr 1727 Jemima ALLEN, b Barrington, RI 7 Apr 1698, d aft Feb 1774, dau Benjamin and Hopestill Allen of Barrington (6:8; Bosworth Gen, p 337). Benjamin came to Br with his parents and bought land there on 21 Apr 1718. He rem with his family to Ashford, Conn where on 9 Sept 1730 he, of Br, bought 100 acres of land with a "mansion house and barn". His will was dtd 30 Aug 1773 and the inv of his est was made

on 21 Feb 1774 (Rounds, 2:175). His will named wife, Jemima; son Ebenezer Bosworth; daus Hopestill, Bridget, Sarah and Elizabeth (no surnames); gdaus Hannah Walker and Abigail Peabody; and son Ebenezer was sole exec (Bosworth Gen, p 343). Benjamin had five ch, b Br, by his first wife, Judith: Judeth, Jonathan, Hannah, Abigail, and Benjamin; and he had nine ch by his second wife, Jemima, the first two b Br and the others at Ashford, Conn: Hannah II, Hopestill, Jemima, Mary, Bridget, Allen, Ebenezer, Sarah and Elizabeth. His dau Hannah m ___ WALKER, and dau Abigail m Ephraim PEABODY, and dau Judith m Ezra SMITH of Ashford (Conn Nutmegger, 23:76-77).

3. Edward, b ca 1691; d Mansfield, Conn bef 21 Feb 1788; m Br prob 1714 Mehitable ___ who was living in May 1742. He was called Edward Jr to distinguish him from his father's brother, Edward, who also lived in Br. By 6 Mar 1729/30 he had rem to Barrington, RI where his first rec land purchase on 5 June 1729 included a home-lot of 73½ acres with houses and barns, and an additional 44 3/4 acres, for L1422. On 12 Mar 1734 he bought 118+ acres in Ashford, Conn, and a farm of 188 acres in Mansfield, Conn. Deeds from 12 Mar 1734/35 on called him Gentleman. Betw Sept 1738 and June 1739 he and his whole family, except for sons Edward and Jonathan, rem to Mansfield. He had ten ch, the first six b Br and the last four at Barrington: Mehitable, Edward, Elizabeth, Jemima, Susannah, Jonathan, Peter, Joseph, Mary, and Samuel (Bosworth Gen, p 346-347, 351, 353, 356, 358).

4. Nathaniel, b 23 Nov 1693; d Br 17 Jan 1771, 78 yr (6:118); m by 1715 Sarah WARDWELL, b 1682, d 11 Oct 1771, 89 yr (Ibid), dau Uzell and Grace Wardwell of Br. He came with his parents from Hull to Br where his father on 11 Dec 1714 deeded him a piece of land in Br betw Thames St and the water. He was a blockmaker. The will of Grace Wardwell of Br, widow, dtd 19 Oct 1739 and pvd 27 May 1741, named her dau Sarah Bosworth, and her son-in-law Nathaniel Bosworth was to be exec (Rounds, 1:308). Nathaniel was termed "Gentleman" when he was imprisoned for debt in Br on 17 Oct 1744. In 1745 and 1746 he was elected Sheriff of the County, and again from 1749 until 1761. In Feb 1748 he was made Justice of the Peace. He was apparently highly thought of, but was a very poor businessman. The inv of his est was taken 15 Jan 1772 and it totaled only L18, 5, 9 and he was an insolvent debtor. Admin of his est was granted to his son, James Bosworth, and son-in-law Bennet Munro. He had five ch, all bp Br in St Michael's Ch (6:63): Sarah who m Bennet MUNRO; Rebecca who m Samuel PAPILLION; Mary who m Edward PAINE; Priscilla who m John HUBBARD; and James, who m Mary HICKS and d 31 Dec 1795, 72 yr (6:118).

5. Sarah, b 7 Jan 1695/96; d 31 July 1696.
6. Jeremiah, b 20 Sept 1697; d Br 26 Sept 1777 ca 80 yr (6:118); m Dorchester, Mass 5 Apr 1727 Susanah FIELD of Braintree, Mass, who d Br 26 Jan 1768, 70 yr (6:117). No issue (Bosworth Gen, p 363).
7. Samuel, b 27 Oct 1699; d 17 June 1770.
8. Jacob, b 22 Nov 1701; d Mansfield, Conn bef 2 July 1782; m (1) (int) 9 Dec 1727 Lydia JONES of Taunton, Mass, who d Barrington, RI soon aft 16 Oct 1742, dau Joseph and Lydia (Neale) Jones of Taunton (NER, 143:128; Bosworth Gen, p 363); m (2) Ashford, Conn 6 Oct 1743 Ruth SQUIRE, b 26 Mar 1722, dau Philip and Elizabeth (Fuller) Squire of Ashford. He was a cordwainer and rem with his parents from Hull to Br, where he lived until his first m. In a deed dtd 17 Feb 1729/30 he was called "of Barrington", and he and his first wife, Lydia, joined the Congre Ch in Barrington on 2 Apr 1732. By Oct 1743 he was in Ashford, Conn where he m (2) Ruth Squire. The div of his est was administered by his widow, Ruth, on 5 Nov 1782. It mentioned sons Nathaniel (eldest), Daniel and Jacob; daus Sarah Blach (eldest), Rebecca Lewis, Hannah Hall, Submit Hall, Ruth Richardson, Elizabeth Cunnell, and Lydia Bosworth (youngest) (Bosworth Gen, p 366-367). He actually had twelve ch, the first six by his first wife, and the last six b Ashford by his second m. The dau "Sarah Blach (eldest)" was Sarah who m Mansfield, Conn 26 June 1781 Varen BALCH.

18. BENJAMIN JONES

Benjamin[2] Jones was bp at Hingham, Mass in Mar 1638, and d Br 12 Jan 1717/18 (6:253; NER, 143:122-124). He was the son of Robert Jones and his first wife, name unkn, who came ca 1636 to Hingham from near Reading, Berkshire, England. Robert had a younger son also named Benjamin, who was bp 27 Aug 1666 and who was also alive when his father's will was written in 1688.

Benjamin[2] signed the Articles on 27 Aug 1680 for a one-third of a thirty-second part of the land which became Br (Munro, p 97). On 20 June 1683 he took the Oath of Fidelity at Br. Bef 1684 he m Bathsheba BOSWORTH, b ca 1654, who d at Br 17 Sept 1740 (6:142), dau Jonathan Bosworth of Hingham and Cambridge, Mass (TAG, 62:55-56). A deed of 10 Dec 1684 by Benjamin Jones of New Bristol in Plymouth Col, husbandman, and Bathsheba his wife, sold to Luke Squire of Hull their dwelling house and land in Hull (NER, 143:122). They had no issue. The VR Br (6:29) rec the m there on 18 Sept 1696 of a Benjamin Jones and Elizabeth Borden, and the b of their first ch, Elizabeth, b 12 July

1697 (6:85). They had six more ch, b Swansea, Mass, and this Benjamin may have been the son of Robert[2] (Robert[1]) Jones, and a nephew of Benjamin[2], the original early settler at Br. Robert[2] had moved from Hull to Swansea by Jan 1666, and he was killed there by the Indians on 24 June 1675 during King Philip's War.

19. ELIASHIB ADAMS (AND HIS BROTHERS)

Henry[1] Adams came from Eng to Braintree, Mass, poss in 1632, where he d and was bur 8 Oct 1646. He left kn sons Peter, John, Joseph, Edward and Samuel. Edward[2] Adams was b 1629 in Eng and became a freeman of Medford, Mass in 1654, where he d 12 Nov 1716. He m (1) by 1653 Lydia "Penniman/poss Rockwood" (Torrey, p 3) who d 1676; and m (2) Abigail (Crafts) (Ruggles) Day, widow John and Ralph (Ibid). Among his fourteen ch was Eliashib[3], b Medford 18 Feb 1659. Edward's will, dtd 19 May 1715 and pvd 3 Dec 1716, divided his est into nine equal parts, of which the ch of his son, Eliashib dec, were to have two parts (Sav, 1:9-10).

Eliashib Adams was admitted as a citizen of Br at its first town meeting on 1 Sept 1681 (Munro, p 79), and he d there in 1698 (Torrey, p 3). The Feb 1689 Census of Br showed him there with no wife or ch (Geneals RI Fams, 1989, 2:401). He m Br 18 Dec 1689 Mehitable CARY, b 24 Dec 1670 Bridgewater, Mass, and d aft 5 Dec 1700, dau John Car(e)y Sr of Bridgewater who m Elizabeth Godfrey. Mehitable m (2) 5 Dec 1700 Miles Standish and rem to Preston, Conn (Torrey, p 700).

Tilden, p 279-280, said that two of Eliashib's brothers, Elisha b 1666, and Edward b 1668, also settled in Br, and that his brother, James b 1661, settled in Barrington, RI. The VR Br (6:61) list the b's of ch to Elisha (sic) and Mehitable Adams, to Edward and Elizabeth Adams, and to James and Mary Adams. Torrey, p 3-4 thought that Eliashib and Elisha might have been the same person; and said that Edward[3] Adams m Br 19 May 1692 Elizabeth WALLEY; and that James[3] Adams m Br 3 or 4 Jan 1689 Mary ALLEN. Eliashib and Mehitable Adams, and James and Mary Adams were all received through bp as members of the Congre Ch of Br on 6 July 1696 (8:239). Eliashib's will, dtd 12 May 1698 and pvd 2 Aug 1698, named wife Mehettabell; and four ch, William, Eliashib, Lydia and Mehettabell, all under age (RIGR, 2:172; Rounds, 1:21).

CHILDREN of Eliashib and Mehitable, b Br (6:61), all bp Congre Ch, Br (Geneals RI Fams, 1989, 2:372-373):
1. Lydia[4], b 17 Jan 1690, bp 22 Dec 1695.
2. William, b 3 June 1693, bp 22 Dec 1695.

3. Mehitable, b 3 Aug 1695, bp 22 Dec 1695.
4. Elisha, b 11 Sept 1697, bp as Eliashib 19 Sept 1697.

These ch rem to Preston, Conn with their mother and her second husband, Myles Standish, and are not found further in the VR Br.

CHILDREN of Edward^3 and Elizabeth Adams, b Br, bp Congre Ch, Br (Geneals RI Fams, 1989, 2:374):
1. Elizabeth^4, b 7 Apr 1693, bp 12 May 1700.
2. Edward, b 28 Aug 1694, bp 12 May 1700.
3. Hannah, b 26 May 1696, bp 12 May 1700.
4. Thomas, b 28 Mar 1698, bp 12 May 1700.
5. Elisha, b 9 May 1699, bp as Eliashib 12 May 1700.
6. Lydia, b 22 July 1701.
7. Nathaniel, b 22 Apr 1704, bp 31 July 1703 (sic) (Ibid, 2:375).
8. Bethia, b 15 Aug 1706, bp 13 Apr 1707 (Ibid, 2:376).
9. Abigail, bp 23 July 1710 (Ibid, 2:378).

CHILDREN of James^3 and Mary Adams, b Br, bp Congre Ch (Geneals RI Fams, 1989, 2:372-374):
1. James^4, b Oct 1691; d.y.
2. James II, b 28 June 1693, bp 25 Aug 1695; d aft father's will of 19 Mar 1732/33.
3. Sarah, b 27 Apr 1695, bp 25 Aug 1695; d.y.
4. Mary b 26 Apr 1697, bp 6 June 1697; d aft father's will of 19 Mar 1732/33.
5. Sarah II, b 21 Jan 1699/1700, bp 27 Jan 1699/1700; m ___ TIFFANY per father's will. Poss he was Hezekiah Tiffany as the VR Br 6:37 list the b of one ch to Hezekiah and Sarah Tiffany in Br: Sarah, b 9 Feb 1727/28.
6. Ebenezer, b 20 Dec 1702; m (int) Br 8 Jan 1736/37 Hannah ALLEN (Bar, 6:5).
7. John, b 18 Dec 1704; d as John Esq 28 Nov 1772 (Bar, 6:20); m (1) Elizabeth ___; m (2) (int) Bar 16 Nov 1745 Martha HUNT (Bar, 6:5). He had four ch b Warren, RI (War, 6:43): Stephen, Newdigate, Sarah and Chloe.
8. Christian, b 26 Nov 1706, bp 1 Dec 1706 (Geneals RI Fams, 1989, 2:376); d Bar 9 Mar 1713/14 (Bar, 6:20).
9. Elizabeth, b 19 Feb 1707; d.y.
10. Elizabeth II, b 26 July 1711; d bef father's will of 19 Mar 1732/33.

This family had rem from Br to Barrington by Mar 1713/14. The will of James Adams of Barrington, yeoman, dtd 19 Mar 1732/33 and pvd 18 Sept 1733, included wife (not named); three sons, James, Ebenezer and John Adams; and daus Mary (no surname) and Sarah Tiffeney (Rounds, 1:222).

Ebenezer[4] (James[3]) Adams was b Br 20 Dec 1702 and m (int) Bar 8 Jan 1736/37 Hannah ALLEN (Bar 6:5), poss b Bar 27 Mar 1717 and d Bar as widow 7 Sept 1777 (Bar 6:20), dau Joseph and Hannah Allen of Bar (Ibid). Capt Joseph Allen's will, he of Rehoboth, Mass, was dtd 8 Jan 1754 and named his dau, Hannah Adams (Rounds, 2:158).

CHILDREN, b Bar (Bar 6:20):
1. Joseph[5], b 25 May 1739.
2. James, b 8 Sept 1740.
3. Mary, b 12 July 1742.
4. Rachel, b 1 June 1744.

20. WATCHING ATHERTON

Humphrey[1] Atherton was in Dorchester, Mass in 1636, and became a freeman on 2 May 1638. He joined the Anc and Honorable Artillery Co in 1638, and was its Captain in 1650. He was often a selectman and Representative, and an Assistant. His wife's name is unkn. As one of his ten or eleven ch, Watching was bp 24 Aug 1651 in Dorchester. He m there 23 Jan 1678 Elizabeth RIGBY, dau Samuel and Elizabeth (George) Rigby of Dorchester (Torrey, p 625). Sav, 1:72-73 said they "had two ch whose names are not told". The VR Br have only one entry for them, the b of a son, Samuel, at Br on 25 June 1686. Torrey said that they lived in Dorchester and Br, but there are no d recs for them in Br, so they prob rem elsewhere aft 1689. The Feb 1689 Census of Br listed Watching Atherton with a wife and four ch living there then (Geneals RI Fams, 1989, 2:402).

21. JOSEPH BASTER

There are no m's, b's or d's in the VR Br of any Basters. Joseph's parentage, and place and date of b, are unkn. However, the 1689 Census of Br listed Joseph Bastor with a wife and one ch (Geneals RI Fams, 1989, 2:402). And early Br horse descriptions listed on 14 June 1696 a horse of Stephen Bedford's "bought of widow Bastar", so Joseph had d bef that date (TAG, 65:118). This was a rare surname in early New England. A Richard Baster came from Dartmouth, Devonshire, England to Newport, RI betw 1620-1650 (Banks Topogr Dict Eng Emigrants, p 21). And a Roger Baster, bachelor and blockmaker, d Newport 23 Apr 1687, age 66 yr and was bur in the Common Bur Ground there (VR RI, Beaman, New Series, 11:34). Poss Joseph of Br was related to them. Sav, 1:137 listed no Basters, but gave a Joseph Bastarr/Bastard of Cambridge, Mass, a tailor with wife, Mary, who rem to Boston in 1647 and had a son, Joseph Jr, b 25 or 29 Sept 1647. Joseph Jr was not the man in Br, as he rem to Fairfield, Conn where he d 1697, leaving a good estate.

22. JOHN BAYLEY

The parentage and place of b of this John Bayley have not been found. Torrey, p 31, said that John Bayley m Rachel ___, had a ch b 1685, and lived in Br, RI. The early recs of Br show his named spelled Bayley, but later it changed to Bailey. Sav, 1:94-95 and 142-143, distinguished between the families with these two spellings. Sav, p 143, and Caulkins, p 290-291, told of a Thomas Bayley who was in New London, Conn on a grant of land in 1652 and m there 10 Jan 1655/56 Lydia, dau of James Redfield of New London. Their ch included a John b Apr 1661, who poss was the John in Br in Sept 1681. The VR Br (6:116) give the d of Bayley ___, about 38 yr, on 4 Mar 1690, who could fit this John, b 1661.

CHILDREN, b Br (6:62):
1. Joshua, b 10 Sept 1685; d Br 5 June 1767, 82 yr (6:115); m by Col Benjamin Church, JP, 9 or 10 Jan 17-11/12 Mary GALLUP (6:7), b Br 22 Oct 1692, d 23 Sept 1771, 79 yr as widow of Joshua (6:115), dau Capt Samuel and Elizabeth (Southworth) Gallup of Br (6:22). (Samuel Gallup, if the son of Capt John Gallup Jr as is now thought, grew up in Stonington, New London Co, Conn.) No issue. Mary, wife of Joshua, became a member of the Congre Ch, Br on 13 May 1741 (8:240). The will of Joshua Bailey of Br, cooper, dtd 14 Mar 1767 and pvd 4 Jan 17-68, named wife Mary; sister Mary Bailey; friend Jonathan Fales; and Richard Smith (RIGR, 6:152).
2. John, b 17 Feb 1687.
3. Mary, b 3 Feb 1699 (sic, 1689 per d rec); d Br 6 Aug 1767, 78 yr, unm (6:115).

23. JOHN BIRGE

John Birge d Br 5 Sept 1733 in his 85th yr (6:116), and so was b ca 1648. He m Sarah ___ who d Br 1717 in 63rd yr. They had a ch b 1683 per Torrey, p 7. Torrey gave John's residences as Boston, Br, RI, and Yarmouth, Mass. He was not the son of Richard of Dorchester, Mass and Windsor, Conn, and who is the only John Birge whom Sav (1:183) described. Chamberlain, p 131-132, said that the will of a John Burge, dtd 1 June 1671, of Weymouth and Chelmsford, Mass, named his two sons, Samuel the elder and John Burge, the younger, by his wife Rebecca. This John Jr might have been the Br settler who named his only son, Samuel.

John and Sarah Birge had only one ch b and rec in Br, Samuel, b 1 Aug 1691 (6:62). This Samuel m St Michael's Ch, Br 9 Nov 1727 Hannah BRAGG (8:200), b 27 Sept 1698 (6:66), d Br 13 Jan 1769, 71 yr, widow (6:116), dau Henry and Elizabeth (Mackmollen) Bragg of Salem, Mass and Br (Torrey, p 93). No issue in VR Br for Samuel or any other Birge. Since John and Sarah d in Br, their stay in Yarmouth, Mass, if in fact they went there, was prob not of long duration. The will of John Birge of Br, taylor, was dtd 4 Oct 1729 and pvd 18 Sept 1733. No wife was mentioned (Rounds, 1:222, 234-235). He named dau, Elizabeth Lewis and son-in-law Joseph Lewis; dau Mary Dolliver and son-in-law John Dolliver; gson John Dolliver under 21; dau-in-law Hannah Birge; Patience (no surname, but apparently dau of Hannah Birge); and Ann Liscomb, widow. Samuel Royal and Samuel Smith, both of Br, were execs. Receipts paid for legacies from the est of John Birge were signed as fols: 1. by Joseph Lewis of Haddam, Hartford Co, Conn for his ch Elezebeth wife of Hezekiah Sharley or Shailey of Haddam; Rebeckah wife of Joseph Lee of Guilford, New Haven Co, Conn; Sarah wife of Thomas Beckwith of Lime (Lyme), New London Co, Conn; and Hannah Lewis of Haddam. 2. by Joseph Lewis of Haddam as guardian of his minor ch, Deborah Lewis and John Lewis. 3. by Joseph Lewis and his wife Elezebeth of Haddam. 4. by Hannah Birge of Br, widow, her father-in-law being John Birge of Br. 5. by Patience Cuthbert of Br, spinster, for legacy from est of her gfather John Birge of Br. 6. by John Doliver and his wife Mary of Greenwich, Co of Kingston, RI.

KNOWN CHILDREN, order uncertain:
1. ch, b 1683; d bef father's will of 4 Oct 1729.
2. Samuel, b prob Br 1 Aug 1691; d bef father's will of 4 Oct 1729; m St Michael's Br 9 Nov 1727 Hannah BRAGG.
3. Elizabeth, d aft father's will of 4 Oct 1729; m Joseph LEWIS. Lived Haddam, Hartford Co, Conn.
4. Mary, d aft father's will of 4 Oct 1729; m John DOLLIVER. Lived Greenwich, RI.

24. THOMAS BLETSOE

Sav did not list any early New England settler of this surname. Torrey, p 78, gave only Thomas with an unnamed wife who had a ch "b 12 June 1696" and lived in Br. The only VR Br entry through 12 June 1696 is their entry then into membership in the Congre Ch, Br. Since these Ch recs used "b" for bp and Torrey used "b" for the birth of a ch, he may have copied the Ch entry verbatim and they did not, in fact, have a ch b then. He was listed as Thomas Blesgo in the 1689 Census of Br with a wife, no ch, and two servants (Geneals RI Fams, 1989, 2:402), and that is the last rec of him in Br.

25. BENJAMIN BOSWORTH

This was either the Benjamin² (Edward¹) Bosworth, b 16-15 England, brother of Nathaniel Bosworth of Hull who settled in Br, or Benjamin's son, Benjamin³ Jr, who was bp 6 Apr 1647 in Hingham, Mass, m Hannah MORTON, and d 5 Nov 1682 at Hull. Neither of these Benjamins ever lived in Br (Bosworth Gen, p 77-93).

26. EDWARD BOSWORTH

Edward³ was the son of Nathaniel² (Edward¹) Bosworth, who bought two-thirds of a thirty-second part of the Mt Hope Lands from the Proprietors, and became an early settler of Br. See No. 17. Nathaniel Bosworth, for an account of Edward Bosworth.

27. WILLIAM BRENTON JR

William² Brenton Jr was the son of Gov William Brenton Sr of Newport, RI, who was President of the RI Col in 1660-61, Deputy Gov in 1663, and Gov from 1666-68, and who d in 1674. Gov Brenton's three eldest sons were Jahleel³ who remained in Newport, and William and Ebenezer, both of whom were in Br at an early date. William Jr was in Br at its first town meeting on 1 Sept 1681 and d there in 1697 (Torrey, p 95). He m Hannah DAVIS, b 1661 and d Br 17 July 1695, 36 or 37 yr (6:119; Torrey, p 95). The 1689 Census of Br listed him as William Brutton, with a wife and two ch (Geneals RI Fams, 1989, 2:402). He was a sea captain and shortly bef his d in 1697 he was "late Master of the Ship Seaflower, recently home from Barbados" (Rounds, 1:17). The acct of his est was presented 22 Feb 1697/98 by his brother, Ebenezer Brenton, admin, and legacies to his ch were: to sons William Jr, Samuel, Benjamin and Jahleel Brenton (Ibid).

CHILDREN, last two rec in Br (6:66):
1. William³, b not rec but poss b 1680, called "eldest son"; d bef his est was settled 30 Jan 1709/10 (Rounds, 1:46); m unkn and had "eldest son" Benjamin, who had a son Benjamin (Geneals RI Fams, 1983, 2:510). An order granting the remaining est of William Brenton, mariner of Br, dtd 30 Jan 1709/10, was to his eldest son, Benjamin, with shares to be paid to the heirs of Major Ebenezer Brenton now dcd, and to his brother, Jahleel Brenton (Rounds, 1:46).
2. Samuel, b not rec but named in acct of legacies paid to ch of William, dtd 1697/98 (Rounds, 1:17).
3. Benjamin, b Br 23 Dec 1686 (6:66); d aft admin of father's est 22 Feb 1697/98.
4. Jahleel, b Br 15 Aug 1691 (Ibid); d Br Mar 1767,

77th yr. He m (1) Frances CRANSTON who d 2 Feb 1740, 47 yr, dau Hon Gov Samuel Cranston of Newport; m (2) Mary ___, who d 1 May 1768, 53 yr. He lived in Newport where his fol kn ch were b, all by his first wife, Frances (VR RI, Beaman, New Series, 11:50): Samuel, Martha who m Robert JENKINS, Hart who m Daniel AYRAULT, Abigail who m Charles HANDY, and Benjamin who m Rachel COOK. If his age is given correctly, he had one kn ch by his second wife: Thomas Jr, d 23 Mar 1772, 26 yr. All of the above ch are bur in the Common Bur Ground of Newport (Ibid). He also had a dau, Frances, who m Mr MUMFORD (Ibid, 10:41). The VR Newport, 4:84, have the fol recs of Jahleel's ch: ___, b Aug 1716; Mary, b 24 Nov 1719; Mercy b 10 July 1721; Heart, b 26 Feb 1723; Martha, b 12 Jan 1726; Elizabeth, b 3 Feb 1727; Jahleel b 22 Oct 1729 and d 9 Nov 1732; ___, b 3 Dec 1730; ___, b 10 Nov 1733; ___, b 18 Apr 1735; ___, b 2 Nov 1736; and Benjamin, b 1737/38?,

William^2 Brenton Jr's brother, Ebenezer Brenton, m Priscilla (BYFIELD) WALDRON (Torrey, p 95), widow of Dr Isaac Waldron who bought a sixteenth part of the Mt Hope lands which became Br. Ebenezer also came at an early date from Swansea, Mass to Br. He had ch b in both places bef he d Br in 1708 (Ibid), and Priscilla d there on 14 May 1705 (6:119). Ebenezer was the admin of the est of his brother, William, in Br in 1697/98 (Rounds, 1:17).

CHILDREN (6:66; Geneals RI Fams, 1983, 2:525):
1. Ebenezer^3, b 7 Dec 1687 Swansea; d ca 1766, prob at So. Kingston, RI. He had two daus: Ann who m Martin HOWARD Jr of Newport, and Elizabeth, who m Edward PERKINS (Geneals RI Fams, 1983, 2:510-511).
2. Martha, b 4 Jan 1689 Swansea.
3. William, b 28 Nov 1694 Br.
4. Sarah, b 6 May 1697 Br.

28. WILLIAM BROWN

Torrey, p 109, said that two William Browns were in Br at an early date: 1. William who d 1689, m 11 Apr 1656 Lydia PARCHMENT who d 1680 ae ca 46; and 2. William who d aft a will dtd 1689, m Jemima/Jennings/Jinnus? WILLIAMS, had a first ch b 1673, and lived ?Portsmouth, RI and Br. Sav, 1:278, said of the first William Brown that he lived in Boston and was perhaps the man called sneeringly William Parchment, which is "wanton folly or inexcusable carelessness". The will of the second William Brown, called of Br, husbandman, dtd 6 Aug 1689 and pvd 20 Apr 1697, named: widow Jinnins; daus Hannah Marshfield, Mary Backaway or Barkaway, Susana Hamond and Deliverance Corps; John Corps to be exec (Rounds, 1:1). It is not poss to be completely sure which of these two William Browns was at the first town meeting of Br, but it was prob the second one.

CHILDREN of William and Jinnins (?), order unkn (Rounds, 1:1):
1. Hannah, poss b 1673; m ___ MARSHFIELD per father's will, and first ch b 1689 (Torrey, p 491, who called Hannah "dau John").
2. Mary, m (1) ___ BACKAWAY/BARKAWAY; m (2) 2 Feb 1697 Portsmouth, RI John HEFFERLAND, and lived Portsmouth (Torrey, p 363).
3. Susannah, d Br 17 Jan 1731 (6:137); m 5 Jan 1684 Br Edward HAMMON (Torrey, p 339) who d Br Jan 1717 (6:137). Susannah had four ch b Br, surname Hammond (6:81): William, Edward, Margaret and Martha. She was called Susana Hamond in her father's will of 6 Aug 1689 (Rounds, 1:1).
4. Deliverance, d aft 13 Mar 1701/02; m (1) by 1679 John CORPS/CORPE of Br who d there 1691 (Torrey, p 184); m (2) by 1696 John GEREARDY of Warwick, RI and Br (Ibid, p 299). Deliverance had six kn ch, all except the first b Br, surname Corps (Geneals RI Fams, 1989, 2:372): John, b 1679; Hope, b 8 Nov 1681 "the first English child b in this town" (Br) (Munro, p 124); Anna; Mary; Elizabeth; and Sarah; and she had two kn ch, surname Gereardy (6:77); John, b Br 22 Dec 1696; and Sweet, b Warwick 15 May 1699.

The VR Br give only the fol recs for any early William Brown, and he is unidentifiable: William of William Brown bur Br 26 Oct 1683 (6:120); William Brown bur Br from Mr Jabez Howland's 3 Dec 1683 (Ibid); Bethia Brown d Br Feb 1689, who poss was of William (Ibid); and Sarah Brown of William and Sarah, b Br 1697 (6:66). No other Brown d's are found in the VR Br until Sept 1794.

29. JAMES BURRILL

James[3] Burrill was b 21 Dec 1657 in Lynn, Mass, and d 1712 in Dartmouth, Mass, son of Francis and Elizabeth Burrill and gson of George and Mary (Cooper) Burrill (Torrey, p 122). George was "one of the richest of the planters", and "the Burrill family was formerly called the royal fam of Lynn, in view of the many famous persons connected with it." (Lewis and Newhall, p 115-116, 489-495). James m (1) Dinah NICHOLSON, b Salem, Mass 21 Mar 1660, dau Joseph and Jane Nicholson of Marblehead and Salem, Mass and Portsmouth, RI (Sav, 3:283); m (2) unkn. A later James Burrill of this Lynn fam settled in Providence, RI where the fam became prominent.

Torrey, p 122 said that James[3] and Dinah had their first ch b 1685 and lived in Br, RI. Aside from James's attendance at the first town meeting of Br, the only other rec for him there was his taking the Oath of Fidelity on 20 June 1683 (Munro, p 114). No m's, d's or b's are given in the VR Br for any early Burrill. James may have rem from Br next to Newport, RI. On 25 Nov 1700 Latham Clarke of Newport, merchant, sold land in the Pettyquamscott Purchase to John Paine of Newport, saddler, and a witness was Jeames Burrill (Geneals RI Fams, 1989, 1:94). He d Dartmouth, Mass betw 7 Aug 1711 and 3 Mar 1711/12. The will of James Burrill of Dartmouth, dtd 7 Aug 1711 and pvd 3 Mar 1711/12, named: sons James (under age) and ffrancis Burrill, and eldest son (unnamed) "who follows the Sea"; daus Elizabeth, Dinah, Hannah, Jane and Sarah; my "sister Ward"; Joseph Nicholson gfather of "my children"; brother Joseph Burrill; payment to be made "aft my Mother's Decease"; and said he deposed of his household goods to his daus "aft the Decease of my first wife" (but he mentioned no later wife) (Rounds, 1:54).

30. JAMES BURROUGHS

James Burroughs, b ca 1650 and d, prob Br, aft 10 Oct 1699, m (1) 8 Dec 1674 at Hingham, Mass Sarah CHURCH, b Hingham prob early 1650's and d Br betw 29 Sept 1688 and 1693, dau Richard Church and Elizabeth Warren, dau Richard Warren of the Myflwr (Myflwr Fams in Progress, Richare Warren, p 3-4, 20-21). Torrey, p 123, said that James and Sarah lived in Hingham, Boston, and Br, RI, and that he m (2) Ann(e) ___, had a ch b by her in 1694, and lived in Br.

The only James Burroughs listed by Sav (1:311) was a tailor in Boston in 1674, who was prob the same James. He was at the first town meeting of Br and took the Oath of Fidelity there on 17 May 1685 (Munro, p 114). James was listed in the 1689 Census of Br with a wife, three ch, and one servant (Geneals RI Fams, 1989, 2:402).

CHILDREN by first wife, Sarah (Myflwr Fams in Progress, Richard Warren, p 3-4, 20-21; 6:67):
1. James, b 28 Jan 1677, Boston; d prob Br Mar 1688.
2. Mary, b 30 Oct 1679, Boston.
3. Elizabeth, d Swansea, Mass bef 7 Aug 1699, shortly aft giving b to an illegitimate ch by a negro servant at the home of Insigne Joseph Kent, where she was also a servant.
4. Thomas, b 12 July 1685 Br (6:67); d 16 Dec 1722, 37 yr 5 mo, and bur Common Bur Ground of Newport, RI (VR RI, Beaman, New Series, 11:70); m prob ca 1706 Abigail

___, who d aft 30 Apr 1736. The admin of the est of Thomas was granted 7 Jan 1722/23 to his widow, now Abigail Toppin, and mentioned bringing up six ch. Thomas was a boatman of Newport and had the fol ch (Myflwr Fams in Progress, Richard Warren, p 83-84): William?, b perhaps ca 1707 prob at Prudence Island, RI; Freeborn?, b ca 1709 prob at Prudence Island; Samuel, b 1712 prob at Prudence Island; Mary?, b ca 1714 Newport; Benjamin, b prob ca 1716 Newport; and Peleg, b perhaps ca 1722 at Newport.

CHILD by second wife, Ann(e) (6:67):
5. Ezekial, b 5 May 1694 Br; d Newport as Deacon of Baptist Ch 26 Aug 1769; m Abigail ___. Ezekial was bur, aged 76 yr, in the Common Bur Ground of Newport (VR RI Beaman, New Series, 11:69-70). He had the fol kn ch; Abigail, who d Newport 14 Dec 1723, 3 yr 5m (Ibid, p 70); Amy, who m 1761 Newport Mr DURFEE; and Desire, who m 1761 Newport Mr HOPKINS (Ibid, 10:61-62).

31. DAVID CAR(E)Y

David^2 Car(e)y was b 27 Jan 1658/59 in Bridgewater, Mass and d 1718 Br, son John and Elizabeth (Godfrey) Car(e)y of Duxbury and Bridgewater. The literature has errors about David. Mitchell, p 311, said of John's sons that "David went to Bristol and Joseph to Windham, Ct", which other writers interpreted to mean that David went to Conn. Col Rev Lin Amer, p 152, said: 7. David, b Jan 27, 1658/59 d in Bristol, Conn in 1718. Seth C. Cary's John Cary, p 65f, had errors in the dates of b, and names, of David's ch. And Arnold's VR RI, vol 6 Br, p 122, stated that the David Cary who d there in 1718 was son$_2$ of Benjamin^3 (John^{2,1}), which is incorrect. It was David^2 (John^1) whose est was inv in 1718.

In 1680 David rem from Bridgewater to Bristol where he became a propr and man of influence. He was a carpenter, and in 1683 became a Deacon of the Congre Ch, which he continued to be until he d in 1718. He was "of Br" when he m 9 Dec 1687 at Billerica, Mass Elizabeth BRACKETT, b 30 Apr 1671, d aft 1726/27, dau Peter^2 (Capt Deacon Richard^1) Brackett and Elizabeth^2 (Jonathan^1) Bosworth of Billerica (Hazen, p 17). Richard Brackett was a Capt in the Ancient and Honorable Artill Co at Boston in 1639. The 1689 Census of Br showed David there with a wife and one ch (Geneal Fams RI, 1989, 2:401). This unkn ch was not listed in Seth C. Cary, or the VR Br, but was given in the IGI RI.

The will of David Cary, carpenter, was dtd 21 July 1718 and apparently was written for him by the town council of Br. It named wife Elizabeth Cary; sons David, Peter and Henry Cary; daus Elizabeth Smith, Mehatable (no surname), Bashua Howland and Bethyah Goreham (RIGR, 3:89). A receipt, dtd 18 Jan 1726/27, was signed by Jonathan and Joseph Glading for legacies from the est of David Cary of Br to their wives, "Sarah and Priscilla two of the Daughters of the said Cary", paid by Elizabeth Kidder, widow, and her son, David Carey (Rounds, 1:140). David Cary's widow m (2) Ephraim Kidder of Billerica, Mass 1 June 1724 (6:12).

See also RIGR, 1990, 13:187-196.

CHILDREN, b Br (6:68):
1. Ch^3, b by 11 Feb 1689; d.y. (IGI RI).
2. Elizabeth, b 7 Mar 1691/92; d 1 Sept 1772, 81 yr (6:163); m by 1712 Daniel SMITH, b Br 2 Mar 1687/88, d 21 Aug 1741 ae 54, son Richard and Joyce Smith of Br (6:103). Elizabeth had seven ch b Br, surname Smith (Ibid): Daniel, John, Elizabeth, David, William, and Nathan and Joyce, twins.
3. Mehitabel, b 14 Aug 1693, twin; d aft father's will of 21 July 1718. Seth C. Cary said she m Mr WARDWELL, who has not been identified.
4. Beersheba/Bathshua, b 14 Aug 1693, twin; m ca 1712 Joseph HOWLAND, b Br 14 Oct 1692, d 16 Aug 1737, son Jabez and Bethiah (Thatcher) Howland and gson of John Howland of the Myflwr. She had three ch b Br, surname Howland (6:83): Lydia, Joseph and Elizabeth.
5. Sarah (per Seth C. Cary), b 11 June 1695; d in childhood.
6. Bethia(h), b 9 Dec 1696 (6:68), or b 22 Jan 1697 (Seth C. Cary, p 65f); d bef 1753; m by 1718 Benjamin GORHAM, b 11 Dec 1695, d 1771/72, son Jabez and Hannah (Sturgis) (Gray) Gorham, and gson of Capt John Gorham who m 1643 Desire Howland, dau John Howland of the Myflwr. Bethia(h) had seven ch, surname Gorham, at least the first four b Br, and the last several prob b in Providence, RI where she and Benjamin rem to (6:80): Benjamin, Bethiah, Sarah, Elizabeth, Jabez, Samuel and Jemima.
<u>7</u>. David, b 22 June 1698; d Nov 1746; m (1) (int) 20 Jan 1721/22 Rachel BATES of Dorchester, Mass; m (2) (int) 2 Oct 1725 Mary CANADA/KENNEDY. Seth C. Cary said he m (2) 9 June 1729. The IGI RI showed the b of this David, and also the b in Br of another David on 20 Feb 1699 (/1700?).
8. Dau, b 24 Nov 1700; d 29 Nov 1700 (6:68). Not in Seth C. Cary.
9. Peter, b 9 Nov 1701; d aft father's will of 21 July 1718.
10. Mary, b 6 Nov 1703. Seth C. Cary said she d in child-

hood. However a Mary Carey m (int) 25 June 1725 Terrance DONNELS at Br (6:12), and they had a ch b Br: Catherine Donelly of Tarence and Mary (6:73), b 6 Oct 1722 (sic?).
11. Sarah, b 21 Jan 1706/07; d 26 Dec 1786; m (int) 2 July 1726 Jonathan GLADDING (6:23), b 5 Jan 1700/01 (6:-78), d 27 Oct 1743 Br, son John Jr and Alice (Wardwell) Gladding of Br, per VR Br. Seth C. Cary omitted this Sarah. She had seven ch b Br, surname Gladding (6:78): Sarah, Elizabeth, Priscilla, Nathaniel, Jonathan, Timothy, and Benjamin.
12. Priscilla, b 9 May 1709; m (int) 2 July 1726 Br Joseph GLADDING (6:23), b 2 Oct 1704 (6:78), son John Jr and Alice (Wardwell) Gladding of Br. They rem to Newport, RI where Priscilla had fourteen ch b, surname Gladding: Samuel, Joseph Jr, Carey (called Cory in VR Newport), Jonathan, Priscilla, Henry, Benjamin, Ebenezer, David, Nathaniel, Alice, Stephen, John and Peter.
13. Rev Henry, b 24 June 1711 per VR Br, or b 4 June 1711 per Seth C. Cary, or b 6 June 1711 per Pat Index, p 118; d 1801 in Vt, 90 yr (6:122); m ca 1734 Abigail PAUL, b ca 1702, d bef 1776, dau Edward and Esther (Babbitt) Paul of Taunton, Mass (Virkus, 5:510). He grad from Harvard College in 1733, earned an AM in 1738, and became a Baptist minister. He lived first in Ashford, Conn where his ch were b, and then rem to Pawling, Dutchess Co, NY. He was chairman of the Committee of Safety in 1775. In the Rev War he gave Patriotic Service from NY (Pat Index, p 118). He had the fol ch, b Ashford, Conn: Mary, Esther, Elizabeth, Mary II, Catherine, Henry, Chloe, and John Paul (Seth C. Cary, p 76-77; IGI Conn).

David^3 (David^2, John^1) Car(e)y was prob b 22 June 1698, and d Nov 1746 (6:122). The IGI RI and Seth C. Cary gave the b of a David on 20 Feb 1699 (/1700?). He m (1) (int) 20 Jan 1721/22 Rachel BATES of Dorchester, Mass (6:12), and m (2) (int) 2 Oct 1725 Mary CANADA/CANADY/KENNEDY (6:-12), or m 9 July 1729 per Seth C. Cary. He had no kn ch by his first wife.

CHILDREN by second wife, Mary, b Br (6:68; Seth Cary, p 76):
1. David^4, b 23 Nov 1729. Seth Cary said he rem to Nova Scotia.
2. Edward, b 1 May 1732 (6:68). Seth Cary said he was b 7 May 1732 and settled in Taunton, Mass. The VR Taunton do not show him, or any other Car(e)y family there. He may have been the ch of David who d 6 Aug 1733 (6:-122).
3. Thomas, b 23 Mar 1733/34; d June 1735 "Thomas of David and Mary". He was the only Thomas shown in the VR Br as being b to David and Mary.

4. ?Thomas, b 19 Jan 1735 "of David Cary/Mary Canada" per IGI RI, and Seth Cary who omitted the first Thomas, b 23 Mar 1733/34, and gave this Thomas as their fourth ch, with Mary as their third ch. Seth Cary said Thomas was b Br 19 Jan 1735, m ca 1764 at Smithfield, RI Sarah BROWN, dau Obadiah Brown, and a desc of Elder Chad Brown and that they had four ch: Ebenezer, Chad, Asa and Sally. It is poss that David and Mary had a Thomas II, but not b 19 Jan 1735 as the VR Br (6:68) give 9 Aug 1735 as the b date of their dau, Mary.
5. Mary, b 9 Aug 1735 (6:68). Seth Cary, p 76 called her their third ch, b 9 Aug 1733, and said she m Mr WIL-BOUR. It has not been poss to identify him.
6. Nathaniel, b 5 Feb 1737/38 (6:68). Seth Cary, p 76 called him Nathan, b 5 Feb 1737 and said he rem to Vt. The 1790 US Census of Vt listed no Nathaniel/Nathan Car(e)y in the State.
7. Michael, b 29 Jan 1739/40 (6:68). Seth Cary said he was b 23 Jan 1739 and d Barrington, RI 1833. He m 26 Aug 1770 at Barrington Martha GARNSEY/GUERNSEY (Bar, 6:9).

Michael^4 (David^{3,2}, John^1) Car(e)y was b 29 Jan 1739/40 (6:68) or 23 Jan 1739 (Seth Cary), and d Barrington, RI in 1833. He may have m (1) an unkn who d by 1770; and he m 26 Aug 1770 at Barrington Martha GARNSEY/GUERNSEY (Bar, 6:9). The VR Bar usually referred to him as "Micha" or "Michah". Martha was prob the "Molly" b Bar 25 Jan 1739/40, dau Ebenezer and Martha Garnsey/Guernsey. Seth Cary, p 94, said he m "Patty Gunsey" of Barrington, Mass, and that he was a soldier in the Rev War and pensioner at his d in 1833. The Pat Index did not list him. But Bicknell, p 382, said that Micah Carey was a Sgt in Capt Thomas Allen's Co in Aug 1775, and a Sgt in Capt Viall Allen's Co in 1780. He told of the battles he was in, said that he lived to be almost 100, and was prob bur at Tyler's Point. Michael rem from Br to Barrington by 1770. The 1790 US Census of RI, Barrington Town, listed him with one male 16 yrs or over, two males under 16, and one female, and he headed the only Car(e)y family in town. Michael Cary left no will, and the Office of Town Clerk of Barrington, RI wrote the author on 20 July 1984 that there were no Carey wills in their files. Since Michael and Martha Garnsey were not m until 26 Aug 1770, his first three ch, as given by Seth Cary, could not be hers. If they were his ch, he must have had a first m, But they are not given in the VR of Br, Barrington, or the IGI RI.

POSSIBLE CHILDREN by "Patty Gunsey"? (Seth Cary, p 94):
? Ebenezer, b ca 1761.
? Nathan, b ca 1767; d without issue.
? Mary, b ca 1769.

KN CHILDREN by Martha Garnsey, b Barrington (Bar, 6:26; IGI RI):
1. Ebenezer Garnsey, b 11 June 1771; m Bar 4 Mar 1798 Polly MOORE (Bar, 6:9, 15). He had four ch b Bar (Ibid, 6:26): Amey Brown, b 18 Sept 1802; Nathan, b 1 Apr 1804; Caleb, b 23 May 1806; and Angeline, b 28 Feb 1812.
2. David, b 9 Dec 1774 (Ibid, 6:26). Not listed by Seth Cary.

32. JOHN CARY

See RIGR, 1988, Vol 11, p 222-225.

33. SAMUEL COBBETT

Samuel^2 Cobbett was b in Lynn, Mass and d in 1713, poss in Br. He m Sarah ___ bef the b of their first ch in 1676 (Torrey, p 164; Sav, 1:414). He was the son of Rev Thomas^1 Cobbett, b 1608 in Newbury, co Bucks, England, who attended Oxford University and was admitted as a freeman at Lynn on 2 May 1638. The Rev Thomas m Elizabeth ___, and was pastor at Lynn until 1656 when he rem to Ipswich, Mass and preached there until he d on 5 Nov 1685 (Lewis and Newhall, p 236). Samuel graduated from Harvard College in 1663 (Ibid, p 238) and became a freeman of the Col on 31 Mar 1674. The Rev Thomas's will of 1686 gave Samuel, already m, a double portion, so he was the eldest son (Hammatt, p 55-59). The 1689 Census of Br listed him as living there alone with no wife or ch (Geneals RI Fams, 1989, 2:402), but Samuel and his wife had a ch b there in Jan 1689 (6:-70). Samuel "Cobbitt" became the first schoolmaster of Br in 1685, and continued as such until 1694 (Munro, p 337).

KNOWN CHILDREN (6:70):
1. Ch^3, b 1676; d.y.? (Torrey, p 164).
2. Sarah, b 3 Jan 1689 Br.
3. Samuel, b 16 Aug 1693 Br.
4. Thomas, b 18 Oct 1695 Br; d 2 Dec 1695 (6:124).
5. John, b 9 Oct 1696 Br.

Samuel prob had other ch b betw 1676 and 1689. No other VR's were found in Br for Samuel or his family, and he poss rem elsewhere after 1696, since Torrey had a kn yr of d for him of 1713.

34. JOHN CORPS/CORPE

The place and date of b of John Corps are not kn, but he d in Br on 1 Nov 1691 (6:125). Torrey, p 184, said that he lived first in Boston and then in Br, and their first ch was b in 1679. He m Deliverance BROWN who d aft 13 Mar 1701/02, dau William and Jinnins/Jeminia? Brown of Br (Rounds, 1:1). John and Deliverance had the "first English child born in this town" (Bristol) when their son, Hope, was b 8 Nov 1681 (Munro, p 124). On 20 June 1683 John Corps signed the Oath of Fidelity at Br (Ibid, p 114). The 1689 Census of Br listed him as "G" (Goodman) Corpe (the only Corpe/Corps in town), with a wife and three ch (Geneals RI Fams, 1989, 2:402). The only Corps recs in the VR Br are those of the b's and bp's of John's ch. Sav did not list anyone of this surname in New England, although he did give families in Boston named Copp (1:456-457). Corpe may have been pronounced Copp.

John's widow, Deliverance, m (2) John GEREARDY/GEREARAY of Warwick, RI and Br (Torrey, p 299). She had two kn ch, surname Gereardy (6:77): John, b Br 22 Dec 1696; and Sweet, b Warwick 15 May 1699. Apparently the Corpe ch rem to Warwick with their mother and step-father. The will of William Brown of Br, husbandman, dtd 6 Aug 1689 and pvd 20 Apr 1697, named widow Jinnins; daus Hannah Marshfield, Mary Backaway or Barkaway, Susana Hamond, and Deliverance Corps; John Corps exec (Rounds, 1:1). William Brown m Jemima/Jinnus? Williams and lived in ?Portsmouth, RI and Br, RI (Torrey, p 109). The settlement of the est of John Corpes of Br, dcd intestate, was dtd 13 Mar 1701/02 and mentioned: eldest son John Corpes aged near 22 yrs with leave of his father-in-law (stepfather) John Geriedi and Deliverance Geraeoli (sic) his natural mother. It said there were six ch (not named) of the dcd (Rounds, 1:24).

CHILDREN (6:71), b Br, all except Hope bp 24 Apr 1691 in the Congre Ch, Br as of "John and Deliverance Corp" (Geneals RI Fams, 1989, 2:372):
1. John, b 1679 (Torrey, p 184; Rounds, 1:24); prob d Warwick betw 12 Mar 1747 and 13 June 1748; m Elizabeth ___. Had three sons and two daus named in his will. The will of John Corpe of Warwick, yeoman, dtd 12 Mar 1747 and pvd 13 June 1748, mentioned wife Elizabeth; son John Corpe eldest, and two youngest sons Benajah and David, both under 21; dau Rebecca Essia (Essex?), and Mary, no surname (RIGR, 3:286). This eldest son, John, may have been the John Corps from Rehoboth, Mass who enlisted in the Continental Army during the Rev War for three years under Capt Carpenter (Supplement, VR Rehoboth, p 925, "from Bliss' History of Rehoboth").
2. Hope, b 8 Nov 1681 Br; poss d bef 24 Apr 1691 when his siblings were bp, although settlement of his father's est dtd 13 Mar 1701/02 said father had six ch then.
3. Anna, b 23 Feb 1683/84 Br.
4. Mary, b 2 Nov 1685, Br.

5. Elizabeth, b 14 Mar 1687/88, Br.
6. Sarah, b 30 Nov 1690, Br.

35. SOLOMON CURTIS

Solomon^2 Curtis was b ca 1642 in Braintree, Mass and d 1711, ae 69 (Torrey, p 197; Sav, 1:484). Solomon m, prob in Braintree, 11 June 1673 Prudence GATLIVE/GATTLIFFE, b 1656 per d rec, and d 1727, ae 76 (Torrey, p 198), dau Thomas and Prudence Gatlive/Gattliffe of Braintree (Ibid, p 296). Solomon was the son of Deodate/Diodatus Curtis and his wife, Rebecca, of Braintree. He took the Oath of Fidelity at Br on 21 May 1684 (Munro, p 114), but no Curtis was listed in the 1689 Census of Br (Geneals RI Fams, 1989, 2:402). Solomon and Prudence had a ch b Br as early as 1683 and brought with them one kn ch, and poss others, from Braintree.

KNOWN CHILDREN (6:71):
1. Solomon^3 Jr, b Braintree, Mass; m Abigail ___ and had the fol ch b Br (6:71): Solomon^4, b 23 Mar 1703/04; Abigail, b 26 July 1705; and Eleazer, b 13 Nov 1709. He and his family apparently rem from Br then as no later recs are found of them.
2. Samuel, b 4 Dec 1683 Br.
3. Nathaniel, b 24 Apr 1687 Br.
4. Mary, b 1 Aug 1695 Br; d 22 Aug 1695.

36. ZECHARIAH CURTIS

There is no rec of Zechariah Curtis in Br, aside from his presence at the first town meeting and the fact that "Zachary" Curtis took the Oath of Fidelity there on 20 June 1683 (Munro, p 114). No m, ch or d's are shown for him in the VR Br. Sav, 1:488 listed only one Zechariah Curtis in early New England, and said he was of Stratford, Conn in 1685, son of William of the same. William Curtis (Sav, 1:487) was in Stratford from 1642 until he d there in 1702. The name of his first wife is unkn, but he had Zechariah, b Nov 1659. Torrey, p 199 said that Zachariah Curtis was b 1659, d 1748, and m by 1690 or 1691 Hannah Porter, b 1665 and d 1738, and that he was of Stratford, Conn. If he was the Zechariah Curtis who was in Br from 1681-1683, he must have returned soon to Stratford.

37. THOMAS DAGGETT/DOGGETT JR

Capt Thomas^3 Daggett/Doggett Jr was b, prob on Martha's

Vineyard, Mass, ca 1658 and d in 1726 (Banks, Martha's Vineyard, 3:127-128). He m 22 Jan 1683 Elizabeth HAWES, b 1662 and d 1732 (Torrey, p 225), dau John and Desire (Gorham) Hawes of Barnstable, Mass (MD, 5:72). He was the son of Capt Thomas Daggett Sr, b ca 1630 and d 1691, and his wife, Hannah Mayhew, b 1635 and d 1722, dau of Gov Thomas Mayhew of Martha's Vineyard. Thomas Sr was the son of John Daggett, who was in Watertown, Mass in 1630, in Rehoboth in 1645, and of Martha's Vineyard by 1667 (Sav, 2:2).

Capt Thomas Jr took the Oath of Fidelity at Br on 17 May 1685 (Munro, p 114), and he was listed in the 1689 Census of Br with a wife, two ch, and two servants (Geneals RI Fams, 1989, 2:402). His ch have a Myflwr desc through his wife, Elizabeth Hawes, who was gdau of Desire Howland, dau of John Howland of the Myflwr (Bowman, p 206-207). He had two ch b Br, and then disappeared from the Br recs after 1689. He may have returned to Martha's Vineyard. The town meeting of Rehoboth on 7 Feb 1689 gave as a proprietor, not inhabitant, there, Thomas Daggett Esq (Bliss, p 128-129). The VR Rehoboth have no recs for him or any of his family.

CHILDREN, order of b of last three uncertain:
1. Samuel[4], b 10 June 1685 Br (6:72), bp Congre Ch, Br, 22 July 1688 (Geneals RI Fams, 1989, 2:371); poss m 11 July 1705 Mary PEASE (Bowman, p 207).
2. Hannah, b 27 May 1687 Br (6:72); bp Congre Ch 22 July 1688.
3. Jemima, m Malachi BUTLER (Bowman, p 207).
4. Thankful, m (1) Zephaniah BUTLER; m (2) Brotherton DAGGETT (Ibid).
5. Timothy, poss m 6 May 1717 Edgartown Mary SMITH (Bowman, p 207 from VR Edgartown).

38, JONATHAN DAVENPORT

Jonathan[2] Davenport was b 6 Mar 1659 in Dorchester, Mass and d 11 Jan 1729 in Little Compton, RI, per LC Fams, p 223, son of Thomas and Mary (Pitman) Davenport. However Jonathan's will was dtd 28 Mar 1729 and pvd 17 June 1729, so he d betw these dates (Rounds, 1:172). Jonathan m Dorchester 1 Dec 1680 Hannah MAYNARD, b 1660 and d 14 Jan 1729 in LC, dau John and Mary (Gates) Maynard of Marlboro, Mass, per LC Fams, p 223-224. However, Hannah was alive when her husband wrote his will on 28 Mar 1729. Although Jonathan was at the first town meeting of Br, his first ch, Thomas, was b 10 Dec 1681 in Dorchester. His second ch was b Br 3 Nov 1684 (6:72). He took the Oath of Fidelity at Br on 20 June 1683 (Munro, p 114). By 1686 he had rem to Little Compton, where he and Hannah lived and d. Jonathan's will, he carpenter of Little Compton, dtd 28 Mar 1729 and pvd 17 June 1729, named wife Hannah; sons Thomas, Jonathan, Simon (unm), Ebenezer, John, Joseph, and Benjamin Davenport; daus Hannah House, and Sarah Davenport (unm); son Joseph to be exec (Rounds, 1:172).

CHILDREN, first b Dorchester, second b Br, rest b LC (LC Fams, p 224):
1. Thomas^3, b 10 Dec 1681; d LC 14 Oct 1751 per LC Fams; m (1) LC 20 July 1704 Catharine WOODWORTH, b 1673, d 1 June 1729, dau Walter Woodworth of LC; m (2) Newport, RI 22 July 1737 Mary PITMAN. He had six ch by his first wife b LC: Eliphalet, Mary, Ephraim, Deborah, Hannah and Oliver; and two ch b Newport by his second wife: Gideon and Susanna (Ibid, p 224-225). The VR RI, Beaman, New Series, 11:124-125 give the burs in the Common Bur Ground of Newport of: Capt Thomas Davenport, d 16 Aug 1745 in 64 yr; adjoining him, Susannah, d 29 Jan 1818 age 70 or 79 yr; and Gideon who d 6 Sept 1810 in 73 yr, and his wife, Phillis, who d 16 Oct 1819 age 86 yr. This may be Thomas^3 and his two ch by his second m, in which case he d Newport and not LC.
2. Jonathan, b 3 Nov 1684; d LC 14 Oct 1751, unm.
3. Hannah, b 23 Dec 1686; d Lebanon, Conn 26 June 1759, ae 83; m 13 June 1710 Nathaniel HOUSE, and rem to Lebanon ca 1721. She had nine ch, surname House, first three b LC and rest in Lebanon (LC Fams, p 350): Nathaniel, Sarah, John, Rebecca, Gideon, Jonathan, Hannah, Simon, and Rebecca II.
4. Simeon, b 27 Dec 1688; d LC 9 Dec 1763, unm.
5. Ebenezer, b 2 Sept 1691; d Newport 4 Aug 1776; m LC 12 Feb 1714 Mary PITMAN, dau John and Mary (Saunders) Pitman of Newport (Torrey, p 588). He rem to Newport where he was a mason and had five ch b (LC Fams, p 225): a dau, Ebenezer, Israel, Elizabeth and Jonathan.
6. John, b 12 Jan 1694; d 20 Apr 1741 Tiverton, RI; m LC 15 June 1726 Elizabeth TAYLOR, b 4 June 1701, dau Peter and Elizabeth (Peckham) Taylor. The b's of his seven ch were rec in Tiverton (Ibid, p 225-226): Noah, Sarah, Jonathan, John, Ephraim, Phebe and Mary.
7. Joseph, b 25 Mar 1696; d LC 2 Sept 1760; m LC 1 Apr 1731 Elizabeth WOOD, b LC 31 Jan 1708, d LC 13 July 1766, dau Jonathan and Elizabeth (Thurston) Wood. He had six ch, rec LC (Ibid, p 226): Hannah, Ruth, William, Jeremiah, Samuel and Mary.
8. Benjamin, b 6 Oct 1698; m Rehoboth, Mass by Rev David Turner 12 May 1731 Sarah BURR of Rehoboth (VR Re, p 74).
9. Sarah, b 10 Dec 1700; unm 28 Mar 1729 when father wrote his will.

39. ROBERT DUTCH

Robert[3] Dutch Jr was b 1647 in Ipswich, Mass and d betw 1695 and 1710, when his widow m (2) (int) Joseph AYRES (Torrey, p 236). He m Ipswich 26 Dec 1677 Hannah LOVELL, dau Thomas and Ann Lovell of Ipswich (Hammatt p 82, 221; Torrey, p 476). He was the son of Robert and Mary (Kimball) Dutch Sr, and gson of Osman Dutch who came from Bridport, Dorset, England to Newport, RI and Gloucester, Mass. Robert attended the first town meeting of Br and signed the Oath of Fidelity there on 9 Aug 1686 (Munro, p 114). The 1689 Census of Br listed him with a wife and three ch (Geneals RI Fams, 1989, 2:401), and his name was on the Br tax roll of Sept 1695. No Dutch m or d recs are in the VR Br, so his fam apparently left Br aft Sept 1695.

KNOWN CHILDREN[4] (Hammatt, p 82; 6:74):
1. Ebenezer, b 29 Jan 1679, Ipswich.
2. Benjamin, b 9 Aug 1680, Ipswich.
3. Robert, b 12 Jan 1692 (sic, 1682?), Ipswich.
4. Hannah, b 31 Aug 1683, Br.
5. Thomas, b 13 Sept 1686, Br.
6. Elizabeth, b 8 Sept 1695, Br.

40. JEREMIAH FINNEY (PHINNEY)

Jeremiah[2] Finney was b in Barnstable, Mass 15 Aug 1662 and d in Br 18 Feb 1748, son John and Elizabeth (Bailey) Finney of Barnstable and Br. He m Br 7 Jan 1684 Esther LEWIS (6:21), b 1664 and d Br 11 Apr 1743, dau Thomas and Mary Lewis. Jeremiah came with his father to Br and was made a freeman in 1680. He took the Oath of Fidelity at Br on 17 May 1685 (Munro, p 114), where he was a sea captain. The 1689 Census of Br listed him with a wife and one ch (Geneals RI Fams, 1989, 2:401). He must have d intestate. No will or inv of his est was given in Rounds through 1762.

CHILDREN b Br (6:132; 8:276; Geneals RI Fams, 1989, 1:449):
1. Jeremiah[3], b 1684; d.y.
2. Mary, b 26 Mar 1686; d bef 1689 Census of Br?
3. Hannah, b 14 Jan 1687/88; d Br 22 Dec 1744; m 14 Jan 1706/07 Thomas DIMAN, b LI, NY 1680, d Br 18 Apr 1754 (Rattray, p 283; 6:128 says he d May 1754), son James and Hannah (James) Diman of South Hampton, LI. Hannah lived with her husband on LI until the fam rem to Br in 1712. She had eight ch, surname Diman, the first five b LI, and the last three in Br (Rattray, p 283): James, John, Rebecca, Deacon Jeremiah, Jonathan, Phebe, Lucretia and Daniel.
4. Mehitable, b 8 May 1687 (sic, 1689?).

5. John, b 3 Aug 1690; d 23 Oct 1690 (6:132).
6. Rebecca, b 24 Feb 1691/92; prob m 11 Mar 1716 Samuel HARRIS of Swansea, Mass.
7. Esther, b 4 May 1693; d Br as widow 26 May 1754 (6:-142) m (int) Br 31 Oct 1719 Joseph JOY of Rehoboth, Mass (6:21), who d Rehoboth 5 Dec 1724 (VR Re, p 842). She had two ch, surname Joy, b Rehoboth (Ibid, p 650): Joseph, b 31 Dec 1720, and Esther, b April 1723.
8. Deborah, bp 20 Oct 1695.
9. John, b 13 Apr 1696; prob d Kingston, Mass 11 Oct 1787; m Mary CAMPBELL, dau Sylvanus and Mary Campbell of Norton, Mass. He lived in Norton where he was a cordwainer, from ca 1717 until ca 1766, when he rem to Easton. No kn issue (Geneals RI Fams, 1989, 1:450). Ca 1724 John was made guardian of Caleb, Ruth and Jeremiah Cambill, ch of Sylvanus Cambill of Norton (Rounds, 1:106). Both Sylvanus and Mary Campbell were dcd.
10. Abigail, b 17 Apr 1697.
<u>11</u>. Capt Jeremiah II (Jr), bp 7 Sept 1700; d Br 21 Oct 1759, 59 yr (6:132); m (int) 17 May 1727 Elizabeth "BRISTON" (6:21) which is incorrect and should be BRISTOW (6:-10), b Br 14 Dec 1706 (6:66), d 8 Nov 1760, 54 yr (6:132), dau Thomas and Elizabeth Bristow of Br (6:66).

Capt Jeremiah II^3 (Jeremiah^2, John^1) Finney was bp 7 Sept 1700 and d Br 21 Oct 1759, 59 yr. He m (int) Br 17 May 1727 Elizabeth BRISTOW (6:10), b Br 14 Dec 1706 (6:66), and d 8 Nov 1760, 54 yr (6:132), dau Thomas and Elizabeth Bristow of Br (6:66). Sav, 1:257 said that the surname Bristow was also called Bristol. Jeremiah was a sea captain.

CHILDREN, b Br (6:76-77):
<u>1</u>. Josiah^4, b 1 July 1728; d Br 23 July 1804, 76 yr (6:-132); m (1) 19 May 1751 Mary/Molly CAREY (6:21), d 18 Sept 1760, 28 yr (6:132), dau Allen and Hannah (Church) Cary of Br; m (2) 16 Sept 1761 Martha GIBBS (6:21), dau James and Martha (Giddings) Gibbs.
2. Ch, d 27 Feb 1730 (6:132).
3. Elizabeth, b 1731; d 14 May 1759, 28 yr (Ibid).
<u>4</u>. Jeremiah, b 19 Mar 1732/33; d Br 17 July 1807, 74 yr (Ibid); m (1) Deborah LORING, b 1740 and d 9 Nov 1791, (-8:369); m (2) St Michael's Ch 14 Apr 1792 Mary COY (8:-205), b 1747, d 20 Sept 1821, 74 yr as widow (8:370), dau Samuel Coy.
5. Thomas, b 19 Mar 1737; d 5 Jan 1791 Plymouth, Mass; m 5 June 1760 Elizabeth CLARK of Plymouth, b 1742, d 3 Mar 1795. Thomas had five or six ch b Br (6:77), and then rem to Plymouth (Geneals RI Fams, 1989, 1:455): Elizabeth Clark, Clark, Molly, Josiah Morton, Ruth, and poss Thomas.
6. Mary, b 14 Nov 1742 and bp same day Congre Ch, Br

(8:276); m 1765 as his second wife Corban BARNES of Plymouth, Mass, who b 1732, son John and Dorcas (Corban) Barnes of Plymouth (Gen Reg Plym Fams, p 12). Mary had eight ch b Plymouth, surname Barnes: Mary, Rebecca, Betsy, Charlotte, Corban, Patty, Deborah and Abigail.
7. Esther, b 14 (sic) Nov 1744, bp Congre Ch, Br 11 Nov 1744 (8:276); d 26 Mar 1745.

Josiah^4 (Capt Jeremiah^3, Jeremiah^2, John^1) Finney was b Br 1 July 1728 and d there as Esq on 23 July 1804, 76 yr (6:132; 8:370). He m (1) Br 19 May 1751 Mary/Molly CAREY (6:21), b Br 3 Dec 1732 (6:68), and d 18 Sept 1760, 28 yr (6:132), dau Allen and Hannah (Church) Carey of Br. He m (2) Br 16 Sept 1761 Martha GIBBS (6:21), b 1739, d 22 or 29 May 1823, 84 yr (6:132; 8:370), dau James and Martha (Giddings) Gibbs (Geneals RI Fams, 1989, 1:452-453). Martha Gibbs Finney became a member of the Congre Ch of Br 1 June 1788 (8:249). Josiah's ch by his first wife have a Myflwr desc through her mother, Hannah Church, from Richard Church of the Myflwr (LC Fams, p 166-167, 172, 174). Josiah was a farmer, and was the postmaster of Br for a time.

CHILDREN by first wife, Molly, b Br and bp Congre Ch Br (6:132; 8:276; Geneals RI Fams, 1989, 1:452):
1. Jeremiah^5, bp 4 Feb 1753; d 25 July 1773, 21 yr, at sea (6:132).
2. Elizabeth, bp 8 Dec 1754; d 21 Sept 1756, 2 yr (Ibid where wrongly called "of Joseph").
3. Allen, bp 20 Mar 1757; d 31 July 1758 (Ibid).
4. Molly, bp 10 June 1759; poss d 19 May 1790 (6:124); m Capt William COGGESHALL who d Br 10 May 1823, 69 yr (Ibid). She had one kn ch, Capt Josiah Coggeshall, b 7 May 1784, who m 1813 Mary Pearse FINNEY, b 19 May 1790, dau Capt Loring Finney of Br (6:15).

CHILDREN by second wife, Martha, b Br and bp Congre Ch Br (6:132; 8:276; Geneals RI Fams, 1989, 1:453):
5. Martha, bp 29 Aug 1762; d Providence, RI 13 Apr 1843; m Br 1783 John FALES, b 13 June 1760, d 4 Oct 1813, son Judge Nathaniel and Sarah (Little) Fales of Br. John was a Sgt under Capt William Throop in the Rev War. Martha had thirteen ch b Br, surname Fales (6:76): Charlotte, Fidelia, Timothy, James Gibbs, James, Betsey P., Abby F., Nancy C., Joseph Jackson, Joseph Jackson II, Henry DeWolf, Henry DeWolf II, and Martha G. These ch have a Myflwr desc through Sarah Little from James Chilton of the Myflwr (Fales Fam, p 75-77; Myflwr Fams thru Five Gens, James Chilton, 2:92-93).
6. Charlotte, b 10 Feb 1764, bp 5 Apr 1764; d Br 15

May 1829, 65 yr, wid of William (6:127); m Br 1 June 1784 William DEWOLF, b 19 Dec 1762, d Br 19 Apr 1829, son Mark Anthony and Abigail (Potter) DeWolf of Br. Charlotte had five ch, b Br, surname DeWolf: Henry, William, Charlotte, Maria and Abigail.

7. Sarah/Sally, b 1767, bp 12 Apr 1767; d 4 May 1820 (6:168); m St Michael's Ch Br 15 Nov 1789 Capt Hezekiah USHER 2nd, bp St Michael's 12 May 1763 (8:180-181), d 15 Sept 1795 at the Gambia River, Africa (6:167), son Rev John and Ann Usher Jr of Br (6:168). Sally had three ch b Br, surname Usher, all bp St Michael's: Anne Francis, George Finney, and Hezekiah.

8. Thomas Gibbs, b 1768, bp 1 Jan 1769; d 4 Oct 1787 at sea. (8:369 says he d 18 Nov 1787, 19 yr.)

9. George, b 1770, bp 7 Apr 1771; d 9 May 1792, 22 yr, at sea unm (6:132).

10. Ann/Nancy, bp 19 Sept 1773; d 17 Dec 1839, unm.

11. Susanna, bp July 1772 (Geneals RI Fams, 1989, 1: 453) or bp July 1775 (8:276); m 23 June 1811 Capt Oliver FITCH (8:333), b 1775, d prob 8 Jan 1814, son Richard and Mary Fitch of Norwich, Conn. Prob no issue.

12. ?Abigail, b 1776; d Br 16 Oct 1796, 20 yr (6:132; 8:369).

13. Elizabeth, bp 18 June 1780.

14. Ruth Thurston, bp 9 Oct 1781; d 4 Feb 1858; m 16 June 1811 Elkanah FRENCH Jr, b 1782, d 22 Sept 1856. She had three ch, surname French: Emily F. (inney?), Abby Finney, and a ch who was b and d 1818. (The VR Re, p 612 have the b of two ch in Rehoboth to Elkanah and Hannah (Walker) French: Esther, b 30 Aug 1777, and Elkanah, b 19 June 1789 (sic, 1779?).

Jeremiah^4 (Capt Jeremiah^3, Jeremiah^2, John^1) Finney was b Br 19 Mar 1732/33 and d there on 17 July 1807, 74 yr (6:132; 8:370). He m (1) Deborah LORING, b 1740 per d rec and d 9 Nov 1791, 51 yr (8:369); m (2) St Michael's Ch 14 Apr 1792 Mary COY (8:205), b 1747, d 20 Sept 1821, 74 yr, widow (8:370), dau Samuel Coy. Jeremiah was a sea captain, and served as a Private in 1778 during the Rev War in Col Nathan Miller's RI Reg't (Pat Index, p 533 under Phinney).

CHILDREN by first wife, Deborah, b Br and bp Congre Ch Br (8:276):

1. Thomas^5, b 1758, d 8 Mar 1760 per Geneals RI Fams, 1989, 1:453. The VR Br 8:276 says "Thomas of Jeremiah and Deborah Finney bp Aug 30, 1772", together with five siblings on that date. Perhaps the first Thomas d and they had Thomas II, although no such b rec was found.

2. Capt Loring, b Br 18 June 1760, bp 30 Aug 1772; d

Br 8 Mar 1827; m 12 Oct 1785 or 1786 Experience (PEARSE) (HERSEY) b Plymouth, Mass 4 May 1764, d Br 11 Dec 1835, dau Samuel and Elizabeth (Atwood) Pearse and wid of Gideon Hersey (Geneals RI Fams, 1989, 1:458).
3. Elizabeth, b 1763, bp 30 Aug 1772; m 26 Feb 1803 Isaac L. NEWTON, son Richard and Lydia Newton of Wrentham, Mass.
4. Deborah, b 1766, bp 30 Aug 1772; m 22 Dec 1785 Lucius RHODES.
5. Rebecca, b 1768, bp 30 Aug 1772; d 2 June 1843; m 10 Nov 1785 Capt Jesse DAVIS, b Freetown, Mass 15 Mar 1764, d bef 1843, son Ichabod and Sylvia (Chase) Davis of Freetown (VR Freetown). Rebecca had six ch, surname Davis (Geneals RI Fams, 1989, 1:453): Polly, Lucinda, Anthony, David, Amanda, and John Jeremiah Finney.
6. Mary, b 1770, bp 30 Aug 1772; d 28 Mar 1835 Providence, RI; m 24 Apr 1788 Capt Parker CLARK, b 26 Apr 1765, d 26 Feb 1839 Providence, son Ezekial and Hannah (Parker) Clark of Rochester, Mass. Mary had three ch, surname Clark: Henry Finney, George Gibbs, and Mary (Ibid, p 453-454).
7. John, b 1772, bp 26 Sept 1773; m 8 July 1798 Avis BOWEN (War 6:9), b 24 Feb 1780, dau James and Ruth (Arnold) Bowen of Warren, RI (Ibid, 6:50). They had one ch, Avis, and rem from Warren, prob to Conn (Geneals RI Fams, 1989, 1:459).
8. Jeremiah Jr, b 1774, bp 25 Nov 1787; d 1 Jan 1799 (Ibid), or d 15 Jan 1799, 25 yr (6:132; 8:369).
9. Hannah, b 1776, bp 25 Nov 1787; d 30 June 1805 Warren, RI; m 5 Nov 1795 Elisha CARPENTER, b 26 Apr 1766, d 21 Nov 1822, son Peter and Abigail (Briggs) Carpenter of Norton, Mass. Hannah had two ch b Warren, surname Carpenter (Geneals RI Fams, 1989, 1:454): Mary and Louisa. Louisa is called Loiza in the VR Warren (War, 6:54).

Capt Loring^5 (Jeremiah^4, Capt Jeremiah^3, Jeremiah^2, John^1) Finney was b Br 18 June 1760, bp Congre Ch Br 30 Aug 1772, and d Br 8 Mar 1827, 66 yr (6:132; 8:370). He m St Michael's Ch 12 Oct 1786 Experience (PEARSE) HERSEY (8:205), b Plymouth, Mass 4 May 1764, d Br 11 Dec 1835 (6:-132), dau Samuel and Elizabeth (Atwood) Pearse, and wid of Gideon Hersey of Plymouth. Experience joined the Congre Ch in Br on 2 Aug 1807 (8:249). Loring was a sea captain, and was a soldier at the Battle of RI during the Rev War (Geneals RI Fams, 1989, 1:458-459).

CHILDREN, b Br (Ibid, 1:458-459):
1. Thomas^6, b 23 Mar 1787; d 12 Sept 1819, 32 yr, in N. Carolina (8:370).
2. Mary Pearse, b 19 May 1790; d 13? Mar 1866; m by Rev

Luther Baker 31 Dec 1813 (6:15) Capt Josiah COGGESHALL, b 7 May 1784, d 14 Mar 1804, son Capt William and Molly (Finney) Coggeshall. She had five ch, surname Coggeshall: Henry, Loring Finney, Martha, William and George.
3. Levi Loring, b 28 Dec 1791, bp Congre Ch 4 Oct 1812 (8:249); d 26 June 1815 at sea, unm (8:370).
4. Eliza Atwood, b 5 May 1794, bp Congre Ch 4 Oct 1812 (8:249); m (1) 17 Apr 1836 Samuel LADIEU, b 19 Apr 1789, son Capt Curtis and Rachel (Tew) Ladieu/Ladue of Barrington, RI (Bar, 6:13, 31); m (2) 5 Dec 1850 John GREGORY Jr, son John Gregory Sr of Seekonk, Mass; m (3) Isaiah SIMMONS. No issue.
5. George, b 4 Jan 1797; d 1821 in N. Carolina (8:370).

41. JOHN FINNEY

John[1] Finney came from England bef 1639 with his mother, brother Robert, and sister Catherine. He settled in Plymouth, Mass where he had a land grant in 1639, and became a freeman in 1644. He then lived in Barnstable and Situate, and joined the group which in 1680/81 settled in Br. He m (1) Christian(a) ___, who d Plymouth 9 Sept 1649 (Sav, 2:160); m (2) 10 June 1650 Abigail (BISHOP) COGGIN who d 6 May 1653, dau Thomas Bishop and wid of Henry Coggin; and m (3) 26 June 1654 Elizabeth BAILEY, who was bur Br 9 Feb 1683/84 (Geneals RI Fams, 1989, 1:448-449). In 1682 he sold his land in Br to his son, Jonathan, who settled there, as did two other sons, Jeremiah and Joshua. In 1702 he was in Swansea, Mass where he prob d soon after. Most of his desc continued to spell their name Finney, except for those of Jonathan[2], who used Phinney. John had no ch by his second wife.

KNOWN CHILDREN by first wife, Christian(a), b Plymouth (Geneals RI Fams, 1989, 1:448):
1. John[2], b 24 Dec 1638; m 1664 Mary ROGERS, and lived Barnstable, Mass. He had thirteen ch (Gen Reg Plym Fams, p 110).
2. Thomas, b ca 1648; d 1653.

CHILDREN by third wife, Elizabeth, b Barnstable (Geneals RI Fams, 1989, 1:448-450):
3. Jonathan, b 14 Aug 1655. Rem to Br, RI. See #42.
4. Robert, b 13 Aug 1656; d 1690 in Phip's Expedition to Canada.
5. Hannah, b 2 Sept 1657; m (1) 1677 Deacon Ephraim MORTON of Plymouth, who d 18 Feb 1732, son Ephraim and Ann (Cooper) Morton of Plymouth; m (2) John COOKE of Kingston, Mass. Hannah had no issue from her second m, but had five ch, surname Morton, prob b Plymouth: Hannah, Ephraim, John, Joseph, and Ebenezer.

6. Elizabeth, b 15 Mar 1659; Geneals RI Fams, 1989, 1: 449 said she prob m 19 Dec 1773 Haile BARTON of Warren, RI and had four ch by him. This is questionable since she was b in 1659 and would have been only fourteen yrs old in 1773. The VR War, 6:7 say he was m in Warren 19 Dec 1773 by Rev Charles Thompson to an Elizabeth Phinney.
7. Josiah, b 11 Jan 1661; lived Plymouth and had a large fam.
8. Jeremiah, b 15 Aug 1662. Rem to Bristol, RI. See #40.
9. Joshua, b Dec 1665; d 7 Sept 1714 Swansea, Mass; m (int) Br 31 May 1688 Mercy WATTS (6:21) who d 12 Feb 1724.

Joshua[2] (John[1]) Finney was b in Dec 1665 in Barnstable, Mass and d 7 Sept 1714 in Swansea, Mass. He m (int) Br 31 May 1688 Mercy WATTS (6:21) who d 12 Feb 1724. Joshua rem with his father to Br in 1680 where he became a freeman, and all of his ch, except two, were b. He went to Swansea by 1707, and three of his four sons rem to Conn (Geneals RI Fams, 1989, 1:450). The div of one-third of the est of Joshua Finney of Swansea, formerly laid out to his widow Mercy Finney, now dcd, dtd 11 Jan 1737/38 is to be div betw his ch: Joshua (eldest son), John (2nd son), Samuel (3rd son), Josiah (youngest son), Mercy wife of John Man (youngest dau), Elezebeth wife of Nathan Luther (2nd dau), and Mary Finney (eldest dau) (Rounds, 1:267).

CHILDREN, all b Br except last two (6:76; Geneals RI Fams, 1989, 1:450):
1. Joshua[3] Jr, b 7 May 1689; d 14 May 1751 Lebanon, Conn; m Br Martha CARTER, b 1671 and d 14 May 1751. He lived in Swansea, and then rem to Conn ca 1750. Joshua had six ch, b Swansea: William, Joshua, Mary/Mercy, Martha, John and Oliver, of whom William, John and Oliver rem to Conn.
2. Elizabeth, b 25 Sept 1691 or 1692; d 19 Sept 1701.
3. Mary, b 12 Apr 1694; d aft div of father's est, dtd 11 Jan 1737/38, and unm then (Rounds, 1:267).
4. Dr John, b 15 Aug 1696; d 6 June 1773 Lebanon, Conn; m Swansea 14 Sept 1716 Ann TOOGOOD who d 11 Aug 1776. He had nine ch, b Swansea: Joel, John, Nathaniel, Joshua, Ann, Mercy, David, Martha and Jabez.
5. Samuel, b 20 May 1699; d Warwick, RI 1765; m 12 Mar 1726/27 Elizabeth (WOOD) TIBBITTS, dau John Wood of Warwick, and wid of Thomas Tibbitts. He had two ch, b Warwick: Benjamin and Mercy.
6. Josiah, b 26 July 1701; will pvd Warren, Conn 22 Aug 1774; m 1 Jan 1723/24 Elizabeth MANN, who d 1775. He had seven ch, b Swansea: Elizabeth, Josiah, Josiah II, Keziah, Lydia, David and Jonathan.
7. Elizabeth II, b 1 May 1707 Swansea; m 4 Nov 1733 Nathan LUTHER of Swansea and had one kn ch, Huldah Luther.

8. Mercy, b unrec, but named in father's div of est, dtd 11 Jan 1737/38 as youngest dau and wife of John MAN (Rounds, 1:267).

42. JONATHAN FINNEY

Jonathan^2 (John^1) Finney was b 14 Aug 1655 in Barnstable, Mass and d in Swansea, Mass in May 1728, son of John and Elizabeth (Bailey) Finney. He m (int) 18 Oct 1682 Joanna KENNICUT/KINNICUTT, b 1669 and prob d 1741, who was incorrectly called the dau of John and Elizabeth Kinnicutt of Br in Geneals RI Fams, 1989, 1:449. Sav, 3:10 showed that in fact she was b Jan 1664, dau of Roger and Joanna (Sheper[d]son) Kennicutt of Malden and Swansea, Mass. She was actually the sister of the above John, b Oct 1669, who Torrey, p 433, said m Elizabeth Luther and lived in Warwick, RI.

Jonathan was one of the first settlers in Br, being made a freeman there in 1680. In 1682 he purchased his father's land at Br, but aft the b of his first one or two ch at Br, he rem to Swansea where his other ch were b. His descs have used the spelling of Phinney. The will of Jonathan Phiney of Swansea, yeoman, dtd 27 Aug 1724 and pvd 20 Aug 1728, named: wife Joannah; son Jonathan Phiney; daus Joannah Clerk, Elizabeth Bradford, Mary Clerk, Lidia Potter, and Hannah Phiney; son Jonathan to be exec (Rounds, 1:163). Apparently Joanna Kennicutt's brother, John, was named as exec of her est. The acct of John Kinicut, admin of est of Joannah Phiney of Swansea, dtd 17 Nov 1741, included payments to her ch: Jeremiah Clark, Elizabeth Luden, Hopestill Potter, Joannah Clerk, and Mercy Phiney "in Right of her Two Children as her late Husband's Double Portion of his mother's Estate" (Rounds, 1:313).

CHILDREN (6:76; Geneals RI Fams, 1989, 1:449-450):
1. Joanna^3, b 30 Nov 1683; m ___ CLARK.
2. Jonathan, b 3 Nov 1686 rec VR Br, but Geneals RI Fams 1:450 said he b Swansea; d Swansea 26 Nov 1736; m Swansea 6 May 1730 Mercy READ, b 1706 and d Nov 1767. He was first a mariner and later a farmer, and had four or five ch b Swansea: Hannah, Jonathan, Jonathan II, Elisha and prob Hannah II. The acct of Mercy Finney, wid and adm of est of Jonathan Finney of Swansea, dcd intest, was dtd 16 Oct 1739 and included "charge of Lying in with a Posthumus Child" (Rounds, 1:286). On 19 Feb 1739 Mercy Finney, widow, was named guardian of Hannah Finney, dau of Jonathan Finney of Swansea (Ibid, 1:290).
3. Mehetabel, bp 19 Jan 1688/89 Swansea. Not named in father's will of 27 Aug 1724.
4. Elizabeth, bp 1695; m (1) ___ BRADFORD; m (2) ___

LUDEN.
5. Lydia, bp 1695; m Hopestill POTTER (not Hopestill COTTON as per Geneals RI Fams, 1989, 1:449). Her father's will of 27 Aug 1724 called her Lidia Potter. "Lidia Potter of Hopestill" joined the Congre Ch, Br in Dec 1723, and was rem from membership (prob through d) on 6 Jan 1770 (8:260).
6. Mary, bp 1695; m ___ CLARK.
7. Ebenezer, bp 23 Apr 1699; d Middleboro, Mass; m (int) 28 May 1726 Jane FAUNCE, b 1692, dau Thomas and Jane (Nelson) Faunce of Plymouth, Mass. He lived for a time in Br, and then rem to Easton, Norton, and Plymouth, Mass. He had one kn ch, Nelson, b Br July 1728, who d aged 2 (6:77). He was not named in his father's will of 27 Apr 1724.
8. Hannah, bp 1 Sept 1700; d 30 June 1730.

43. JOSEPH FORD

The date and place of b of Joseph Ford are not kn for certain. He may have been the son of Andrew and Eleanor (Lovell) Ford of Weymouth and Hingham, Mass. Chamberlain, p 226, said that this Andrew's second son was Joseph who "perhaps rem to Hingham or Bristol, RI and d bef 25 Feb 1692/93" (the date of Andrew Ford's will). Joseph Ford was prob b by 1661/62 as he m in Br 6 Dec 1683 Deborah WALDO, who was b 1661 (6:55). He took the Oath of Fidelity in Br on 20 June 1683 (Munro, p 114), but he was not listed in the 1689 Census of Br (Geneals RI Fams, 1989, 2:401-402). He had two ch b Br (6:77): Deborah, b 27 Sept 1684 (VR Br 6:77 say 27 Sept 1784, a typographical error), and Joseph, b 26 July 1686. Joseph's widow, as Deborah (Waldo) Ford, m 15 Mar 1694 Samuel DANIEL, and they lived in Boston, Mass (Torrey, p 203, 275).

44. ANTHONY FRY

Anthony Fry was prob b by 1650, place and parentage unkn. He m Hannah ___, poss in Yarmouth, Mass, bef the b of their first ch there in 1671. Torrey, p 287, said that he lived in Yarmouth and Bristol, RI. Sav did not mention an Anthony Fry, and named no Fry(e) surname in Yarmouth. Anthony was at the first town meeting in Br and was living there by early 1685. He and Hannah had five ch b Yarmouth, and two ch b Br. The 11 Feb 1689 Census of Br gave him there with a wife, seven ch and no servants (Geneals RI Fams, 1989, 2:401). Both Anthony and Hannah became members of the Congre Ch, Br on 12 June 1695 (8:249). Anthony had d and his wid, Hannah, had m (2) prob Deacon John BUT-

TERWORTH of Br bef 3 Oct 1706, date of the will of Anthony's son, Lt Thomas Fry of Br (Rounds, 1:37, 51). Anthony's son John m in Br and raised a fam there, and the only Fry recs of m's in Br are those of him and his ch.

CHILDREN, first five b Yarmouth, Mass and last two in Br (VR Yarmouth in MD, 3:37, 247; 6:77):
1. John ffray, son of Anthony ffray, b 28 June 1671; d Br 12 Jan 1705/06 (6:133); m Deliverance ___ by 1694.
2. Lt Thomas, b 11 Nov 1673; d bef 3 Oct 1706. The inv of the est of Lt Thomas Fry of Br, mariner, was dtd 3 Oct 1706 and presented by Samuel Penfield and Hannah (Fry) Penfield, his wife, admins. (Hannah was the sister of Lt Thomas Fry.) It consisted of his personal est "found to be with his mother Mrs Hannah Butterworth in Br". There was no other kn Thomas Fry in Br except the son of Anthony and Hannah. This shows that Hannah, wid of Anthony Fry, m (2) a Butterworth of Br (Rounds, 1:37). Hannah prob m (2) Deacon John BUTTERWORTH of Br. The acct of John and Joseph Butterworth, admins of the est of their father, Deacon John Butterworth of Br, was presented 2 Apr 1711 and mentioned cash paid to "Mrs Butterworth for her part of her dower in said est (Rounds, 1:51).
3. Hannah ffry, b 20 Oct 1676; m by 1700 Samuel PENFIELD Jr of Br (Torrey, p 569; Rounds, 1:37). She had four ch b Br, surname Penfield (6:99): Samuel, Peter, Abigail, and Nathaniel.
4. (worn) siar, b 8 Apr 1678.
5. Nathanell, b 18 June 1680.
6. James, b 7 Mar 1684/85 Br (6:77), bp Congre Ch Br 17 July 1687 (Geneals RI Fams, 1989, 2:371).
7. Mercy, b 15 Apr 1687 Br, bp as Mary in Congre Ch Br 17 July 1687 (Ibid).

John^2 (Anthony^1) Fry was b Yarmouth, Mass 28 June 1671 and came with his father's family to Br by 1685. He d in Br 12 Jan 1705/06 (6:133). All of his ch were bp in Br in 1710 as "of Deliverance Fry", and his last rec ch was b in Dec 1705. Both the VR Br, 6:22 and Torrey, p 287, said that John m 18 June 1695 Elizabeth HUMMERY. All of the b's of his ch appear in the VR Br, 6:77 as of "John and Deliverance", and the surname Hummery does not exist in Sav or elsewhere in Torrey. The inv of the est of John Fry of Br was dtd 7 Feb 1705(/06) and presented by Deliverance Fry, his widow (Rounds, 1:34).

CHILDREN, b Br (6:77), all except Anthony bp Congre Ch Br (Geneals RI Fams, 1989, 2:377-378):
1. Stephen^3, b 19 June 1695.

2. John, b 18 Dec 1696; m Br by Rev Nathaniel Cotton 26 Mar 1724 Abigail SPINK (6:22). No ch in VR Br.
3. Anthony, b 4 Sept 1698; m Br 24 June 1724 Mercy TAYLOR of Freetown, Mass (Ibid). He had two ch b Br (6:77): John, b 9 May 1725, and Anthony, b 19 Nov 1726. He prob then rem from Br.
4. Mary, b 24 July 1700; m Br 12 Dec 1723 Capt John INGRAHAM (6:29), b 8 Dec 1701 (6:84), d 17 Feb 1786, 85 yr (6:141), son Timothy and Sarah (Cowell) Ingraham. Mary had ten ch b Br, surname Ingraham (6:84): Timothy, Mary, John, Abigail, Jeremiah, Rachel, Thomas, Joseph, Samuel and Martha.
5. Hannah, b 4 June 1702; m 21 Apr 1725 Thomas RICHMOND of Taunton, Mass (6:46).
6. Martha, b 29 Apr 1704.
7. Nathaniel, b 26 Dec 1705.

45. CAPT SAMUEL GALLOP/GALLUP

See also: RIGR, 1990, Vol 13, p 205-214.

Samuel Gallop/Gallup was prob at least 21 yrs of age, and had enough money to purchase land in the new settlement, when he attended the first town meeting of Br on 1 Sept 1681. All of the Samuel Gallop/Gallups then in New England were studied and their histories examined, with the result that only one Samuel was found who could have lived in Br in this time period.

Capt John[2] Gallop Jr, bp at St Mary's, Bridport, Dorset, England on 25 Jan 1620, came with his mother, Christabell (Brushett) Gallop and three siblings, Samuel, Nathaniel, and Joan, in 1633 to join his father, Capt John[1] Gallop Sr, who had come in 1630 to Nantasket, Mass. Capt John Jr m in 1643, prob in Boston, Hannah LAKE, dau John dcd and Margaret (Reade) Lake, and he gained the reputation as a great Indian fighter in the Pequot War. He applied for a home lot in New London, Conn by 1650/51, and in 1654 rem with his family to 450 acres of land he owned on the west side of the River Mystick in what is now Stonington, Conn. He was killed 19 Dec 1675 in the Narragansett Swamp Fight of King Philip's War, where he was a Capt.

The div of his est gave L100 to his wid, L137 to his eldest son John, L90 to his son Benadam, L89 each to his sons William and Samuel, and L70 each to his five daus. The Gallup Fam, p 24-27 said that of John Jr's sons, there were only two living lines, those from John and Benadam. "His son William left no sons, and of Samuel there is no record." Sav, 2:222-223 named John Jr's sons as John, Benadam b ca 1656, William b 1658, and "Samuel who died probably unm". Since Samuel and William received the same amount of money from their father's est, they may have been about the same age. Samuel would therefore have been 21 yrs old by the time of Br's first town meeting in 1681, and have had L89 available to buy land there.

The only other Samuel Gallup in New England of the right age was Samuel^3 (Samuel^2, John^1) of Boston, and the Gallup Fam, p 24, said that he was a sea captain and "died in the disastrous expedition to Canada under William Phips in 16-80. By his death the male line of this family became extinct." So it seems very prob that the Samuel^3 (Capt John^{2,1}) of whom it was said "there is no record", was the Samuel Gallop/Gallup who settled in Br in 1681. He took the Oath of Fidelity at Br on 17 May 1685 (Munro, p 114).

Among the other early Br settlers at its first town meeting there was one woman, "widow Elizabeth Southard", whom the VR Br, 6:164 called Southworth, Elizabeth at the date of her d in Br on 24 June 1682. The VR Br give only two early Southworth m's in Br: Elizabeth Southworth who m 12 May 1685 Samuel Gallup of Br, and Prissilla Southworth who m 1 Mar 1689 Samuel Talbot/Talbee (6:50). All of the widowed Elizabeths who m Southworth males and had daus named Elizabeth, old enough and free to m in 1685, were traced.

It appears that there could be one, and only one, who fitted these requirements. Constant^2 (Edward^1) Southworth, b 1615 in Leyden, Holland, and d 10 Mar 1679 Duxbury, Mass, m 2 Nov 1637 Elizabeth Collier, dau William Collier of Duxbury, the Ass't Gov of the Plymouth Colony. Constant went with his fam to the Br area bef its first town meeting, and then rem to Little Compton, RI. His will, dtd 27 Feb 1678 and pvd Mar 1678/79, named his wife, Elizabeth, and among his ch, "To my dau Elizabeth Southworth my next bed and furniture, provided she doe not marry William Fobbes, but if she doe then to have five shillings. To dau Prissila Southworth my next best bed and furniture. Unto my son William Southworth my next best bed." (reproduced in LC Fams, p 628).

LC Fams, p 271, and the Gen Reg Plym Fams, p 246-248, stated that Elizabeth Southworth m William Fobes. However, Torrey, p 272, said "no", William Fobes did not m (1) Elizabeth Southworth, and this seems to be correct. It seems clear that Elizabeth (Collier) Southworth, wid of Constant, left LC aft his death, and rem to Br with her two youngest daus, Elizabeth and Priscilla. And her son, Capt William, also lived in Br for a time and his eleven cn were all bp on 29 June 1709 at the Congre Ch of Br.

This clarifies the identity and parentage of the Elizabeth Southworth whom Capt Samuel Gallup m in Br on 12 May 1685. She joined the Congre Ch in Br on 12 June 1695, and d 15 Aug 1709 from a fall from a horse. Capt Samuel joined the Congre Ch on 6 July 1696, and d Br 24 Mar 1717.

CHILDREN, b Br (6:77):
1. Elizabeth[4], b 26 Apr 1688; d aft 19 Feb 1728/29, date of div of est of brother Nathaniel; m Br 20 Apr 1710 Samuel BOWERMAN (6:22), b 22 Oct 1685, d 29 Dec 1729, son Tristram and Ann (Hooper) Bowerman of Br (6:9, 65). Elizabeth had two ch b Br, surname Bowerman: Edward, b 22 Nov 1711, and Elizabeth, b 25 Feb 1713/14.
<u>2</u>. Capt Samuel Jr, b 9 Oct 1690; d bef son William's will of 11 Feb 1752; m by 1716 Mary____ of Groton, Conn, who d Br 12 Mar 1750.
3. Mary, b 22 Oct 1692; d 23 Sept 1771, 79 yr, wid Joshua Bailey (6:115); m by Col Benjamin Church, JP, 9 or 10 Jan 1711/12 Joshua BAYLEY (6:22), b 10 Sept 1685, d 5 June 1767, 82 yrs (6:115), son John and Rachel Bayley of Br. No issue in VR Br.
4. William, b 18 Aug 1695; d Nov 1774, 80 yr, Cambridge, Mass (6:133); m by Rev James McSparran 19 Dec 1721 Mary ANTILL (6:22), who d Br 20 Feb 1762 (6:133), dau Edward and Sarah Antill Sr of New York City.
5. Nathaniel, b 5 June 1698; d by 18 Feb 1728/29, unm. The appt of his brother, Samuel Gallop of New London, Conn, was dtd 18 Feb 1728/29, naming him admin of the est of Nathaniel Gallop of Br, who d intestate. His est was divided 19 Feb 1728/29 among his brothers and sisters, namely Samuel Gallop, William Gallop, Elizabeth Bowerman, and Mary Bailey (Rounds, 1:167, 169).

Capt Samuel[4] Jr (Capt Samuel[3]) Gallup was b Br 9 Oct 1690 (6:77), and d bef his son William "Jr's" will of 11 Feb 1752 (RIGR, 3:136). He m by 1716 Mary____ of Groton, Conn, who d Br 12 Mar 1750 (6:133). He became a freeman of RI from Br in 1747 (MacGunnigle, p 24). At the town meeting held in Br on 10 Feb 1746/47 he took the Oath of Bribery and Corruption as Capt Samuel Gallop (Munro, p 161). He was prob a sea captain, and he may have d at sea as there is no d entry for him in the VR Br. In 1728/29 he was of New London, Conn. The IGI Conn do not list his m or the b of any of his ch in Conn.

CHILDREN, order not certain (6:77; will of William Gallup "Jr" in RIGR, 3:136):
1. Mary[5], b 16 Dec 1716 (6:77), prob in Groton, Conn, or 16 Dec 1714 (IGI RI); d aft brother William's will of 11 Feb 1752; m St Michael's Ch, Br 15 July 1736 Capt BRAGG, prob b 14 Feb 1714/15 (6:66), and bp Congre Ch,

81

Br 24 July 1715, as John, and d 18 Apr 1746 at St "Estatious" (6:119), son Henry and Susanna Bragg of Br. Mary had five ch b Br, surname Bragg (6:66): John, Susannah, Susannah II, Ann, and Henry.
2. Samuel, b 26 Oct 1718 (6:77), prob in Groton, Conn; prob d unm bef brother William's will of 12 Feb 1752 as not named in it.
3. William "Jr", b unrec Br, prob b Conn; d Br 12 Feb 1752; poss m Eliza___, who d 4 Feb 1752 as Mrs Eliza Gallup. No issue. The will of William Gallup "Jr" of Br, was dtd 11 Feb 1752 and named his sister, Mary Bragg, and two youngest sisters, Annah and Abigail Gallup; uncle Joshua Bailey to be sole executor and a father for his orphan sisters (RIGR, 3:136).
4. Ann/Anna, b unrec Br, prob b Conn; d Br 7 Mar 1791; m Congre Ch, Br 18 Oct 1756 Nathaniel DIMAN (6:22), b 29 Jan 1734 (6:73), d 24 May 1812 (6:128), son Deacon Jeremiah and Sarah (Giddings) Diman of Br. The Diman Fam, p 118 said that Ann(a) was dau of Samuel Gallup. She had five ch b Br, surname Diman (6:73; Diman Fam, p 118): William, Mary, Deacon Jeremiah, Nancy and John.
5. Abigail, prob b Conn, bp Congre Ch, Br 13 Sept 1741 as dau Capt Samuel and Mary Gallop (Geneals RI Fams, 1989, 2:384), d 1 Jan 1779, 38 yr, "wife of Nathaniel" (6:149); m 13 Nov 1766 as his first wife, Nathaniel MUNRO (6:38), b 1 Aug 1741 (6:92), d 9 Dec 1804, 62 yr (6:-149), son Nathaniel and Mary (Jolls) Munro of Br. Abigail had four ch b Br, surname Munro (6:92-93): Samuel, Lydia, Abigail, and Nathaniel. Nathaniel Munro m (2) Abigail WARDWELL and had three more ch, including a second dau named Abigail.

William^4 (Capt Samuel^3) Gallup was b Br 18 Aug 1695 and d in Cambridge, Mass in Nov 1774, 80 yr. He m Congre Ch, Br 19 Dec 1721 Mary ANTILL (6:22), or m her 19 Oct 1721 at Narragansett, Washington Co, RI (per IGI RI). Mary was bur St Michael's Ch, Br, 22 Feb 1762 (8:226), and was dau of Edward and Sarah Antill Sr who were of New York City, NY, where Edward was a well-known merchant and owner of large grants of land in NJ. William Gallup became a freeman of RI in Br in 1747 (MacGunnigle, p 24), and on 10 Feb 1746/-47 he took the Oath of Bribery and Corruption at Br (Munro, p 161). After the d of Edward Antill Sr, his wid, Sarah, m a Mr Smith. The will of Sarah (Antill) Smith of Br, wid, dtd 26 Dec 1725 and pvd 6 Mar 1728/29, named her dau, Mary Gallup; gdau Elizabeth Gallop, dau of her dau Mary and son-in-law William Gallop, who was exec of her est (Rounds, 1:188, 259). On 17 May 1737 William Gallop of Br, Joyner, was appted guardian of his dau, Mary Gallop, under 14, niece of Elezebeth Davis of Br (Ibid, p 238, 259). The will of Elezebeth Davis, wife of Simon Davis of Br (called gentleman elsewhere), dtd 29 May 1730 and pvd 16 June 1730, named two kinswomen, Elesebeth Gallop and Mary Gallop, both under 21 and unm, daus of her kinswoman, Mary Gallop (Rounds, 1:190, 297).

The acct of the surviving exec of the est of Elezebeth Davis, wife of Simon Davis of Br, namely William Munro, was dtd 23 July 1740 and included legacies "to Mr Gallop's ch"; and mentioned cash paid "to Isaac Royal Esq, father of Isaac Royal Junr who m Elizabeth, one of the minors" (Rounds, 1: 259). At first it seemed that the Elizabeth, minor, was Elizabeth^5 Gallup. However this was not the case. The will of (Col) Henry Makentosh (McIntosh) of Br, Esq, dtd 1 July 1725 and pvd 8 Nov 1725, named wife Elisebeth and gdaus Elizebeth and Mary Mcintosh, both under 21. Madam Elizabeth McIntosh was exec of the est of Col Henery Mcintosh of Br (Ibid, 1: 128). Simeon Davis m Br 2 June 1728 Madam Elizabeth McIntosh (6:17). Wyman, p 26, said that Isaac^3 Royal Jr, son of Isaac^2 Sr of Dorchester and Medford, Mass, m 27 Mar 1738 Elizabeth McIntosh who d 14 July 1770. He was a Representative to the General Court and a Loyalist, and fled to England in 1775 where he d 1781. So the connection of Elizabeth McIntosh Davis to William Gallop's ch must have been through William's wife, the Antills, and does not refer the m of his dau, Elizabeth Gallup.

CHILDREN, all bp St Michael's Ch, Br except Elizabeth (8:-156):
1. Elizabeth^5, bp 9 June 1723 Trinity Ch, Newport, RI; prob m St Michael's Ch, Br, 13 June 1742 Nathaniel PAINE, b Br 17 June 1719, and d 15 Jan 1747 at Annapolis (prob Nova Scotia), son Col Nathaniel and Sarah Paine Jr (6:41, 96; 8:214).
2. Mary, bp 19 Sept 1725; d aft 17 May 1737 (Rounds, 1: 259).
3. Samuel, bp Oct 1727.
4. Edward, bp 25 Jan 1729/30; bur St Michael's 28 Apr 1730 (8:226).
5. Sarah, bp 21 Nov 1731; m St Michael's 12 June 1756 (8:205), or m 12 June 1758 (IGI RI) Nathaniel LUTHER. No issue in VR Br.
6. Rebecca, bp 10 Mar 1733/34.
7. Ann, bp 23 Jan 1736/37; bur St Michael's 4 July 1737 (8:226).
8. Ann II, bp 6 Aug 1738.
9. Antill, bp 3 Aug 1740.
10. William, bp 17 June 1744 (8:156), or bp 1749 (IGI RI).

46. JOHN GLADDING JR

For John[1] Gladding Sr, the original settler at Br, and his ch, and the names of their ch, see: John[1] Gladding of Newbury, Mass and Bristol, RI by Dorothy Chapman Saunders in TAG (July 1989), vol 64, p 143-147.

CHILDREN of John[2] Jr and first wife, Alice Wardwell, b Br (6:78):
<u>1</u>. John[3], b 18 Sept 1694; d Br 8 Feb 1732, ae 38; m 12 July 1716 Martha poss SMITH, b ca 1694, d Br 6 June 1767, 73 yr.
2. Mary, b 30 Nov 1696; poss m (int) 14 Feb 1718 Robert "GOOF" (GOFF) (6:23); or poss m 25 Feb 1720/21 John LAWLESS (Ibid). No issue in VR Br or Rehoboth.
3. William, b 13 Oct 1698; d 22 Oct 1735, 38 yr (6:134) or d betw 14 and 18 Oct 1735, dates of writing and probating of his will (Rounds, 1:245), which called him "joyner" and named wife, Esther, to be guardian of his sons William and Solomon, both under 21, and his exec. He m 24 Oct 1726 Esther DROWNE, b 26 Oct 1708, d 18 Nov 1787, 79 yr, wid (6:134), dau Solomon and Esther (Bosworth) Drowne of Br. They had the fol ch b Br (6:78): Esther, b 30 July 1727; William, b 1 June 1730 who prob m Susannah WARDWELL (6:23); Bathsheba, b 15 Jan 1731/32; Esther II, b 19 Apr 1733; and Solomon, b 20 Mar 1734/-35.
4. Jonathan, b 5 Jan 1700/01; d 27 Oct 1743; m Br 24 Oct 1726 (6:23) or 2 July 1726 (Repre Men RI, p 134) Sarah CAREY, b 21 Jan 1706/07, d 26 Dec 1786, 83 yr, dau Deacon David and Elizabeth (Brackett) Carey of Br. His four sons rem to Providence, RI and founded the branch of the fam there. He had the fol ch b Br (6:78): Sarah, b 1 Sept 1727; Elizabeth, b 22 Sept 1729; Priscilla, b 9 Apr 1733; Nathaniel, b 6 Oct 1735 and rem to Providence where he m; Jonathan, b 12 Oct 1737 who m Br Susannah CAREY and rem to Providence; Timothy, b 18 Nov 1740 and rem to Providence where he m; and Benjamin, b 22 June 1743 who rem to Providence where he m.
5. Ebenezer, b 8 Dec 1702; d 26 Feb 1737; m Br 16 Nov 1725 Experience BRAGG (6:10), b 2 Apr 1700 (6:66), dau John and Elizabeth Bragg of Br. They had the fol ch b Br (6:78): John, b 28 Oct 1726; Rebecca, b 8 June 1728; and Elizabeth, b 22 July 1730.
6. Joseph, b 2 Oct 1704; m Br 24 Oct 1726 (int w July 1726, 6:23) Priscilla CAREY, b 9 May 1709 (6:68), dau Deacon David and Elizabeth (Brackett) Carey of Br. Joseph rem to Newport, RI where he was made a freeman in 1748 (6:23; MacGunnigle, p 25). He had fourteen ch, of whom the VR Newport give only two (4:98; GB, p H): Cory (sic Cary), b 10 Dec 1732, and Jonathan, b 29 Apr 1735. The GB, p I gave three more: Joseph who m and had four

kn ch: Lillis, Joseph, Cary and Samuel; Henry who m and had: Joseph, Sarah, Rhoda, and Henry; and John who m and had: Elizabeth, Joseph, Henry and John. Another son, David, d 13 Jan 1754 age 2 or 12 yrs, and he and his parents, Joseph and Prissilla, are bur in the Common Bur Ground, Newport, RI (VR RI, Beaman, New Series, 11:181).
7. Alice, b 24 Mar 1705/06; d 25 Aug 1734, 30 yr (6:-134); m (int) 25 Jan 1728 James GLADDING (6:23), b 21 Sept 1707, son William "Jr" and Mary Gladding (6:78). She had one ch b Br, surname Gladding: James, b 19 Apr 1731 (Ibid).
8. Elizabeth, b 13 Sept 1708.
9. Nathaniel, b 16 Dec 1709; d 13 Sept 1735, 27 yr (6:-134); m Br 2 Apr 1733 Jemima CAREY (6:23), b 25 July 1711 (6:68), dau Josiah and Ruth (Reynolds) Carey of Br. Ruth Reynolds was dau of Nathaniel Reynolds of Boston and Br, a member of the Anc and Hon Artillery Co in 1658 (Sav, 3:526). Nathaniel had one ch, Rebecca, b Br 14 Aug 1734 (6:23, 68, 78, 134).
10. Sarah, b 27 May 1712; d 3 June 1712, ae 8 days (Ibid, p 134).
11. Sarah II, b 21 May 1715; poss d 5 Aug 1730 (Ibid).

John^3 (John$^{2, 1}$) Gladding was b Br 18 Sept 1694 and d Br 8 Feb 1732, ae 38 (TAG, 64:146). He m 12 July 1716 Martha (poss) SMITH, b ca 1694 per d rec, and d Br 6 June 1767, 73 yr, whose parentage is unkn. She m (2) Br, 21 Aug 1744 Samuel SMITH (6:23), son Richard Smith of Br. John Gladding lived and d in Br, and it is from his Journal, reproduced in The Gladding Book, that details about his ch are kn. He was a ship owner and sea captain, and was also a shoemaker (GB, p 43-46).

CHILDREN, b Br (6:78):
1. Capt John^4, b 30 June 1717; d 16 Nov 1785, 69 yr (6:134); m (1) Br, he "of Newport", 25 Sept 1738 Mary DROWNE of Br (6:23), b 7 June 1719 (6:73), d Br 15 Apr 1759, 40 yr (6:134), dau Solomon and Esther (Bosworth) Drowne of Br; m (2) 6 Sept 1759 Hannah SHORT, b 1719/20, d Br 29 Feb 1788, 69 yr (Ibid), dau Philip Short of Warren, RI.
2. Charles, b 10 June 1719; d bef 28 Sept 1762; m Rehoboth, Mass by Rev John Greenwood 2 Feb 1743/44 Judith BOSWORTH, b Re 9 Jan 1723/24, dau Joseph and Lydia (Kent) Bosworth of Re (VR Re, p 52, 152, 619). They had six ch b Re betw 1745/46 and 1756. On 28 Sept 1762 Judeth Gladding of Re m by John Wheaton, Justice, John Wilson LOW of Warren, RI (War, 6:28). This must have been the wid of Charles, as his dau, Judeth, was not b until July 1756. The GB, p H2 and IV said that Charles rem to Barrington, RI, which seems to be an error unless he moved

there aft the b of his ch. His ch, b Re, were (VR Re, p 619): Lydia, b 2 Oct 1745 or 1746; Sarah, b 3 June 1747; Charles, b 4 Dec 1748; George, b 10 Sept 1750; Joseph, b 8 Nov 1752 who m Amanda MARTIN, dau Capt Nathaniel and Susan Martin of Barrington and had six ch; and Judith, b 26 July 1756.
3. Daniel, b 20 May 1721.
4. Martha, b 10 Apr 1723; m (int) 27 Feb 1740 Zephaniah PEASE of Newport (6:42).
5. George, b 26 Mar 1724/25; d at sea 29 Dec 1747 coming home from Surinam (6:34); m Br 28 July 1745 Elizabeth CUMMINGS (6:23). No issue in VR Br.
6. Samuel, b 25 Mar 1728; d 16 Apr 1762, 34 yr (6:134); m Br 9 Sept 1751 Mary GIBBS, b 21 Oct 1732, dau John and Sarah (Jones) Gibbs (6:22, 23, 134). He had five ch b Br (6:78): Samuel Jr, b 19 Oct 1751; Nathaniel, b 28 Apr 1754; George, b 9 Apr 1756; Mary, b 2 Sept 1758, who m Deacon ___ HAMMOND (GB, p H2); and John, b 23 June 1761. The GB, p I said that Samuel m Elsa___ and had the fol ch b Br: Samuel, Mary, Betsey, Martha T., Nathaniel, Samuel II, Philip and Benjamin. They are not given in the VR Br.
7. Phebe, b 21 Aug 1730.
8. Mary, b 23 Aug 1732; d 19 Mar 1810, 78 yr (6:141; 8:-375); m Br 24 June 1750 John INGRAHAM Jr (6:29), b 25 Jan 1727/28, d 3 Aug 1799, 72 yr (6:141; 8:375), son Capt John and Mary (Fry) Ingraham (6:22).

Capt John^4 (John^{3,2,1}) Gladding was b Br 30 June 1717 and d 16 Nov 1785, 69 yr (6:134). He m (1) Br 25 Sept 17-38 Mary DROWNE, b 7 June 1719 and d Br 15 Apr 1759, 40 yr (6:134), dau Solomon and Esther (Bosworth) Drowne of Br; m (2) 6 Sept 1759 Hannah SHORT, b 1719/20, d Br 29 Feb 17-88, 69 yr (6:134), dau Philip Short of Warren, RI. Philip Short's will, dtd 3 July 1761 and pvd 7 Nov 1763, named his dau Hannah wife of John Gladding of Br (RIGR, 4:261). Capt John owned a sloop and was both a ship's captain and a shoemaker. He kept a journal in which he described the British attacks against Br in 1775 and 1776 when 130 of their ships came into Br harbour, and fourteen families, including Capt John's, fled to Dighton where they remained until Apr 1779. He owned a house in Br on Bradford St, and was bur in the Old Br burial ground on the east side of the Common (GB, p 45-46). He had no issue by his second m.

CHILDREN by first wife, Mary, b Br (8:276; GB, p H2, J):
1. John^5, b 3 Jan 1739/40 (only ch of Capt John^4 rec in VR Br, 6:134); d 25 Sept 1820, 81 yr; m 17 Sept 1761 Lucretia SMITH, b 7 May 1743, d 5 May 1813, 70 yr, dau Richard and Lucretia (Diman) Smith of Br (6:50, 130, 134).

2. Josiah, bp Congre Ch, Br 13 Sept 1741; d 5 Sept 1804 (GB, p 47). He rem to Middletown, Conn ca 1780 where he m and had the fol ch (Ibid, p 112, I): Ezra who had three ch; Josiah who had fourteen ch; Polly; Joseph who rem to Albany, NY; Timothy who also went to Albany, NY; Susan; John who went to Ashtabula Co, Ohio; James S.; and Daniel S. who lived in New Haven, Conn.
3. Peter, bp 6 Nov 1743; d 6 Dec 1779, 35 yr (Ibid, p 16). No m or ch in VR Br.
4. Martha, bp 8 Dec 1745; d.y.
5. Capt Daniel, bp 20 Dec 1747; m Br 2 Aug 1769 Susannah WARDWELL (6:56), b 15 Jan 1750/51 (6:110), d 15 Aug 1808, dau John and Phebe (Howland) Wardwell.
6. Martha II, bp 28 Jan 1749/50.
7. Mary, bp 14 June 1752; d 29 Aug 1837, 87 yrs, unm (6:135).
8. Solomon, bp 30 Mar 1753; d 20 Mar 1778, 24 yr (GB, p 46). No m or ch in VR Br.
9. Capt Joshua, bp 31 July 1757; d 3 Feb 1828, 71 yr (6:135); m Sarah WARDWELL who d 27 Jan 1819, 60 yr (6:-135). She was prob the Sarah b 4 Dec 1758 to Isaac and Sarah (Waldron) Wardwell of Br (6:135; 8:371). No ch of Capt Joshua are rec in the VR Br, but GB, p I gave them as fols: Lydia; Hannah who m Samuel SWAN; Solomon who m Nancy WALDRON; Sarah; Joshua; George who d.y.; Abigail who m Henry MUNROE; and George II.

Capt John[5] (John[4,3,2,1]) Gladding was b Br 3 Jan 1739/40 (6:134), and d Br 25 Sept 1820, 81 yr (6:135). He m 17 Sept 1761 Lucretia SMITH (6:23), b 7 May 1743 and d 5 May 1813, 70 yr (6:135), dau Richard and Lucretia (Diman) Smith of Br (6:50, 130, 134). John was a well-known builder of fast ships, and had his home and boatyard on the south side of Constitution St betw Hope and High Sts in Br. He and his wife were bur in the Old Bristol bur grounds on the east side of the Common.

CHILDREN, b Br (6:78-79; GB, p 46-47):
1. John[6], b 19 Nov 1762; d 20 Oct 1821, 59 yr; m 11 Jan 1784 Rachel TALBY/TALBEE, b 3 Nov 1764, d 14 Sept 1849, aged 85, dau Edward and Anstis (Waldron) Talby of Br (6:51, 105, 135).
2. Hannah, b 27 Aug 1764; d aft 19 Nov 1807; m Congre Ch, Br 3 Apr 1786 Ambrose WALDRON (8:334), b 1 June 1764 (6:109), d Br 7 Sept 1846, 82y 3m (6:170), son Nathaniel and Hannah (Throop) Waldron (6:55). Hannah had the fol ch b Br, surname Waldron (6:109): Leonard, Nancy, Billings "2nd" who m Hannah DIMAN, Polly, John, Nathaniel, Marshall, Hannah, Rebecca, Abby Cary, and Richard S.
3. Lucretia, b 25 July 1766; d 22 Feb 1786, 22 yr (sic)

(6:169); m as his first wife Thomas WALDRON (GB, p I),
b 16 Jan 1762, d 11 Sept 1821, 59 yr (6:109, 169), son
Nathaniel and Hannah (Throop) Waldron. She had two ch b
Br, surname Waldron (6:7; 8:354): Hannah, and Richard
Smith.
4. Capt Samuel, b 4 Apr 1768; d as Samuel 2nd 8 Dec
1813; m St Michael's, 20 Mar 1789 Charlotte INGRAHAM
(8:206), b 2 July 1767, d 6 Nov 1836, 69 yr, wid Capt
Samuel (6:135; GB, p L, f1), dau Capt Joshua and Mary
(Richmond) Ingraham of Br (8:206). Capt Samuel was a
ship owner and merchant-captain at Br (GB, p L, 72). He
had the fol ch b Br (6:79; GB, p 46-47): Eunice, b 12
Oct 1789 who m Joseph COIT (8:206); Allen Ingraham, b
16 Aug 1791; Samuel, b 22 Feb 1794; Richard Smith, b
25 Feb 1796 who m Martha CLARKE; John, b 8 May 1798;
Edmund, b 8 Oct 1800; Gilbert Richmond, b 4 Mar 1802;
Samuel II, b 28 Feb 1804; Martha James, b 7 Sept 1806;
and Mary Ingraham, b 14 Sept 1808.
5. Richard, b 8 May 1770; d 13 Jan 1775.
6. Benjamin, b 11 Sept 1772; d 3 Sept 1778.
7. Polly/Molly, b 27 Apr 1775; m (1) Congre Ch, Br 6
Feb 1793/94 Samuel MUNRO; poss m (2) Mr ___ HOWLAND per
GB, p I. No ch or d's given in VR Br. Poss he was the
Samuel Munro who rem to Sharon, Conn where he had ch.
8. Richard II, b 22 Jan 1779; d 6 Aug 1780.
9. Rebecca (GB, p I).
10. Sarah, b 5 Apr 1781; m Congre Ch, Br 18 Aug 1805
Nehemiah COLE Jr, son Nehemiah and Judeth Cole (8:329,
334). No ch in VR Br.
11. Lucretia II, b 14 July 1785; d aft 10 Jan 1834; m
Congre Ch, Br 17 June 1810 Otis CHASE of Providence, RI,
blacksmith (8:335). Otis's will, dtd 20 Dec 1833 with
codicil dtd 10 Jan 1834, and pvd 20 May 1834, named wife
Lucretia; sons Samuel eldest, Otis Jr, John Gladding,
and Henry Clay Chace; and dau Lucretia Gladding Chace
(RIGR, 6:122).

John^6 (John^{5,4,3,2,1}) Gladding was b Br 19 Nov 1762 and
d there 20 Oct 1821, 59 yr. He m 11 June 1784 Rachel TALBY/-
TALBEE, b 3 Nov 1764, d 14 Sept 1849, aged 85, dau Edward
and Anstis (Waldron) Talby of Br (6:51, 105, 135). John
owned a three-cornered lot in Br which extended from High,
Walley and Water Sts, and included a dwelling, windmill and
shore lot. He was a garden farmer, and was also deputy-sher-
iff of Br County for many years (GB, p 48, L). Edward "Tal-
ber"'s will, dtd 29 Apr 1806 and pvd 6 Apr 1807, named his
dau, Rachel, wife of John Gladding, Jr (RIGR, 6:158).
John's will, dtd 20 June 1821 and pvd 5 Nov 1821, named
wife Rachael; sons John, Edward, Benjamin, Stephen T., and
James D. Gladding; daus Lydia wife of John Winslow; Hannan

(no surname), and Rachael wife of Samuel Sparks (RIGR, 7:-172).

CHILDREN, b Br (6:79; GB, p 48-49):
1. John[7], b 23 Oct 1784 (GB) or 1785 (6:79); d Pharsalia, NY 1 Jan 1839, ca 46 yr (GB, p 51) or 53 yr (6:135); m 1 May 1808 by Rev Joseph Snelling Nancy COGGESHALL, dau James and Patty Coggeshall of the Narrows on Mt Hope Bay (6:15, 24).
2. Edward Talbee, b 21 or 22 Dec 1787; d aft father's will of 20 June 1721.
3. Lydia, b 17 Jan 1790; m John WINSLOW of Fairhaven, Mass. She had six ch, surname Winslow (GB, p L).
4. Benjamin, b 9 Feb 1792; d 12 Sept 1847, 56 yr, in Waterville, Oneida Co, NY (6:135); m Mehitable COGGESHALL, dau James and Patty Coggeshall (6:135; GB, p 50).
5. Hannah T., b 6 Aug 1794; m (1) Mr ___ LINDSEY and had two ch, surname Lindsey; m (2) Congre Ch, Br 9 Nov 1828 (8:335) Joseph SPARKS and had one dau, surname Sparks (GB, p L).
6. Samuel, b 16 Apr 1797; not named in father's will of 20 June 1721.
7. Rachel, b 21 Oct 1800; m Congre Ch, Br 31 Dec 1818 Samuel SPARKES (8:335). She had four kn ch b Br, surname Sparkes (8:391): ch of Samuel d 11 Dec 1814, 5 mo; ch of Samuel d 12 May 1819; Amanda of Samuel d 21 Oct 1822, 20 mo; and Samuel of Samuel d 1823, 17 mo.
8. Samuel T., b 21 Feb 1803; d aft 1850 prob at Smithfield, Bradford Co, Pa; m by Rev Arthur A. Ross 13 Apr 1830 Hannah V. HARDING (6:24) who d 29 July 1849, 40 yr at Smithfield, Pa, dau James Harding (6:135). The 1850 US Census of Pa listed Stephen Gladding in Smithfield Boro, Bradford Co, farmer, with one son, Samuel, aged 17; nearby in Springfield Township was another son, John G., aged 19, a carpenter.
9. James Nickerson, b 4 Oct 1807; d 3 July 1864 (6:-135); m 26 Feb 1838 Lucretia G. COLE (6:24). He had the fol ch b Br (6:79): Lucretia James, Julia Ann T., Rachel Talbee, Alzada, James Nickerson, John, Sarah Cole, Anne, Ella Frances, Ella Fales, Daniel, and Benjamin S.

John[7] (John[6,5,4,3,2,1]) Gladding was b Br 23 Oct 1784 (GB, p 48-49) or 1785 (6:79). He m by Rev John Snelling 1 May 1808 Nancy COGGESHALL, dau James and Patty Coggeshall of the Narrows on Mt Hope Bay (6:15, 24). Nancy's sister, Mehitable, m John's brother, Benjamin. John was apprenticed to the rope-making trade with Major Howland, who had his rope walk on Br Common. In the early winter of 1816 John and Benjamin, with their wives and four small ch, left Br in a two-horse wagon provided by a Mr

Bosworth of Br who had gone on ahead, to join a group of families who had left Br and settled in Chenango Co, NY. They crossed the Hudson River on the ice, and then traveled through the woods. John located in the town of Pharsalia in Chenango Co, where he established a cordage business which continued to be run by his descs until after 1900. He was an active member of the Methodist Ch in Pharsalia until an accident caused his d on 1 Jan 1839. He left his widow and five ch (GB, p 49-51).

CHILDREN (6:79; GB, p 49-50):
1. Martha Turner^8, b 4 Aug 1810, Br.
2. Anstress T., b 25 Nov 1811, Br.
3. James Coggeshall, b 12 Nov 1813, Br.
4. Rachel, b 7 Sept 1819, Pharsalia, NY.
5. John, b 28 Apr 1822, Pharsalia, NY.

Capt Daniel^5 (Capt John^4, John^{3,2,1}) Gladding was bp 20 Dec 1747 and m Br 2 Aug 1769 Susannah WARDWELL (6:56), b 15 Jan 1750/51 (6:110) and d 15 Aug 1808, dau John and Phebe (Howland) Wardwell (6:56). The GB, p I is incorrect in saying that Susannah was dau of "Col S. Wardwell". Phebe Howland was a desc of John Howland of the Myflwr, so Daniel Gladding's ch have a Myflwr desc (Sav, 2:479; 6:56). Capt Daniel was a ship owner and merchant-captain, and he owned a wharf on Thames St in Br (GB, p 105).

CHILDREN, b Br (6:79; GB, p I):
1. Nancy Ann^6, b 24 Dec 1770; m Congre Ch, Br 24 Jan 1790 Nathaniel LISCOMB (8:334, 340), b 19 Feb 1768, bp St Michael's Ch, Br 20 Oct 1771, prob d 30 Aug 1802 (8:-378), son Samuel and Leah (Waldron) Liscomb of Br (6:88; 8:219). She had two kn ch b Br, surname Liscomb: ch d 1792, 2 days (6:145); and Nathaniel who m Congre Ch Br 27 Mar 1819 Sarah LAWLESS, dau John and Sarah Lawless (6:33; 8:340).
2. Polly, m Capt William PIERCE.
3. Susan, m (1) D. WALDRON; m (2) William RICH; m (3) S. SHERMAN.
4. Capt Nathaniel, b 14 Aug 1777 (6:79); d 28 Mar 1838, 60 yr, on passage home from New Orleans (6:135); m Congre Ch Br 27 July 1800 (6:24) Nancy PECK, b 1777 per d rec, d 5 Jan 1836, 57 yr, wife of Nathaniel (6:135), dau Capt Jonathan and Mary Peck (8:334). Capt Nathaniel was a sea captain and had the fol ch b Br (6:79): Nathaniel, Jonathan Peck, John, Nancy, and Susannah W.
5. Major Lefavour Howland.
6. Daniel, m Sarah ALGER of Warren, RI (GB, p 105). He was apprenticed to the sailmaking trade with Mr Alger, and later owned a sail business in Br. He had six ch.

7. Peter, d at sea ae 20 (GB, p 105).
8. Sally, m 16 May 1808 Bennet MUNRO 2nd (6:24) and had three ch b Br, surname Munro (6:93): Edward, Phebe Howland, and Eleanor.
9. Patty, m Capt Allen WALDRON.
10. Phebe, m 24 Nov 1799 LeFavour HOWLAND (6:24) and had one ch, Daniel LeFavour Howland, b Br 1803 (6:83).

47. JABEZ GORHAM

Jabez^3 (Capt John^3, Ralph^1) Gorham was b 3 Aug 1656 in Barnstable, Mass, and d in Br betw the date of his will, 16 Mar 1724/25 and 20 Apr 1725 when it was pvd. He m by 1677 Hannah(STURGIS) GRAY (MD, 5:180), who aft his d returned to Cape Cod where she d 17 Oct 1736 and was bur in Brewster, Mass. She was dau of Edward Sturgis Sr of Barnstable and Yarmouth (Torrey, p 313, 720), and wid of John Gray. All of Jabez's ch have a Myflwr desc through his mother, Desire Howland, who was dau of John and Elizabeth (Tilley) Howland of the Myflwr.

Jabez had rem with his family from Barnstable to Br bef the date of its first town meeting, when he was admitted as a citizen of the town (Munro, p 79). The 1689 Census of Br listed him with a wife and four ch. Hannah, the wife of Jabez, on 6 July 1696 became a member of the Congre Ch of Br (8:251). Jabez's will, he of Br, yeoman, dtd 16 Mar 1724/25 and pvd 20 Apr 1725, named wife Hannah; eldest son Jabez Gorham, sons Isaac, Joseph and Benjamin; dau Elizabeth wife of Shobael Baxter; and gsons Edward, William and Samuel Downs (Geneals Myflwr Fams, 2:99; Rounds, 1:119).

CHILDREN, b Br except first and poss second ch (6:80; Geneals Myflwr Fams, 2:99):
1. Hannah^4, b 23 Dec 1677 Barnstable, Mass; d 28 Mar 1682 Br in a tub of slush and water (6:136).
2. Elizabeth, b unrec; d aft 16 Mar 1724/25; m (1) ca 1700 William DOWNS, and m (2) ca 1711 Shubael BAXTER (Bowman, p 208). She had three ch, surname Downs: Edward, William and Samuel, per her father's will of 16 Mar 1724/25, and she had two kn ch, surname Baxter (Bowman, p 213): Richard who m (1) Yarmouth, Mass Jane BAXTER, and m (2) Nantucket, Mass Mary/Molly COFFIN; and Thankful who m (1) Thomas THACHER, and m (2) Samuel LAMBERT.
3. Samuel, b 15 Apr 1682 Br. Not named in, and d bef, father's will of 16 Mar 1724/25 as Jabez was called eldest son.
4. Jabez Jr, b 31 Jan 1683/84; d 21 Nov 1745 (6:136); m (1) Leah___, who bur St Michael's Ch, Br 15 May 1739 (6:136; 8:227); m (2) St Michael's 31 July 1744 (int

30 Mar 1744, 6:24) Mary (WARDWELL) MAXFIELD (8:206), wid Daniel, who m (3) 13 Oct 1763 Stephen SMITH (6:25).
5. Shubael, b 12 Apr 1686. Not named in father's will of 16 Mar 1724/25.
6. Isaac, b 1 Feb 1689; d New Haven, Conn 1739/40; m (1) Mary___ who d Br 11 Sept 1716 (6:136); m (2) 6 Aug 1717 Hannah MILES, b 27 Oct 1697 New Haven, dau Richard and Hannah (Eaton) Miles of New Haven (Fams Anc New Haven, 3:674).
7. John, b 8 Nov 1690; d Jan 1717.
8. Joseph, b 22 Aug 1692, bp Congre Ch, Br, 11 Aug 1695. He rem to Fairfield, Conn where he was living 16 June 1725 when he gave a receipt for his share of his father's est. He m twice and had many descs, per Geneals Myflwr Fams, 2:99.
9. Hannah II, b 21 Feb 1693/94, bp Congre Ch 11 Aug 1695.
10. Benjamin, b 11 Dec 1695; d betw 18 Oct 1771 and 1 Feb 1722; m by 1718 Bethiah CAR(E)Y, b Br 9 Dec 1696 (6:68) or b 22 Jan 1697 (Seth C. Cary, p 65f); d bef 1753, dau David and Elizabeth (Brackett) Car(e)y of Br (Geneals Myflwr Fams, 2:101).
11. Thomas, b 30 Oct 1701. Not named in father's will of 16 Mar 1724/25.

Jabez^4 Jr (Jabez^3, Capt John^2, Ralph^1) Gorham was b Br 31 Jan 1683/84 and was bur St Michael's Ch, Br, 23 Nov 1745 (8:227). He m (1) by 1707 Leah___, who was bur St Michael's 15 May 1739 (Ibid); and m (2) St Michael's 31 July 1744 Mary (WARDWELL) MAXFIELD, wid Daniel (8:206), who m (3) 13 Oct 1763 Stephen SMITH (6:25). Jabez Jr had no issue by his second wife. His first wife, Leah, was bp by Rev John Sparhawk at the Congre Ch, Br, together with four of her ch, Samuel, Shubael, Elizabeth, and Hannah Gorham, on 27 Oct 1717 (Geneals RI Fams, 1989, 2:380). Her dau, Mary, was bp there by Rev Nathaniel Cotton on 10 Oct 1721 (Ibid, 2:381).

CHILDREN by first wife, Leah (6:80; Geneals Myflwr Fams, 2:100):
1. Samuel^5, b 27 Nov 1707 Newport, RI; bur St Michael's 25 Nov 1739 (8:227).
2. Elizabeth, b 9 Apr 1710 Newport; bur St Michael's 28 Aug 1726 (Ibid).
3. Shubael, b 29 Mar 1713 Br; bur St Michael's 11 Sept 1734 (Ibid).
4. Hannah, bp 27 Oct 1717; d 27 July 1802, ae 85; m St Michael's 30 May 1737 John KINNICUTT (8:206). She had ten ch, surname Kinnicutt, bp St Michael's Ch, Br (8:163).
5. Mary, bp 10 Oct 1721; m St Michael's 30 May 1738 Samuel OSBORNE (Ibid, p 206).

6. Rebecca, bp 5 Jan 1723 St Michael's (8:157); bur St Michael's 25 Mar 1725 (Ibid, p 227).
7. Nathan, b 8 Jan 1725/26, bp St Michael's 30 Jan 1725/26.
8. Deborah, bp St Michael's 24 Sept 1732.

Isaac^4 (Jabez^3, Capt John^2, Ralph^1) Gorham was b Br 1 Feb 1689 and d in New Haven, Conn by 1739/40 when the inv of his est was made. He m (1) by 1712 Mary___ who d Br 11 Sept 1716; and m (2) 6 Aug 1717 Hannah MILES, b New Haven 27 Oct 1697 (Fams Anc New Haven, 3:674), dau Richard and Hannah (Eaton) Miles of New Haven. Isaac bought land in New Haven on 1 Mar 1719/20 where he was a cooper. The admin of his est was by his father-in-law, Lt Richard Miles, and it named his eldest son, Isaac, and seven other ch.

CHILDREN by first wife, Mary, b Br (6:80; Geneals Myflwr Fams, 2:104):
1. Isaac^5, b 28 May 1713, bp 10 July 1715 Congre Ch, Br; d Br 1 Dec 1760, 50 yr (6:136), bur St Michael's 3 Dec 1760 (8:227); m Br 19 Oct 1742 Jemima POTTER, b 1718 per d rec, d 10 Oct 1806, 88 yr (6:136), dau Hopestill and Lydia (Hubbard) Potter.
2. Hezekiah, b Feb 1714/15, bp 10 July 1715 Congre Ch, Br; d 15 Dec 1715 (6:136).

CHILDREN by second wife, Hannah, b New Haven, Conn (Geneals Myflwr Fams, 2:104; Fams Anc New Haven, 3:674-676):
3. John, bp 10 July 1720 New Haven; d 1768; m New Haven 25 Dec 1745 Lydia DORMAN, b 12 Mar 1726/27, d 9 Jan 1782, ae 55, dau Benjamin and Sarah (Tuttle) Dorman of New Haven (Fams Anc New Haven, 3:674).
4. Mary, b 10 Oct 1721; d 1 Apr 1773 New Haven; m 12 Feb 1746/47 William PUNCHARD.
5. Timothy, b 13 Nov 1723; m (1) 12 Mar 1746/47 New Haven Mary PUNCHARD, dau William and Mehitabel (Perkins) Punchard of New Haven, who d 1747/48; m (2) 4 Jan 1749/50 Sarah BROWN, who d 16 July 1778, ae 52, dau Eleazer and Sarah (Rowe) Brown.
6. Hezekiah II, b 5 Dec 1725; d 11 May 1790 ae 65 New Haven; m New Haven 19 Jan 1748/49 Abigail DICKERMAN who d 21 July 1798 ae 70, dau Isaac and Mary (Atwater) Dickerman of New Haven.
7. Elizabeth, bp 21 Jan 1727/28; d New Haven 30 Aug 18-07 ae 80; m New Haven 25 Oct 1749 David GILBERT, b 9 July 1725, d 20 Apr 1807, son David and Experience (Perkins) Gilbert of New Haven.
8. Samuel, bp 12 July 1730; d unm 1755.
9. Hannah, bp 5 May 1733; d New Haven 1 Oct 1803 ae 71; m (1) 10 Oct 1753 Leonard LEWIS; m (2) 19 July 1767 Stephen BRADLEY.

10. Sarah, bp New Haven 6 July 1735; d bef 1740.
11. Richard, bp New Haven 21 Aug 1737; d bef 1740.

Isaac[5] (Isaac[4], Jabez[3], Capt John[2], Ralph[1]) Gorham was b Br 28 May 1713 and bp 10 July 1715 at the Congre Ch, Br. He d Br 1 Dec 1760, age 50 (6:136), and was bur at St Michael's Ch 3 Dec 1760 (8:227). He m Br 19 Oct 1742 Jemima POTTER, b 1718 per d rec, and d 10 Oct 1806, 88 yr (6:136), dau Hopestill and Lydia (Hubbard) Potter (Geneals Myflwr Fams, 2:104).

CHILDREN, b Br, bp St Michael's Ch (Ibid, 2:104; 6:80; 8:157):
1. Mary[6], b 28 July 1743 (6:80), bp 7 Aug 1743; d 12 Jan 1785 (6:163); m 13 Oct 1763 Stephen SMITH of Br, b 22 Apr 1741 (6:103), d Br as Esq 3 Nov 1799, 59 yr, son Samuel[3] and Elizabeth (Drowne) Smith Jr of Br.
2. Hannah, b 25 Sept 1745 (6:80), bp 17 Mar 1748/49.
3. Capt Isaac, b 1747, bp 17 Mar 1748/49; d Sept 1795, ae 48, at sea (8:371); m 4 Sept 1774 Sarah THOMAS of Warren, RI (War, 6:38), prob b 3 Sept 1749, dau Amos and Jemima Thomas of Warren (Ibid, p 92).
4. Althea, b 1751, bp 24 May 1752; d 17 June 1823; m 1774 Gilbert RICHMOND, b Little Compton, RI 27 Apr 1754, d 19 Mar 1782 at sea, son Dr Ichabod and Mary Richmond of LC (LC Fams, p 517).
5. Lydia, bp 9 May 1759; bur St Michael's 12 May 1759 (8:227).
6. William, bp 9 Dec 1759; d 26 Dec 1778 in shipwreck at Martha's Vineyard.

Benjamin[4] (Jabez[3], Capt John[2], Ralph[1]) Gorham was b Br 11 Dec 1695. He d in Providence, RI betw 18 Oct 1771 when he signed a deed and 1 Feb 1772 when his will, dtd 14 May 1764, was sworn to by witnesses. He m by 1718 Bethia CAR(E)Y, b Br 9 Dec 1696 (6:68) or 22 Jan 1697 (Seth C. Cary, p 65f), and d bef 1753, dau David and Elizabeth (Brackett) Car(e)y of Br. Benjamin was the first Gorham to settle in Providence, and he started the line of the family which continued there. Benjamin's will, he tanner and curier of Providence, dtd 14 May 1764 and pvd 23 May 1772, named his son, Jabez; daus Elizabeth Grainger and Sarah Whipple; and gson Samuel Owen.

CHILDREN, first b Br, last three prob b Providence (6:80; Geneals Myflwr Fams, 2:101-103):
1. Benjamin[5], b 22 Aug 1718, bp 5 Aug 1722 Congre Ch, Br; prob d.y. and unm.
2. Bethia, b 10 Oct___, bp 5 Aug 1722 Congre Ch, Br; d bef father's will of 14 May 1764; m Providence 19 Jan

1738 Abner BROWN.
3. Sarah, b 15 Sept 1723, bp 24 Nov 1723 Congre Ch, Br; m Providence 14 Mar 1745 Rowland TAYLOR; m (2) bef 14 May 1764 ___ WHIPPLE.
4. Elizabeth, bp 21 Jan 1727/28 Congre Ch, Br; d 3 Sept 1785; m Providence 21 Feb 1748 Thomas GRAINGER.
5. Jabez, b not rec; d aft father's will of 14 May 17-64; m Providence by Richard Waterman, JP, 4 Oct 1753 Abigail FIELD, b 27 Jan 1730, dau Jeremiah and Abigail (Waterman) Field. Jabez was a tanner in Providence.
6. Samuel, b not rec; d bef father's will of 14 May 1764.
7. Jemima, b not rec; d bef father's will of 14 May 1764; m 26 Nov 1749 Joseph OWENS per Geneals Myflwr Fams, 2:101. The VR Providence, p 142 say that Joseph Owens m Jemima York. No rec has been found of a first m of Jemima to a York, but that may have been the case.

48. RICHARD HAMMOND

Sav, 2:346 mentioned only one Richard Hammond in early New England, who was of Kennebeck in 1665 and was killed by the Indians in 1676, "when all of his family of sixteen were either killed or carried into captivity." Perhaps the Richard who was at the first town meeting of Br was a son. Whoever he was, he did not settle in Br as the VR Br have no m, ch or d pertaining to him. Torrey, p 339, listed only one Richard Hammond who d in 1676, m Elizabeth Smith, widow of James, aft 29 May 1660, and lived in Salem, Mass.

The only Hammond/Hammon family in the VR Br was that of Edward and Susannah Hammon (6:81). Torrey, p 339 said that Edward Hammon m "Susannah Bradley/Brown?" 5 June 1684 and lived in Br, RI. The VR Br 6:26 give the m of Edward Hammon and Susanna Bradley in Br 5 Jan 1684. But the will of William Brown of Br, dtd 6 Aug 1689, named his dau Susana Hammond (Rounds, 1:1). Perhaps Susannah Brown m (1) a ___ Bradley.

Edward d Br Jan 1717, and Susannah Hammon d there 17 Jan 1731 (6:137). Whether Edward was a son or other relative of Richard's is unkn. He may have been left, or purchased, Richard's land. Edward and Susannah had four ch b Br (6:81): William, b 31 Dec 1685; Edward, b 1 Dec 1687; Margaret, b 24 June 1690; and Martha, b 10 Mar 1694/95. A William Hammon m (1) at Rehoboth, Mass 25 Apr 1706 Rebecca ORMSBEE "both of Rehoboth" (VR Re, p 458) who may have been Edward's son William, b 1685.

49. HENRY HAMPTON

Torrey, p 340 said that Henry Hampton, bef the b of his ch in 1683, m Sarah Barney, who was b 1662, and that he lived first in Salem, Mass and then went to Br, RI. Sarah Barney was b at Salem 12 Sept 1662, dau Jacob Barney Jr and his second wife, Ann Witt, of Salem (Sav, 1:123). The will of Jacob Barney of Rehoboth, Mass, yeoman, dtd 30 July 1692 and pvd 10 Jan 1692/93, named wife Ann, and dau Sarah Hampton (Rounds, 1:4-5).

Henry and Sarah had three ch b Br (6:81): Katheren, b 25 June 1683; Henry, b 25 Feb 1684/85; and Abigail, b 2 Mar 1687. There are no other Hampton m's or d's in the VR Br. He was prob the man listed as Goodman Hampden, with a wife and four ch, in the 1689 Census of Br (Geneals RI Fams, 1989, 2:402). He and his fam rem to Newport, RI, and he and his wife, Sarah, and their son, Henry, who d 9 May 1704 age nearly 20 yr, are bur in the Common Burial Ground at Newport (VR RI, Beaman, New Series, 11:201). It is poss that the fourth ch listed for Henry in the 1689 Census of Br was a son, John. The only Hampton b in the VR Newport, p 100, is the b of a son, Henry, to John and Mary (Davis) Hampton on 24 Dec 1732.

50. WILLIAM HEDGE JR

William[2] Hedge Jr was b, prob in Yarmouth, Mass, son of William Sr and his unkn first wife. William Sr was a freeman of Lynn, Mass in 1634, but then moved to Sandwich in 1637, and on to Yarmouth (Sav, 2:400). William Jr m Elizabeth STURGES, who was b 20 Apr 1648 in Yarmouth, dau Edward Sturges/Sturgis of Charlestown 1634 and Yarmouth 1643 (Sav, 4:229) and his first wife, Elizabeth Hinckley (Torrey, p 720). William Jr and Elizabeth had the b's of three ch rec in the VR Br (6:82); Elizabeth, b 15 Feb 1682/83, d 16 Feb 1682/83; John, b 4 Apr 1685, d 17 July 1687 (6:138); and Elizabeth II, b 5 May 1687. He was listed in the 1689 Census of Br with a wife and three ch (Geneals RI Fams, 1989, 2:401), so he had at least two more unkn ch. The Hedges disappeared from the VR Br aft then, so must have rem elsewhere.

51. WILLIAM HOAR

A William Hoar was in Salem, Mass in 1659. He was almost certainly the same man who was a baker in Boston and m there in 1669 Hannah WRIGHT, dau Robert Wright, and who was a freeman of Boston in 1671 (Sav, 2:432; Torrey, p 376).

Hannah was prob the dau of the only Robert Wright of Boston whom Sav listed (4:659), who was a member of the Anc and Honorable Artillery Co there in 1643 and had a wife, Mary. Although William Hoar was admitted as a citizen of Br at its first meeting, he apparently remained in Boston through the b of his dau, Hannah, on 5 Mar 1687. He and his wife had rem to Br, however, prior to the b there of another Hannah II on 26 Aug 1689. He was listed in the 1689 Census of Br with a wife, three ch, and three servants (Geneals RI Fams, 1989, 2:402). William and Hannah both became members of the Congre Ch of Br on 6 July 1696 (8:252). The will of William Hoar of Br, baker, dtd 23 July 1697 and pvd 27 Dec 1698, named wife Hannah "the wife of my Youth and the Naturall Mother of all the Children that Ever I had". No ch were named (Rounds, 1:6). William d Br 27 Nov 1698 (6:139), and his widow, Hannah, d 28 Sept 1746 (6:139; 8:252).

CHILDREN (Sav$_2$ 2:432; 6:82):
1. William^2, b 1 Feb 1671 Boston; d ae 2 mos.
2. Samuel, b 6 May 1673 Boston; d ae 7 mos.
3. Joseph, b 15 Mar 1675 Boston.
4. Benjamin, b 5 Sept 1680 Boston; m Br 10 Apr 1699 Rebecca SMITH (6:27) and had three ch (6:82): Hannah, b Br 15 Aug 1700; Rebecca, b Br 17 Aug 1702 and d 21 Aug 1702 (6:139); and Benjamin, b Newport, RI 11 Oct 1711.
5. Paul, b 23 Dec 1682 Boston.
6. William II, b 1 Mar 1685 Boston.
7. Hannah, b 5 Mar 1687 Boston; d.y.
8. Hannah II, b 26 Aug 1689 Br.
9. Mary, b 10 Mar 1692 Br; bur St Michael's Ch, Br 19 May 1737, unm (8:228).

William^2 (William^1) Hoar was b Boston 1 Mar 1685 and m by 1709 Sarah___. He had one ch rec in the b recs of Br (6:82): 1. William^3, b Br 21 May 1710 (6:82).

William^3 (William^{2,1}) Hoar was b Br 21 May 1710 (6:82) and d there 23 Oct 1786, 77 yr (6:139; 8:374). He was m by Rev John Usher at St Michael's Ch, Br 17 Nov 1734 Susannah BRAGG (8:207), who was b Br 28 July 1712 (6:66), dau Henry and Susannah Bragg of Br.

CHILDREN, b Br (6:82), bp St Michael's Ch (8:159):
1. Hannah^4, b 27 Oct 1735, bp 2 Nov 1735.
2. Mary, bp 23 Jan 1736/37; she or Hannah was prob the ch of William Hoar who d Br 18 May 1737 (6:139).
3. William Jr, b 28 July 1743 (sic), bp 16 Oct 1742; d betw 10 June and 5 Nov 1787 (RIGR, 4:264); m Br 31 May

1764 Mrs Phebe CAREY (6:27).
4. Benjamin, b 19 Oct 1743; bur St Michael's 24 Feb 1743/44 (8:228).
5. Sarah, b 4 Feb 1744/45, bp 10 Mar 1744/45.
6. Ann, b 30 Jan 1745/46, bp 2 Feb 1745/46.
7. Mary II, bp 6 Apr 1747.
8. Eliza, bp 10 July 1748.
<u>9</u>. Benjamin II, bp 30 July 1749; prob d Br 21 Mar 1829 (6:139); m St Michael's 12 June 1785 Priscilla WALDRON, b 4 Jan 1758 (6:109), d Br 16 Apr 1835, 77 yr, wid Benjamin (6:139), dau John and Elizabeth Waldron of Br.
10. Susannah, bp 7 Oct 1750.
11. Abigail, bp 26 Apr 1752; bur St Michael's 17 Nov 1754 (8:228).
12. ?Elizabeth, or #8, Eliza?, bur St Michael's 7 Apr 1754 (Ibid).

William^4 Jr (William^{3,2,1}) Hoar was b Br 28 July 1742 and bp St Michael's Ch 16 Oct 1762. He m Br by Rev John Burt 31 May 1764 Phebe CAREY (6:27), who was prob the Phebe of Allen Cary dec and Hannah now Clarke, bp Congre Ch, Br 23 July 1749 (8:272). William had rem to Warren, RI by 1774 and d there in 1787. As William Jr he was a Private from RI in the Rev War (Pat Index, p 333, which said that he d aft 1790). But the will of William Hoar of Warren, blockmaster, dtd 10 June 1787 and pvd 5 Nov 1787, named wife Phebe; sons William, eldest, Allen, Benjamin, Samuel, and Lewis Hoar; and daus Elizabeth, Phebe and Hannah, no surnames (RIGR, 4:264). The 1790 US Census of RI, p 11, gave Phebe Hoar in Warren as head of a household of two males 16 or over, two males under 16, and three females.

CHILDREN, first six bp St Michael's Ch, Br (8:159-160; War, 6:71):
<u>1</u>. William^5, bp 30 June 1765;m Warren by Rev John Pitman 30 Nov 1788 Molly BOWEN (War, 6:24).
2. Elizabeth, bp 17 Aug 1766; m Warren 16 Mar 1788 William CARR (War, 6:24). She had one ch b Warren, surname Carr: William, b 14 Apr 1790 (Ibid, p 54).
<u>3</u>. Major Allen, bp 14 Aug 1768; m Warren by Rev John Pitman 14 Mar 1790 Hannah SANDERS (Ibid, p 24).
4. Phebe, bp 22 July 1770.
5. Lewis, bp 25 Oct 1772; d.y.
6. Benjamin, b 12 June 1774, bp St Michael's 6 Nov 1774; m Warren bef 1796 Elizabeth ___ and had two ch b Warren (Ibid, p 72): Nancy in 1796; and Lydia Burr on 13 Feb 1808 who m 3 Feb 1833 Alvin COLE (Ibid, p 24). Benjamin had no d recs in the VR Warren.
7. Hannah, b 19 July 1778 Warren; m Warren 4 Dec 1796

Oliver CHILD (War, 6:24), b Warren 28 Jan 1775 (Ibid, p 57), son Jeremiah and Patience (Cole) Child of Warren (Ibid, p 14). Hannah had one ch, surname Child, rec as b in Warren: Betsey, b 18 July 1797 (Ibid, p 57).
8. Samuel, b 15 Aug 1781.
9. Lewis II, b 30 Jan 1786; m by 1812 Frances___, and had three ch b Warren (Ibid, p 72): Elizabeth, b 15 June 1813; John R., b 5 Sept 1816 who m by 1840 Sarah B___ and had two ch b Warren, Mary Rogers and Henry Irvine (Ibid, p 72); and Maria Rogers, b 26 Nov 1817.

William^5 (William^{4,3,2,1}) Hoar was bp St Michael's Ch, Br, 30 June 1765 and m Warren, RI by Rev John Pitman 30 Nov 1788 Molly BOWEN (War, 6:24). The 1790 US Census of RI, p 11, showed him as head of a household in Warren of one male and two females. He had the fol ch b Warren (Ibid, p 71): Betsey, b 10 Sept 1789; William, b 18 Aug 1791; Pardon Bowen, b 18 June 1793; George, b 30 June 1796, twin; John, b 30 June 1796, twin and d.y.; John II, b 26 Sept 1799; Nathan, b 10 Sept 1801; Benjamin, b 20 June 1804; Mary Bowen, b 6 Aug 1806; and Lewis Thomas, b 3 Nov 1810. William's wife, Molly Bowen, was prob the Mary b 20 Sept 1768, dau Jonathan and Elizabeth (Munroe) Bowen of Warren, as she had a brother, Pardon, b 7 June 1764 (Ibid, p 49), and Mary and William Hoar named their second son Pardon Bowen.

Major Allen^5 (William^{4,3,2,1}) Hoar was bp St Michael's Ch, Br, 14 Aug 1768, and m in Warren, RI by Rev John Pitman 14 Mar 1790 Hannah SANDERS (War, 6:24). He did not appear in the 1790 US Census anywhere in RI, but he was in Warren on 13 Feb 1791 when a ch, Phebe, was b to him there. He d in Warren in Oct or Nov 1837. His will, dtd 18 Oct 1837 and pvd 13 Nov 1837, named wife Hannah; sons Allen C., David and Joseph Hoar; daus Phebe (no surname) and Hope Sherman widow; and gson Allen, son of Joseph Hoar (RIGR, 7:259). It is not kn where he earned the title of Major, but poss it was in the War of 1812. He and Hannah had five ch b Warren (War, 6:71-72): Phebe, b 13 Feb 1791; Allen Carey, b 8 Oct 1793 who m War 20 Mar 1817 Mary CHAMPLAIN "of Capt John, dec" (Ibid, p 24, 55); Joseph Sanders, b 23 July 1795 who m War 28 Aug 1836 Mrs Lucy GOFF, wid of Jeremiah; Hope Sanders, b 27 Jan 1798 who m 7 Sept 1817 Levi SHERMAN "of Levi" (Ibid, p 24, 36); and David, b 20 June 1803.

Benjamin^4 (William^{3,2,1}) Hoar was bp 30 July 1749 in St Michael's Ch, Br, and prob d Br 21 Mar 1829 (6:139). He m at St Michael's 12 June 1785 Priscilla WALDRON, b 4

Jan 1758 (6:109) and d Br 16 Apr 1835, 77 yr, wid of Benjamin (6:139), and dau John and Elizabeth Waldron of Br. The VR Br (6:397 and 8:207) incorrectly state that on that date Benjamin m Priscilla Gladding. That he m Priscilla Waldron is pvd by deeds and mortgages given in Geneals RI Fams, 1989, 2:702-703. The 1790 US Census of RI, p 10, listed him in Br as head of a household of one male 16 and over, one male under 16, and four females.

CHILDREN, bp St Michael's Ch, Br (8:160):
1. Elizabeth^5, bp 17 Apr 1786, twin.
2. Hannah, bp 17 Apr 1786, twin.
3. John Waldron, bp 2 May 1790.
4. Mary, bp 2 May 1790.
5. William, bp 4 Aug 1793; m 1 Oct 1816 Congre Ch, Br, Mary BROWN (8:337), b 5 Nov 1794 and rec as Polly (6:66) and d 27 Aug 1848, 54 yr (6:139), dau James and Mary Brown of Br.
5. Abner, bp 24 May 1795.

52. JABEZ HOWLAND

Jabez^2 Howland was b 1644 Plymouth, Mass and d Br in 1711 or 1712 (Torrey, p 394). He was the son of John Howland of the Myflwr who d 1692/93 Plymouth, and his wife, Elizabeth Tilley, b 1607, and d 1687 in Swansea, Mass. Jabez lived first in Duxbury, Mass and m ca 1668 Bethiah THACHER who d 1725, only dau of Anthony Thacher and his second wife, Elizabeth Jones, of Yarmouth (MD, 18:70; Torrey, p 394, 733). Jabez had five ch b Duxbury, and then rem to Br where five more ch were b (Sav, 2:479). Munro, p 93 said that Jabez had been a Lt with Capt Benjamin Church's forces in King Philip's War, and "was a man of great force and energy...throughout his long life he was honored with many and important trusts by his fellow-townsmen." He kept an inn in Br, and in 1689 and 1690 he was elected Representative from there to the General Court of Plymouth Col (Sav, 2:479; Munro, p 384). The 1689 Census of Br listed him with a wife, four ch and two servants (Geneals RI Fams, 1989, 2:402).

The will of Jabez Howland of Br, blacksmith, was dtd 14 May 1708 and pvd 21 Feb 1711/12, and the div of his est was held 26 Nov 1714. He named wife Bethiah; four sons, Jabez (eldest), Josiah, Samuel and Joseph Howland; only dau Elizabeth, wife of Nathan Townsend of Newport (she was dec bef 26 Nov 1714); and Nathan Townsend only son of late and only dau Elizabeth Townsend, late wife of Nathan Townsend (RIGR, 3:88; MD, 7:198-208).

CHILDREN (6:82-83; Sav, 2:479):
1. Jabez³ Jr, b 13 Sept or 13 Nov 1669 Duxbury; d Br 17 Oct 1732, 64 yr (6:139), bur St Michael's 19 Oct 1732; m ca 1697? Patience STAFFORD, b 1669, d 1721, ae 52 (Torrey, p 394). The VR Br, 8:228 say that Patience, wife of Jabez Howland was bur St Michael's in June 1726. She was dau of Samuel and Mercy (Westcott) Stafford of Warwick, RI (Sav, 4:160).
2. John, b 15 Jan 1673; d 16 Jan 1673 Duxbury.
3. Bethiah, b 3 June 1674 Duxbury; d bef father's will of 14 May 1708.
4. Josiah, b 6 Aug 1676 Duxbury; d 8 Feb 1717 (6:139); m 24 Nov 1709 Yetmercy SHOVE (Bowman, p 226-228) Barnstable, Mass, who b 7 Nov 1682 and d aft 26 Dec 1747, dau George and Hannah (prob Walley) Shove of Taunton, Mass (Sav, 4:90). He had two ch, b Br (6:83): Yetmercy, b 11 Mar 1712/13, and m (1) 17 Oct 1731 Capt Isaac PALMER (6:28), and m (2) 6 Dec 1733 (6:41) Nathaniel HOWLAND (Bowman, p 226); and Josiah Jr, b 9 Apr 1717 and d unm betw 26 Dec 1747 and 3 Apr 1748. Josiah Jr's will, he yeoman of Br, was dtd 26 Dec 1747 and pvd 3 Apr 1748. He mentioned only his mother, Yet Mercy Howland, living (RIGR, 3:134).
5. John II, b 26 July 1679 Duxbury; d bef father's will of 14 May 1708.
6. Elizabeth, b unrec, but b ca 1681 per gs rec, and named in father's will; d Newport, RI 20 May 1707 age 26 yr (VR RI, Beaman, New Series, 11:413); m Nathan TOWNSEND of Newport (Bowman, p 225). She had one ch, Nathan Townsend Jr, per her father's will, who took an A.M. degree and d 7 Jan 1742 in 36 yr, so b ca 1706. Nathan and Elizabeth and their son, Nathan Jr, are all bur in the Common Bur Ground of Newport.
7. Judah, b 7 May 1683 Br; d 6 mos.
8. Seth, b 5 Jan 1684/85 Br; bur 12 Apr 1685 (6:139).
9. Deacon Samuel, b 24 May 1686 Br (Sav, 2:479) or 16 May 1686 (6:82); d 15 May 1748 (8:252); m (1) by Rev John Sparhawk 6 May 1708 Abigail CAREY (6:27), b Br 31 Aug 1684, d 6 Aug 1737 (8:252; RIGR, 11:223), dau Deacon John and Abigail (Allen) Carey of Br; m (2) (int) 10 Feb 1741/42 Madame Rachel () ALLEN of Barrington, RI; m (3) Rehoboth, Mass 4 June 1747 Mrs Dorothy HUNT (VR Re, p 197, 200).
10. Experience, b 19 May 1687 Br; d.y.
11. Joseph, b 14 Oct 1692 Br; m ca 1714 Bathsheba CAREY (Bowman, p 226), b 14 Aug 1693, dau David and Elizabeth (Brackett) Carey of Br. He had three ch, b Br (6:83): Lydia, b 6 Nov 1715 who m Capt Edward BELCHER; Joseph, b 6 Dec 1717 who m Sarah BAKER; and Elizabeth, b 14 Feb 1719/20 who m Constant TABER (Bowman, p 276).

Jabez[3] Jr (Jabez[2], John[1]) Howland was b Duxbury, Mass 13 Sept of 13 Nov 1669, and d Br 17 Oct 1732, 64 yr (6:-139), being bur at St Michael's Ch 19 Oct 1732. He m, ca 1697 prob, Patience STAFFORD, b 1669 per d rec, and d Br 1721, ae 52 (Torrey, p 394). Patience, wife of Jabez Howland, was bur St Michael's in June 1726 (8:228), dau Samuel and Mercy (Westcott) Stafford of Warwick, RI (Sav, 4:-160). When the first vestry of St Michael's Ch was elected in the spring of 1724, Jabez Howland was made one of the ten vestrymen, and was also named one of its two wardens (Munro, p 145). The div of his est was made 21 May 1734 and named sons Jabez (eldest) and Thomas; daus Bethiah Davis, Mercy Martindal, Elizabeth Little, Sarah Lawton, and Patience Howland (Rounds, 1:230).

CHILDREN, b Br (6:83):
1. Bethiah[4], b 5 Dec 1702; d aft 4 July 1734, date of will of Simon Davis of Br; m (1) St Michael's 19 May 1725 Capt Nicholas BRAGG (6:10; 8:207), b Br 23 May 1696 (6:66); d 8 Feb 1732 at Surinam (6:119), son Henry and Elizabeth (Mackmollen) Bragg of Salem, Mass and Br (Torrey, p 93). She m (2) St Michael's 29 Aug 1733 Simeon/Simon DAVIS of Br (6:10), b 1660 per d rec, d 11 Sept 1736, 76 yr (6:126). She had no issue by her second m. The will of Simon Davis of Br, gentleman, being aged, was dtd 4 July 1734 and pvd 20 Oct 1736. He named wife Bethiah who rcvd all of the est she brought with her; and Bethiah's son, Nicholas Bragg (RIGR, 3:262). She had two ch b Br, surname Bragg: Nicholas, bp 2 June 1728; and William, b 25 Feb 1729/30 (6:66), bp 8 Mar 1729/30 (8:148), and bur St Michael's 8 Feb 1730/31 (Ibid, p 223).
2. Mary/Mercy, b 27 Jan 1704; d aft div of est of her father, 21 May 1734 (Rounds, 1:230); m (1) by Rev James Orem 22 Nov 1722 Capt George PEARSE (6:42); m (2) Br St Michael's 9 July 1724 Isaac MARTINDALE (6:35; 8:214). The VR Br have no recs of ch b to these m's.
3. Elizabeth, b 15 May 1707; d prob 5 Oct 1707 (6:139).
4. Elizabeth II, b 17 July 1709; d aft 21 May 1734, date of div of father's est; m as "Eliza" St Michael's 3 Oct 1733 Otis LITTLE (6:28; 8:207, 210), son Isaac Little of Marshfield, Mass, a desc of Richard Warren of the Myflwr (Bowman, p 225, 292). No issue in the VR Br.
5. Sarah, b 30 Apr 1711; d aft 7 Mar 1746/47; m St Michael's 27 Aug 1732 (6:31) Isaac LAWTON (8:207, 209), prob b 6 Oct 1709 and d 7 Mar 1749 (6:143), son Thomas and Margaret Lawton (6:86). The will of Thomas Lawton of Br, gentleman, was dtd 29 Mar 1749/50 and mentioned his son, Isaac Lawton dec, leaving unnamed ch (RIGR, 3:136). Sarah had four ch b Br, surname Lawton: ch of Isaac 4 June 1733 (6:143); John, b 22 Nov 1734; William, b 3 Oct 1737; and Joshua, b 8 Mar 1746/47.

6. Jabez, b 20 July 1713; d aft 21 May 1734, date of div of father's est.
   7. Patience, b 23 Mar 1716/17; m St Michael's 6 Dec 1739 Samuel BARKER Jr of Scituate, Mass (8:207).
   8. Thomas, b 5 Feb 1719/20; d aft 21 May 1734.

Deacon Samuel[3] (Jabez[2], John[1]) Howland was b Br 24 May 1686 (Sav, 2:479) or 16 May 1686 (6:82), and d there 15 May 1748 (8:252). He m (1) Br 6 May 1708 Abigail CAREY (6:27), b Br 31 Aug 1684, d 6 Aug 1737, 53 yr, "wife of Samuel" (6:139), dau Deacon John and Abigail (Allen) Carey of Br. He m (2) (int) as Samuel Howland Esq of Br 10 Feb 1741/42 Madame Rachel ( ) ALLEN of Barrington, RI (Bar, 6:-15; 6:28); and m (3) at Rehoboth, Mass by Rev John Greenwood 4 June 1747 Mrs Dorothy HUNT (VR Re, p 197, 200). His will, he of Br, Esq, dtd 29 Apr 1748 and pvd 27 June 1748, gave to his wife, Dorothy, the goods that were hers at the time of their m; named sons Samuel, eldest, and John; daus Abigail Smith, Tabitha Peckham, Phebe Wardwell, Mary Wardwell and Mehitable Wardwell; dau-in-law Abigail m to son Samuel, now at sea, and their two daus Abigail and Elizabeth, both under 21; sister-in-law Bathsheba Howland, wid; Rev John Burt of Ch of Christ in Br; and Rev Solomon Townsend of Warren (RIGR, 3:134).

CHILDREN, by first wife, Abigail, b Br (6:83):
   1. Samuel[4] Jr, b 3 Apr 1709; d aft 29 Apr 1748, date of father's will; prob m (1) (int) 29 July 1738 as Samuel Jr of Br, Sarah SMITH, b Oct 1714 New Haven, Conn, dau William and Mary (Collins) Smith of New Haven (Fams Anc New Haven, 7:1661); m (2) by 1743 Abigail___. On 10 Feb 1746/47 as a freeman of Br, he took the Oath of Bribery and Corruption (Munro, p 161). His name did not appear in the 1774 Census of Br. He was a mariner and perhaps d at sea, as his father's will made provision for his wife and ch in case he did not return from sea. He had two ch b Br (6:83): Abigail, b 4 Aug 1744; and Elizabeth, b 16 Mar 1745 (prob 1745/46).
   2. Abigail, b 18 Oct 1710; d 9 Aug 1751, 40 yr, wife of Benjamin Smith (6:162); m (1) Br by Timothy Fales, JP, 23 Oct 1729 Israel CHURCH of Little Compton, RI, b 22 Apr 1707, d 29 Aug 1735, 28 yr (6:123), son Joseph and Grace (Shaw) Church of LC (LC Fams, p 166, 172); m (2) 31 May 1739 Benjamin SMITH (6:14), b 1716, son Samuel and Sarah Smith of Br (6:103). Abigail had three ch b Br, surname Church (6:69) who also have a Myflwr desc from Richard Warren: Nathaniel, b 10 Mar 1730/31; Abigail, b 13 Jan 1732/33; and Sarah, b 19 Feb 1734/35. Abigail also had five ch b Br, surname Smith (6:103): Benjamin, b 1 Mar 1739/40 who m Mrs Jemima WARDWELL (6:50); Josian, b 7 June 1742 who m Mrs Eleanor TAYLOR (Ibid); Nathaniel,

b 30 Jan 1744/45 who m Parnel TAYLOR (6:50); Joseph, b 25 Aug 1747 who m Molly MILLER "both of Warren" (Ibid); and Samuel, b 28 June 1749 and d 2 Aug 1751.

3. Deacon John Sr, b 27 Sept 1713; d 21 Aug 1786, 73 yr (8:374); m Br by Rev Barnabus Taylor 24 Oct 1736 (6:-28) Martha WARDWELL, b Br 29 Nov 1716, d 4 July 1794, 78 yr, wid (6:140), dau Joseph and Martha (Giddings/Giddens) Wardwell of Br. On 10 Feb 1746/47 as a freeman of Br, John signed the Oath of Bribery and Corruption (Munro, p 161). In the 1774 Census of Br he was listed as head of a household of one male over 16 and one female over 16 (Ibid, p 189). He gave Public Service from RI during the Rev War (Pat Index, p 349), and he was made Deacon of the Congre Ch in Br (8:337). The will of John Howland Esq of Br, advanced in age, dtd 5 Oct 1775 and pvd 1 Oct 1789, mentioned wife Martha and unnamed only son (RIGR, 6:155). He had two ch b Br (6:83): John, b 29 Jan 1736/37 and d.y.; and John II Jr, b 9 Mar 1738/-39, d as John Esq Br 6 Dec 1792, 54 yr (6:140), who m (1) Br 25 Oct 1759 Elizabeth LEFAVOUR (6:28), and m (2) 7 Dec 1785 Elizabeth (MARTIN) DEWOLF (6:17; 8:307, 337). See his following acct.

4. Tabitha, b 13 Jan 1715; d aft father's will of 29 Apr 1748; m (1) 12 May 1734 (6:12) Nathaniel CAREY (6:28) of Newport (6:12), prob b 6 Feb 1713/14, son Josiah and Ruth (Reynolds) Carey; m (2) Br 22 Apr 1742 John PECKHAM of Newport (6:42). Tabitha had one kn ch b Newport, surname Carey: Josiah, b 24 Feb 1738/39 (6:68); and she had the fol ch b Newport, surname Peckham (6:98): Robert, b 16 Jan 1742/43 (Br rec); Abigail, b 4 Nov 1744 (Br rec); and Samuel, b 19 Mar 1746 (Br rec). A ch of John Peckham d 4 Sept 1750 Br (6:155). There are no b recs of her ch in the VR Newport. Her father's will of 29 Apr 1748 called her Tabitha Peckham.

5. Seth, b 9 July 1719; d 6 Aug 1719.

6. Phebe, b 9 Mar 1720/21; d 30 Nov 1794, 74 yr, wid (6:171); m 12 Oct 1741 John WARDWELL (6:28), b 12 Oct 1721, d betw 25 Jan 1770 and 7 Jan 1771, son Joseph and Martha (Giddings/Giddens) Wardwell of Br. In 1754 John was a Lt in one of the four Br Companies which went on the Expedition against Crown Point (Repre Men RI, 1:392). The will of John Wardwell of Br, gentleman, dtd 25 Jan 1770 pvd 7 Jan 1771, named wife Phebe; sons John, eldest, Nathaniel 2nd, Joseph, Samuel, Daniel and Allen, some of whom were under 21; daus Phebe, m but no surname given, Susanna, m but no surname given, Mary, Elizabeth, and Tabitha, no surnames given, some under age (RIGR, 6:153).

7. Mary, b 18 Mar 1722/23; m Br 26 Sept 1742 William WARDWELL (6:28), b 1722, d 1760 at sea, son Benjamin and Mary Wardwell of Br (6:56, 83, 170). Mary had nine ch b Br, surname Wardwell, and bp Congre Ch, Br (8:290): Will-

liam, bp 8 Jan 1743/44; Abigail, bp 9 June 1745; Mary, bp 25 Oct 1747; William II, bp 28 Jan 1749/50; Major Benjamin, bp 9 Feb 1752 who m (1) Sarah SMITH, dau Richard Smith of Br, and m (2) Huldah GOFF, dau Joseph and Patience Goff (8:355); Sarah, bp 3 Mar 1754; Martin, bp 29 June 1756; Samuel, bp 27 Aug 1758; and Capt Samuel II, bp 25 May 1760 who m Elizabeth CHURCH, dau Samuel and Ann Church (8:354). A ch of William Wardwell d 18 Apr 1754, and an infant of William d 19 June 1757 (6:-170).

8. Mehitabel, b 1 Feb 1724/25; d 13 Feb 1764, wife of Stephen (6:170); m Br as his first wife, 18 Dec 1746, Stephen WARDWELL (6:28, 56, 83, 170-171; Repre Men RI, 1:372-373), b 1722 and d 6 Aug 1799, 77 yr (6:171), son Joseph and Martha(Giddings/Giddens) Wardwell of Br. Stephen owned a tavern on Hope St. Mehitabel had six ch b Br, surname Wardwell (6:110): Elizabeth, b 7 July 1749; Abigail, b 24 Dec 1751; Stephen Jr, b 5 Nov 1754; Josiah, b 20 July 1757; James, b 9 Jan 1760; and Hannah, b 6 Nov 1762. A child of Stephen Wardwell d 15 Dec 1722 (6:170).

John[5] Jr (Deacon John[4] Sr, Deacon Samuel[3], Jabez[2], John[1]) Howland was b Br 9 Mar 1738/39 and d there as John Esq 6 Dec 1792, 54 yr (6:140). He m (1) Congre Ch, Br 25 Oct 1759 Elizabeth LEFAVOUR (6:28), prob b Br 28 May 1741 (6:86) and d 1784 (8:374), dau Timothy and Elizabeth (Bosworth) LeFavour; m (2) Congre Ch, Br 7 Dec 1785 Elizabeth (MARTIN) DEWOLF, b Br 10 Oct 1747 (8:89), dau William and Elizabeth Martin Jr and wid of Capt Mark Antony DeWolf (6:17; 8:307, 337). John Howland Jr was listed in the 1774 Census of Br as head of a household of two males above 16, five males under 16, one female above 16, and three females under 16 (Munro, p 189). As John Jr he gave Public Service from RI during the Rev War, as did his father, called John Sr (Pat Index, p 349). The will of John Howland, Esq of Br, dtd 29 Nov 1792 and pvd 4 Feb 1793, named wife Elizabeth; sons John, Peleg dec, Lefavour, Josiah, and William Martin Howland under 15; daus Martha and Sarah, no surnames (RIGR, 6:156).

CHILDREN by first wife, Elizabeth LeFavour, b Br and bp Congre Ch, Br (6:83; 8:278):
1. Samuel[6], b 13 June 1760, bp 17 Aug 1766; d bef father's will of 29 Nov 1792.
2. John, b 20 Sept 1761, bp 17 Aug 1766; d aft 3 Dec 1826; m (1) Congre Ch, Br 20 Dec 1789 Rebecca MUNRO (8:-337), b 17 Apr 1768 (6:93), d 19 Sept 1823 (8:252), or Aug 1824 (8:375), dau Capt Daniel and Rebecca Munro; m (2) Congre Ch, Br as "John of John Esq and Elizabeth" 3 Dec 1826 Mary (GLADDING) MUNRO, dau John and Lucretia

Gladding, wid of ___ Munro (8:306). He had no issue by his second m, but by his first wife, Rebecca, he had seven kn ch, all of whom d in Br (8:374-375): John Jr, ch of, d 24 Sept 1792; John, of John, d 16 Sept 1794, 1 yr; Nancy Burt, of John, d 24 Dec 1796, 17 mo; Ann Burt, of John, d 20 Feb 1800, 2 yr; prob Josiah, d 25 Sept 1821, 21 yr, who m Congre Ch, Br 27 Aug 1720 Mary L. BRADFORD (8:337); Rebecca, of John, d 3 June 1824, 17 yr, and Charles, "last of John's family", d 28 June 1825, 21 yr.
3. Elizabeth, b 8 Sept 1763, bp 17 Aug 1766; d bef father's will of 29 Nov 1792.
4. Daniel, b 11 Feb 1765, bp 17 Aug 1766; d Sept 1795, 31 yr (8:374) at Gambia river, Africa (6:140), but not named in father's will of 29 Nov 1792; m Congre Ch, Br, 22 Oct 1786 Rebecca WALDRON, b 16 June 1766 (6:109), dau Nathaniel and Hannah (Throop) Waldron of Br (8:337). He had three ch bp Congre Ch, Br (8:278): Samuel and Abigail, both bp 18 May 1794; and Daniel, bp 9 Nov 1794.
5. Martha, b 7 Nov 1766, bp 19 Apr 1767; m as second wife Congre Ch, Br 11 June 1797 Major Samuel Viall PECK (8:337), b 22 Oct 1763, bp Congre Ch, Br 10 Sept 1769 (8:284); drowned in Br harbor 21 Feb 1804, 40 yr (8:386), son Thomas and Mary (Richmond) Peck of Br (6:43; 8:345). Martha had one kn ch b Br, surname Peck (8:386): Martha of Samuel V., d 3 Sept 1798, 5 mo.
6. Abigail, b 5 Feb 1768, bp 8 May 1768; prob m Congre Ch, Br 24 May 1792 Capt Simeon MUNRO (8:337), who was lost at sea Dec 1796 (8:381). Abigail had two ch bp Congre Ch, Br, surname Munro (8:282): Hannah Carey, bp 18 Mar 1804 who m Samuel WARDWELL (8:343); and Abigail Howland, bp 18 Mar 1804 who m James NEWMAN (Ibid).
7. Peleg, b 26 Aug 1769, bp 13 May 1770; d Oct 1790 (6:140; 8:374).
8. Child of John, b 1771, stillborn (6:140).
9. Capt Nathaniel, b 9 Sept 1772, bp 10 Jan 1773; d 18 Mar 1805, 32 yr (8:374); m Congre Ch, Br 27 Sept 1797 (8:345) Hannah PECK, dau Capt Jonathan and Mary (Throop) Peck of Br (8:33). He had four ch of whom three were bp Congre Ch, Br (8:278): John 2nd, b 12 July 1798, bp 17 Nov 1805; Frederick, d 16 Nov 1803, 19 m (8:374); Nathaniel, and Frederick II, both bp 17 Nov 1805.
10. Sarah, b 7 Aug 1774, bp 30 Oct 1774; d 31 Dec 1775 (6:140).
11. Sarah II, b 17 Dec 1775, bp Oct 1776; m Congre Ch, Br 13 or 30 Sept 1798 Capt Samuel PITMAN (6:44; 8:337), son Peleg and Mary (Wardwell) Pitman (6:44). Sarah had eight ch b Br, surname Pitman (6:99): Josiah Howland who m Hannah LINDSEY (6:44); Samuel; Sarah; George; Abigail; Ann who m Samuel S. MUNRO (6:44); John Howland who m Eliza F. SLADE (6:44; 8:215); and Elizabeth Lefavour who m Nathan B. HEATH (6:44).

12. Lefavour, b 6 June 1778, bp 27 June 1799; d aft 1802; m Congre Ch, Br 24 Nov 1799 Phebe GLADDING, dau Capt Daniel and Susannah (Wardwell) Gladding of Br (6:28). He had one kn ch, b Br: Daniel LeFavour, b 16 June 1803 (6:83).
13. Josiah, b 6 Mar 1780, bp 15 Oct 1780; d Dec 1796, lost at sea (8:374).

CHILD by second wife, Elizabeth (Martin) DeWolfe, b Br, bp Congre Ch (6:83; 8:278):
14. William Martin, b 26 June 1788, vp 12 Oct 1788; d 1804 at Africa (6:140; 8:374).

53. BENJAMIN INGELL/INGALLS

It is not kn when or where Benjamin Ingalls was b, or who his parents were. Sav mentioned no Benjamin as a son of any Ingalls he listed. Torrey, p 409, gave Ingell, Benjamin of Br, RI, who d 1690, with a wife, Waitstill who m (2) 1697 Gershom Marble and d 1728. Benjamin had no entries in the VR Br. A "Ben Ingle" was listed in the 1689 Census of Br, who was prob he, but he was then living alone with no wife or ch (Geneals RI Fams, 1989, 2:402). The will of Benjamin Ingell of Br, "saylor", dtd 4 Oct 1690 and pvd 19 Nov 1690, mentioned wife Weightstill "who is now in child", and son, Benjamin under 21 (Rounds, 1:3). His wife and ch left Br upon her second m on 29 Dec 1697 to Gershom Marble of Scituate, Mass (Torrey, p 487).

54. JOSEPH JACOB(S)

Joseph^2 Jacob(s) was b 1 May 1646 in Hingham, Mass, bp 10 May 1646 (Sav, 3:534), and d in Br 9 Feb 1708 (6:141), son of Nicholas and Mary (Gilman) Jacob(s). Nicholas was in Watertown, Mass in 1633, but rem to Hingham where he lived thereafter and d. Joseph m ca 1670 in Hull, Mass Hannah BOSWORTH, b Hull 30 Apr 1650, bp Hingham 16 July 1650 (Bosworth Gen, p 112), and d Br prob aft 1722 (8:253), dau Nathaniel and Bridget () (Bellamy) (Lobdell) Bosworth of Hull and Br. On 20 June 1683 Joseph took the Oath of Fidelity in Br (Munro, p 114), where he was a carpenter. He was termed Mr Joseph Jacob when he rec his ear mark for cattle, sheep etc in Br on 13 June 1700 (TAG, 65:118). His will was dtd 26 Mar 1703 and pvd in Boston 22 Apr 1708 (Rounds, 1:40), or pvd 1705 (RIGR, 2:172). In it he named his wife, Hannah, and only surviving son, Nathaniel.

CHILDREN (6:85, 141; Sav, 2:533):
1. Joseph^3, b 20 Feb 1673 Hingham; d.y.
2. Joseph II, Jr, b 10 Apr 1675 Hingham; d Br 1 Nov

1703 (6:141).
3. Benjamin, b 10 Apr 1680 Hingham; d Br 17 Aug 1703 (Ibid).
4. Nathaniel, b 29 Jan 1683 Hingham; d aft 29 July 1722 (8:253).
5. Mary, b 16 July 1686; d Hingham 22 Mar 1696 (6:141).

Nathaniel^3 (Joseph^2, Nicholas^1) Jacob(s) was b Hingham, Mass 29 Jan 1683 and d aft 29 July 1722. He rem to Br in 1683 with his father's family. He m by 1714 Mercy___, and they both joined the Congre Ch in Br on 29 July 1722 (8:253). They had four ch bp in that Ch and then they disappeared from the VR Br, and prob rem from town.

CHILDREN, b Br (6:84):
1. Mary^4, b 28 Aug 1715, bp Congre Ch, Br 5 Aug 1722 (Geneals RI Fams, 1989, 2:381).
2. Joseph, b 12 July 1717, bp Congre Ch, Br 5 Aug 1722 (Ibid). A Joseph Jacobs became a freeman of Newport, RI in 1750, who may have been this man (MacGunnigle, p 30).
3. Benjamin, b 26 Apr 1719, bp Congre Ch, Br 5 Aug 1722.
4. Hannah, bp Congre Ch, Br 17 Mar 1722/23 (Geneals RI Fams, 1989, 2:382).

55. DANIEL LANDON/LANGDON

Little is kn about Daniel Landon. Neither his parents, b date, nor d date are given by Sav or Torrey. The latter (p 449) said only that he m Ann/Anna ?Lobdell, had a ch b 1682, and lived in Charlestown, Mass and Br, RI. Wyman gave only one line to him, the only Landon mentioned, and said that he m Ann___. The only rec of him in the VR Br is that of the b's of three ch there to Daniel and Anna Landon (6:86): Mercy, b 2 June 1682; Martha, b 4 Feb 168?-/84; and James, b 29 Mar 1685. No Landon d's or m's are found in the VR Br, and Daniel did not take the Oath of Fidelity there betw June 1683 and Aug 1686 (Munro, p 114). He was listed in the 1689 Census of Br as Dan Langdon with a wife and seven ch (Geneals RI Fams, 1989, 2:402), and he prob rem from Br not long aft then. Two m's in Boston may poss be those of two of Daniel's ch, b Br: Martha Landon m Elnathan Satley 7 June 1709; and James Langdon m Mary York 4 Apr 1711 (Boston Mars, p 25, 35). Among his seven ch listed in the 1689 Census of Br was poss a son, Daniel, who rem to Colchester, New London, Conn. A man of this name had the fol ch b there: Samuel, b 19 Feb 1723; Deborah, b 16 Feb 1725; William, b 25 Apr 1727; and Joshua, b 13 Apr 1729 (Early b's, m's and d's in Colchester, cited in Hurd, p 393).

56. THOMAS LEWIS

Thomas[2] Lewis was b in England and came in the Elizabeth from Ipswich in 1634, aged 9 mos, with his parents, Edmund and Mary Lewis. They were first at Watertown, Mass, but rem in 1639 to Lynn, Mass where Edmund and Mary d. They had four sons, two of whom, John and Thomas, were named in Edmund's will, dtd Lynn 18 Jan 1651 and pvd 25 Feb 1651 (Sav, 3:85-86); Lewis and Newhall, p 181-182).

Thomas m in Lynn 11 Nov 1659 Hannah BAKER, prob dau Edward Baker of Lynn, and they were in Br by 1681. Thomas d there 26 Apr 1709 ca 76 yr, and Hannah, wid, d Jan 1717 (6:144). Thomas did not take the Oath of Fidelity in Br betw 1683 and 1686, as many new settlers did, and the VR Br show no ch b to them in Br. He was listed in the 1689 Census of Br as G(oodman) Lewis, with a wife and six ch (Geneals RI Fams, 1989, 2:401). As Goodman Lewis he described a horse of his in Br on 9 May 1700, branded with an R (TAG, 65:118). The will of Thomas Lewis of Br, dtd 11 Aug 1708 and pvd 6 July 1709, named aged wife Hannah; "my sons and daus", but only named dau Hepzebath (Rounds, 1:45).

CHILDREN, all b Lynn, Mass, order unkn (Sav, 3:88):
1. Edward[3], b 28 July 1660.
2. Hannah, d Br Dec 1717 (6:148); m Br 22 Jan 1683 George MOWRY, per VR Br 6:32. Torrey, p 517 said she m on this date George MOREY of Br, which is correct. Hannah had nine ch b Br, surname "Mowry" (6:90): John, b 3 Oct 1684; Mary, b 24 Mar 1687/88; Sarah, b 4 Mar 1690/91 who m Br 24 Sept 1713 Ephraim ANDROS (6:37) and had ch b Swansea (VR Re, p 524); Hannah, b 18 Mar 1693/94; George, b 31 Aug 1696; Martha, b 12 Mar 1698/99, who m (int) Br as Martha Moorey 24 June 1723 Thomas TABER of Taunton, RI (6:37, 51); Abigail, b 27 Feb 1701/02; Benjamin, b 18 Apr 1705; and Thomas, b 1 Jan 1708/09.
3. Esther, b 1664?; d 1743; m Br 7 Jan 1684 Jeremiah FINNEY of Br (6:21, 32; Torrey, p 579), b 15 Aug 1662, d Br 7 Jan 1748, son John Finney and his third wife, Elizabeth Bayley, of Br (Geneals RI Fams, 1989, 1:448-450). The 1774 Census of Br gave Jeremiah Finney as head of a household of eleven persons (Munro, p 188): two males above 16, two males under 16, three females above 16, and four females under 16. Esther had eleven ch b Br, surname Finney (6:132; 8:276; Geneals RI Fams, 1989, 1:449): Jeremiah, b 1684 and d.y.; Mary, b 26 Mar 1686; Hannah, b 14 Jan 1687/88, d Br 22 Dec 1744, and m 14 Jan 1706/07 Thomas DIMAN; Mehitable, b 8 May 1687 (sic, 16-89?); John, b 3 Aug 1690; Rebecca, b 24 Feb 1691/92 and prob m 11 Mar 1716 Samuel HARRIS of Swansea, Mass; Es-

ther, b 4 May 1693 who m (int) 31 Oct 1719 Joseph JOY of Rehoboth, Mass (6:21); Deborah, bp 20 Oct 1695; John, b 13 Apr 1696 who m Mary CAMPBELL of Norton, Mass; Abigail, b 17 Apr 1697; and Capt Jeremiah Jr, bp 7 Sept 1700, and m (int) 17 May 1727 Elizabeth BRISTON or BRISTOW (6:21, 66) of Br.
4. Thomas Jr, b 29 Apr 1668; m 10 Apr 1689, poss at Swansea, Mass Elizabeth BROOKS (Torrey, p 464). He had two ch b Br and then disappeared from the Br recs (6:87): Nathaniel, b 14 Dec 1689, and Abigail, b 8 Jan 1691.
5. Mary, of Thomas and Hannah, d Br 26 Mar 1686 (6:144).
6. Sixth ch, per 1689 Census of Br, prob dau, Hepzebath, named in father's will dtd 11 Aug 1708 (Rounds, 1:45).

57. JOHN MARTIN JR

John Martin Jr was bp 1 May 1642 in Charlestown, Mass and d in Lebanon, Conn where Torrey, p 492 said he rem to from Br. He lived first in Malden and then in Swansea, Mass, bef settling in Br. He was the son of John Martin Sr and his first wife, Rebecca, who were in Charlestown, Mass in 1638 (Sav, 3:162). On 14 Apr 1671 John Jr m in Malden Mary MUDGE, dau of Thomas Mudge, a tailor, who was in Malden by 1658 (Sav, 3:252; Conn Nutmegger, 22:574). Wyman, ɔ 658 said that John Martin Sr was prob the son of Robert Martin of Weymouth, Mass, and mentioned a sale of ten acres of land of John Sr's in Malden in 1650 to J. Greenland.

John Jr took the Oath of Fidelity in Br on 20 June 1683 (Munro, p 114). On 12 June 1695 both he and his wife, Mary, became members of the Congre Ch in Br (8:255), which is prob an error for 1685 as they had ch bp in this Ch in 1687. The 1689 Census of Br listed him as G(oodman) Martin with a wife and six ch (Geneals RI Fams, 1989, 2:401). John d in in Lebanon, Conn bef 26 Oct 1722 when his son, Joseph, as exec of his est, received a receipt from Robert Jolls of Br, who was guardian of Thomas Martin, son of John Martin Jr, and gson of John Martin of Lebanon (Rounds, 1:89, 225).

CHILDREN, bp Congre Ch, Br (6:89; Geneals RI Fams, 1989, 2:371-372);
1. Mary$^{4?}$, b 19 Apr 1674 Malden; bp Br 21 Aug 1687.
2. Thomas, b 8 June 1675 Malden; bp Br 21 Aug 1687.
3. John "Jr", b 14 Sept 1679 Malden, bp Br 21 Aug 1687; d Br bef 23 Sept 1711; m ca 1700 Hannah DARLING (Torrey, p 492).
4. Abigail, b 19 July 1681 Swansey, bp Br 21 Aug 1687.
5. Joseph, b 15 Jan 1684/85 Br, bp Br 21 Aug 1687; m Mary___, and had one ch, Jonathan, b Br 17 or 19 Jan 1707/08 (6:89), or b Br 20 Dec 1707 (letter from town clerk of Br). They rem to Lebanon, Conn, where Joseph

bought a grist mill and forty acres of land in 1729, and where he d 13 May 1750, 66 yr, and his wife, Mary, d 25 Jan 1745/46, 63 yr (VR Windham; Joseph Martin of Windham, Conn, H. Scholl, in The Conn Nutmegger, 1989, 22:573-4).
6. Benjamin, b 24 May 1686 Swansey, bp Br 21 Aug 1687.
7. Ebenezer, b 28 Sept 1689, Swansey.
8. Martha, b 11 Feb 1691 Swansea per 6:89, bp Congre Ch, Br 19 Apr 1696.

John$^{4?}$ "Jr" (John^3) Martin was b 14 Sept 1679 in Malden, Mass and bp Br 21 Aug 1687. He d Br bef 23 Sept 1711, and m ca 1700 Hannah DARLING, b 14 Apr 1677 Braintree, Mass, dau Denice/Dennis and Hannah (Francis) Darling of Braintree and Mendon, Mass (VR Braintree, Mass; Darling Fam, p 5-8; Cutter, 1:385; Torrey, p 492). Hannah, wife of John Martin Junr, was bp 14 July 1706 as an adult and became a member of the Congre Ch, Br (Geneals RI Fams, 1989, 2:376).

CHILDREN, b Br (6:89):
1. John$^{5?}$, b 14 May 1703; prob m 10 Dec 1726 wid Experience RUE of Norton, Mass (6:35).
2. May, b 7 Jan 1704/05.
3. Thomas, b 18 Aug 1706, bp Congre Ch, Br 23 Sept 1711 "its father being dead" (Geneals RI Fams, 1989, 2:379); prob m St Michael's Ch, Br 3 Dec 1727 Ann MUNRO (8:211).

John Martin Jr had a prob ninth ch, William$^{4?}$, b 1677 per d rec; d 30 Apr 1767, 91 yr (6:147); m Br Mary___, who d Br bef 7 May 1706, and m(2) by Rev John Sparhawk, Br, 7 May 1706 Christian PELTON (6:35). His was the first Martin m in the VR Br, vol 6. He was b during the four years betw Thomas on 8 June 1675 and John on 14 Sept 1679, during which no b was rec of any ch of John Jr. And his d rec says he d Br 30 Apr 1767, 91 yr (6:147). His three sons were all named the same as were three sons of John and Mary (Mudge) Martin Jr's, and there were no other kn Martins in Br at this time, except John Jr's family.

CHILD of William$^{4?}$ by first wife, Mercy/Mary, b Br (Geneals RI Fams, 1989, 2:375):
1. Mary$^{5?}$, bp Congre Ch, Br 24 June 1705.

CHILDREN by second wife, Christian, b Br (6:89):
2. William, b 20 Dec 1707, bp Congre Ch, Br 20 Mar 1709 (Geneals RI Fams, 1989, 2:376); prob d.y.
3. John, b 19 Mar 1708/09, bp Congre Ch, Br 20 Mar 1709 (Ibid, 2:377).
4. Charity, bp 24 Dec 1710 (Ibid, 2:378); d Br 5 Apr 1776, 65 yr, unm (6:147).

5. William II, b 17 Feb 1712/13, bp 17 May 1713 (Geneals RI Fams, 1989, 2:379); m (1) St Michael's 23 July 1741 Martha NEWTON; m (2) St Michael's 19 Sept 1745 Eliza LINDSEY (8:211). He had ten ch b Br (6:89-90; 8:167).
6. Thomas, b 7 Apr 1715, bp 10 July 1715 (Geneals RI Fams, 1989, 2:379); d at Antigua, WI 1758 (6:47); m (1) St Michael's 21 Nov 1736 Hannah SMITH, b 4 Apr 1715 Br, d 13 July 1746, dau Nathaniel and Abigail Smith of Br (6:103); m (2) St Michael's 17 July 1748 Rachel WALDRON (8:211), b 1723 (6:147) who d as wid 13 Mar 1769, 43 yr and bur St Michael's 14 Mar 1769 (6:147; 8:231). He had seven ch b Br (6:89; 8:166-167).
7. Susanna, b 9 Sept 1717, bp 23 Oct 1717 (Geneals RI Fams, 1989, 2:380); d 29 Jan 1745 (6:143); m St Michael's 22 Feb 1736/1737 Thomas LAWTON Jr (8:211), b 14 Oct 1714 Prudence Isle, d June 1744 at Surinam (6:143), son Thomas and Margaret Lawton of Prudence Isle and Br (6:86). Susanna had three kn ch, surname Lawton, bp St Michael's (8:163): Ruth, bp 21 Oct 1739; Thomas, bp 21 Mar 1741/42; and Eliza, bp 29 Apr 1744.

58. NICHOLAS MEAD

Nothing is kn about the parentage, or place and date of b, of Nicholas Mead. Sav, 3:191 said he was in Charlestown, Mass by 1680 and that his wife, Elizabeth, joined the Ch there on 6 Mar 1681. Torrey, p 501, gave no dates for him, but said he was of Charlestown, then Br, RI, and finally Mendon, Mass. Wyman, p 663, said he was a tanner and was admitted to the Ch in Charlestown on 26 June 1681, and that his est was on the tithe list of 1680/81. The Selectmen's recs there noted the removal of Nicholas and his family on 18 (12) 1682/83 (18 Feb 1683). He was in Br on 20 June 1683 when he took the Oath of Fidelity there (Munro, p 114). The Congre Ch recs of Br say that both Nicholas and Elizabeth Mead joined on 12 June 1695, which is apparently an error for 1685, since they had a ch bp there in July 1687. The 1689 Census of Br listed Nicholas with a wife and six ch (Geneals RI Fams, 1989, 2:401). He was in Mendon, Mass by Oct 1690 when he had a ch bp there.

KNOWN CHILDREN:
1. Susanna, b 5 Sept 1679, bp 13 Mar 1681 Charlestown, Mass (Wyman, p 663; Sav, 3:191), or bp 13 Jan 1681 (IGI Mass).
2. Elizabeth, b and bp 14 Aug 1681 Charlestown (Wyman, p 663).
3. Ebenezer, b 22 Mar 1685/86 Br, bp Congre Ch, Br 10 July 1687 (Geneals RI Fams, 1989, 2:371).
4. Katherine, bp Congre Ch, Br 10 July 1687 (Ibid).

5. John, bp Congre Ch, Br 13 May 1688 (Ibid).
6. Ch listed in 1689 Census of Br (Ibid, p 401).
7. Joseph, bp 7 Oct 1690 Mendon (IGI Mass).

59. GEORGE MOREY/MOWRY

The date of b, and parentage, of George[1] Morey/Mowry are not kn. He m in Br as George Mowry 22 Jan 1683 Hannah LEWIS (6:37; Torrey, p 517). She was the dau of Thomas and Hannah (Baker) Lewis of Lynn, Mass and Br, and she d in Br as Hannah of George Morey in Dec 1717 (6:148). George signed the Oath of Fidelity in Br on 17 May 1685 as George Morye (Munro, p 114). George and Hannah Moorey both joined the Congre Ch in Br on 6 July 1696 (8:257). Virkus, 6:94 said that George Morey came from England, settled at Br, and rem to Norton, Mass; m 1683 Hannah Lewis who d 1717. He apparently followed his sons to Norton aft his wife's d, and he prob d there.

CHILDREN, b Br (6:90), bp Congre Ch, Br (Geneals RI Fams, 1989, 2:373-375, 377):
1. John[2], b 3 Oct 1684, bp 13 June 1697; m Margaret LINSFORD and had two kn ch: Linsford, bp Congre Ch, Br 29 Aug 1708, and John Jr, b Br 13 May 1712. John Jr rem to E. Haddam, Conn where he m (1) ___ and had two ch, Mary, bp 1755, and Ruth, b 1757. He was of Lebanon, Conn when he m (2) Desire (FULLER) SAWYER, b Colchester, Conn 2 or 22 Feb 1723, d aft 1 Sept 1760, dau Samuel and Naomi (Rowley) Fuller of Colchester. Desire's ch, if any, have a Myflwr line from Edward Fuller of the Myflwr (Myflwr Fams Through Five Gens, Edward Fuller, 4:44-45, 137-138). John and Desire had no Conn land or probate recs aft their m, and apparently rem elsewhere.
2. Mary, b 24 Mar 1687/88, bp 13 June 1697.
3. Sarah, b 4 Mar 1690/91, bp 13 June 1697; m Br as Sarah Mowry 24 Sept 1713 Ephraim ANDROS (6:37). Sarah had three ch b Br, surname Andros (6:62): Abigail, b 13 July 1717; Ephraim, b 10 Jan 1718 (prob 1718/19); and Hannah, b 2 Sept 1720. They rem from Br to Swansea, Mass where Sarah had four more ch b (VR Re, p 524): Elizabeth, b 5 May 1723; John, b 7 Mar 1726; Nathaniel, b 16 Mar 17-28; and Patience, b 11 June 1732.
4. Hannah, b 18 Mar 1693/94, bp 13 June 1697.
5. George Jr, b 31 Aug 1696, bp 13 June 1697; d betw 24 Feb and 6 Mar 1753 in Norton, Mass; m (1) Elizabeth HODGES, dau John Hodges of Norton, whose will dtd 7 Jan 1743/44 and pvd 16 Feb 1743/44, named wife Mary and a dau Elizabeth, wife of George Morey (Rounds, 1:335). The will of Marcey Hodges of Norton, wid of John Hodges dec, dtd 23 Oct 1746 and pvd 5 Sept 1749, named dau

Elizabeth Mory, eldest, dec; gch Elizabeth Mory, dau of
her dau Elizabeth Mory dec (Rounds, 2:67-68). George Jr
m (2) Mary HODGES, dau Ebenezer and Esther Hodges of
Norton. The will of George Morey Jr of Norton, gentleman, dtd 24 Feb 1753 and pvd 6 Mar 1753, named wife Mary,
and his two ch, George Morey (under 21), and Mary Morey
(Ibid, 2:129). Mary Morey of Norton, wid, was appted the
guardian of Mary and George Morey, both under 14, ch of
George Morey of Norton, on 24 Sept 1753 (Ibid, 2:304).
The div of the est of Ebenezer Hodges of Norton, dtd 9
Nov 1750, was betw his wid, Esther, and his only ch,
Mary Morey (Ibid, 2:98).

6. Martha, b 12 Mar 1698/99, bp 23 Apr 1699; m (int) as
Martha Moorey, Br 24 June 1723 Thomas TABER of Tiverton,
RI (6:37, 51). Martha had three ch, surname Taber, rec
in the VR Br (6:105): Timothy, b 13 May 1724; Benjamin,
b 26 Jan 1725/26 Swansey; and Thomas, b 14 Aug 1728. A
ch of "widow Tabor" d Br 10 Feb 1730 (6:165), which may
refer to a ch of Martha's.

7. Abigail, b 27 Feb 1701/02, bp 21 June 1702.

8. Benjamin, b 18 Apr 1705, bp 17 June 1705. He poss
rem to Norton, Mass with his brothers, George and Thomas,
as a Benjamin Morey on 22 Apr 1752 witnessed the will of
Phillip Atherton of Norton (Rounds, 2:120).

9. Thomas, b 1 Jan 1708/09, bp 20 Mar 1709; prob m Mehitable HODGES who d bef 12 Feb 1749/50, date of her
father's will, dau Nathaniel and Hannah Hodges of Norton,
Mass. Thomas had one kn ch, Thomas Jr. The will of Nathaniel Hodges of Norton, yeoman, dtd 12 Feb 1749/50 and
pvd 6 Mar 1749/50, mentioned wife Hannah; and Mehittable
Morey dec, late wife of Thomas Morey of Norton; and Thomas Morey son of my dau Mehittable dec (Rounds, 2:77).

60. JEREMIAH OSBORNE

It has not been poss to identify the parentage, date,
or place of b, of this Jeremiah Osborne. The given name
of Jeremiah was used for several generations by the ch and
desc of Thomas[1] Osborne, who was in New Haven, Conn in
1639, and rem to East Hampton, LI in 1650. Fams of Anc New
Haven gave the wives and ch of several of these Jeremiahs
and none went to Br, RI. Sav, 3:317-318 said that the Thomas[1] of New Haven was "perhaps brother of Richard"; and
that Richard was of Hingham, Mass in 1635 and went to New
London, Conn bef 1640, and in 1666 had lands in Newtown,
LI. He mentioned his sons, but gave no Jeremiah. Sav also
said that a Jeremiah of New Haven, "perhaps brother of
Richard", tanner, by wife, Mary, had a Jeremiah b 1652 who
d soon, and Jeremiah again b 28 Nov 1656. This last Jeremiah was not the Br man as Sav said that his "son Jeremiah

and other heirs were proprietors in 1685" in New Haven.

The Jeremiah Osborne who was at the first town meeting of Br in 1681 d there in 1709, and m by 1683 Mercy DAVIS, who d Br 16 Feb 1732/33 (6:153). Torrey, p 546, said only that they lived in Br, RI. Mercy Davis's parentage is not kn. But a Simeon Davis Jr m in Br 24 Sept 1685, and he was the son of Simeon Sr of Concord, Mass, who was the son of the emigrant, Dolor Davis. Sav, 2:21 said that Simeon Sr had a dau, Mary, b 3 Oct 1663. She may also have been called Mercy, and have come to Br with her brother, Simeon. Jeremy Osborn was listed in the 1689 Census of Br with a wife, one ch, and one servant (Geneals RI Fams, 1989, 2:402). The will of Jeremiah Osborne of Br, dtd 27 July 1708 and pvd 6 Apr 1709, named wife, Mercy, and small ch; only John Osborn was mentioned "who is to have a double portion as the law directs". Simon Davis was one of the two appraisers of the inv of Jeremiah's est, dtd 24 Mar 1709 (RIGR, 3:88; Rounds, 1:44).

CHILDREN, b Br (6:95 incorrectly calls him Osband):
1. Robert^2, b 11 Aug 1684; bur 2 Sept 1685, 1 yr 3 w (6:153).
2. Katherine, b 12 Nov 1686; d bef 15 Jan 1760, date of husband's will; m Br 24 May 1708 Jonathan WOODBURY (6:40, 60), b 5 May 1685, d as Jonathan Esq 21 Jan 1766, 81 yr (6:174), son Samuel and Mary Woodbury of Br. No issue. The will of Jonathan Woodbury was given in RIGR, 6:151.
3. John, b 31 Oct 1689; m Sarah___ and had one kn ch, John, bp Congre Ch, Br 27 Mar 1715 (Geneals RI Fams, 1989, 2:379).
4. Jeremiah, b 25 July 1693; d 24 Jan 1693/94 (6:153).
5. Margaret, b 27 May 1695; d Oct 1730 (6:174); m (int) Br 7 July 1721 Capt Samuel WOODBURY (6:40), b 5 Nov 1688 (6:113), d 24 Mar 1757, 69 yr (6:174), son Samuel and Mary Woodbury of Br. He m (2) Br 18 June 1739 Mrs Elizabeth SAMPSON (6:60). Margaret had four ch, b Br, surname Woodbury (6:113): Jonathan, b 11 Apr 1722 and d bef 15 Jan 1760, date of uncle Jonathan Woodbury's will (RIGR, 6:151); Sarah, b 16 Sept 1723, and m 27 Oct 1745 John COY (6:60); Margaret, b 30 Nov 1724 and m ___SWAN; and Samuel, b 1 Nov 1726.
6. Sarah, b 11 May 1701.
7. Jeremiah II, b 21 June 1706.

61. PETER PAPILLON/PAMPELION

See: The Papillons of Boston and Bristol by Estelle Wellwood Wait, NER, July 1970, 124:161-182, reprinted in Geneals RI Fams, 1989, 2:29-50.

62. SAMUEL PENFIELD SR

Samuel[1] Penfield Sr was apparently the first of this surname to appear in New England, and it is not kn where or when he was b, or who his parents were. He was in Lynn, Mass by 1650 where he m (1) 30 Nov 1675 Mary LEWIS (Sav, 3:388; Lewis and Newhall, p 228). After the b of his first two ch in Lynn, he was in Rehoboth, Mass by May 1681, and in 1685 was living in Br, and having ch b there. He m (2) by 1692 Anne___ who d by 1695; and he m (3) by 1695 Mary ___. He was the same Samuel Penfield (the only man of this surname) given by Colket, p 219 as of Lynn, Mass ca 1650, Rehoboth 1681, Providence, 1681, d Guilford 30 Nov 1710/1, freeman, captain. Steiner, p 137 said that Samuel Penfield came to Guilford, Conn from Br and was admitted as a planter on 17 Dec 1710 and d 22 Nov 1714. However, it was Samuel Jr who d in 1714, not Samuel Sr, who d in 1710. Colket quoted as a ref "Penfield Gen". This is The Genealogy of the Descendents of Samuel Penfield by Florence B. Penfield, Harris Press, Reading, Pa, 1963, not seen by this author. The Pat Index, p 525, gave as accepted Rev War ancestors thirteen Penfield men, all of whom served from Conn, and two of whom were named Samuel.

CHILDREN by first wife, Mary (6:99; Sav, 3:388):
1. Samuel[2] Jr, b 17 Sept 1676 Lynn, Mass; d Guilford, Conn 22 Nov 1714; m Br Hannah FRY, b 20 Oct 1676 Yarmouth, Mass, dau Anthony and Hannah Fry of Br (VR Yarmouth; Rounds, 1:37). He had four ch b Br (6:99): Samuel, b 19 July 1700; Peter, b 14 July 1702; Abigail, b 22 Dec 1704; and Nathaniel, b 10 Feb 1706/07. He rem to Guilford, Conn with his father.
2. Mary, b 24 Oct 1678 Lynn; m at Taunton, Mass (Sav, 3:388) or Br (6:43) 14 Apr 1698 Jeremiah FAIRBANKS of Taunton, b 1676 per d rec, who lived in Br and d there 28 Mar 1736, 60 yr (6:130). Mary had the fol ch b Br, surname Fairbanks (6:75): Mary, b 22 Aug 1692 (sic, prob 1699); David, b 7 Feb 1700/01; Abigail, b 17 Apr 1703; Sarah, b 4 Apr 1705; Elizabeth, b 4 Apr 1707; Jerusha, b 5 Sept 1708; Hannah, b 28 Apr 1710; Deborah, b 8 Feb 1712/13; Jonathan, b 29 Mar 1714; Nathaniel, b 2 Mar 1716; Jeremiah, b 8 Jan 1717/18; Rebecca, b 25 Jan 1719/20; and Benjamin, b 23 May 1722.
3. Sarah, b 20 Feb 1680 Rehoboth (VR Re, p 713). Not mentioned by Sav.
4. John, b 30 May 1681 Rehoboth (Sav, 3:388) or b "last of May, 1683" Rehoboth (VR Re, p 713); m 1714 Ann CORNWALL (Virkus, 5:412).
5. Isaac, b 27 July 1685 Br. An Isaac Penfield was on the muster roll from Guilford, Conn in the old French War (Steiner, p 424).

   6. Hannah, b 29 Oct 1687 Br.
   7. Jonathan, b 21 Nov 1689 Br.

CHILDREN by second wife, Anne, b Br (6:99):
   8. Rebecca, b 23 Oct 1692, twin.
   9. Abigail, b 23 Oct 1692, twin.

CHILD by third wife, Mary, b Br (6:99):
  10. Benjamin, b 26 Apr 1696.

63. JOHN POPE

The only rec in Br of John Pope is his name at the 1681 town meeting. The VR Br have no m's, b's or d's of early Popes. He apparently never lived in Br, and prob he soon sold his land there. Colket, p 228 listed only one John Pope, who came to New England in 1637, was in Dorchester, Mass in 1643, and d there 18 Oct 1686. Torrey, p 593 listed John Pope Sr who was in Dorchester and d there in 1649, and his poss son, John Jr, also of Dorchester, who d in 1686. Perhaps John Jr bought the land in Br, or his own son, John, b Dorchester 1 July 1658, did so (Sav, 3:458).

64. EDMUND RANGER

The parentage, date and place of b of Edmund Ranger are unkn. He was a stationer or binder in Boston, and lived there from 1671 until 1681. He lived in Br from 1682 until at least 1689, and then prob returned to Boston. He m three times, prob in Boston: m (1) by 1672 Sarah FULLER, dau Robert, who d bef 1676; m (2) Anna SMITH by 1676; and m (3) by 1680 Mary (PEARSE?)/GATLINE (Sav, 3:507; Torrey, p 611). He was a freeman of Boston in 1671. His third wife and ch came to Br with him. He apparently had no ch by his second m, and his first wife, Sarah, did not have a Myflwr desc. The 1689 Census of Br showed him there with a wife, four ch, and no servants (Geneals RI Fams, 1989, 2:402) so he rem from Br aft then.

CHILDREN by first wife, Sarah (Sav, 3:507):
   1. Prudence, b 5 Nov 1672 Boston.
   2. John, b 16 Apr 1674 Boston; m (int) Boston 9 Oct 1695 Elizabeth WYLLS (Torrey, p 611).

CHILDREN by third wife, Mary (Sav, 3:507; 6:100):
   3. Samuel, b 29 Mar 1681 Boston. (sic, prob earlier).
   4. Stephen, b 24 Mar 1681/82 Br.
   5. Mary, b 9 Sept 1685 Br.
   6. Amos, b 17 Feb 1687 Br.
   7. Sarah, b 15 Sept 1692, poss Boston.

65. INCREASE ROBINSON SR

Increase[2] Robinson Sr was b Dorchester, Mass 14 Mar 1642 and d Taunton, Mass 1699 (Sav, 3:555; Torrey, p 629), son of William Robinson. William was in Dorchester in 1636 and was a member of the Anc and Hon Artill Co in 1643. Increase m 19 Jan or Feb 1663/64 Sarah PENNIMAN (Torrey, p 629). Sarah was prob of Braintree, Mass since Sav, 3:555 said that Increase's sister, Waiting, m Joseph Penniman of Braintree, and that Joseph's father, James Penniman of Boston and Braintree, and his wife Lydia, had a dau Sarah b 6 May 1641 (Ibid, 3:389). Although Increase was at the first town meeting of Br, he apparently never lived there, as there are no recs for his family in the VR Br. He prob lived in Taunton. The ch of Increase Sr were named in the will of his son, Josiah Robinson of Taunton, dtd 16 Aug 1703 and pvd 4 June 1705, he "being pressed to goe forth to the Eastward against the Indians". Josiah named brothers Increase and Ebenezer Robinson; four sisters, Sarah Dean, Hannah Williams, Bethia Pitts and Abigail Robinson; honored mother (unnamed); and mentioned his lands in Taunton, Dorchester and in the North Purchase (Rounds, 2:33).

CHILDREN b Taunton, order of b unkn:
1. Increase[3] Jr, d 1738; m 11 Feb 1695 Mehitable WILLIAMS, b 7 June 1676, dau Joseph and Elizabeth (Watson) Williams of Taunton (Torrey, p 820; Sav, 4:563). He lived in Taunton (Torrey, p 629). The will of Joseph Williams, dtd 5 July 1695, named eldest dau, Mahettabell Robinson (Rounds, 1:11). Joseph was the son of Richard[1] and Frances (Deighton) Williams, and all of his desc have a number of royal lines from Frances Deighton, dau Dr John and Jane (Basset) Deighton of Gloucester, Eng (TAG, 1933, 9:212-222).
2. Ebenezer, named in brother, Josiah's will dtd 16 Aug 1703.
3. Josiah, d betw his will dtd 16 Aug 1703 and its proving 4 June 1705, prob unm. No issue. See his will above (Rounds, 2:33).
4. Sarah, b 1667?; d 1741; m 15 Dec 1692 Samuel DEAN, b 24 Jan 1667 and d 1731 Taunton (Torrey, p 212), son John and Sarah (Edson) Dean Jr of Taunton (Sav, 2:29).
5. Hannah, b 8 Mar 1670; d 2 Dec 1757; m by 1701 John WILLIAMS, b 27 Aug 1675, d Taunton 18 Aug 1724, son John and Elizabeth (Rogers) Williams of Taunton (Torrey, p 820). Her six ch have a Myflwr desc from Thomas Rogers (Myflwr Fams thru Five Generations, 2:205-206). They were b Taunton, surname Williams: Nathaniel who m Sarah DEAN, Experience who m Capt Nathan(iel) HODGES (Ibid, p 310), Silas, John, Timothy and Simeon.
6. Bethiah, m Peter PITTS of Taunton (Torrey, p 589).
7. Abigail, named in brother, Josiah's will.

66. JOHN ROGERS JR

John^3 Rogers Jr was b ca 1640 prob in Duxbury, Mass, and d in Barrington, RI 28 June 1732, son of John and Anna (Churchman) Rogers Sr (Myflwr Fams thru Five Generations, Thomas Rogers, 3:158, 164-165). John Jr does not appear in the VR of Barrington. He m (1) Duxbury Nov 1666 Elizabeth PABODIE, b Duxbury 24 Apr 1647 and d betw 4 May 1677 and Oct 1679, dau William and Elizabeth (Alden) Pabodie. She was a gdau of John Alden of the Myflwr. John Rogers m (2) 21 Oct 1679 Hannah (HOBART) BROWNE, b Hingham, Mass 15 May 1638 and d Br 11 Sept 1691, dau Rev Peter Hobart of Hingham and wid of John Browne of Salem, Mass; and he m (3) aft 22 Mar 1692/93 Marah (COBHAM) BROWNING, b Salisbury, Mass 21 May 1652 and d 1739 in Rehoboth, dau Josiah and Mary (Haffield) Cobham and wid of Joseph Browning (Bruning?) of Boston. John had no issue by his second and third wives. He was a merchant, and lived in Boston, Taunton, Swansea, Br, and Barrington. At the time of his d he had been blind for some time.

CHILDREN by first wife, Elizabeth, b Duxbury (Myflwr Fams thru Five Generations, Thomas Rogers, 2:165):
 1. Hannah^4, b 16 Nov 1668, d prob Hingham betw 1 June 1747 and 5 Nov 1754; m Plymouth, Mass 31 July 1689 Samuel BRADFORD, b Plymouth ca 1667, d Duxbury 11 Apr 1714 ae 46, son William and Alice (Richards) Bradford. Samuel was a desc of William Bradford of the Myflwr. Hannah had seven ch b Plymouth, surname Bradford (Ibid, p 190): Hannah, b 14 Feb 1689/90; Gershom, b 21 Dec 1691; Perez, b 28 Dec 1694; Elizabeth, b 15 Dec 1696; Jerusha, b 10 Mar 1699; Welthea, b 15 May 1702; and Gamaliel, b 18 May 1704.
 2. John, b 22 Sept 1670; d Boston 2 Nov 1696, unm.
 3. Elizabeth, b 16 Apr 1673; d Little Compton, RI 23 Oct 1724, 52 yr; m 1693 Silvester RICHMOND, b LC ca 1673, d Dartmouth, Mass 20 Nov 1754, 81 yr, son Edward and Abigail (Davis) Richmond. Elizabeth had eleven ch b LC, surname Richmond (Ibid, p 191): William, b 10 Oct 1694; Elizabeth, b 10 May 1696; Sylvester, b 30 June 1698; Peleg, b 25 Oct 1700; Perez, b 5 Oct 1702; Ichabod, b 27 Feb 1704; Ruth, b 7 Mar 1705; Hannah, b 9 July 1709; Sarah, b 31 Oct 1711; Mary, b 29 Nov 1713; and Rogers, b 25 May 1716.
 4. Ruth, b 18 Apr 1675; d 28 Apr 1725, 50 yr LC; m Br 12 July 1694 James BENNETT, b Charlestown, Mass 31 May 1666, d LC 17 Feb 1729/30, 64 yr, son John and Mary (Cobham) Bennett. No kn issue (Ibid, p 165).
 5. Sarah, b 4 May 1677; d LC 19 Jan 1769 or 1770, 92 yr; m LC 1694 Nathaniel SEARLE, b Dorchester, Mass 9 June 1662, d LC 5 Feb 1749/50, 88 yr, son Robert and Deborah (Salter) Searle. Nathaniel was the first school-

master at Little Compton, RI. Sarah had four ch b LC, surname Searle (Ibid, p 191-192): Deborah, b 17 Nov 1695; John, b 12 Mar 1698, and drowned 20 Mar 1714; Sarah, b 2 Apr 1700; and Nathaniel, b 26 Apr 1703.

67. JOHN SAFFIN

The Hon John[1] Saffin was the only person of this surname listed in either Sav, 4:3-4, or Torrey, p 646. The latter gave his date of b as "?1634", and he d in Br 29 July 1710 (Sav, 4:4). He was a lawyer, and was in Scituate by 1643, was a selectman in 1653, and owned a part of the Narragansett Lands in 1663-65. He m (1) 2 Dec 1658 Martha WILLET, b Plymouth, Mass 6 Aug 1639 and d 11 Dec 1678 of smallpox, dau Capt Thomas and Mary (Brown) Willet of Plymouth; m (2) 1680 Charlestown, Mass Elizabeth (SCAMMON) LIDGETT, who d 1682, dau Humphrey Scammon of Kittery and wid of Peter Lidget of Boston and Charlestown (Wyman, p 619, 849); and m (3) in 1688 Rebecca LEE, dau Rev Samuel Lee of Br (NER, 144:233). She m (2) 26 July 1712 Rev Joseph Baxter of Medfield, and d in 1713.

It seems unlikely that John was b as late as 1634, since he would have been only nine years old when in Scituate by 1643, and nineteen when a selectman in 1653. Aft the d of his first wife in 1678, he rem to Boston where he was made Judge of the Superior Court. In 1686 Judge Saffin was speaker of the Mass General Assembly (NER, 144:233). Sav said that by 1690 he was living in Br, where he was appointed the first Judge of Probate when Br changed to the new county and became part of RI. He was Representative from Br to the General Court of Plymouth Colony in 1689 and 1691, and to the General Court of Mass in 1692 (Munro, p 384).

The only time his name appears in the VR Br is when he was received as a member of the Congre Ch of Br on 12 July 1695, and he was rem from its membership list on 29 July 1710 (8:262). He had no ch by his second or third wives. A disagreement with his third wife caused their separation, and he left her nothing in his will. Sav, 4:3-4 said that his first "wife with two of their ch d in 1678 of smallpox, and the rest of the ch all d young". John Saffin's family was armigerous and their coat of arms was carved on the tombstone of his son, Thomas, at the Ch of St Dunstans in Stepney, London, where he d 18 June 1687 of smallpox. John Saffin's "only surviving son" was "bur Boston 15 Oct 1687 just about the time arrived the news of Thomas Saffin's death in London" (Eng Origins New Eng Fams, Second Series, 1985, 3:57).

CHILDREN by first wife, Martha (Sav, 4:3-4):
1. John[2], b 13 Sept 1659; d ae 2 yrs.
2. John II, b 14 Apr 1662.
3. Thomas, b 18 Mar 1664; d 18 June 1687 London.
4. Simon, b 4 Apr 1666.
5. Josiah, b 30 Jan 1668.
6. Joseph, b 2 Feb 1670; d.y.
7. Benjamin, b 15 June 1672; d soon.
8. Joseph II, b 24 Jan 1676.

68. JOSEPH SANDY

This surname was prob at times written Sandye, Sandys or Sands. His b date and parentage have not been discovered. Sav did not mention a Joseph of any of these surnames. Torrey, p 649, said that he was b 1660 and m Br, RI 18 Oct 1682 Bethia LUCAS. The VR Br, 6:47 calls him Sandye in the rec of this m. The date of his d is unkn. On 17 May 1685 he signed the Oath of Fidelity in Br (Munro, p 114), and he was listed in the 1689 Census of Br under Joseph Sardy with a wife and three ch (Gens RI Fams, 1989, 2:402). Since there are no m's for his family, and only the d of one dau in the VR Br, he and his family prob left Br after the b of his son, John.

CHILDREN, b Br (6:102):
1. Joseph[2], b 2 Mar 1682/83.
2. Mary, b 23 Jan 1684/85.
3. Sarah, b 7 Oct 1687.
4. Benjamin, b 30 July 1689.
5. Elizabeth, b 7 May 1691; d 27 Aug 1694 "by a blow from a horse" (6:161).
6. Bethia, b 11 May 1693.
7. John, b 21 Jan 1694/95.

69. JOHN SMITH

The parentage, and date and place of b, of the John Smith who was at the first town meeting of Br, are not kn. Torrey, p 684 said he m Susanna, surname unkn, had a ch b 1678, and was of Portsmouth, RI, Newport, RI, and ?Br, RI by 1686. Sav, 4:123 said of him only that he was of Newport and by wife, Susanna, had Rebecca, b 14 Oct 1678. The VR Br (6:103) list three ch b Br betw 1686 and 1692 to them, and then they disappeared from the recs, and must have rem elsewhere. They prob had other ch b betw 1678 and 1686. The VR Newport, 4:115 do not give any ch b there to a John and Susanna Smith.

KNOWN CHILDREN (6:103; Sav, 4:123):
1. Rebecca[2], b 14 Oct 1678, prob Portsmouth or Newport, RI.
2. Mary, b 14 Aug 1686 Br.
3. John, b 28 Oct 1689 Br.
4. Thomas, b 19 Oct 1692 Br.

70. RICHARD SMITH

See also: RIGR, 1990, Vol 13, p 234-254.

Richard[1] Smith was b 1643 in London, England and in 1673 came to Boston, Mass. He rem to Br, RI on 9 Nov 1680, and lived there until he d in 1696. He was the second town clerk of Br, a mason and stonecutter, and built his house near the corner of Hope and Constitution Streets. He took the Oath of Fidelity in Br on 20 June 1683 (Munro, p 93, 114). Another Richard Smith from Gloucester, Eng in 1641 bought land from the Narragansett Indians in what became RI, and was the first white man to build a house, which he used as a trading post, near Wickford Cove in what is now No. Kingston. His son, Major Richard Smith Jr, was on the Council of Sir Edmund Andros and was Assistant for RI in 1672-1673. These two families should not be confused.

Richard Smith of Br m in Eng Joyce___, who d Br aft 10 June 1710, the date of the div of his est. This div named wife Joyce Smith; his five ch, viz: dau-in-law Mercy Smith, wid of his eldest son, John, on behalf of John's one son and two daus; Nathaniel Smith; Samuel Smith; Daniel Smith; and Hannah Eddy wid (Rounds, 1:28).

KNOWN CHILDREN (6:103). He prob had others b betw 1672 and 1681, who d.
1. John[2], prob b Eng; d bef div of father's est 10 June 1710; m Mercy___. Had one son and two daus, names unkn (Rounds, 1:28).
2. Hannah, b ca 1672, poss in Eng; d Br 16 Jan 1755, age 83, as Mrs Hannah Adey (6:114); m Br 19 July 1697 William ADY/EDDY (6:49; Torrey, p 242) who d bef 10 June 1710. Hannah's will, dtd 13 Apr 1740 and pvd 3 Feb 1755, named her sons Joseph, William and John Eddy; dau Elizabeth "Daks"; and her brother Samuel Smith, exec. There are no recs of the surname Daks in Br or Newport. The VR Br, 6:17 give the m on 30 Apr 1723 of Elizabeth Eddy and David DEAUR of Newport, RI. The recs of the b of Hannah's above named four ch are in 6:74; her will RIGR, 3:137.
3. Nathaniel, b 17 May 1681 (6:103); d 22 Mar 1751, 70 yr (6:162); m Abigail___ who d Br as wid, 9 Dec 1759 (6:162). He had nine ch b Br (6:103): Mary, b 12 Apr

1709, d 6 Nov 1775, m 7 Apr 1732 John HASKILL who d Nov 1737 at Woodstock; Abigail, b 18 Feb 1711, m Br 28 Mar 1736 Ralph STANHOPE of Newport; Nathaniel, b 29 June 1713, d 26 Dec 1747 in shipwreck returning from Surinam, m as Nathaniel Jr, Br 21 May 1746 Mrs Phebe MANCHESTER; Hannah, b 4 Apr 1715, d 13 July 1746, m (int) 6 Nov 1735 Thomas MARTIN, b 7 Apr 1715 Br, d Antigua, WI 1758, son William and Christian (Pelton) Martin; Priscilla, b 16 May 1717, d 19 Feb 1753, m Br 29 May 1738 Charles MUNRO, b 9 Jan 1716/17, d 11 Jan 1798, 82 yr, son Benjamin and Mary Munro of Br; Mercy, b 29 Jan 1719/20; Lydia, b 8 June 1722; Martha, b 11 Mar 1724/25 who prob m Br 28 May 1749 Esbon/Eben SAN(D)FORD of Newport who d there 22 Jan 1759; and William, b 14 Jan 1727/28, d 13 Aug 1736, 8 yr.
<u>4</u>. Samuel, b 24 June 1683; d 18 Nov 1766, 85 yr (sic) (6:163); m (1) Sarah___ who d Apr 1744; m (2) Br 21 Aug 1744 Martha () GLADDING, wid of John Gladding.
<u>5</u>. Daniel, b 2 Mar 1687/88; d 21 Aug 1741, 54 yr (6:-162); m by 1712 Elizabeth CAREY, b 7 Mar 1691/92 (6:68), d 1 Sept 1772, 81 yr, Br (6:163), dau David and Elizabeth (Brackett) Carey of Br.

Samuel^2 (Richard^1) Smith was b Br 24 June 1683 (6:103), and d there 18 Nov 1766, 85 yr (sic) (6:163). He m (1) Sarah___ who d Apr 1744; and m (2) 21 Aug 1744 Martha () GLADDING, wid of John. She d 6 June 1759, 73 yr per GB, p 43-44 (which is incorrect), or d Br 6 June 1767, 73 yr as Martha Smith (6:163). She was alive 17 Aug 1765 when named in Samuel's will. Samuel was made a freeman of RI from Br in 1747 (MacGunnigle, p 41). The will of Samuel Smith of Br, gentleman, advanced in age, dtd 17 Aug 1765 and pvd 1 Dec 1766, mentioned an unnamed former wife; wife Martha who received "stuff she brought to me at the time of our marriage"; two sons, Benjamin and Richard Smith; gsons Stephen and James Smith, and Samuel (no surname); gdaus Sarah Allen, Elizabeth West, Esther Ormsby, Mary Smith, and Sarah Hull (RIGR, 6:152). The identity of the parents of gdau Sarah Hull has not been found.

CHILDREN, all by first wife, Sarah, b Br (6:103):
<u>1</u>. Samuel^3 Jr, b not rec but bef 1710; d as Samuel Jr 6 Sept 1746 (6:162); m Br 10 May 1731 Elizabeth DROWNE (6:49).
2. Sarah, b 24 Apr 1710; prob d 17 Dec 1738 (6:162).
3. Eliza, bp 12 July 1713 Congre Ch, Br (Geneals RI Fams, 1989, 2:379); prob d bef father's will of 17 Aug 1765.
<u>4</u>. Benjamin, b 2 July 1716; d 4 Apr 1784, 68 yr (8:390); m (1) 31 May 1739 Abigail CHURCH (6:50) who d 9 Aug

1751, 40 yr (6:162); m (2) Br 29 Oct 1752 Mrs Sarah MAY (6:50) who d 17 Mar 1764 (6:163).
5. Richard, b 25 May 1720; d 6 Feb 1813, 92 or 93 yr (6:163); m (1) Br 24 Dec 1741 Lucretia DIMAN (6:50), who d Br 31 Jan 1790, 71 yr (8:390); m (2) 25 Jan 1792 Mrs Ruth JAMES of Providence, RI (6:50).

Samuel^3 Jr (Samuel^2, Richard^1) Smith was b Br bef 1710 and d there as Samuel Jr 6 Sept 1746 (6:162). He m Br 10 May 1731 Elizabeth DROWNE (6:49), b Boston, Mass 8 Sept 1710 and d Br 6 May 1765, 56 yr, as wid (6:163), dau Solomon and Esther/Hester (prob Bosworth) Drown. The will of Samuel Smith Jr of Br, cordwainer, dtd 18 Aug 1746 and pvd 4 Nov 1746, named wife Elizabeth; his eight ch, Samuel (eldest) (sic, eldest son), Stephen, James, Sarah, Elizabeth, Easther, Mary and Hannah (no surnames); his wife to be exec (Rounds, 2:18).

CHILDREN, all b Br (6:103):
1. Sarah^4, b 16 Feb 1731/32; d Br 14 Dec 1772, 41 yrs, wid (6:114); m Br 9 June 1751 James ALLEN (6:50), bp St Michael's Ch, Br, 19 July 1730 (8:145), d at sea 7 Dec 1769 (8:114), son William and Lydia Allen. Sarah had five ch, surname Allen, bp Congre Ch, Br (6:270): Sarah, James, Hannah, Samuel and Lydia.
2. Elizabeth, b 14 Dec 1733; m Br 7 June 1753 Benjamin WEST (6:50). She was named as Elizabeth West in the will of her gfather, Samuel Smith (RIGR, 6:152).
3. E(a)sther, b not rec but named in father's will; m (1) as Esther 15 Dec 1757 Capt James GOFF of Rehoboth, Mass (6:50), prob b Re 8 June 1736 (VR Re, p 454, 620), son James and Mary (Ormsbee) Goff of Re (VR Re, p 152); m (2) 12 Oct 1764 Capt Ezra ORMSBY (6:24). The Pat Index, p 506 listed Ezra Ormsby, b 1734, d 23 Mar 1796, m (2) Esther (Smith) Goff, and who was a Capt from RI in the Rev War.
4. Mary, b 25 Jan 1736/37; prob the gdau, Mary Smith, named in her gfather, Samuel Smith's will of 17 Aug 1765.
5. Samuel, b 11 Apr 1739.
6. Stephen, b 22 Apr 1741, bp 14 June 1741 Congre Ch Br (8:286); d 3 or 4 Nov 1799, 59 yr as Esq (6:163); m (1) Br 13 Oct 1763 Mary GORHAM (6:50); m (2) 1 Dec 1785 Ruth BOSWORTH (8:350).
7. Hannah, b 30 Apr 1743, bp 1 May 1743 Congre Ch Br (8:286).
8. James, b 3 May 1745, bp 5 May 1745 Congre Ch Br (Ibid); d 30 June 1826 (Pat Index, p 626); m Br 2 Dec 1767 Phebe WARDWELL (6:50), b Br 23 Jan 1748/49 (6:110),

d 23 Sept 1840, 92 yr, wid of James (6:164), dau John and Phebe (Howland) Wardwell. Phebe Howland's desc have a Myflwr line from John Howland. The Pat Index, p 626, listed James Smith as a Soldier, Guard, and with Public Service from RI during the Rev War, and his wid, Phebe, was granted a pension. James had the fol ch, b Br (6:104): Martha, Phebe and Elizabeth, who were all bp 19 July 1772 at the Congre Ch, Br, and Nathaniel Wardwell, bp there 9 Oct 1774 (8:287).

Benjamin^3 (Samuel^2, Richard^1) Smith was b 2 July 1716 and d Br 4 Apr 1784, 68 yr (8:390). He m (1) Br 31 May 1739 Abigail (HOWLAND) CHURCH (6:14, 30), b ca 1711 from d rec, and d 9 Aug 1751, 40 yr (6:162), dau Deacon Samuel and Abigail (Carey) Howland, and wid of Israel Church (LC Fams, p 172).He m (2) Br 29 Oct 1752 Mrs Sarah MAY (6:50), who d Br 17 May 1764 (6:163). The 1774 Census of Br showed Benjamin as head of a household there of three males above 16, one male under 16, two females above 16, and one female under 16 (Bartlett, p 183). Abigail's ch have a Myflwr desc from Richard Warren.

CHILDREN by first wife, Abigail, b Br (6:103):
1. Capt Benjamin Jr, b 1 May 1740; d 6 May 1801; m Br 18 Sept 1764 Mrs Jemima (LINDSEY) WARDWELL (6:50), b Br 20 May 1719 and d 9 Sept 1796, 78 yr (6:163), dau John and Elizabeth (Munro) Lindsey of Br (6:87), and wid of Joseph Wardwell Jr (6:56). No issue.
2. Josiah, b 7 June 1742; d Br 22 June 1837, 95 yr (6:164); m (1) Br 5 July 1764 "Mrs" Eleanor TAYLOR who d bef 22 Aug 1776; m (2) Aug 1776 "Mrs" Elizabeth REYNOLDS who d 2 Oct 1797, 47 yr (6:163); m (3) Mary WARDWELL who d Br 26 Mar 1821.
3. Nathaniel, b 30 Jan 1744/45; d 9 Oct 1828, 84 yr (6:163); m (1) Br 27 Oct 1768 Parnel TAYLOR who d aft 9 Jan 1781; m (2) as Nathaniel 1st Br 26 Feb 1791 Mrs Amarentia (FALES) MUNRO (8:350).
4. Joseph, b 25 Aug 1747, bp Congre Ch, Br 30 Aug 1747; d aft 16 Feb 1804; m 18 May 1769 Molly MILLER "both of Warren" (6:50; War, 6:37), b Warren, RI 14 Feb 1750 (War, 6:81), d aft 22 June 1793, last ch b 23 June 1793 (War, 6:90), dau Barnard and Elizabeth (Hicks) Miller of Swansea and Warren (War, 6:31). He had the fol ch b Warren (War, 6:90): Barnard who m Elizabeth DEWOLF; Benjamin; Joseph; William; James; Anthony; Job and Molly, twins; Sally, and Eliza.
5. Samuel, b 28 June 1749, bp Congre Ch, Br 2 July 1749; d 2 Aug 1751 (6:162).

CHILD by second wife, Sarah, b Br (6:103):
6. Samuel II, bp 22 Mar 1761 Congre Ch, Br; d Br 14

Sept 1823, 63 yr (6:163); m 1785 Phebe PEARSE of Rehoboth. "Phebe Smith of Samuel" joined the Congre Ch, Br 7 June 1795 and was rem from membership on 9 Aug 1858, prob by d (8:263). He had three ch bp Congre Ch, Br, all on 14 June 1795 (8:287): Benjamin, Sarah, and Ruth. Samuel's will, he of Br, husbandman, dtd 12 Sept 1823 and pvd 3 Nov 1823, named wife Phebe Smith; son Benjamin Smith; daus Sarah wife of James Smith, and Ruth wife of Allen Munro (RIGR, 9:58-59).

Josiah[4] (Benjamin[3], Samuel[2], Richard[1]) Smith was b Br 7 June 1742 (6:103), and d there 22 June 1837, 95 yr (6:164). He m (1) Br 5 July 1764 "Mrs" Eleanor TAYLOR (6:50) who d bef 22 Aug 1776; m (2) by Joseph Reynolds 22 Aug 1776 "Mrs" Elizabeth RAYNOLDS (6:50), by Br 21 Sept 1750 (6:100), and d 2 Oct 1797, 47 yr (6:163), dau Joseph and Lydia (Greenwood) Reynolds Jr; m (3) Mary WARDWELL, b Br 6 Jan 1753 (6:110), d Br 26 Mar 1821, dau John and Phebe (Howland) Wardwell of Br. Josiah had no issue by his third m. He was a Private from RI in the Rev War (Pat Index, p 627). The 1774 Census of RI shows Josiah in Br, head of a household of twelve: two males above 16, two males under 16, four females above 16, three females under 16, and one black (Bartlett, p 182).

The will of Josiah Smith of Br, yeoman, advanced in age, was dtd 10 Apr 1817, codicil of 26 Mar 1821, and pvd 3 July 1837 (RIGR, 10:152-153). He mentioned his wife, Mary, who received "furniture she brought" to their m; three daus, Abigail wife of Allen Wardwell, Rebecca Smith, and Elizabeth wid of the late Allen Bourne; gson Josiah Smith Wardwell, and gdau Eleanor Taylor Wardwell, dau of Allen and Abigail Wardwell; gdau Ruth Waldron Bourne under 18, dau of late Allen Bourne. His codicil named his seven gch of son-in-law Allen Wardwell, viz: gsons Allen Wardwell Jr, George S. Wardwell, Josiah S. Wardwell, and William T. Wardwell, and gdaus Eleanor T. Wardwell, Nancy R. Wardwell, and Mary S. Wardwell; also four gch, the ch of late son-in-law Allen Bourne dec, viz: gson George J. Bourn and gdaus Ruth W. Bourn, Rebecca S. Bourn, and Elizabeth A. Bourn.

CHILDREN by first wife, Eleanor, b Br, and bp Congre Ch, Br (6:103-104):
1. Abigail[5], b 3 Oct 1765, bp 27 Oct 1771 (8:287); d 6 Oct 1844, 79 yr; m Congre Ch, Br 3 Sept 1786 Allen WARDWELL (8:350), b 1 Mar 1765 (6:111), d 31 Mar 1840, 76 yr (6:171), son John and Phebe (Howland) Wardwell (6:56). Abigail had seven ch, surname Wardwell, named in the will of her father, Josiah Smith, above. Her ch all have a Myflwr desc through Phebe Howland from John Howland.

2. Rebecca, b 13 Dec 1767, bp 27 Oct 1771 (8:287); d 4 June 1846, 79 yr "Rebecca of Josiah", unm (6:164).
3. Benjamin, b 8 Nov 1769, bp 27 Oct 1771 (8:287), d bef father's will of 10 Apr 1817; m Br Congre Ch 6 Nov 1794 Elizabeth BOURNE (8:350), b 14 July 1774 (6:64), d 11 Oct 1796, 23 yr (6:163), dau Shearjashub and Ruth (Waldron) Bourne Jr of Br. No kn issue.
4. Susannah, b 5 Dec 1771, bp 24 May 1772 (8:287); d 15 Oct 1797, 25 yr, unm (6:163; 8:390).
5. Barnabus Taylor, b 22 Jan 1774, bp 5 June 1774 (8:-287; d 19 Jan 1775, 1 yr (6:163).
6. Ch "of Josiah" b and d __ __ 1775.

CHILDREN by second wife, Elizabeth, all bp Congre Ch, Br on 11 Sept 1788 (8:287):
7. Josiah Jr, b 24 Aug 1779 (6:104); d 18 Sept 1796, 21 yr (sic) at Charleston, SC (6:163).
8. George Reynolds, b 5 Sept 1781; d 29 Apr 1805, 25 yr, unm (6:163). The will of George Reynolds Smith of Br, dtd 16 Feb 1804 and pvd 3 June 1805, named father Joseph (sic, Josiah) Smith, living; sisters Abigail wife of Allen Wardwell, Rebecca Smith, Elizabeth Smith, and Mary Smith (RIGR, 6:158-159). The will of George's father, Josiah, given above, proves his parentage by naming his four sisters.
9. Jonathan, b 15 May 1784; d 13 Oct 1797 (6:163; 8:-390).
10. Elizabeth, b 27 Feb 1786; d aft 10 Apr 1817, date of father's will; m Congre Ch, Br 7 June 1805 Allen BOURNE (8:350), b 25 June 1779 (6:64), d 8 Dec 1814, 35 yr (6:118), son Shearjashub and Ruth (Waldron) Bourne Jr. Elizabeth had four ch b Br, surname Bourne, named in her father's will above.
11. Mary, b 4 Feb 1788; d 19 Apr 1806, 18 yr (6:163).
12. Eleanor, b 1789; d 21 Oct 1797, 8 yr, "Eleanor of Josiah" (8:390).

Nathaniel[4] (Benjamin[3], Samuel[2], Richard[1]) Smith was b Br 30 June 1744 (6:103) and d there 9 Oct 1828, 84 yr (6:163). He, "of Benjamin", m (1) Br by Rev John Burt 27 Oct 1768 Parnel TAYLOR (6:50), who d aft 9 Jan 1781, dau Rev Barnabus Taylor, dec. He m (2) as Nathaniel 1st, in Congre Ch, Br 26 Feb 1791 Amarentia (FALES) MUNRO, b 31 Mar 1754 (6:75), d 1 May 1841, 87 yr (6:164), dau Jonathan and Hannah (Peck) Fales (6:20), and wid of (poss Henry) Munro. No rec of Amarentia's m to a Munro was found. She joined the Congre Ch, Br on 5 June 1796. The will of Nathaniel Smith of Br, yeoman, was dtd 8 Feb 1815 with codicils of 26 May 1817 and 14 Jan 1828, and pvd 5 Jan 1829. He named wife Amarenthia; sons Allin Taylor

Smith under 21, and Nathaniel Smith Jr dec, leaving wid Rebecca Smith and unnamed ch; daus Eleanor wife of Capt John Munro, Polly wife of Capt William Bradford, and Nancy dec, wife of John W. Russell late dec, leaving unnamed ch; gdau Paniel (sic, Parnel) Taylor Russell; and brother Josiah Smith. The first codicil said his dau Eleanor Munro d last winter; the second codicil named friend John Wardwell to be joint exec with his wife and son (RIGR, 9:-61).

CHILDREN by first wife, Parnel, all b Br except Eleanor (6:104), and bp Congre Ch, Br (8:287):
1. Nancy^5, b 16 Jan 1770; d 24 Sept 1775, 6 yr (6:163).
2. Martha, b 1 Dec 1771; prob d bef father's will of 8 Feb 1815 as not named in it.
3. Nathaniel Jr, b unrec, bp 14 Jan 1772 Br per IGI RI; d bef 8 Feb 1815, poss June 1811 (6:163); m 1 Feb 1801 Rebecca SMITH of Dighton, per Elder Wight's Publishments (8:317). His father's will mentioned his unnamed ch. The VR Br (6:104) give one ch of his: John Munro Smith, b 3 June 1802.
4. Allen Taylor, b 25 Apr 1773; d "Allen of Nathaniel" 18 Sept 1775, 2 yr 2 mo (6:163).
5. Nancy II, b 7 May 1775; d 5 Sept 1810, 36 yr (6:160); m Congre Ch Br 1 June 1802 Capt John Willard RUSSELL, who d 20 Aug 1814, 44 yr (6:160), son Nathaniel and Elizabeth Russell. Nancy had four ch b Br, surname Russell (6:101): Betsey Bourne, Parnell Taylor, Nancy Smith and John.
6. Eleanor, b 11 Feb 1777 Rehoboth, Mass; d winter of 1816/17; m Congre Ch, Br 19 May 1799 Capt John MUNRO who d 12 Sept 1807, 31 yr (6:150). No issue found in VR Br.
7. Mary/Polly, bp as Polly 1779 Br per IGI RI; m as Mary Congre Ch, Br 1 Feb 1804 Capt William BRADFORD 3rd (6:50; 8:350), b Rehoboth 2 Feb 1781 (6:65) and d Br 23 Apr 1851, 70 yr (6:119), son Major William and Elizabeth Bradford Jr of Rehoboth. Polly had four ch b Br, surname Bradford (6:65): William Parnell, Edward James, Allen Taylor Smith, and Nancy Smith. The VR Re do not show any ch b to William and Elizabeth Bradford.
8. Allen Taylor II, b 10 Jan 1781; d 28 July 1795, 15 yr "of Nathaniel 1st" (6:163).

CHILD by second wife, Amarentia (6:104):
9. Allen Taylor III, b 27 June 1797, bp Congre Ch, Br 10 Sept 1797 (8:287); d Br 11 May 1842, 44 yr (6:164). No m or issue found in the VR Br.

Richard^3 (Samuel^2, Richard^1) Smith was b Br 25 May 1720 and d Br 6 Feb 1813, 92 or 93 yr (6:163). He m (1) Br 24 Dec 1741 Lucretia DIMAN (6:50), b 1719, d 31 Jan 1790, 71 yr (6:163), dau Thomas Diman of Br, yeoman, whose will, dtd 6 July 1749 and pvd 4 July 1754, named his dau Lucritia wife of Richard Smith (RIGR, 3:137). He m (2) 25 Jan 1792 Mrs Ruth JAMES of Providence, RI. The will of Richard Smith Esq of Br, in old age, dtd 1 Mar 1808 and pvd 1 Mar 1813, named wife Ruth; son Richard Smith; daus Lucretia Gladding and Rebecca Munro; gsons John Gladding Jr and Josiah Munro; gdaus Lucretia Sabin and Sarah Church; gtgsons Richard Gladding and Richard son of Ambrose Waldron (RIGR, 7:165).

CHILDREN, all by first wife, Lucretia, b Br (6:103), bp Congre Ch, Br (Geneals RI Fams, 1989, 2:385-391):
  1. Lucretia, b 7 May 1743, bp 8 May 1743; d 5 May 1813, 70 yr (6:135); m Br 17 Sept 1761 John GLADDING Jr (6:50), b 3 Jan 1739/40 (6:78), d 25 Sept 1820, 81 yr (6:135), son Capt John and Mary (Drowne) Gladding of Br. She had ten ch surname Gladding, b Br (6:78-79): John, Hannah, Lucretia, Capt Samuel, Richard, Benjamin, Polly/Molly, Richard II, Sarah, and Lucretia II.
  2. Thomas, b 11 Mar 1744/45, bp 14 Apr 1745; d 29 Oct 1746 (6:162).
  3. Richard, b 10 Mar 1747/48, bp 20 Mar 1748; d 26 Sept 1749 (Ibid).
  4. Rebecca, b 1 July 1750, bp 5 Aug 1750; d 3 Nov 1827, 78 yr, wid (6:150); m 28 Nov 1769 Br Deacon Archibald MUNRO of Br (6:50), b 11 Nov 1746 (6:91), d 15 Jan 1812, 65 yr (6:150), son Simeon and Rebecca (Wardwell) Munro of Br.The VR Br (6:93) list five of her ch b Br, surname Munro: Josiah, Mary, George, Rebecca, and Jeremiah. Archibald Munro was a Private from RI in the Rev War (Pat Index, p 474).
  5. Richard II, b 16 Apr 1753, bp 25 May 1753; d Br 17 Oct 1832, 80 yr, as Esq (6:163); m by 1784 Susanna TREBY (prob of Newport, RI) who d Br 31 Aug 1841 as "Susan, wid of Richard". A Peter Treby m 2 Apr 1741 Susannah Church in the 2nd Congre Ch of Newport (8:477), and they may have been her parents. They and six of their ch are bur in the Common Bur Ground of Newport (VR RI, Beaman, New Series, 11:415). This surname does not appear in the VR Br. No b's of ch of Richard Smith Jr are given in the VR Br, but they list the fol d's (6:163): Richard, d 23 Aug 1785, 3w; ch d 18 Sept 1790, 12 hours; Samuel, d 23 June 1801, 14 yr. Richard Jr's will, he of Br far advanced in life, dtd 28 May 1832 and pvd 5 Nov 1832, named: father Richard Smith dec; wife Susanna; daus Sarah wife of William Pearse 2nd, Susanna wid of Thomas Moore dec, and Mary P. wife of Nathaniel P. Paine; and unfortunate gson Jeremiah Pearse son of Sarah and William Pearse 2nd (RIGR, 10:150). None of these m's is in the VR Br. Richard Jr was a Sgt and gave Public Service

from RI in the Rev War, and his wid, Susanna, received a pension for his service (Pat Index, p 629).
6. Sarah, bp 3 Aug 1755.
7. Hannah, bp 12 Nov 1758.

Stephen[4] (Samuel[3,2], Richard[1]) Smith was b Br 22 Apr 1741 (6:103), bp Congre Ch, Br 14 June 1741 (8:286), and d Br 3 or 4 Nov 1799, 59 yr as Esq (6:163). He m (1) Br 13 Oct 1763 Mary GORHAM (6:50), b 28 July 1743 (6:80), d 12 Jan 1785 (6:163), dau Isaac and Jemima (Potter) Gorham. Mary's desc have a Myflwr line from Capt John Gorham who m Desire Howland, dau of John Howland. Stephen m (2) 1 Dec 1785 Ruth BOSWORTH (8:350), b Br 28 July 1760 (6:64), d 25 Mar 1823, 63 yr, wid (6:163), dau Samuel and Elizabeth (Peck) Bosworth of Br.

The will of Stephen Smith Esq of Br, dtd 1 Apr 1799 with a codicil dtd 17 July 1799, and pvd 2 Dec 1799, named present wife Ruth, who was pregnant at date of codicil; brother-in-law Samuel Bosworth Esq; sons Samuel, Henry and Benjamin Bosworth Smith, last two under 21; daus Mary Fales, Hannah Dury, Lydia D'Wolf, Sukey Jarvis Spaulding Sarah Crossman, Harriot Smith unm, and Elizabeth Peck dec; each of the daus by my present wife, viz: Louisa (Smith), Ruth (Smith), and Elizabeth Bosworth (Smith), all under 21 and unm; and the ch of my dec dau Elizabeth Peck, viz: Nicholas, John and Mary Peck (RIGR, 7:167-168). The will of Jemima Gorham of Br, wife of Isaac Gorham, was dtd 13 May 1806 and pvd Nov 1806. Among others it mentioned her dau (unnamed) wife of Stephen Smith; to the ch of Stephen Smith and his wife my dau (no name) $1000., viz: Hannah wife of Dr Dury, Mary Fales wid, Susan Spaulding wid, Sally Prossman (sic, Crossman), Harriot Smith, Samuel Smith, and Lydia wife of Levi D'Wolfe, and ch of Elizabeth Peck dec, namely Mary, Nicholas and John (RIGR, 6:159-161).

CHILDREN by first wife, Mary, b Br, order of b unkn for last three (6:103):
1. Mary[5], b 18 July 1764; d 5 Oct 1814, 50 yr, wid (6:131); m by 1783 William FALES, b 6 Mar 1758 (6:75), d 22 Jan 1797, 39 yr (6:131), son Nathaniel and Sarah (Little) Fales of Br. Mary had five ch b Br, surname Fales (6:76), bp Congre Ch, Br (8:275): Stephen Smith, b 24 Nov 1783, bp 17 Nov 1789; William, b 5 Mar 1788; Lydia Smith, bp 17 Apr 1791; Edward, bp 28 July 1793; and Charlotte, bp 26 July 1795.
2. Elizabeth, b 5 June 1766; d 20 May 1796, 30 yr (6:-156); m Congre Ch, Br 2 Oct 1785 Nicholas PECK, b Br 6 May 1762 (6:98); d 1847, 86 yr (6:156), son Jonathan

and Mary (Throop) Peck of Br. Elizabeth had three kn ch b Br, surname Peck, named in the will of Jemima Gorham of Br. The VR Br, 8:284 say that on 23 Mar 1794 four persons were bp at the Congre Ch of Br, namely, Elizabeth, wife of Nicholas Peck, and Mary, Nicholas, and John "of Nicholas and Mary". This is obviously an error for of Nicholas and Elizabeth Peck. 8:284 also give the bp at the Congre Ch, Br, of other ch of theirs: Frances on 17 Aug 1794, and Elizabeth of Nicholas and Elizabeth on 5 June 1796. 6:98 gives the b of only one of these ch: John 2nd of Nicholas and Elizabeth, b 26 Sept 1791.

3. Hannah, b 23 Mar 1768; m St Michael's Ch 24 May 1787 Dr John DRURY/DEWRY (8:213) or m 18 Feb 1787 Dr John DRING (8:30). He was called Dury in the will of Hannah's father, dtd 1 Apr 1797. She had two kn ch bp St Michael's 2 May 1790 (8:155) of "Dr ___Drury": Austin and John People. Drury is prob the correct spelling.

4. Lydia Potter, b 11 Mar 1770; d Br 16 May 1825 (6:-129); m (1) Br Congre Ch 19 Aug 1792 Capt Levi DEWOLF, bp Congre Ch, Br 26 Oct 1766 (8:274), son Mark Antony and Abigail (Potter) DeWolf of Br. She had six ch b Br, surname DeWolf, bp Congre Ch (8:274): Lydia Potter, bp 21 Dec 1794 who prob m Luke DRURY; Mark Antony, bp 16 July 1797; Mary, bp 30 June 1799; Levi, bp 27 June 1802; Abigail, bp 30 June 1805; and Sarah, bp 11 Sept 1808.

5. Susannah, b 26 May 1773; d Br 21 Apr 1809, 36 yr, as "Susan, wid" (6:164); m (1) as Sukey Smith, ___ JARVIS; m (2) 1 Jan 1797 Congre Ch, Br as Sukey Jarvis Smith, Capt Edward SPAULDING (8:350), prob b 23 Aug 1767 (VR Providence, 2:247), d Br 9 Feb 1804, 36 yr (6:164), son Edward and Audr(e)y (Stafford) Spaulding of Providence, RI. The VR Br, 8:391 give the d of one ch of hers: Spaulding, Capt Edward, ch of, d 4 Aug 1803, 2w. Her father's will called her Sukey Jarvis Spaulding.

6. Stephen, b 24 Dec 1774; d Br 6 Oct 1797, 15 yr (sic) as Stephen of Stephen Esq (6:163).

7. Sarah, b unrec but named in father's will; m as "Sally" in Congre Ch, Br 19 Feb 1795 Dr Luther Andrews CROSSMAN, (8:350) who d at sea 10 June 1804 as Dr Luther Andrew Crossman (6:126). Sarah Crossman was bp as an adult at St Michael's 20 July 1806, and her two ch, John Andrews and Julia Augusta Crossman, "of Sarah", were bp there 14 Sept 1806 (8:152).

8. Samuel, b unrec but named in father's will; m Congre Ch, Br 10 Dec 1799 as "Samuel Smith of Stephen Esq and Mary" Hannah BOURNE (8:350), prob bp 10 Aug 1781, dau Shearjashub and Ruth (Waldron) Bourne Jr of Br. No ch or d's in VR Br.

9. Harriot, b unrec but named in father's will; alive and unm on 13 May 1806 when named in will of her gmother, Jemima (Potter) Gorham. The IGI RI has an entry: bp Harriot 9 Sept 1784 Providence, of Turpin Smith and Mary

131

in which the "Turpin" may be an error for Stephen. No Turpin Smith is found in the recs of Providence or Br.

CHILDREN by second wife, Ruth, bp Congre Ch, Br (8:287):
10. Louisa "of Stephen" d 22 Sept 1787, 1 yr (6:163).
11. Capt Henry, b 10 Dec 1787 (6:104), bp 30 June 1799; d 23 Aug 1821, 33 yr (8:391); m Congre Ch, Br 27 Sept 1812 Amelia MAYBERRY. He had one ch rec in the VR Br (6:104): Samuel, b 20 July 1816.
12. Louisa II, b 25 Apr 1789 (6:104), bp 30 June 1799; d 21 Apr 1834, 45 yr (6:139); m Congre Ch, Br 7 Dec 1806 John HOWE (8:350). She had one ch rec in the VR Br, surname Howe (6:82): Mark Antony DeWolf, b 5 Apr 1809.
13. Ruth, b 8 Jan 1792 (6:104), bp 30 June 1799.
14. Rev Benjamin Bosworth, b 13 June 1794 (6:104), bp 30 June 1799; d bef July 1831; m as "Rev Benjamin B." at St Michael's Ch, Br 4 June 1818 Elizabeth BOSWORTH (8:200), who m (2) St Michael's 6 July 1831 Rev Sylvester NASH (8:213). He had no issue in the VR Br.
15. Ann "of Stephen and Ruth", bp 12 Oct 1798; d 13 Oct 1798, 2 mos (8:390).
16. Elizabeth Bosworth, b unrec but named in father's will, bp 30 June 1799.
17. Ann II, b posthum, bp 4 May 1800 "of Stephen dec, and Ruth". Codicil of father's will, dtd 17 July 1799, mentioned ch his wife, Ruth, was pregnant with.

Daniel^2 (Richard^1) Smith was b Br 2 Mar 1687/88 (6:103) and d there 21 Aug 1741, 54 yr (6:162). He m by 1712 Elizabeth CAREY, b 7 Mar 1691/92 (6:68) and d Br 1 Sept 1772, 81 yr (6:163), dau David and Elizabeth (Brackett) Carey of Br. Daniel's will, dtd 14 Aug 1741 and pvd 24 Aug 1741, named wife Elizabeth; sons Daniel, eldest, John, David, William, and Nathan Smith; daus Elizabeth James, and Joyce (no surname); brother Samuel Smith to be exec (RIGR, 3: 262; Rounds, 1:311). An order to Samuel Smith of Br, cordwainer, to be exec of the est of his brother, Daniel Smith of Br, bricklayer, was dtd 24 Aug 1741. Daniel's wife, Elizabeth, of Br was apptd 12 Aug 1745 as guardian of Nathan and Joyce, minors over 14, ch of Daniel Smith dcd.

CHILDREN, all b Br (6:103):
1. Daniel^3 Jr, b 7 July 1713; d aft father's will of 14 Aug 1741. No m, d or ch found in VR Br. The will of Daniel Smith of Newport, dtd 10 Aug 1764 mentioned wife Mary; sons Sumner Smith "who received all estate in Br". Daniel and Joseph, and daus Mary and Bath___(sheba) may be of this Daniel (RIGR, 13:49).
2. John, b 20 Jan 1714/15; poss d at sea Apr 1746 (6:-162).

3. Elizabeth, b 15 Mar 1717/18, bp Congre Ch, Br Dec 1721 (Geneals RI Fams, 1989, 2:381); m Br 6 July 1738 Capt Benjamin JAMES (6:49). Elizabeth had two kn ch, surname James, bp Congre Ch, Br (8:279): Samuel, bp 27 Sept 1741 and William bp 1 July 1744.
4. David, b not rec but named in father's will, bp Congre Ch, Br Dec 1721 (Geneals RI Fams, 1989, 2:381); d Oct 1748 at Newport, RI (6:162).
5. William, b 3 Mar 1724/25; d aft father's will of 14 Aug 1741.
6. Nathan, b 1 July 1730, twin; d at sea Sept 1752, unm (6:162).
7. Joyce, b 1 July 1730, twin; d 16 Jan 1804, 77 yr, wid (6:175); m Br 22 Dec 1753 Isaac YOUNG of Newport, RI who d Br 15 Oct 1773 (6:175). Joyce had five ch b Br, surname Young (6:113): Elizabeth, George, William, Sarah and David.

71. WIDOW ELIZABETH SOUTHARD/SOUTHWORTH

The VR Br (6:164) give the d of this person as Southworth, Elizabeth, wid, on 24 June 1682. Only two early Southworth m's appear in these VR Br: Elizabeth Southworth who m Br 12 May 1685 Samuel Gallup of Br; and Priscilla Southworth who m Br 1 Mar 1689 Samuel Talbot/Talbee (6:50). All of the widowed Elizabeths who m Southworth males and had a dau, Elizabeth, old enough and free to m in 1685, were traced. At first it seemed that none existed, as all of their daus named Elizabeth were said to have m other men than Samuel Gallup. Then it appeared that one, and only one, fitted these criteria.

Constant^2 (Edmund^1) Southworth was b 1615 in Leyden, Holland, and d Duxbury, Mass 10 Mar 1679. He m 2 Nov 1637 Elizabeth Collier, dau William Collier of Duxbury, who was the Ass't Gov of the Col for twenty-eight years (Sav, 1: 433). Constant and his family rem to Br at its settlement and then went on to Little Compton, RI. His will, dtd 27 Feb 1678 and pvd Mar 1678/79, named wife Elizabeth, and among his ch, "To my dau Elizabeth Southworth my next best bed and furniture, provided she doe not marry William Fobes, but if she doe then to have five shillings. To dau Prissila Southworth my next best bed and furniture. Unto my son William Southworth my next best bed." (LC Fams, p 628). LC Fams, p 246-248, and other refs stated that Elizabeth Southworth m ca 1679, as his first wife, Lt William Fobes, and d in 1681 (LC Fams, p 271). However, Torrey, p 272, said "No", William Fobes did not m (1) Elizabeth Southworth.

It seems certain that Elizabeth Southworth, wid of Constant, rem from LC to Br to live aft his d, and was at the first town meeting. She took with her their two youngest daus, Elizabeth and Priscilla, both of whom m at Br. Her son, Capt William Southworth, m (1) Rebecca Pabody of Duxbury, and also lived in LC, and then in Br (LC Fams, p 628-630). Two of William's sons, Samuel and Thomas, continued to live in Br for some time bef moving on to Conn.

CHILDREN of Constant^2 and Elizabeth Southworth (LC Fams, p 627-628):
1. Mercy^3, b ca 1638; d 25 Nov 1712; m 12 May 1658 Samuel FREEMAN Jr.
2. Edward, d ca 1727; m Mary PABODIE, dau William and Elizabeth (Alden) Pabodie.
3. Alice, b 1646; d 5 Mar 1719; m 26 Dec 1667 Col Benjamin CHURCH, the Indian fighter who lived in LC and Br.
4. Nathaniel, b 1648; d 14 Jan 1711; m 10 Jan 1672 Desire GRAY, dau Edward and Mary (Winslow) Gray (LC Fams, p 292).
5. Mary, b prob ca 1650; m ca 1670 David ALDEN, son John and Priscilla (Mullins) Alden.
6. Elizabeth, d Br 15 Aug 1709 (8:250); m Br 12 May 1685 Capt Samuel GALLUP (6:50).
7. Priscilla, m (1) Br 1 May 1689 Samuel TALBOT/TALBY (6:50); m (2) May 1708 John IRISH of LC.
8. Capt William, b 1659; d LC 25 June 1719; m (1) 1680 Rebecca PABODY, dau William and Elizabeth (Alden) Pabody, who d LC 23 Dec 1702; m (2) Saybrook, Conn Mrs Martha (KIRTLAND) BLAGUE.

Elizabeth^3 (Constant^2, Edward^1) Southworth m Br 12 May 1685 Capt Samuel GALLUP of Br, and d there 15 Aug 1709 due to a fall from a horse (6:22; 8:250). Capt Samuel Gallup was prob b ca 1658, the prob son of Capt John Gallup of Boston, New London, and Stonington, Conn, an Indian fighter (Gallup Fam, p 24-27; Sav, 2:222-223; RIGR, 13:205-214). He was also an early settler of Br, and was present at its first town meeting (Munro, p 79), and d Br 24 Mar 1717 (6:133). Both he and Elizabeth joined the Congre Ch, Br in 1695 (8:250). Elizabeth had five ch b Br, surname Gallup (6:77): Elizabeth, b 26 Apr 1688, m 20 Apr 1710 Samuel BOWERMAN (6:9, 22); Capt Samuel, b 9 Oct 1690 who m by 1716 Mary___ of Groton, Conn; Mary, b 22 Oct 1692 who m 9 or 10 Jan 1711/12 Joshua BAYLEY (6:22); William, b 18 Aug 1695 who m 19 Dec 1721 Mary ANTILL (Ibid); and Nathaniel, b 5 June 1698 who d unm by 18 Feb 1728/29 (Rounds, 1:167). It should be noted that all of Elizabeth's ch, except Elizabeth named for herself, and Samuel named for her husband, had similar names to those of her siblings.

Priscilla[3] (Constant[2], Edward[1]) Southworth m (1) Br 1 May 1689 Samuel TALBOT/TALBY (6:50), who was poss b Boston 9 Jan 1665, son Stephen and Hannah Talby of Boston (Sav, 4:250); and m (2) May 1708 as his second wife John IRISH Jr, b 1641 Duxbury, Mass and d 21 Feb 1717 LC, son John and Elizabeth Irish Sr of Duxbury (LC Fams, p 370-371; Torrey, p 726). Priscilla had two ch b Br, surname Talbee (6:105), but had no issue from her second m: Stephen, b 26 Aug 1693 who m Alice___ and had three ch b Br betw 1725-1730 (6:105); and Hannah, b 21 Sept 1698. Hannah's stepfather, John Irish, in his will dtd 9 Nov 1715 and pvd 20 Mar 1717, left "To dau Hannah Talbee ten sheep" (LC Fams, p 371).

Capt William[3] (Constant[2], Edward[1]) Southworth was b 1659 Duxbury, Mass and d in LC 25 June 1719 (LC Fams, p 628-630). He m (1) Rebecca PABODY, b 16 Oct 1660 Duxbury and d LC 23 Dec 1702, dau William and Elizabeth (Alden) Pabody. Rebecca's mother was dau of John and Priscilla (Mullins) Alden of the Myflwr, so her ch have a Myflwr desc. William m (2) Saybrook, Conn Mrs Martha (KIRTLAND) BLAGUE, b 1667 and d 7 Feb 1737/38, dau Nathaniel and Parnell Kirtland of Lynn, Mass, and wid of Joseph Blague of Saybrook (Torrey, p 75). Capt William lived in Duxbury, LC and Br. He was a selectman and deputy in Duxbury, and was in LC by 1686 where he was a large landowner. In 1689 he was made a Lt, and later was a Captain.

CHILDREN by first wife, Rebecca, all bp Congre Ch, Br 29 June 1701 (LC Fams, p 629-630; Geneals RI Fams, 1989, 2: 374):
1. Benjamin[4], b LC 16 Apr 1681; d LC aft 1729; m (1) LC 18 Dec 1701 Elizabeth WOODWORTH; m (2) LC 14 Mar 1717 Alice CHURCH; m (3) LC 18 July 1722 Susanna (PALMER) BLACKMAN. He had seven ch b LC (LC Fams, p 630).
2. Capt Joseph, b LC 1 Feb 1683; d LC 20 Apr 1738; m LC 20 Apr 1710 Mary BLAGUE, dau Joseph and Martha (Kirtland) Blague, b 1691, d LC 29 Oct 1770. He was town clerk of LC for nine yrs, and had eleven ch b LC (Ibid, p 630).
3. Edward, b Duxbury 23 Nov 1684; d 1735 or later; m (1) 17 Mar 1708 Mary FOBES, b 1689, d LC 29 Feb 1712, dau William and Martha (Pabodie) Fobes; m (2) LC 11 Oct 1716 Elizabeth PALMER, b LC 17 Nov 1691, d Lebanon, Conn 13 Oct 1784, dau John and Elizabeth (Richmond) Palmer of LC. He had two ch by his first wife, and eight ch by his second wife, all rec LC (Ibid, p 631).
4. Elizabeth, b 23 Sept 1686; d 10 Apr 1743; m LC 2 Dec 1703 David LITTLE, son Ephraim and Mary (Sturtevant) Little of Marshfield and Scituate, Mass. She had nine ch b Scituate, surname Little (Ibid, p 399).
5. Alice, b LC 14 July 1688; d 25 Apr 1770; m LC 25 May

1709 John COOK, b Tiverton, RI 5 Nov 1685, d LC 1754, son John and Ruth (Shaw) Cook of Tiverton. She had nine ch, surname Cook, the first three b LC, and the rest in Tiverton (Ibid, p 207, 629).
6. Samuel, b 26 Dec 1690; d Stratford, Conn 1758; m Abigail___. He lived in Br and then rem to Lyme, Conn. They had five ch, b Br (6:104).
7. Nathaniel, b 31 Oct 1692; m by 1719 Mary TORREY, dau Josiah and Sarah (Wilson) (Batt) Torrey. They had three ch b Br (6:104), and then rem to Mansfield, Conn. He was a ship carpenter, and never returned from a voyage to the Mediterranean Sea ca 1730 (Virkus, 6:158).
8. Thomas, b 13 Dec 1694; m LC 21 Feb 1723 Patience THURSTON, b 16 Feb 1702, dau Jonathan and Sarah Thurston of Newport, LC, and Dartmouth, Mass (LC Fams, p 674-675). He lived in Br, and then rem to Mansfield, Conn (Ibid, p 629).
9. Stephen, b 31 Mar 1696.

CHILDREN by second wife, Martha (LC Fams, p 629-630):
10. Gideon, b LC 31 Mar 1707; d 1772 Rochester, Mass; m LC 25 Sept 1728 Mary WILBORE, b LC 13 Apr 1711, dau John and Sarah (Palmer) Wilbore of LC. He graduated from Yale College in 1727 and was a school master in 1732 in Rochester, Mass. He had fourteen ch, the first three b LC (Ibid, p 632).
11. Andrew, b 12 Dec 1709; m 27 Dec 1731 (LC Fams, p 630) or m 27 Jan 1731/32 (VR Saybrook Col, 2:213) Temperance KIRTLAND, b Saybrook, Conn 10 Nov 1710, d 19 Dec 1794, aged wid, at Chester, Conn (Chester, Conn Congre Ch Recs, 2:153 in Saybrook Col Ch Recs, Fourth Ecclesiastical Soc, p 571), dau John and Temperance (Buckingham) Kirtland Jr of Saybrook (VR Saybrook Col, 2:4 or 6). He had eight ch b Saybrook (Ibid, 2:213).

72. ROBERT TAFT SR

Robert[1] Taft/Taffe Sr was b ca 1640 and came from England to Braintree, Mass by 1678, where he was a carpenter and shipwright. In 1679 he bought land in Mendon, Mass, and was an original settler there. He was a member of the first Board of Selectmen in 1680 and for several years thereafter. In 1695 he was constable, and in 1709 his sons and he built a bridge over the Great River (Blackstone) (Austin, 160 Fams, p 231-232). He m Sarah___ by 1671, and they both d in 1725. He and Sarah lived in Br during 1683 and 1684, and on 20 June 1683 Robert took the Oath of Fidelity there (Munro, p 114). The only entry for his family in the VR Br is that of the b of their son, Benjamin, on 31 Mar 1684 (6:105), and they returned to Mendon.

CHILDREN (Austin, 160 Fams, p 229-231):
1. Thomas[2], b 1671; d 1755; m 1692 Deborah GENERY, dau Isaac and Elizabeth (Gamlyn) Genery/Chenerie of Medfield (Sav, 2:241). They had the fol ch: Joseph, Sarah, Eleazer, Hannah, Rebecca, Deborah, Rachel, Martha, Isaac, Susannah, and Thomas.
2. Robert Jr, b 1674; d "4-29-1748" (29 June 1748); m 1694 Elizabeth WOODWARD who d aft 1748. Their ch were: Elizabeth, Robert, Israel, Mary, Elizabeth II, Jane, Alice, Eunice, John, Jemima, Gideon, and Rebecca.
3. Daniel, b 1677; d "8-24-1761" (24 Oct 1761); m (1) ca 1702 Hannah___ who d "8-8-1704"; m (2) "12-5-1706" Lydia CHAPIN, b 9-29-1677, dau Josiah and Lydia (Brown) Chapin. Sav, 1:360 said that Josiah Chapin m Mary___ and was in Braintree in 1676 and Mendon in 1689. Daniel had one ch by his first wife, Daniel, who d.y.; and he had the fol ch by his second wife, Lydia: Abigail, Josiah, Lydia, Daniel II, Ephraim, Japhet, and Caleb.
4. Joseph, b 1680; d "7-18-1747"; m 1708 Elizabeth EMERSON who d aft 1747, dau James Emerson. Sav, 2:117 gave one James Emerson of Ipswich, Mass who, by wife Sarah, had a dau Elizabeth b 6 Mar 1687. Joseph had the fol ch: Lucy, Moses, Peter, Sarah, Joseph, Elizabeth, Aaron, Margaret, and Ebenezer.
5. Benjamin, b 31 Mar 1684 (6:105); d 1766; m "3-22-1707" Sarah THOMAS. His ch were: Samuel, Stephen, Mijamin (sic, Benjamin?), Tabareh, Silas, and Paul.

73. MAJOR ROBERT THOMPSON

Major Robert Thompson's name on the list of land owners of Br at its first town meeting is the only mention of him in the recs of Br. He obviously did not settle in Br, and nothing more is kn about him. Torrey, p 738 gave only one Robert Thompson, who m a Hopkins, poss by 1639, d in 1695, and was in Boston and then returned to England.

74. WILLIAM THROOPE SR

William[1] Throope Sr, poss of Scots descent, was prob b 1637/38, and d Br 4 Dec 1704 (8:265; Torrey, p 754). He m prob in Barnstable, Mass 14 May 1666 Mary CHAPMAN (VR Barnstable, Mass in MD, 14:86, he called Wm Troop), b 31 Oct 1643 and d aft 1732, dau Ralph and Lydia (Wills) Chapman of Marshfield, Mass (Sav, 1:362; Torrey, p 145). William was of Barnstable when he m, but rem to Br prob betw June 1684 and July 1686. He came with his family and household goods by ox-cart, being the first of the new settlers of Br to come in "by team" (Munro, p 92). He was a surveyor

and selectman, and was Representative from Br in 1691 to
the General Court of Plymouth Col (Munro, p 384). He joined the Congre Ch in Br on 3 May 1687 (8:265), and was its
Deacon when he d. As Deacon William Throope of Br, yeoman, in his 67th yr, his will, dtd 12 June 1704 and pvd 1
Jan 1704/05, named wife Mary; sons Dan, John and William,
and his youngest son, Thomas Throope; two eldest daus,
Mary wife of John Barney, and Elizabeth wife of Jonathan
Peck; and two youngest daus, Mercy Throope and Lidiah.
The acceptance of this will by his heirs on 4 June 1705
called Lidiah the wife of Eliazer Cary (RIGR, 2:172;
Rounds, 1:32-33).

CHILDREN, order of some b's unkn:
1. Mary^2, b 6 Apr 1667 Barnstable (MD, 14:86); d aft
1728; m Br 4 Nov 1686 John BARNEY (6:52), b Salem, Mass
1 Aug 1665 (Sav, 1:123), d 1728, son Rev Jacob and Ann
(Witt) Barney Jr of Salem and Rehoboth, Mass. Mary had
seven ch b Br, surname Barney (6:62): Mary, John, Elizabeth, Anna, Jacob, John II, and William.
2. Daniel/Dan, b 1670 Barnstable; d 3 Dec 1737, 67 yr
Lebanon, Conn (Myflwr Fams in Progress, Richard Warren, p 71); m (1) Br 23 Aug 1689 Dorcas BARNEY (6:52);
m (2) Br 5 Jan 1697/98 Deborah MACEY (Ibid); m (3) LC
21 Jan 1712/13 Deborah (CHURCH) GRAY (LC Fams, p 294).
3. Elizabeth, b not rec; d 14 June 1729 (6:156); m Br
31 Mar 1695 Jonathan PECK (6:52), b 5 Nov 1666 Seekonk,
Mass and d bef 3 July 1717 when his wid presented his
est for probate (Peck Gen, p 130, 133, 135), son Nicholas Peck Esq and his second wife, Rebecca Bosworth,
of Seekonk. Jonathan owned large tracts of land in Br,
and settled on Peck's Hill. Elizabeth had eight ch,
surname Peck, b Br and bp Congre Ch, Br (6:98; Geneals RI Fams, 1989, 2:373): Mary, Jonathan Jr, Nicholas, William who rem to New Haven, Conn, Isaac, Elizabeth, Mercy, and Deacon Thomas.
4. Deacon John, b 1676 Barnstable; d Br as Deacon
John 25 Jan 1772, 96 yr (6:166; 8:265); m (1) Br 25 or
26 Nov 1697 Rebecca SMITH (6:52; Torrey, p 754), who
d Br 19 Dec 1731 (6:166); m (2) as "Deac John of Br"
(int) 9 Oct 1732 Mrs Susannah TAYLOR "of Barnworth"
(6:52), b ca 1683 per d rec, d 13 Oct 1768, 85 yr, Br
(6:166).
5. Capt William Jr, b ca 1679/80 Barnstable; d Lebanon, Conn 3 Feb 1737/38, 59 yr; m Br 20 Mar 1698/99
Martha COBLEIGH/COBLYE, b ca 1674/75 and d Lebanon 13
Feb 1736/37, 63 yr, dau John and Mary (Bosworth) Cobleigh of Swansea, Mass.
6. Thomas, b 4 Sept 1681, bp 17 Sept 1683 as Thomas
of Willm and Mary Troop, by Pastor Russell of Barnstable (Myflwr Source Recs, p 611); d Br 18 Sept 1756,
75y, 0m 14d (6:166); m (1) by 1703 Abigail___ who d

Br July 1740; m (2) 7 Apr 1742 Ziporah MANN of Wrentham, Mass (6:52), b 1681 and d as "wid of Thomas", Br 25 Jan 1767, 84 yr (6:166).

7. Mercy, no b or m found, but named in father's will of 12 June 1704 as one of his two youngest daus. A Mary Throope was bp by Pastor Russell at Barnstable in June 1684 as Mary of Willm and Mary Troop (Myflwr Source Recs, p 611), who may have been she.

8. Lidiah/Lydia, b Br 15 July 1686 (6:106); m Br 1700 Eleazer CAR(E)Y, b Bridgewater, Mass 27 Sept 1678, d Br 28 July 1754, son John and Abigail (Allen) Car(e)y Jr of Br (RIGR, 11:222-223). Lydia had seven ch b Br, surname Car(e)y (6:68): Abigail, Lydia, Ann, Elizabeth, Eleazer, Mary and Martha.

Daniel/Dan^2 (William^1) Throope was b 1670 Barnstable, Mass and d 3 Dec 1737, 67 yr, at Lebanon, Conn (Myflwr Fams in Progress, Richard Warren, p 71). He m (1) Br 23 Aug 1689 Dorcas BARNEY (6:52; Myflwr Source Recs, p 35), b 22 Apr 1671 (Sav, 1:123-124), d bef Jan 1697/98, dau Jacob and Ann (Witt) Barney of Salem and Rehoboth, Mass; m (2) 5 Jan 1697/98 Deborah MACEY (6:52); m (3) LC 21 Jan 1712/13 Deborah (CHURCH) GRAY, b 13 Mar 1676/77 Hingham, Mass, d 8 June 1752, 69 yr, Lebanon, Conn, dau Joseph and Mary (Tucker) Church and wid of Samuel Gray of LC (LC Fams, p 294). Dan's ch by Deborah (Church) Gray have a Myflwr desc from Richard Warren. All of his ch by his three wives, except one ch b 1700, were b Br, so he did not rem to Lebanon until aft Feb 1717. He was there bef Dec 1724 when his dau, Deborah, was m in Lebanon (IGI Conn).

CHILDREN by first wife, Dorcas, b Br (6:106):
1 Mary^3, b 31 Oct 1691; poss d 11 Apr 1696 (6:166).
2 Dorcas, b 3 Dec 1693.
3 William, b 30 Sept 1695; bur 28 Mar 1696 (Ibid).

CHILDREN by second wife, Deborah Macey, b Br (6:106):
4. Mercy, b 14 Oct 1698.
5. Samuel, b 25 Apr 1700 Taunton, Mass; d bef 25 Feb 1729 Lebanon, Conn when his wife m (2) Ebenezer HYDE; m (int) "of Br" 31 Mar 1722 Dorothy GRAY, called "of Newport" (6:52) which is not correct. She was of LC, and was the dau of Samuel and Deborah (Church) Gray. Samuel's father, Dan, m wid Deborah (Church) Gray, so Dorothy, b LC 14 Jan 1704, was Samuel's step-sister. Through Deborah's mother, she and Samuel's descs have a Myflwr line from Richard Warren. They had the fol ch b Lebanon (VR Lebanon in IGI Conn): Samuel, bp 17 Jan 1725 who m Lebanon 27 May 1747 Submit CLARKE; Mary, bp

23 July 1726; and Macey, bp 29 Jan 1727/28 who m Lebanon 11 Mar 1753 Dorcas TERRY. A Mary, perhaps Mary II, was b 23 Jan 1727 per Hurd, 2:515. This could also have been an error for Macey.
6. Deborah, b 17 Mar 1702; m Lebanon 3 Dec 1724 Samuel WILLIAMS (Hurd, 2:516; IGI Conn). She had eleven ch b Lebanon, surname Williams: Deborah, Priscilla, Joanna, Submit, Rebecca, George, Bathsheba, Mary, Nathaniel, Theody, and Samuel (Ibid).
7. Submit, b 25 Dec 1706; m First Congre Ch, Lebanon, 3 June 1725 Samuel MURDOCK (Bailey, Book 2, p 39). She had four kn ch, surname Murdock, first, second and fourth b at Windham, Conn, and the third b Lebanon (IGI Conn): William, Samuel, Submit and William II.

CHILDREN by third wife, Deborah (Church) Gray, b Br (6:106; Myflwr Fams in Progress, Richard Warren, p 16-17, 71):
8. Dan Jr, b 31 July 1715; m as "Dann Jr" of Lebanon, Conn (int) 12 Mar 1736/37 Susannah CAREY "Jr" of Br, b 1717 and d 1754, prob dau of Benjamin and Susannah (Kent) Carey. He had seven ch, all bp First Congre Ch, Lebanon, and all of whom have a Myflwr desc from Richard Warren (IGI Conn): Bethiah, b 18 Dec 1738 (Hurd, 2:515) who m Lebanon William HUNTINGTON; Dan, b 19 Apr 1740, m 31 Jan 1760 Rachel TERRY, had eleven ch, and was a Capt of Conn Militia in 1776 in the Rev War (Pat Index, p 357); Susannah, b 18 Mar 1742, m Lebanon Benjamin THROOPE, b 3 Nov 1744, bp 26 Dec 1744, d 16 May 1822, son Rev Benjamin and Sibel (Dyer) Throope, and he was a Major from Conn in the Rev War (Pat Index, p 678); Benjamin, b 3 June 1745; Joseph, b 23 Dec 1748, d 13 Sept 1836, m Lebanon 8 Nov 1770 Zerviah BISSELL, and was a Sgt from Conn in the Rev War and had three ch; Mary, bp 11 Aug 1754; and Carey, bp 1765, who m Lebanon 26 Nov 1788 Elizabeth LYMON. Mary and Carey were not given in Hurd, 2:515 as ch of Dan Jr, but are in the IGI Conn.
9. Joseph, b 26 Feb 1716/17; prob d Litchfield, Conn where he rem to bef 1752; m First Congre Ch, Lebanon 20 Mar 1740 Deborah BUELL (Bailey, Book 2, p 41). His ch have a Myflwr desc from Richard Warren. He had ten ch, the last four bp Litchfield, the others bp Lebanon (IGI Conn; Hurd, 2:515): Deborah, bp 22 Apr 1741 and m Ira BISHOP; Benjamin, bp 13 Sept 1742, d.y.; Joseph, bp 22 Apr 1743/44 (sic, 1744); William, bp 26 Dec 1745 and m Litchfield Sarah HAND; Elizabeth, bp 10 Jan 1747 Lebanon and m Alexander WAUGH who was a Capt and had Civil Service from Conn in the Rev War and who d 1800 in Hamilton, NY (Some Conn Nutmeggers Who Migrated, p 256); Daniel, b 8 or 18 Nov 1748 Lebanon, d 1 Nov 1833, m Amy BARNES and was a Lt from Conn in the Rev War (Pat Index, p 678); Benjamin II, bp 13 Sept 1752 Litchfield, who m (1) Mary BURGESS, m (2) Mary (BATEMAN) SMITH and was a

Private from Conn in the Rev War (Pat Index, p 678); Martha, bp 12 July 1753 Litchfield; Rhoda, bp 10 June 1758 Litchfield; and Samuel, bp 8 Nov 1761 Litchfield.

Deacon John[2] (William[1]) Throope was b 1676 and d Br 25 Jan 1772, 96 yr (6:166). He m (1) Br 26 Nov 1697 Rebecca SMITH who d Br 19 Dec 1731; and m (2) (int) as "Deac John of Br" 9 Oct 1732 Mrs Susannah TAYLOR "of Barnworth" (6:-52), b ca 1683 per d rec, d Br 13 Oct 1768, 85 yr (6:166). He had no issue from his second m. On 13 June 1697 John joined the Congre Ch of Br and later became its Deacon; Susannah joined on 13 May 1741 (8:265). John and his son, John Throope Jr, both of Br, became freemen of RI in 1747 and both took the Oath of Bribery and Corruption on 10 Feb 1746/47 (Munro, p 161; MacGunnigle, p 44). The will of John Throope of Br, yeoman, dtd 12 Apr 1762 and pvd 3 Feb 1772, named wife Susanna; only son John Throope; daus Anne Waldron, Mary Morey and Rebecca Lyon; gsons John and Amos Throope and Nathaniel Waldron; and gdaus Anstis Talby and Phebe Champlin (RIGR, 6:153-154).

CHILDREN by first wife, Rebecca, b Br (6:106-107):
1. John[3], b 24 Jan 1698; d bef 27 May 1716, unm.
2. Ann(e), b 27 Dec 1699; d Br 7 Aug 1790, 91 yr, wid (6:169); m (int) Nov 1718 Cornelius WALDRON, b 4 Sept 1697 (6:108), d 22 Sept 1778, 81 yr, at Rehoboth, Mass (6:169), son George and Rachel (Baker) Waldron of Br (Torrey, p 772). She had ten ch b Br, surname Waldron, whom the VR Br, 6:109 do not identify correctly, mixing them with the ch of Joseph and Martha Waldron. The wills of Cornelius and Joseph Waldron show their proper parentage (RIGR, 6:155 for Cornelius's will). Ann(e)'s ch were: Anne, Priscilla, Rachel, Anstis, Leah, Nathaniel, Sarah, Willoughby, John "2nd", and Isaac.
3. Rev Amos, b 28 Mar 1702; d Woodstock, Conn bef 1 Feb 1737 when Simon Davis's settlement of est called his dau, Frances, the wid of Rev Amos Throope (Rounds, 1:322). He m Br 7 Jan 1724/25 Frances DAVIS, b Br 23 Sept 1703, dau Sim(e)on and Ann (Low) Davis of Br (6:-17, 72). She m (2) at Woodstock, Pennel or Penuel BOWEN (Bailey, Book 1, p 109). Rev Amos rem to Woodstock where he was pastor of the First Congre Ch from Jan 17-28 until his d. The will of Simon Davis, gentleman of Br, dtd 4 July 1734 and pvd 20 Oct 1736, named a dau "Francis Throop" (sic) (Rounds, 1:255, 322). Amos had seven ch, all bp Woodstock except Nathaniel who was b Br (IGI Conn): Nathaniel, b 11 Mar 1725/26 and d Br 17 Sept 1726 (6:107); Frances, bp 17 Mar 1727; Amos, bp 29 May 1730 and d.y.; Amos II, bp 9 May 1731 and d.y.; John, bp 11 Sept 1733 who m 17 Dec 1755 Frances DANA at Pomfret, Conn, and was a Private in the Rev War from

Conn (Pat Index, p 678); Nathaniel II, bp May 1735; and Amos III, bp 30 Apr 1736.
4. Mary, b 9 Sept 1704; d aft 8 Apr 1746, date of b of last ch in Woodstock, Conn; m Br 31 May 1728 Joseph MARCY of Woodstock (Bailey, Book 1, p 108). Her father's will called her Mary Morey which seems to be incorrect. Mary had ten ch b Woodstock, surname Marcy (IGI Conn): Joseph, Stephen, Esther, Nathaniel, Rebeckah, Ichabod, Hadlock, Smith, Lidia, and Thomas.
5. Hester/Esther, b 31 Dec 1706; d bef father's will of 12 Apr 1762; m (int) Br as Esther 19 June 1730 Thomas KENTON,and m Br 15 Oct 1730 Thomas KEMPTON (6:52), prob the same man. No ch found in the VR Br or IGI Conn.
6. Rebecca, no b rec but named in father's will as Rebecca Lyon (Virkus, 5:606 gave her dates as b 1707 and d 1801); m Br 8 Mar 1731/32 Ebenezer LYON (6:52) b 1675, d 1741, son William and Deborah (Colburn) Lyon of Woodstock, Conn (Virkus, 5:606). But Bailey, Book 1, p 108 said that Ebenezer Lyon of Woodstock, Conn m Rebecca Throop 28 Jan 1731/32 by Josiah Dwight in Woodstock. Rebecca had five kn ch surname Lyon, all bp Woodstock Twp, Windham Co, Conn (IGI Conn): Amos who m Bethia DANA, Frances, Moses, Ebenezer, and Wareham. It seems prob that Rebecca may have m a younger Ebenezer Lyon than the son of William and Deborah, b 1675, who would have been 57 yrs old in 1732.
7. Lydia, b 15 Mar 1713/14.
8. John II, b 27 May 1716; d Br as John Esq 2 Dec 1802, 86 yr (6:166); m (1) (int) as "John Jr of Br" 6 Oct 1739 Phebe HALL of Swansey, Mass (6:52) who d 18 Dec 1740 (6:166); m (2) by 1753 Sarah___; m (3) 2 Aug 1784 Mrs Elizabeth (COLE) (COLE), wid of Warren, RI (8:319), b 25 Apr 1753, d 10 Nov 1828, dau Isaiah and Eleanor (Nichols) Cole and wid of Luther Cole of Warren (War, 6:59, 60).
9. Ebenezer, b 25 Nov 1718; d Br 10 Aug 1736, 17 yr.

John[3] Jr (Deacon John[2], William[1]) Throop was b Br 27 May 1716 (6:107), and d there 2 Dec 1802, 86 yr (6:166). He m (1) (int) 6 Oct 1739 Phebe HALL of Swansea, Mass (6:-52) who d 18 Dec 1740 (6:166); m (2) by 1753 Sarah___; and m (3) 2 Aug 1784 Mrs Elizabeth (COLE) (COLE) of Warren, RI (8:319), b 25 Apr 1753, d 10 Nov 1828, dau Isaiah and Eleanor (Nichols) Cole, and wid of Luther Cole (War, 6:59, 60; Cole, p 96). John was a freeman of RI from Br in 1747 (MacGunnigle, p 44, and took the Oath of Bribery and Corruption at Br on 10 Feb 1746/47, when his father did (Munro, p 161).

The will of John Throop of Br, advanced in age, dtd 14

Mar 1796 and pvd 6 Jan 1803, named wife Elizabeth; only son John Throop under 21; daus Phebe Champlin dec, and Sarah Coggeshall dec; gch, ch of his dau Phebe Champlin, dec, viz: John, James and William Champlin, Phebe wife of Gideon Hull of Providence, Martha wife of John Hill of Providence, and Nancy wife of Samuel Burr of Br; gch, ch of his dau Sarah Coggeshall dec, viz: William Coggeshall and Patience (no surname) (RIGR, 6:157-158). If it were not for John Throop's will, it would be thought unlikely that the same man had three ch, one b 1740, another 1753, and a third in 1786. The will of Elizabeth Throop of Br, wid, dtd 4 June 1823 and pvd 1824, named her son Thomas Cole (RIGR, 9:59).

KNOWN CHILD$_4$ by first wife, Phebe, b Br (6:106):
1. Phebe^4, b 18 Nov 1740; d 14 Sept 1778 (6:122); m Br 5 Feb 1759 Thomas CHAMPLAIN of Warren, RI (6:13). Phebe had nine ch b Br, surname Champlain (6:69): Thomas, Phebe Hall, Martha, Nancy, Bridget, Capt John who m Elizabeth CARR of Warren (8:300), Joshua, James and William. Phebe's dau, Phebe Hall, was named for her sister, Phebe. Although her father's will said she m Gideon Hull, Elder Wight's Publishments (8:300), gives her m in Br to Gideon Hall on 9 Oct 1785.

KNOWN CHILD by second wife, Sarah, b Br (6:106):
2. Sarah, b 29 Oct 1753; d 9 June 1785, 32 yr (6:124); m by Rev Charles Thompson 17 Dec 1772 as his first wife, George COGGESHALL Jr (6:53), b Br 8 Feb 1752 (6:70), d Br 18 July 1812, 62 yr (6:124), son George and Hannah Coggeshall, Sr. George Jr was a Private, and also had Naval Service, in the Rev War from RI (Pat Index, p 142). Sarah had two ch b Br, surname Coggeshall (6:79): Patience, b 4 Sept 1773; and William, b 4 Nov 1778.

CHILD by third wife, Elizabeth, b Br (6:106):
3. John, b 7 July 1786; d Br 15 Sept 1820, 34 yr (8:-392); m Br 15 Nov 1807 Eliza COGGESHALL (8:301), who d Br as wid Oct 1823 (8:392). No issue found in VR Br. The will of William Coggeshall of Br, gentleman, dtd 29 Mar 1823, codicil of 25 Apr 1823, and pvd 7 July 1823, named his dau, Eliza Throop (RIGR, 9:58).

Capt William^2 Jr (William^1) Throope was b ca 1679/80 in Barnstable, Mass and d Lebanon, Conn 3 Feb 1737/38, 59 yr. He m Br 20 Mar 1698/99 Martha COBLEIGH/COBLYE (called Martha Collye in VR Br 6:52), b ca 1674/75 and d Lebanon, Conn 13 Feb 1736/37, 63 yr. She was the dau of John Cobleigh who d ca 1679/80 in Swansea, Mass, and his wife, Mary Bosworth, b 1647, dau Jonathan Bosworth Sr of Rehoboth, Mass

(Recs Town of Attleboro of 28 May 1672, listing "John Cobley, one share [of the North Purchase] that he had of his father Jonathan Bosworth", in Bosworth Gen, p 68). Jonathan^2 (Edward^1) Bosworth and his wife, Elizabeth, had two daus, Mary who m John Cobleigh, and Bathsheba who "m (prob) Benjamin JONES" (TAG, 62:55-56). A deed from Benjamin Jones of Br, yeoman, and Bashua (Bathsheba) Jones, gave...to our well-beloved Kinsman William Throope "Ssaltmonger" and his now wife, Martha, etc (Bosworth Gen, p 175). William had rem from Br to Lebanon, Conn by 5 Apr 1730, the date he was admitted as a member of the Congre Ch there.

The will of Capt William Throope of Lebanon, Conn, dtd 27 Dec 1737 and pvd 16 Feb 1737/38, mentioned no wife, but named two sons, William and Benjamin; daus Elizabeth, Martha, Bathsheba, Mary and Lydia (no surnames); son-in-law Daniel Vaughan; dau-in-law Sarah Throop; gson William Throop; his Aunt Jones at Br; and his land at Br and Ashford, Conn; son Benjamin to be exec and residual legatee (Windham, Conn Probate District, Rec Book 2:317-320, given in TAG, 62:55-56).

CHILDREN, b Br^3 (6:106-107):
1. William^3, b 8 Jan 1699/1700; d prob aft Oct 1743 at Lebanon, Conn; m (int) Br as William Jr 19 Sept 1719 Elizabeth STANBURY of Pembroke, Mass (6:52).
2. Joseph, b 23 July 1701; d bef father's will of 27 Dec 1737; m Br 24 Feb 1724/25 Sarah SMITH. They had one dau, Sarah, b Br 26 Sept 1726 (6:106).
3. Elizabeth, b 27 May 1703; d 18 Apr 1731 (Fams Anc New Haven, p 1409); m Br 13 May 1725 as his first wife William PECK (6:52), b Br Nov 1702 and d 1758 New Haven, Conn, son Jonathan and Elizabeth (Throope) Peck of Br. Elizabeth had four ch, surname Peck (Fams Anc New Haven, p 1409): Elizabeth and Mary both b New Haven, and Martha and Nicholas both b Newport, RI. Nicholas m New Haven Abigail ATWATER.
4. Martha, b 30 June 1705; d aft father's will of 27 Dec 1737, prob at Lebanon, Conn; m Br 23 Nov 1725 Daniel VAUGHAN (6:54). Martha had at least five ch, surname Vaughan: Mary, b 3 Sept 1726 Br (6:108); John, bp 9 Aug 1732 Lebanon; and Elizabeth, Martha and Daniel, all bp Lebanon (IGI Conn).
5. Bathsheba, b 11 Jan 1707/08, twin; d aft 10 May 1742, prob Lebanon, Conn; m First Congre Ch, Lebanon, 8 Jan 1730 John SIMMS/SYMS (Bailey, Book 2, p 40). She had five kn ch, surname Simms, bp Lebanon (IGI Conn): John, Mary, Martha, John II, and Lydia.
6. Mary, b 11 Jan 1707/08, twin; d aft 25 May 1749; m First Congre Ch, Lebanon, Conn 26 Feb 1729/30 Thomas CHAPMAN (Bailey, Book 2, p 40). They rem to Ashford,

Windham Co, Conn, where Mary had the fol kn ch, surname Chapman (IGI Conn): Thomas, Mary, Martha, Bathshua, Throop who m Susanna BARNEY at Ashford, Sybbel, Ann, Joseph, and Elias.
7. John, b 11 Mar 1710/11; d 7 May 1711 "about 3 months" (6:166).
<u>8</u>. Rev Benjamin, b 9 June 1712; d Bozrah, Conn 16 Sept 1785; m Canterbury, Conn 27 Nov 1735 Sybil DYER/DYAR (Bailey, Book 2, p 123; IGI Conn).
9. Lydia, b not rec, but named in father's will of 27 Dec 1737.

William^3 (Capt William^2, William^1) Throop was b Br 8 Jan 1699/1700 (6:106), and d prob aft Oct 1743 at Lebanon, Conn. Fams Anc New Haven, p 1786 said he d 1738 Lebanon, which would seem to be incorrect since he had ch bp in the First Congre Ch there in May 1739, Jan 1741, and Aug 1744. He m (int) as William Jr in Br 19 Sept 1719 Elizabeth STANBURY of Pembroke, Mass (6:52), and they had rem to Lebanon by Jan 1729/30. Fams Anc New Haven, p 1786, mentioned only five ch of theirs, of whom four were b Br and one in New Haven, Conn. In addition, the IGI Conn listed six more of their ch, bp Lebanon "of William Throop and Elizabeth Stanbury" or of "Wm Throop and Elizabeth". And Bailey, Book 2, p 43 and 46; Book 5, p 50, 53-54, gave the m's in Lebanon of these last six ch.

CHILDREN:
1. Rev William^4, b 11 July 1720 Br (6:107); d 29 Sept 1756 Southold, LI, NY; m New Haven, Conn Mercy MANSFIELD, b 3 Mar 1718/19, d 7 July 1793 ae 75, dau Moses and Margaret (Prout) Mansfield of New Haven. William graduated in 1743 from Yale College and was the fifth pastor of the Congre Ch of Southold, LI until his d (Whitaker, p 260). He had three sons, one of whom was John Rutherford Throop, who was a Second Lt in the 2nd Continental Artillery in the Rev War (Heitman, p 542-543).
2. Joseph, b 24 Jan 1721/22 New Haven; m Bozrah, Conn 29 Mar 1744 Susannah GALLOP (Bailey, Book 5, p 50). Bozrah was originally part of Norwich, Conn in New London Co.
3. George, b 10 Mar 1723/24 Br (6:107); m Lebanon, Conn 5 Nov 1746 Mehitable BLISS (Bailey, Book 2, p 43).
4. Elizabeth, b 9 Mar 1725/26 Br (6:107); d 29 Aug 1727, ca 17 mos (6:166).
5. Josiah, b 13 July 1727 Br (6:107). No m or ch in IGI Conn.
6. Benjamin, b 19 Jan 1729/30 Lebanon (Hurd, 2:515; IGI Conn). No m or ch in IGI Conn.

7. John, b 12 Oct 1731 Lebanon (Hurd, 2:515).
8. Thomas, b 9 Sept 1733 Lebanon (Ibid; IGI Conn). No m or ch in IGI Conn.
9. Elizabeth II, b 8 Jan 1734/35 Lebanon (Hurd, 2:515); m Bozrah, Conn 24 Oct 1764 Charles HINCKLEY (Bailey, Book 5, p 54) or m at Lebanon (IGI Conn). No issue seen.
10. Martha, b 17 May 1739 Lebanon (Hurd, 2:515); d 4 July 1763; m First Congre Ch, Lebanon 8 Jan 1761 Lt Israel GILLETT, b 17 Sept 1738 Lebanon, d 8 July 1829, ae 91, prob at Hartford, Vt, son Ebenezer Gillett. Israel was a soldier from Vt and gave Public Service in the Rev War (Pat Index, p 268; Bailey, Book 2, p 46). One kn ch, Daniel Ordway Gillett (IGI Conn).
11. Priscilla, prob b 1 July 1741 Lebanon (Hurd, 2:515); m Bozrah, Conn 16 Aug 1759 Caleb OWEN (Bailey, Book 5, p 53), b 20 May 1741 Lebanon, son Caleb and Elizabeth (Brewster) Owen. She had three ch b Lebanon, surname Owen(s): Esther, Martha and Joel (IGI Conn).
12. Mary, b 11 Aug 1744 Lebanon (Hurd, 2:515).

Rev Benjamin^3 (Capt William^2, William^1) Throop was b Br 9 June 1712 (6:107) and d 16 Sept 1785, at Bozrah, formerly part of Norwich, New London Co, Conn. He graduated from Yale College in 1734 and rem first to Windham Co, Conn where he m at Canterbury 27 Nov 1735 Sybil DYER/DYAR (Bailey, Book 2, p 123; IGI Conn). They moved to Norwich, Conn where he was the first pastor of the Congre Ch at what became Bozrah, from its organization 3 Jan 1739 until his d on 16 Sept 1785 (Hurd, 1:375), and where his ch were b and bp. Sybil's parents were John Dyer of Canterbury who m Congre Ch there 22 Oct 1713 Abigail FITCH, dau Major James Fitch. Major James Fitch m 8 May 1687 Alice BRADFORD, dau William Bradford Jr, son of William Sr of the Myflwr (Bowman, p 39-40). So all of Benjamin Throop's ch have a Myflwr desc. When Bozrah was separated from Norwich in 1786, Benjamin was the moderator of its first town meeting on 20 June 1786, and he was then elected as one of the three Selectmen (Hurd, 1:375). This obviously refers to Benjamin Jr, son of Rev Benjamin.

CHILDREN, all bp Norwich (Bozrah), Conn (IGI Conn):
1. Chloe^4, bp 20 Sept 1736.
2. Issabella, bp 25 Oct 1737.
3. Dyer, bp 17 Sept 1738 who was a Col in the Conn Militia during the Rev War (Heitman, p 542).
4. Benjamin, bp 9 Mar 1743; d.y.
5. Benjamin II Jr, bp 26 Dec 1744 (IGI Conn), b 3 Nov 1744 (Pat Index, p 678); d 16 May 1822; m Congre Ch, Lebanon, Conn 11 Dec 1766 Susannah THROOPE (Bailey, Book 2, p 48), who bp 18 Mar 1742 in Lebanon, dau Daniel and

Susannah (Carey) Throope Jr of Lebanon. Benjamin was a Major in the 4th and 5th Regt's from Conn in the Rev War and was given pension S42492 (Heitman, p 542; Pat Index, p 678; Conn Rev Pens, p 148). He lived in that part of Norwich which became Bozrah, and had five kn ch bp Congre Ch Bozrah: Dan, bp 27 Apr 1768 who m Mary GAGER, and was a fifer from Conn in the Rev War, with Mary receiving pension W20088 for his service; Clarissa; John; Dyar; and prob Susannah (IGI Conn).
6. Sybil, bp 20 Jan 1746; m Congre Ch, Bozrah 19 Nov 1767 Joseph HARRIS. No issue found in IGI Conn.
7. Abigail, bp 23 Aug 1749.
8. Sarah, bp 19 Dec 1751.
9. Octavia, bp 7 July 1754; d 18 Aug 1839; m Congre Ch, Bozrah 30 Aug 1781 (Hale, House, p 294), or m 30 Sept 1781 (IGI Conn) Enoch HALE, b 28 Oct 1753 Coventry, Conn and d 4 Jan 1837 Westhampton, Mass, son Deacon Richard and Elizabeth (Strong) Hale of Coventry. Enoch graduated in 1773 from Yale College. Octavia had eight unnamed ch, surname Hale (Hale, House, p 294). None was found in the IGI Conn, but six were in the IGI Mass, all b Westhampton, Hampton Co, Mass: Sally, Nathan, Octavia, Enoch, Richard and Sibilla.

Thomas^2 (William^1) Throope was b 4 Sept 1681 and bp 17 Sept 1683 by Pastor Russell at Barnstable, Mass (Myflwr Source Recs, p 611), and he d Br 18 Sept 1756, 75y, 0m, 14d (6:166). He m (1) by 1703 Abigail___ who d July 1740 (Ibid), and m (2) 7 Apr 1742 Ziporah MANN of Wrentham, Mass (6:53), who was b 1683 and d Br as wid of Thomas 25 Jan 1767, 84 yr (6:166). He had no issue by his second m. Thomas, and Thomas Throope Jr, both of Br, were made RI freemen in 1747 (MacGunnigle, p 44), and both took the Oath of Bribery and Corruption at the town meeting of Br freemen on 10 Feb 1746/47 (Munro, p 161). The will of Thomas Throope of Br, yeoman, dtd 3 May 1754 and pvd 4 Oct 1756, mentioned wife Ziporah who received the furniture she brought to their m; only son Thomas Throope; dau Mercy Raynolds; gsons Thomas and John Raynolds and gdau Mary Raynolds, all under age; and two gdaus, Abigail and Mary Nicholson, both under eighteen (RIGR, 5:93).

CHILDREN by first wife, Abigail, b Br (6:106):
1. Abigail^3, b 17 Nov 1703; d Jan 1717 (6:166).
2. William, b 29 Nov 1706; d 1712/13 (Ibid).
3. Lydia, b 10 May 1708; d bef father's will of 3 May 1754.
4. Thomas Jr, b 26 May 1710; d 12 June 1771, 61 yr (Ibid); m (1) 6 Mar 1733 Mary BILLINGS of LC, RI, b LC 19 Oct 1712, d Br 20 Dec 1743 (Ibid), dau Rev Richard

and Sarah (Little) Billings of LC (LC Fams, p 43); m (2) (int) 10 Apr 1744 Elizabeth MANN of Wrentham (6:53).
5. William II, b 25 Jan 1712/13, twin; d bef father's will of 3 May 1754.
6. Mercy, b 25 Jan 1712/13, twin; d as "Marcy, widow" Br 23 Sept 1795, 83 yr (6:159); m Br 6 May 1733 Eleazer REYNOLDS, b Br 12 Mar 1703/04 (6:100), d 1745 Cape Breton, Canada (6:159), son Peter and Mary (Giles/Gills) Reynolds of Br. Mercy had three ch, surname Reynolds, named in her father's will of 3 May 1754: Thomas, Mary and John. The VR Br (6:100) give only the b of John on 26 June 1744.
7. Mary, b 29 Oct 1717; prob d bef father's will of 3 May 1754 as not named in it; m Br 10 Nov 1736 John NICHOLSON of Wrentham, Mass (6:40, 52). Mary had two daus surname Nicholson, Abigail and Mary, who were both under eighteen when mentioned in her father's will.

Thomas^3 Jr (Thomas^2, William^1) Throope was b Br 26 May 1710 (6:106) and d there 2 June 1771, 61 yr (6:166). He m (1) 6 Mar 1733 at LC, RI Mary BILLINGS, b 19 Oct 1712 and d Br 20 Dec 1743 (Ibid), dau Rev Richard and Sarah (Little) Billings of LC (LC Fams, p 43); m (2) (int) 10 Apr 1744 Elizabeth MANN of Wrentham, Mass (6:53). Mary Billings' ch have a Myflwr line from Richard Warren through her mother, Sarah Little (Myflwr Fams in Progress, Richard Warren, p 66-67). Thomas Jr of Br was made a freeman of RI in 1747 (MacGunnigle, p 44). On 10 Feb 1746/47 he took the Oath of Bribery and Corruption at Br and that same day, as a freeman, he was elected as one of the six members of the Town Council (Munro, p 160-161). The will of Thomas Throope of Br, yeoman, dtd 31 Oct 1770 and pvd 5 Aug 1771, named wife Elizabeth; sons Billings Throope eldest, William, Samuel, Thomas, George and Benjamin Throope; daus Hannah Waldron, Mary Peck, Sarah (no surname) who is somewhat weakly, Esther (no surname), Elizabeth Richmond, Lydia (no surname), Susanna and Abigail, last two poss under eighteen and unm; and sister Mercy Reynolds (RIGR, 6:153).

CHILDREN by first wife, Mary, b Br (6:106):
1. Hannah^4, b 20 Oct 1733; d Br 22 June 1811, 78 yr, "wife of Nathaniel" (6:169); m Br 19 Oct 1755 Nathaniel WALDRON (6:55), prob b 25 Mar 1731 (6:109), d Br 22 Jan 1817, 87 yr (6:169), son Cornelius and Ann(a) (Throop) Waldron of Br. Hannah had eleven ch b Br, surname Waldron (6:109): Nathaniel Jr who m Lydia SALISBURY of Caleb (6:55), Billings, John, Abigail, Thomas who m Ruth GRAY of Col Thomas, and Ambrose, Rebecca who m David BAILEY (Ibid), Joseph, Benjamin, William Throop, and Samuel. Cornelius Waldron's will in RIGR, 6:153-154,

named his son, Nathaniel.

2. Capt Billings, b 31 May 1735; d Br 24 Jan 1776 (6:-166) or 27 Jan 1776 (Pat Index, p 678); m by 1758 Hannah MORTON, b 1733 Plymouth, Mass, dau Thomas and Abigail (Pratt) Morton of Plymouth (Gen Reg Plymouth Fams, p 189, 192, 209). Billings was a Capt in Col William Richmond's RI Reg't in the Rev War (Pat Index, p 678). He had seven or eight kn ch, b Br (6:106): Abigail, Molly, Hannah, Sarah, Betsey, Peggy and Thomas. The Gen Reg Plymouth Fams, p 263, said that he also had a son, Billings Jr. The VR Br, 6:166 list the fol d's: Billings, ch of d 11 Sept 1770; and Capt Billings, ch of d 23 Sept 1775.

3. Mary, b 30 May 1737; m Br 29 Oct 1757 Capt Jonathan PECK (6:43), b 4 Jan 1724/25, d 7 Oct 1797, 73 yr, son Jonathan Peck of Br and his first wife, Hannah Wood, of LC (6:43, 98, 156). Jonathan Peck Jr was a Major from RI in the Rev War (Pat Index, p 523). His ch have a Myflwr desc from Richard Warren through his mother, Hannah Wood, whose mother was Mary Church (Myflwr Fams in Progress, Richard Warren, p 70; LC Fams, p 780). The ch of Mary, surname Peck, were (6:98): Abigail, Jonathan, Nicholas, John, Sarah, Mary, Lydia, and poss Nancy.

4. Capt William, b 13 June 1739; d Br 26 Feb 1817, 78 yr (8:392); m (1) Br 20 Mar 1765 "Mrs" Alathea FALES (6:53), b Br 5 Mar 1742/43 (6:75) and d 19 June 1789, 46 yr (6:166; 8:392), dau Nathaniel and Sarah (Little) Fales of Br (6:20); m (2) (int) 22 Jan 1790 Br Mrs Mary HEAL(E)Y (8:319), b 1744 per d rec, d Br "widow of Capt Wm" 17 June 1834, 90 yr (6:166). William was a Capt in the Rev War from RI (Pat Index, p 678). He had no issue by his second wife. By his first wife, Alathea, he had the fol kn ch, b Br (6:106, 166): ch of William d 2 Jan 1770 ca 5 yr; infant ch of William d 1767; and William, b 15 Aug 1771, who d Br as Hon William Esq 30 May 1850, 79 yr. The Hon William m at Tiverton, RI 22 Oct 1795 Hannah WALKER, dau David dec and Sarah Walker (6:53).

5. Abigail, b 9 July 1741, bp Congre Ch, Br 13 Sept 1741 (8:288); d Br 12 Oct 1756 in 16th yr (6:166).

6. Sarah, b 1 Oct 1743, bp Congre Ch, Br 6 Nov 1743 (8:288); d prob unm aft father's will of 31 Oct 1770 which called her "somewhat weakly".

CHILDREN by second wife, Elizabeth, b Br and bp Congre Ch, Br (6:106; 8:288):

7. Samuel, b 18 Mar 1744/45, bp 5 May 1745; d 28 Jan 1776, 31 yr (6:166); m Br St Michael's Ch 8 Dec 1768 Eliza PEARSE (6:42; 8:174, 180), bp St Michael's 21 Aug 1748, dau William Pearse of Br and his wife, Lydia Brown of Barrington, RI. Samuel had three ch, bp St Michael's (8:180): Pamella, Mary and George. His wid, Eliza, m (2) Jeremiah WHEELER.

8. Esther, b 16 Mar 1745/46, bp 27 Apr 1746; d aft father's will of 31 Oct 1770, and unm then.
9. Elizabeth, b 15 Sept 1747, bp 11 Oct 1747; m Br 25 Oct 1770, she as "Eliza Throop, of Thomas of Br", Edward RICHMOND (6:53), b 5 Aug 1736 LC, son Capt Perez and Deborah (Loring) Richmond, whose homestead was partly in LC and partly in Westport Harbor, Dartmouth, Mass. No issue found in VR Br, but their ch, if any, have a Myflwr desc from John Alden and Priscilla Mullins (LC Fams, p 514, 517).
10. Lydia, b 4 Mar 1748/49, bp 14 May 1749; d aft father's will of 31 Oct 1770. No m or d in VR Br.
11. Dau, b 21 May 1750; d.y.
12. Jerusha, b 12 June 1751; d 3 July 1751 (6:166).
13. Thomas, b 4 June 1752, bp 26 July 1752.
14. George, b 15 Mar 1754, bp 19 May 1754; d 14 Sept 1756 in 3d yr (Ibid).
15. Susannah, b 20 May 1755, bp 27 July 1755; d aft father's will of 31 Oct 1770.
16. George II, b 21 Nov 1756, bp 12 June 1757.
17. Benjamin, b 25 June 1758, bp 3 Sept 1758.

75. JOHN THURSTON

It has not been poss to find the parentage or date of b of this John Thurston. He does not fit any of the John Thurstons in Sav or Torrey. The only entry concerning him in the VR Br is the b of a son, David, in Br 30 Jan 1684/-85 to him and his wife, Sarah (6:107). Torrey does not include this m. He signed the Oath of Fidelity in Br on 9 Aug 1686 (Munro, p 114), and aft that he disappeared from the Br recs and must have rem elsewhere.

76. GEORGE WALDRON

George Waldron of Br was poss the son of George (1603-1680+) and Bridget (Rice) Waldron, who were m in Alcester, England on 21 May 1635, and came to Dover, NH (Torrey, p 772). The George of Br was the brother of Dr Isaac Waldron of Boston, Mass, who purchased a sixteenth part of the Mount Hope Lands which became Br, and of Samuel Waldron of Dighton, Mass, who named George in his will of 8 Aug 1727 as his brother (Rounds, 1:174-175).

George d in Br 12 Dec 1739 (6:168). He m, prob by 1675, Rachel BAKER, who d in Br 25 Nov 1706 as "Rachel of George" (Ibid). He was the only freeman by the name of Waldron who signed the Oath of Fidelity on 20 June 1683 in Br (Munro, p 114). At the meeting of freemen in Br on 10 Feb 1746/47 when Br changed from Mass to RI, among those who took the

Oath of Bribery and Corruption were Cornelius Waldron, Joseph Waldron, and Joseph Waldron Jr (Munro, p 161).

CHILDREN, first two b Boston, rest b Br (6:108; Sav, 4:-389):
1. John^2, b 25 Aug 1676; d 17 Dec 1756? (6:169).
2. Prob Benjamin, b 22 May 1679.
3. Isaac, b 7 Mar 1683/84 (6:108); d 28 June 1740 (6:-168); m Hannah poss HOAR, b 1689 per d rec, d 30 Jan 1768, 79 yr, wid (6:169). No issue. The will of Isaac Waldron of Br, dtd 26 June 1740 and pvd 15 July 1740, named wife Hannah Waldron; brother Cornelius Waldron and his unnamed ch; and sister Martha Nibbs (RIGR, 3:-262; Rounds, 1:295). The will of Hannah Waldron of Br, wid, dtd 18 Nov 1767 and pvd 7 Mar 1768, mentioned only her cousin (nephew?) William Hoar (RIGR, 6:152). It is poss that Isaac's wife, Hannah, was b 26 Aug 1689 to William and Hannah Hoar of Br (6:82).
4. Thomas, b 29 Apr 1686.
5. Jacob, b 23 Apr 1689.
6. Samuel, b 26 July 1691; d 25 Oct 1691 (6:168).
7. Hannah, b 2 Sept 1692.
8. Joseph, b not rec, but ca 1693/94 per d notice; d 14 Aug 1760, 67 yr (6:169); m by 1718 Martha (NEWTON) TOMAN, b 1682 per d rec, d 10 Dec 1759, 77 yr, dau Thomas Newton, and wid of Stephen Toman of Br (Ibid).
9. Cornelius, b 4 Sept 1697; d 22 Sept 1778, 81 yr at Rehoboth, Mass (6:169); m (int) Nov 1718 Ann(a) THROOP (6:52, 55), b Br 27 Dec 1699 (6:106), d 7 Aug 1790, age 91, wid (6:169; 8:394), dau John and Rebecca (Smith) Throope of Br (6:52).
10. Martha, b 30 Dec 1701; d 4 Apr 1775, 74 yr (6:153); m (1) by 1725 Thomas NIBBS and m (2) 23 Dec 1744 St Michael's Ch John A. OLDRIDGE (8:213) who d 29 Jan 1776, ca 83 yr (6:153). She was named in her brother, Isaac's will of 20 June 1740 as Martha Nibbs. Martha had two ch b Br, surname Nibbs: Thomas and Ebenezer, twins, b 11 July 1726 (6:95). Thomas Nibbs, of Thomas and Martha, was bur St Michael's Ch 19 Nov 1726 (8:232), and Ebenezer Nibbs d Nov 1744 at Surinam (6:152). Martha had no issue by her second m.

Joseph^2 (George^1) Waldron did not have his b rec, but was b ca 1693/94 per his d rec, and d Br 14 Aug 1760, 67 yr (6:169). He m by 1718 Martha (NEWTON) TOMAN, who was b 1682 per d rec, and d Br 10 Dec 1759, 77 yr, dau Thomas Newton and wid of Stephen Toman of Br (6:169). At the meeting of freemen in Br on 10 Feb 1746/47, Joseph took the Oath of Bribery and Corruption (Munro, p 161). The will of Thomas Newton of Br, mariner, was dtd 2 Dec 1725 and pvd 21 Dec 1725. He, being aged and infirm, named daus Abigail wife of Joseph Carpenter, and Martha now wife of Joseph Waldron and formerly wife of Stephen Toman dcd; and gch Thomas, Stephen and Martha Toman (Rounds, 1:129). A receipt from Joseph Waldron of Br, "glassier", for money received by his wife, Martha, from the est of her father, Thomas Newton, and paid by Samuel Vial, exec, was dtd 13 Mar 1726/27 (Ibid, 1:142). The will of Joseph Waldron of Br, shopkeeper, dtd 27 Aug 1752 and pvd 1 Sept 1760, named his living unnamed wife; and sons Joseph, Daniel and John Waldron (RIGR, 5:95).

CHILDREN, b Br (6:109):
1. Joseph^3 Jr, b 6 Oct 1718; m Br 16 July 1741 Rebecca PECK (6:55), prob b 26 Sept 1721, dau Jonathan and Hannah (Wood) Peck (6:98).
2. Nathaniel, b 9 Aug 1721; not mentioned in father's will of 27 Aug 1752 and prob d bef then.
3. Capt Daniel, b 14 Dec 1724; d 27 Dec 1767, 44 yr on coast of Africa (6:169); m Br 28 Sept 1746 Phebe REYNOLDS (6:55), b 3 Aug 1725, d 3 Mar 1789, 64 yr, wid (6:-169; 8:394), dau Joseph and Phebe (Leonard) Reynolds.
4. John, b 26 Mar 1727; d as John Esq 28 Nov 1798, 72 yr (6:169); m by 1751 Elizabeth ALLIN, b 31 Oct 1726 Barrington, RI (Bar, 6:21; Geneals RI Fams, 1989, 2:702-703), d Br 19 July 1801, wid (6:169), dau Mathew and Ruth (Stockbridge) Allin of Barrington (Geneals Myflwr Fams, 3:510). The will of Mathew Allin Esq of Warren, RI, dtd 28 Apr 1761 and pvd 6 July 1761, named dau Elizabeth, wife of John Waldron of Br (RIGR, 4:260). The will of John Waldron of Br, dtd June 1797 and pvd 4 Feb 1799, mentioned wife Elizabeth; unnamed dau, wife of son-in-law Shearjashub Bourne Esq; gsons John Waldron Bourne and Allen Bourne under 25, sons of Shearjashub Bourne; all his unnamed gch and unnamed gdaus; and brother Joseph Waldron (RIGR, 6:157). The will of Elizabeth Waldron of Br, dtd 10 July 1801 and pvd 1 Feb 1802, mentioned unnamed daus, wives of son-in-law Shearjashub Bourne and son-in-law Samuel S. Peck; gson Allen Bourne; four gdaus: Nancy Ruth Waldron, Hannah Smith, Martha Bourne, and Mary Bourne (RIGR, 6:157). (Hannah Smith was also a dau of Shearjashub Bourne.) The 1774 Census of Br showed John Waldron as head of a household of six persons: one male above 16, one male under 16, one female above 16, one female under 16, and two blacks (Bartlett, p 183). John and Elizabeth had the fol ch b Br (6:109): Ruth who m Shearjashub BOURNE Jr (6:55); Allen; Priscilla who m Benjamin HOAR of Br; Hannah who m Samuel Vial PECK of Br; and poss Thomas whose dau, Nancy Ruth Waldron, was named as a gdau in the will of Elizabeth (Allin) Waldron.

Joseph[3] Jr (Joseph[2], George[1]) Waldron was b Br 6 Oct 1718, and poss d 4 Mar 1788 in 73 yr (sic) at Newport, RI, and was bur in the Common Bur Ground of Newport (VR RI, Beaman, New Series, 11:432). He m Br 16 July 1741 Rebecca PECK (6:55), prob b 26 Sept 1721, dau Jonathan and Hannah (Wood) Peck (6:98). Hannah Wood was b LC, RI, dau Lt John and Mary (Church) Wood. Through her mother she and her descs have a Myflwr line from Richard Warren (LC Fams, p 166-167, 780). At the meeting of freemen in Br on 10 Feb 1746/47, Joseph Jr took the Oath of Bribery and Corruption (Munro, p 161).

CHILDREN, bp Congre Ch, Br (8:289; IGI RI):
1. Capt Nathaniel[4], b 16 Mar 1741/42 (IGI RI), bp 22 Aug 1742; d 26 or 27 Jan 1769, 27 yr, Newport, RI (6:-169) and bur in the Common Bur Ground, Newport (VR RI, Beaman, New Series, 11:432).
2. Martha, bp 22 Apr 1744; prob d 12 Dec 1831, 88 yr, in Newport; prob m Capt George BUCKMASTER of Newport. Both bur in Common Bur Ground, Newport (Ibid).
3. Joseph, b 22 Dec 1747 (IGI), bp 27 Dec 1747; d 10 Oct 1756, 9 yr (6:169).
4. Jonathan, b 15 Jan 1749/59 (IGI), bp 25 Mar 1750.
5. Rebecca, b May 1752 (IGI), bp 7 June 1752.
6. Ch, b and d 1754 (6:169).
7. Hannah, b 4 Mar 1756 (IGI), bp 25 Apr 1756.
8. Elizabeth, b 14 Apr 1759 (IGI).
9. Joseph II, b 27 Mar 1762 (IGI), bp 8 Aug 1762.
10. Elizabeth, bp 8 Aug 1762. (Poss the same as #8.)
11. Abigail, bp 16 Nov 1766; prob d as Miss Abby 13 Dec 1831, 68 yr, and bur Common Bur Ground, Newport (VR RI, Beaman, New Series, 11:432).
12. Nathaniel II, b unrec, but called "of Joseph and Rebecca" when m Congre Ch, Br by Rev Henry Wight 19 May 1799 Ruth BOURNE "of Shearjashub Esq (Jr) and Ruth" (8:353).

Capt Daniel[3] (Joseph[2], George[1]) Waldron was b Br 14 Dec 1724 and d 27 Dec 1767, 44 yr, on the coast of Africa (6:169). He m Br 28 Sept 1746 Phebe REYNOLDS (6:55), b 3 Aug 1725, and d 3 Mar 1789, 64 yr, wid (6:169), dau Joseph and Phebe (Leonard) Reynolds of Br. He was a sea captain. The will of Daniel Waldron of Br, mariner, dtd 5 Sept 1761 with codicils of 23 Aug 1765 and 12 Aug 1767, and pvd 2 Oct 1769, mentioned wife Phebe; four sons Daniel, Newton, George and Leonard, all under age; dau Molly; the ch wife is pregnant with; brother John Waldron exec (RIGR, 6:152-153). The will of Phebe Waldron, dtd 13 July 1786 and pvd 4 Jan 1790, named her father Joshua (sic, Joseph) Reynolds late of Br dec; son Newton Waldron; and all of her (unnamed) ch (RIGR, 6:156). Capt Daniel's wid was the Phebe Waldron listed in the 1774 Census of Br as head of a household of nine persons: two males above 16, one male under 16, two females above 16, three females under 16, and one black (Bartlett, p 183).

CHILDREN, bp Congre Ch, Br (8:290):
1. Ch^4, d July 1747 (6:169).
2. Daniel, b 22 Dec 1749 (IGI RI), bp 1 July 1750; d 9 Mar 1775, 26 yr (6:169).
3. Newton, bp 16 Feb 1752; d 17 Mar 1827, 75 yr (Ibid); m 3 Apr 1794 Frances BOSWORTH (8:353), b 1769 per d rec, d "wid Newton" 27 Jan 1851, 82 yr (6:170), dau Major Benjamin and Mary Bosworth. Major Benjamin Bosworth m (2) Mary CHURCH of Br 19 July 1764 (Pat Index, p 73; 6:8) and was then of Newport, RI. He was a Major from RI in the Rev War. The will of Newton Waldron Esq of Br, advanced in age, dtd 28 Oct 1823 and pvd 27 May 1827, named wife, Frances; sons Leonard and Benjamin Bosworth Waldron; and daus Frances Waldron and Ann Waldron (RIGR, 9:60). Newton had four ch, b Br (6:109-110): Leonard, Benjamin Bosworth who m Mary FALES (8:333, 354), Frances, and Ann who m Col Arnold Howland BUSH.
4. Capt George, b 7 Apr 1754 (IGI RI), bp 21 Apr 1754; d 9 Oct 1786, 33 yr, at sea (6:169); m Sarah MARTINDALE, b 1759, d 4 Aug 1834, 75 yr, "wid Capt George" (6:169), prob dau Sion and Sarah (Park) Martindale of Newport, RI. Capt George had one kn ch, George Jr, who m at St Michael's ch 18 Oct 1798 Sarah MUNRO (8:219). There is a "Daniel of Capt Daniel" Waldron who d Apr 1800, 20 yr at Africa (8:394) who now can not be placed, if these statements are correct. If he were of Capt George^4 (Capt Daniel^3) Waldron, his dates could place him in this family.
5. Samuel, b 11 Oct 1755 (IGI RI), bp 19 Oct 1755; d 4 4 Aug 1756 (6:169).
6. Phebe, b 22 May 1758 (IGI RI), bp 28 May 1758; d unm as "Miss Phebe" 13 Aug 1826, 68 yr (6:169). Her will, dtd 24 Dec 1821 and pvd 2 Oct 1826, named her sister, Elizabeth Diman; nephews Leonard and Benjamin B. Waldron; and nieces Frances and Ann Waldron (RIGR, 9:59).
7. Leonard, b 26 May 1760 (IGI RI), bp 15 June 1760; d aft father's will of 5 Sept 1761.
8. Elizabeth, bp 30 May 1762; d "wife of Thomas Diman" 20 July 1834, 72 yr (6:128); m Congre Ch, Br, as 2nd wife 25 July 1819 Thomas DIMAN, son Deacon Jeremiah and Sarah (Giddens) Diman of Br (6:8). No issue.
9. Molly, b 5 Jan 1764 (IGI RI), bp 8 Jan 1764; m Br 15 Oct 1786 Benjamin REYNOLDS (8:347), bp Congre Ch, Br 17 Apr 1757 (8:285), or 17 Mar 1757 (6:100), son John and Dorothy Reynolds Jr of Br (Ibid). Molly had one kn ch, surname Reynolds, bp Congre Ch, Br: Mary, bp 11 Sept

1/91 (8:285).
10. Nancy/Mercy, b Dec 1767 and rec as Nancy (6:109), but bp 10 Jan 1768 as Mercy (8:290).

Cornelius[2] (George[1]) Waldron was b Br 4 Sept 1697 and d Rehoboth, Mass 22 Sept 1778, 81 yr (6:169). He m (int) Nov 1718 Ann(a) THROOPE (6:55), b Br 27 Dec 1699 (6:106), and d 7 Aug 1790, 91 yr, wid (6:169; 8:266), dau John and Rebecca (Smith) Throope of Br (6:52). At the meeting in Br of freemen on 10 Feb 1746/47, Cornelius took the Oath of Bribery and Corruption (Munro, p 161). The will of Cornelius Waldron of Br, blacksmith, dtd 4 Oct 1774 and pvd 6 Oct 1778, named his wife, Ann; sons Isaac, Nathaniel and John Waldron; daus Willoby (no surname), Sarah Wardwell, Anstis Talby, Ann Rawson and Leah Liscomb; and "rest of my estate to my nine children at decease of their mother" (but only eight ch were named); and brother (in-law) John Throope (RIGR, 6:155). The will of John Throope of Br, yeoman, dtd 12 Apr 1762 and pvd 3 Feb 1772, named dau Anne Waldron and gson Nathaniel Waldron, and gdaus Anstis Talby and Phebe Champlin (RIGR, 6:153-154). The VR Br, 6:109 do not have all of Cornelius and Ann's ch correctly identified as theirs, but mixes them up with the ch of Joseph and Martha Waldron. The wills of Cornelius (RIGR, 6:155) and Joseph (RIGR, 5:95) show their ch's proper parentage. The 1774 Census of Br listed Cornelius as head of a household of three persons, one male above 16 and two females above 16 (Bartlett, p 183).

CHILDREN, b Br:
1. Anne[3], b 25 Sept 1720; m Br 14 Apr 1737 Thomas RAWSON (6:45, 56). Anne had one rec ch b Br, surname Rawson: William, b 11 Nov 1738 (6:100). They prob rem from Br. There is a poss that Thomas Rawson was the son of Wilson Rawson of Uxbridge, Suffolk Co, Mass. On 16 Feb 1730/31 Benjamin Raynolds of Br, cordwainer, was appted guardian of this Thomas Rawson, over 14 (Rounds, 2:191).
2. Priscilla, b 1724; d 15 Sept 1741 "wife of Robert Carr" (6:121, 169); m (int) 3 May 1740 Robert CARR 96:13, 55). No issue in VR Br.
3. Rachel, b 27 Dec 1726; d 13 Mar 1769, 43 yr, wid (6:147); m St Michael's Ch 17 July 1748, as his second wife, Thomas MARTIN, b Br 7 Apr 1715, d 1758 at Antigua (6:147), son William and Christian (Pelton) Martin (6:-35, 89). There are several recs of her ch b Br, surname Martin (8:166-167): ch of Rachel, wid, d 26 Sept 1759 (6:147); Rachel of Rachel d 28 Sept 1759 (8:231); ch bp St Michael's 16 Sept 1754; Thomas, bp St Michael's 12 Sept 1756; and Eliza, bp St Michael's 3 Sept 1758. The recs of St Michael's call these last three the ch of

Thomas and his first wife, Hannah. But Hannah d July 1746 and Thomas m (2) Rachel on 17 July 1748.

4. Anstis, b 5 Jan 1728; d 26 Sept 1796, 70 yr, wife of Edmund (6:165); m Congre Ch, Br 17 Oct 1751 as his first wife, Edward TALBY/TALBEE Sr (6:51, 55), bp St Michael's 19 July 1730 (6:105; 8:179), d 22 Mar 1807 (Geneals RI Fams, 1989, 2:113) or d 19 Mar 1807 (Pat Index, p 664), son Stephen and Alice (Rosbotham) Talbee of Br (6:105; 8:179). Stephen was a Private from RI in the Rev War. Alice Rosbotham, and her descs, have a Myflwr line from Richard Warren (Geneals RI Fams, 1989, 2:109-113). Anstis had six ch b Br, surname Talby/Talbee, bp Congre Ch, Br (8:288): Lydia, Hannah, Edward Jr, Priscilla, Rachel and Stephen.

5. Leah, b 17 May 1729; d 7 June 1815, 86 yr, wid (6:-145; 8:378); m St Michael's 7 Jan 1749/50 (8:219) Samuel LISCOMB, b 13 Mar 1726/27 (6:87), d 17 May 1804, 77 yr (6:145), son John and Rebecca (Thurston) Liscomb Jr (6:33). Leah had nine ch b Br, surname Liscomb (6:-88): Priscilla, Leah, Samuel, Rebecca, John, Isaac, Isaac II, Nathaniel, and Benjamin.

6. Nathaniel, b 25 Mar 1731; d 28 Jan 1817, 87 yr (8:-395) or d at 80 yr (8:266); m Br 19 Oct 1755 Hannah THROOPE (6:55), b 20 Oct 1733 (6:106), d 22 June 1811, 78 yr (6:169; 8:395), dau Thomas and Mary (Billings) Throope Jr of Br (6:52).

7. Sarah, b 10 Feb 1734; d 5 July 1812, 79 yr, wid Isaac (6:171); m Br 9 Sept 1756 Isaac WARDWELL of Providence, RI (6:56), b 1730 per d rec, d 7 May 1810, 80 yr (6:171). Sarah had five ch rec in Br and bp Congre Ch, Br, surname Wardwell (6:111; 8:291): Lydia, Sarah, Jonathan, Anna who was bp as Nancy, and Willoby.

8. Willoby/Willoughby, b 13 Nov 1736; d unm as "Miss Willoughby" 6 Nov 1818, 82 yr (6:169).

9. John 2nd, b 20 Dec 1738; d 18 Aug 1790 ae 54 of cholera morbus (8:394; Geneals RI Fams, 1989, 2:703), m 22 Feb 1759 Eliza MARTIN (8:219), b 20 Dec 1738, dau Cornelius and Anne Martin (Geneals RI Fams, 1989, 2:-703). No issue in VR Br. As John Waldron 2nd he gave a quit claim to Nathaniel Waldron, gentleman, for his interest in the house and land left to the ch of Cornelius Waldron by their uncle, Isaac Waldron (reprinted in Geneals RI Fams, 1989, 2:703). John 2nd was a blacksmith, and the 1774 Census of Br showed him as a head of a household of two males above 16, one male under 16, two females above 16, and two blacks, for a total of seven (Bartlett, p 183).

10. Isaac, b 1 June 1742; d 21 June 1824, 82 yr (6:169); m Br 14 Feb 1765 Abigail WEST (6:55, 57), b 1740 or 17-43 per d rec, d 25 June 1824, 81 yr (6:169), or d 84 yr (8:395). The 1774 Census of Br listed Isaac as head

of a household of six persons: one male above 16, four males under 16, and one female above 16 (Bartlett, p 183). The 1790 Census of RI, p 11, showed Isaac in Br, head of a household of two males 16 and upward, and two females. He had the fol ch b Br (6:109): William, b 1 Feb 1766; George, b 22 Mar 1767; Isaac Jr, b 16 Apr 1770 who m Feb 1793 Martha DROWNE (8:303, 353) and had seven ch; Daniel, b 6 Feb 1773 and prob m Susanna___; Elizabeth, b 23 Apr 1776 and m 4 May 1794 Jeremiah EDDY; and Anne, b 9 Feb 1779.

Nathaniel[3] (Cornelius[2], George[1]) Waldron was b Br 25 Mar 1731 and d 22 Jan 1817, 87 yr (8:395). He was m Br 19 Oct 1755 to Hannah THROOPE (6:55), b Br 20 Oct 1733 (6:-106), d 22 June 1811, 78 yr (6:168; 8:395), dau Thomas and Mary (Billings) Throope Jr of Br (6:52). The 1774 Census of Br showed Nathaniel as head of a household of ten persons: two males above 16, four males under 16, two females above 16, and two females under 16 (Bartlett, p 183). The 1790 US Census of RI, p 11, gave him as head of a household of eight people: four males 16 or above, one male under 16, and three females. Nathaniel was ca eighty years old when he became a member of the Congre Ch of Br on 28 Jan 1810 (8:266).

CHILDREN, all bp Congre Ch, Br except William Throop (6:-109; 8:290):
1. Nathaniel[4] Jr, b 10 June 1756 (6:109), bp 26 Sept 1756 (8:290); d June 1829 (Pat Index, p 711); m by Daniel Bradford, J.P., 20 Nov 1781 Lydia SALISBURY "of Caleb" (6:47, 55). Nathaniel Jr was a Private from RI in the Rev War (Pat Index, p 711). There is a rec of the m in the Congre Ch, Br, of one ch, "Nathaniel of Nathaniel and Lydia", on 9 Feb 1815 to Betsey WALDRON, dau William Throop and Jemima (Oxx) Waldron (8:354), who was his first cousin. The will of William Throop Waldron of Br, dtd in 1843, named his dau, Betsey, wife of Nathaniel Waldron of Woodstock, Conn (RIGR, 13:4), and three of her ch, Eveline, Frederick and Henry. So Nathaniel and his family rem to Woodstock.
2. Billings, b 4 Feb 1758, bp 28 May 1758; d 1 Nov 1823, 66 yr (6:169; 8:395); m Elizabeth___ and had no issue. The will of Billings Waldron of Br, yeoman, dtd 1 June 1820 and pvd 5 Jan 1824, named wife Elizabeth; brothers Nathaniel, John dcd leaving unnamed heirs, Thomas, Ambrose, Joseph, Benjamin, William T., and Samuel Waldron; sisters Polly wife of Stephen Talbee, Abigail wife of Ephraim Cory, and Rebecca Bailey dcd leaving unnamed heirs, being the late wife of Daniel Bailey; nephew David Waldron son of brother Samuel Waldron; Betsey Cartee dau of Stephen Talbee and Polly his wife; and item: to the daus of my brother-in-law Stephen Talbee and

Polly his wife, now living, and to the heirs of Alice Freeborn dcd, i.e. Hannah Nooning wife of Jonathan Nooning, Betsey Cartee wife of Benjamin Cartee, the heirs of Alice Freeborn dcd wife of Isaac Freeborn; to Polly wife of Thomas Waldron Jr, Nancy wife of John Fletcher, Abigail wid of Wing Spooner dcd, Priscilla wife of Nathan Warren, and Rachel Talbee (RIGR, 9:59).

3. John, b 13 Feb 1760 (Pat Index, p 711), twin, bp 2 Mar 1760; d 29 Sept 1818; m Elizabeth HOWLAND, poss bp Congre Ch, Br with three siblings on 17 Aug 1766 (8:-278), dau John and Elizabeth (LeFavour) Howland Jr (6:-28). John was a Private from RI in the Rev War (Pat Index, p 711). No issue in VR Br, but his brother, Billings, in his will of 1 June 1820, said John was dcd and had unnamed heirs (RIGR, 9:59).

4. Abigail, b 13 Feb 1760, twin, bp 2 Mar 1760; m by Daniel Bradford, J.P., 18 July 1779 Lt Ephraim CAREY of Scotland, Conn, son of Benjamin Carey (6:12).

5. Thomas, b 16 Jan 1762 (6:109), bp 6 June 1762; d 11 Sept 1821, 59 yr (6:169; 8:395); m (1) Lucretia GLADDING (Pat Index, p 711), b 25 July 1766 (6:78), bp Congre Ch, Br 4 Oct 1767 with two siblings, d as "Lucretia wife of Thomas" 22 Feb 1786, 22 yr (sic) (8:394), dau John and Lucretia (Smith) Gladding Jr; m (2) as Thomas "of Nathaniel" by Daniel Bradford, J.P., 1 Feb 1778 Ruth GRAY "of Col Thomas" (6:55). The IGI RI says he m her 20 Nov 1778), b 1764 per d rec, d 19 June 1850, 85 yr, wid, a Rev War pensioner (6:170). The date of 1778 for his second m must be incorrect; perhaps it was 1788.

Thomas Gray m Abigail Brown and was a Lt Col from RI in the Rev War (Pat Index, p 282). The will of Thomas Gray of Br, yeoman, dtd 7 Nov 1803 and pvd 5 Dec 1803, named wife Abigail, and a dau, Ruth Waldron (RIGR, 7: 167). Thomas Waldron was a Private from RI during the Rev War (Pat Index, p 711). The 1790 US Census of RI, p 11, showed him as head of a household in Br of four persons: one male 16 or over, one male under 16, and two females. His kn ch, b Br, were, by first wife, Lucretia: Hannah, "dau Thomas and Lucretia" m Br 6 Jan 1807 Capt James BATT, son James and Mary Batt of Dorsetshire, Eng (6:7); and Richard Smith "of Thomas and Lucretia" m Br 10 Feb 1807 Lydia M. GRAY, dau Pardon and Reliance Gray (8:354). By his second wife, Ruth, he had: Thomas Jr, b 22 Aug 1790; and John, b 12 Apr 1797, both "to Thomas and Ruth".

<u>6</u>. Ambrose, b 1 June 1764, bp 24 June 1764; d 7 Sept 1846, 83y 3m (6:170), or d same date, 82 yr (8:492); m Congre Ch, Br 3 Apr 1786 Hannah GLADDING (8:353), b 27 Aug 1764 (6:78), d 25 June 1850, 85 yr, wid of Ambrose (6:170), dau John and Lucretia (Smith) Gladding Jr of Br.

7. Rebecca, b 16 June 1766, bp 12 Oct 1766; d bef brother Billings's will of 1 June 1820; m (1) Congre Ch, Br as "of Nathaniel and Hannah" 22 Oct 1786 Daniel HOWLAND, son John and Elizabeth Howland (8:337); m (2) Br as Mrs Rebecca Howland 18 Jan 1801 (8:298) David BAILEY of Woodstock, Conn, son David and Elizabeth Bailey (6:-6; 8:324). No issue in VR Br. She left unnamed heirs per will of her brother, Billings, who were prob b in Conn.
8. Joseph, b 8 Feb 1768, twin, bp 13 Nov 1768; d 1 Feb 1840, 72 yr (6:169); m Congre Ch, Br, 1 Sept 1793 (8:-328, 353) Charlotte COGGESHALL "of Mrs Hannah", b 1767 per d rec, d 16 Sept 1824, 57 yr as "wife of Joseph" (6:169; 8:395). His kn ch, b Br were: d of a ch of Joseph 25 Aug 1794, 3w (8:394); Joseph of Joseph b 1 Sept 1795 (IGI RI) and d as ch of Joseph 10 Sept 1795, 10d (8:394); Hannah, b 1796 (IGI RI) and d 17 July 1803, 7y (8:394); William Coggeshall, b Mar 1797 (IGI RI); and Lucy C. who m (1) Br 1 Aug 1819 ___PHILLIPS (8:346), and m (2) she "of Joseph and Charlotte" Congre Ch, Br 3 Jan 1825 John H. THINGLEY, son Barton and Lorana Thingley (8:352). The will of Joseph Waldron of Br, 3 score and 6 yrs old, dtd 13 Jan 1834 and pvd 2 Mar 1840, named his two daus, "Lucy B. Waldron late wife of John H. Kingsley, and Maria Waldron"; his brothers Ambrose, William T., Samuel Waldron, and Benjamin Waldron dec; Abby Sammana and Harriet Jones, daus of my brother Benjamin Waldron dec (RIGR, 13:1).
9. Benjamin, b 8 Feb 1768, twin, bp 13 Nov 1768; d 30 Apr 1822 (8:395); m Congre Ch, Br 20 Sept 1790 Sarah WARDWELL, b 1771 per d rec, bp Congre Ch, Br with two siblings 23 Oct 1774 (8:291), d 1 Oct 1826, 55 yr, wid (6:169), dau Deacon Joseph and Elizabeth (May) Wardwell of Br (6:156; 8:353). Benjamin's ch, bp Congre Ch, Br, were (8:290): Abigail, bp 4 Dec 1796, m Br 31 May 1812 John SEMANATT (8:349) who was named as John SAMMENATTER in the will of his brother-in-law, Capt Thomas Jones, dtd 15 Nov 1815 (RIGR, 7:171); Harriet, bp 4 Dec 1796, m Br 30 Aug 1813 Capt Thomas JONES (8:338); John Wardwell, bp 7 July 1799 and alive 15 Nov 1815 when named in will of Capt Thomas Jones; and Ellen Smith, bp 20 Apr 1800, d 16 Oct 1804, 4½ yr (8:394).
10. William Throop, b 29 Aug 1770; d 10 July 1843, 73 yr (6:170); m Congre Ch, Br 26 Feb 1793 (8:344, 353) or 10 Oct 1792 (IGI RI) Jemima OXX, bp Congre Ch, Br 25 Sept 1774 (8:283), d aft husband's will of 14 July 18-43, dau Capt Samuel Oxx Jr and his second wife, Rebecca Lindsey (6:41). Capt Samuel Oxx Jr was a Private from RI in the Rev War (Pat Index, p 510). Capt Samuel Oxx's will, he of Br, dtd 19 Mar 1806 and pvd 1 Dec 1806, named his wife Rebecca, and as one of his daus, Jemima Waldron (RIGR, 6:158). The Methodist Ch was formed in

Br with a first class that met in May 1792 at the home of Capt Daniel Gladding, and among its approximately sixteen members was William Throop Waldron (Munro, p 263). Two of his ch are kn from their m's in the Congre Ch, Br (8:354): Betsey Waldron, of William Throop and Jemima, m 9 Feb 1815 Nathaniel WALDRON of Nathaniel and Lydia; and Allen, of William Throop and Jemima, m 19 Oct 1817 (8:335) Martha GLADDING of Capt Daniel and Susanna Gladding. Allen d 13 Mar 1848, 54 yr (6:170). The will of William T. Waldron of Br, dtd 14 July 1843 (sic) and pvd 4 Sept 1843, named: wife Jemima; sons Allen whose wife is Patty, William T. Jr who has three unnamed sons, John, Henry, and Levi Waldron; daus Betsey wife of Nathaniel Waldron of Woodstock, Conn, Rebecca wife of Perez Mason, Jemima wife of James Hathaway, and Harriot wife of Augustus N. Miller; the three ch of dau Betsey wife of Nathaniel Waldron, viz: Eveline, Frederick and Henry (RIGR, 13:4).

11. Samuel, b 11 May 1772, bp 24 Oct 1773; d 4 June 1840, 68 yr (6:169); m St Michael's Ch, Br, 23 Dec 1794 (8:219) Molly/Mary INGRAHAM, b 5 Sept 1771 (6:84), d 11 Sept 1828, 57 yr, "wife of Samuel" (6:169; 8:395), dau Joshua Ingraham and his second wife, Mary Richmond (8:208). Mary Richmond had a Myflwr desc from John Alden through her father, Rogers Richmond of LC, RI, whose mother was Elizabeth Rogers, dau of John Rogers of Duxbury, Mass (LC Fams, p 514-515). The first two of Samuel's kn ch were bp in the Congre Ch, Br (8:290): Ambrose, bp 13 Sept 1798 and d 14 Sept 1798, 8w (8:394); Eliza, bp 13 July 1800, m Congre Ch, Br 29 Oct or 29 Nov 1819 Nathaniel WALDRON, b 8 Oct 1795 (6:109), son Ambrose and Hannah (Gladding) Waldron, who was her first cousin (8:354); Mary Billings "of Samuel Waldron" d 13 Oct 1813, 18m (8:395); and David, named in his uncle Billings Waldron's will of 1 June 1820 (RIGR, 9:59).

12. Mary/Polly, b not rec, but named in her brother, Billings's will of 1 June 1820, which said she was wife of Stephen Talbee and had offspring. The VR Br (6:165) give the d of Polly, wife of Stephen Talbee, 28 Dec 1832, 98 yr (sic). She prob d ca her 58th yr, and was b ca 1774, to fit into the b dates of her siblings. Stephen Talbee was prob b Br 3 Oct 1766, son Edward and Anstis (Waldron) Talbee (6:105), in which case he was Polly's first cousin. The will of Polly's brother, Billings, dtd 1820, named several ch of hers (RIGR, 9:59): Hannah who m Jonathan NOONING; Betsey who m Benjamin CARTEE; Alice who m Isaac FREEBORN; and Rachel.

Ambrose[4] (Nathaniel[3], Cornelius[2], George[1]) Waldron was b 1 June 1764 and bp Congre Ch, Br 24 June 1764. He d 7

Sept 1846, 82y 3m (6:170), and m Congre Ch, Br 3 Apr 1786 Hannah GLADDING (8:353), b 27 Aug 1764 (6:78) and d 25 June 1850, 85 yr "wid of Ambrose" (6:170), dau John and Lucretia (Smith) Gladding Jr (6:23). The 1790 US Census of RI, p 11, listed Ambrose as head of a household in Br of six persons: two males 16 or over, two males under 16, and two females. The will of Ambrose Waldron of Br, dtd 19 Jan 1835 and pvd 5 Oct 1846, named: wife Hannah, sons Leonard and Billings (two eldest sons), John, Nathaniel, Marshal and Richard S. Waldron; daus Nancy (eldest) wife of Ephraim Cary, Mary Anthony widow, Hannah wife of John Dimon, Rebecca wife of Sanford Pearse, and Abby wife of Joseph Liscomb (RIGR, 13:6).

CHILDREN, B Br (6:109):
 1. Son^5, d 10 June 1802, 16 yr (8:394).
 2. Leonard, b 2 Feb 1787/88; d 27 Mar 1863, 76 yr (8:-237); m by 1808 Elizabeth____. His kn ch b Br, were (6:-110): Lydia, b 27 July 1809; Ambrose; John H. who m Martha F. COLE, of Nehemiah (6:55); and ch of Leonard d 4 Mar 1817, 2d (8:395).
 3. Nancy, b 22 Dec 1788 or 1789; m (1) Br 6 Nov 1806 Solomon GLADDING, b 1784 per d rec, d 7 May 1811, 27 yr (6:135), or d 5 June 1811 (8:371), son Capt Joshua and Sarah Gladding (6:24); m (2) Ephraim CARY per her father's will of 19 Jan 1835. No issue found in VR Br.
 4. Billings 2d, b 27 Aug 1790; m by Rev Jordan Rexford 16 Feb 1812 Hannah DIMAN (6:55); b 1787 per d rec, d 26 July 1839, 52 yr, wife of Billings (6:168), dau Jonathan and Dolly (Fales) Diman of Br (6:18). The will of Dolly Diman, wid Jonathan, dtd 7 Feb 1821, named dau Hannah wife of Billings Waldron Jr (2d) (RIGR, 9:61). He had three ch rec in the VR Br (6:110): Jonathan Diman, b 8 Dec 1812; Elizabeth Jackson, b 17 Oct 1814; and d of Harriet Newell of Billings, 16 July 1821, 4yr (8:395). Note: Did he also have a son, Billings, who m 12 Oct 1840 Martha HADWIN of Providence (IGI RI)?
 5. Mary/Polly, b 6 Apr 1792; m St Michael's Ch 18 Jan 1819 Joseph ANTHONY (8:199) who d bef 4 July 1825. Mary was bp as an adult at St Michael's 2 Apr 1820 (8:146). The will of Joseph Anthony of Br, dtd 2 June 1825 and pvd 4 July 1825, mentioned unnamed living wife; ch Hannah W. Anthony; bros (in-law?) Leonard Waldron and Billings Waldron, trustees and execs (RIGR, 9:59). Molly/Polly had the fol ch, surname Anthony, bp St Michael's Ch, Br (8:146): Mary, bp 24 Dec 1819; Hannah Waldron bp 2 Aug 1822; and Mary Abby and Joseph Augustus, both bp 15 Sept 1826.
 6. John, b 9 Mar 1794; d aft father's will of 19 Jan 1835.
 7. Nathaniel, b 8 Oct 1795 (6:109); d aft 19 Jan 1835;

m Br 29 Oct or 29 Nov 1819 Eliza WALDRON (8:354), bp
Congre Ch 13 July 1800, dau Samuel and Mary (Ingraham)
Waldron, his first cousin. No issue in VR Br.
8. Marshall, b 24 Aug 1797; d aft father's will of 19
Jan 1835.
9. Hannah, b 7 Mar 1799; d 23 Aug 1839, 40 yr (6:129);
m Congre Ch, Br 26 Oct 1819 John DIMAN (8:331), b 2 Jan
1794 (6:73), son William and Nancy (Munro) Diman of Br
(6:38, 73). Hannah had the following ch bp St Michael's
Ch, Br, surname Diman (8:154): George Waters; Serephine who m David Sands WILCOX (8:204); Nancy Munro; and
John Williams. A ch of John and Hannah d 1 Aug 1830
(8:225); and poss the "John of John" who d 12 Oct 1821,
14m, was hers (8:367).
10. Son d 8 June 1802, 14 days (8:394).
11. Rebecca, b 20 May 1803; m Congre Ch, Br 31 Dec 1822
(8:354), or 1832 (8:345) Sanford Munro PEARSE, son Capt
Jeremiah and Mary (Munro) Pearse (8:345). No issue in
VR Br.
12. Abby Cary, b 4 May 1805; m St Michael's Ch 3 Sept
1826 Joseph Diman LISCOMB (8:219), bp St Michael's 13
July 1806 and bur there 24 Sept 1863, 58 yr (8:165, 230),
son Isaac and Margaret (Diman) Liscomb. Abby had three
kn ch, surname Liscomb, bp St Michael's (8:165): Hannah
Pearse, Catherine, and Margaret D.
13. Richard S.(mith?), b 20 Nov 1807; d aft father's
will of 19 Jan 1835.

77. THOMAS WALKER

The place of b, and parentage, of Thomas[1] Walker are
not kn. He was b ca 1654 per his d rec, and was living in
Br by 20 June 1683 when he signed the Oath of Fidelity
there. He d Br 7 Aug 1724, 70 yr, and was bur in the old
graveyard of the Walker family (Munro, p 141; 8:237). He
m 4 Nov 1684 Elizabeth PARRIS (Torrey, p 775) who, from
her d rec, was b 1648 and d Br 6 Nov 1742, 94 yr (6:170).
The will of Thomas Walker of Br, tanner, being aged and
infirm, dtd 20 Feb 1721/22 and pvd 26 Oct 1724, named wife
Elizabeth; son William Walker; dau Mary (Little?); and
gdau Jane Walker now in Barbados (Rounds, 1:109). The will
of Elizabeth Walker of Br, wid, being aged and infirm,
dtd 23 June 1735 and pvd 8 Apr 1743, named son William
Walker; dau Mary wife of Edward Little; gdaus Mary Little
and Elizebeth Little, both under 18 and unm; gch: John and
Thomas Bowen, and Sarah, Esther and Elizebeth, ch of my
dau Elizebeth Bowen dcd; gdau Jane Walker of Barbados dau
of my son Thomas Walker dcd; Sarah Little, under 18 and
unm, eldest dau of Edward Little; and friend Samuel Howland of Br to be exec and guardian of my gch (Rounds, 1:

329). On 12 Mar 1741 Joseph Russell of Br, gentleman, was appointed guardian of Elizebeth Walker of Br, wid, who was "non compus mentis" (Rounds, 1:315).

CHILDREN, b Br, order unkn (6:110):
1. John^2, b 1 Oct 1685; d Br 3 May 1719, 34 yr, bur in old graveyard of the Walker family. "Hee was furst born of this race, and furst buried in this place." (Munro, p 141).
2. Capt William, b 5 Aug 1687; d 17 July 1735 (6:170): m Hannah___, b 1692 per d rec, d Br 2 May 1774, 82 yr (Ibid), bur St Michael's Ch (8:237).
3. Thomas, b unrec; called dcd in mother's will of 23 June 1735; m unkn and had one dau, "Jane Walker of Barbados" named in his mother's will. No recs in VR Br.
4. Mary, b 28 July 1693 (6:110) or b 28 July 1698 (Myflwr Fams in Progress, Richard Warren, p 68); d 25 Jan 1739/40 (6:145); m Br 7 Nov 1717 as his first wife Edward LITTLE (6:33, 55), bp 17 July 1698, d betw Apr 17-76 and 2 Oct 1777, prob at New Haven, Conn, son Lt Samuel and Sarah (Gray) Little of LC and Br (Myflwr Fams in Progress, Richard Warren, p 67-68). Edward Little's ch have a Myflwr desc from Thomas Little who m Ann, dau Richard Warren of the Myflwr (LC Fams, p 398-399). Mary had nine ch b Br, surname Little (6:88): Sarah, b 15 Oct 1718; Edward, b 1 July 1720, d.y.; Mary, b 15 May 1721, m Thomas RANNEY and was living in Middletown, Conn 2 Sept 1774; Thomas, b 18 Oct 1722, living in Litchfield, Conn 2 Sept 1774; Elizabeth, b 8 Mar 1724/25, m ___WALLACE and was living in Middletown, Conn 2 Sept 1774; Lemuel, b 26 Aug 1726; Nathaniel, b 10 Apr 1729; Edward II, b 16 May 1733 and living in Simsbury, Conn 2 Sept 1774; and Rebecca, b 22 Feb 1736/37, m Matthew GREGORY and was living in Danbury, Conn 2 Sept 1774.
5. Elizabeth, b unrec; called dcd in mother's will of 23 June 1735; m ___BOWEN and had the fol ch, surname Bowen, named in mother's will: John, Thomas, Sarah, Esther and Elizabeth. Not in VR Br.

Capt William^2 (Thomas^1) Walker was b Br 5 Aug 1687 and d there 17 July 1735 (6:170). He m Hannah___ who was b 1692 per d rec and d Br 2 May 1774, 82 yr (Ibid), and bur St Michael's Ch (8:237). The first services of the Protestant Episcopal Ch in Br (St Michael's) were conducted by laymen in the early 1700's in Mr William Walker's house, betw High and Wood Sts, a little north of the road that skirts the head of Walker's Cove (Munro, p 141). At Easter of 1724 when the first vestry of St Michael's Ch was elected, William was made one of the vestrymen (Ibid, p 145). The will of William Walker of Br, gentleman, dtd 4 June

1735 and pvd 13 July 1735, named wife Hannah; son John Walker; daus Rachel, Elesebeth and Mary (no surnames); his negro men Peleg and Ceaser; his tanyard; wife and son to be execs (Rounds, 1: 242-243).

CHILDREN, b Br (6:110):
1. John^3, b 17 Mar 1714/15; d Br 3 Apr 1773, 59 yr (6:-170); m St Michael's 6 Nov 1746 Patience COGGESHALL (8:-220), b 1725 per d rec (6:170), d 28 Feb 1791, 66 yr, wid (Ibid), bur St Michael's (8:237).
2. Rachel, b 24 Oct 1716.
3. Elizabeth, b 15 Jan 1720/21; m as Eliza at St Michael's 3 Oct 1745 Stephen RAWSON (8:220). She had one ch bp Congre Ch, Br, surname Rawson: George, bp 10 May 1747 (8:285).
4. Mary, b 23 Oct 1722; m St Michael's 2 Oct 1742 Elisha WEAVER (6:55; 8:220). She had two ch b Br, surname Weaver (6:111): John, b 10 Mar 1743/44, and William, b 15 Mar 1744/45.

John^3 (Capt William^2, Thomas^1) Walker was b Br 17 Mar 1714/15 and d there 3 Apr 1773, 59 yr (6:170). He m at St Michael's 6 Nov 1746 Patience COGGESHALL, b 1725 per d rec, d 28 Feb 1791, 66 yr, wid (Ibid), and bur St Michael's (8:327). Patience was bp at St Michael's as an adult on 6 Nov 1765 (8:183). John was one of the freemen who on 10 Feb 1746/47 took the Oath of Bribery and Corruption at Br (Munro, p 161). On 9 Mar 1747 he was chosen Vendue Master of Br and was empowered to hold public auctions. On the same date he was made one of the two Church wardens of St Michael's (Ibid, p 150, 163). The 1774 Census of Br gave Patience as head of the only Walker family there, which was made up of three females above 16, and one black (Bartlett, p 183).

CHILDREN, b Br, bp St Michael's (6:110; 8:182-183):
1. William^4, b 25 July 1748; bur St Michael's 8 Dec 1748 (8:237).
2. Elizabeth, b 25 Dec 1750.
3. John, b 28 Oct 1753, bp 7 Feb 1755; bur St Michael's 19 Feb 1755 (Ibid).
4. Abigail, b 16 Mar 1758.
5. Rebecca, b 6 Nov 1759, bp 29 Oct 1765; bur St Michael's 31 Oct 1765 (Ibid).

78. UZELL/UZAL WARDWELL

See also: RI Roots, 1990, 16:69-73, 104-111.

Uzell/Uzal^2 Wardwell was b 7 Apr 1639, prob in Exeter,

NH, and d 25 Oct 1732 in Br, eldest son of William and Alice Wardwell of Boston, Mass, and briefly of NH and Me. Uzell was a carpenter and settled in Ipswich, Mass where he m (1) 3 May 1664 Mary (KINSMAN) RINDGE/RING, who d betw June 1673 and 1676, dau Robert and Mary (Boreman) Kinsman Sr of Ipswich, and wid of Daniel Rindge/Ring Sr (Gen Dict Me & NH, p 720; Torrey, p 779). He m (2) by 1677 Grace___ who d Br 9 May 1741 (6:170). The b's of his ch were rec at Ipswich from 1665-1677, and at Br from 1684-1693 (VR Ipswich, 1:382; 6:110). On 17 May 1685 he took the Oath of Fidelity at Br (Munro, p 114). The 11 Feb 1688/89 list of families at Br showed that he then had a wife, six ch, and no servants there (Early Rehoboth, 1: 72-76).

The will of Uzal Wardwel of Br, yeoman, dtd 10 Jan 1728 and pvd 7 Dec 1732, named wife Grace; five sons, Joseph, Uzal, James, William and Benjamin; and six daus, Mary Barker, Grace Giddeons, Sarah Bosworth, Alec (Alice) Glading, Abigail Green, and Hannah Crompton (Rounds, 1: 210). The will of Uzal's second wife, Grace Wardwel of Br, wid, dtd 19 Oct 1739 and pvd 27 May 1741, named sons Uzal (eldest), James, Joseph, Benjamin dcd; daus Mary Barker, Grace Giddins and Sarah Bosworth; gson Uzal Wardwel, son of my son Benjamin dcd; and daus-in-law (stepdaus) Abigail Green, Hannah Crompton and Mary Lawles; son-in-law Nathaniel Bosworth to be exec (Ibid, 1:308).

CHILDREN by first wife, Mary, all b Ipswich (VR Ipswich, 1:382):
1. Abigail^3, b 27 Oct 1665; d aft step-mother's will of 19 Oct 1739; m 1684 John GREENE Jr of East Greenwich and Warwick, RI (RI Roots, 16:104), d 6 Oct 1729 Warwick, RI, son John Greene Sr of London, England.She had eleven ch, surname Greene (Gen RI Fams, 1983, 1:368, 372-374): James, John, Jane, Usal, Ebenezer, Robert, William, Enfield, Mary, Hannah and Andrew.
2. Hannah, b 1667; d aft step-mother's will of 19 Oct 1739; m by 1693 Francis CROMPTON/CRUMPTON of Ipswich, Mass (Torrey, p 195). She had four ch b Ipswich, surname Crompton/Crumpton (VR Ipswich, 1:105; Hammatt, p 283; IGI Mass): Francis, Hannah, Mary and Francis II.
3. Alice, b 27 Dec 1670; d Br 23 Mar 1729 (not 3 Mar 1720 as per Rep Men RI, 1:134); m Br 31 Oct 1693 John GLADDING Jr of Br (6:23), b 11 Oct 1670 Newbury, Mass, d Br 29 Aug 1754, son John and Elizabeth (Rogers) Gladding Sr of Newbury and Br (TAG, 64:143-147). She had eleven ch b Br, surname Gladding (6:78): John, Mary, William, Jonathan, Ebenezer, Joseph, Alice, Elizabeth, Nathaniel, Sarah, and Sarah II.
4. Mary, b June 1673 (Hammatt, p 393); d aft step-mother's will of 19 Oct 1739; m ___LAWLES(S). No recs

of her m, or b's of ch, in the VR Br or IGI Conn. They prob left town.

CHILDREN by second wife, Grace:
5. Mary II, b Sept 1677 (VR Ipswich); d aft mother's will of 19 Oct 1739; m Branford, Conn by Rev Samuel Russell 13 June 1700 Jonathan BARKER of Branford, son Edward Barker (Torrey, p 41; VR Branford). She had nine ch b Branford, surname Barker (VR Branford, in Conn Nutmegger, 1969, 2:239; Bailey, 2:101-104; Fams Anc New Haven, 1:114; IGI Conn): Anne, Jonathan, Mary, Uzel, James, Rebecca, Sarah, Abigail, and Joseph.
6. Grace, b 1678 (not rec Ipswich); d 1 May 1768, 90 yr; m Br 25 Dec 1701 Joseph GIDDINGS/GIDDENS Jr, b 9 June 1672 (6:134), son Joseph and Susannah (Rindge) Giddings Sr of Ipswich (IGI Mass). She had four ch, surname Gidding, first one or two b Ipswich, rest in Br (6:77; Gidding Fam, p 23): Mary, Susannah, Sarah and Martha.
7. Uzal, b unrec, "eldest son"; d aft mother's will of 19 Oct 1739; m by 1707 Phebe BASSETT, b 9 Oct 1681, dau Samuel and Mary (Dickerman) Bassett of New Haven, Conn. Rem to Branford, Conn (Fams Anc New Haven, 1:135; Bailey, 2:101-104; Gen Conn Fams, 2:121). He had eight ch, all b Branford (Bailey, 2:101-104; IGI Conn): Mary, b 8 June 1708; Sarah, b 13 Jan 1709/10, who m 24 Jan 1734 Jacob HARRISON of Branford; Phebe, b 18 July 1712, who m 10 Apr 1740 Thomas ALLEN; Hannah, b 4 Jan 1714, who m 28 Dec 1737 Joseph TYLER Jr of Branford; Rebeccah, b 21 Nov 1716; Abigail, b 14 Dec 1718, who m 20 Apr 1740 John BALDWIN; Joseph, b 31 May 1721, who m 30 May 1745 Lois FRISBIE; and Uzal, b 20 Oct 1723.
8. Sarah, b 1682 per d rec (not rec Ipswich); d 11 Oct 1771, 89 yr and bur St Michael's Ch, Br 13 Oct 1771; m Nathaniel BOSWORTH, b 23 Nov 1693 Hull, Mass, bur 19 Jan 1771 St Michael's, 78 yr, son John and Sarah Bosworth (6:63, 118; 8:223; IGI Mass). She had five ch b Br, surname Bosworth (6:63): Sarah, Rebecca, Mary, Priscilla, and James.
9. James, b 30 June 1684 Br; d 14 Mar 1757, 74 yr; m Sarah INGRAHAM (6:110, 170).
10. Joseph, b 30 July 1686 Br; d 10 Mar 1755, 69 yr; m (int) 22 Dec 1709 Martha GIDDINGS/GIDDENS (6:23, 56, 110, 170).
11. Benjamin, b 9 Apr 1688 Br; d 1739; m (1) Mary___ who d 2 May 1733; m (2) (int) 18 Jan 1734 wid Elizabeth HOLMES of Norton, Mass, who d 6 June 1737 (6:110, 170).
12. William, b 13 May 1693, twin; d aft mother's will of 19 Oct 1739. No m or ch in VR Br.
13. Rebecca, b 13 May 1693, twin; prob d.y. as not named in mother's will of 19 Oct 1739 (6:110).

James[3] (Uzell[2], William[1]) Wardwell was b Br 30 June 1684 and d there 14 Mar 1757, 74 yr (6:170). He m by 1714 Sarah INGRAHAM, b 23 Sept 1695, d as wid 2 Apr 1761, dau Timothy and Sarah (Cowell) Ingraham of Br (6:83, 170; Torrey, p 410; Repre Men RI, 1:372). James was a freeman of Br when he took the Oath of Bribery and Corruption at Br on 10 Feb 1746/47 (Munro, p 161).

CHILDREN, b Br (6:110):
1. Rebecca[4], b 22 Mar 1714/15; d 28 Sept 1761 (6:149); m St Michael's Ch 19 Dec 1732 as his first wife, Simeon MUNRO (6:56), b Br 30 July 1713, d Br 23 May 1789, 76 yr (6:149), son George and Mary Munro (6:91). She had seven ch b Br, surname Munro (6:91): Dorcas, Rebecca, Mary, William, Simeon, Archibald and Sarah. Two of them, Deacon William and Dr Archibald, were in the Rev War from RI (Pat Index, p 474-475).
2. James "Jr", b 4 May 1717; d 9 Apr 1745; m Br 3 Mar 1742 Ann LISCOMB, b 8 Feb 1718/19, d 9 Feb 1796, dau John and Rebecca (Thurston) Liscomb Jr of Br. He was made a freeman of RI at Br in 1747 (MacGunnigle, p 46; 6:33, 56, 87, 170; 8:237). He had one kn ch b Br, Rebecca, b 21 Jan 1743/44, who m David MUNRO (Repre Men RI, 1:372).
3. Hannah, b 5 Apr 1720; prob d as wid 5 June 1759; m (int) 6 July 1740 Samuel SANFORD of Newport, RI. She had one ch b Br, surname Sanford, Hannah, b 25 June 17-45 (6:47, 56, 102, 161).
4. Sarah, bp 2 Feb 1723; m (int) 28 Nov 1741 Archibald SALISBURY who d Newport, RI 22 May 1743. She had one ch b Br, surname Salisbury, Sarah, b 30 Jan 1742/43 and d Mar 1745/46. Sarah poss m (2) (int) 14 Dec 1745/46 (sic) Joseph KELLEY (6:47, 56, 102, 161; 8:183).

Joseph[3] (Uzell[2], William[1]) Wardwell was b Br 30 July 1686 and d there 10 Mar 1755, 69 yr. He m (int) 22 Dec 1709 Martha GIDDINGS/GIDDENS, b 1687 and d 11 Aug 1755, 88 yr, dau Joseph and Susanna (Rindge) Giddings of Ipswich, Mass (Virkus, 5:709). Joseph was a cordwainer, and as a freeman of Br he took the Oath of Bribery and Corruption there on 10 Feb 1746/47 (Munro, p 161; 6:23, 56, 110, 170). His will, dtd 6 Sept 1753 and pvd 7 Apr 1755, he being aged, mentioned wife Martha; sons Joseph dec, John and Stephen; daus Mary Lindsey, Martha Howland, Elizabeth Phillips and Susanna Glading; and three gdaus of son Joseph dec: Jemima, Martha and Lydia (RIGR, 5:92).

CHILDREN, b Br (6:110):
1. Mary[4], b 22 Sept 1710; d 7 Aug 1712 (6:170).
2. Mary II, b 2 Aug 1713; d Rehoboth, Mass 3 June 1777,

65 yr (6:144); m Br 23 Nov 1737 William LINDSEY, b 2 July 1713, d Rehoboth, Mass 17 May 1777, 64 yr (Ibid), son John and Elizabeth (Munro) Lindsey Jr. The d's of Mary and William Lindsey were not in the VR Re, p 846. Mary had seven ch, b Br, surname Lindsey (6:32, 56, 87): Mary, Rebecca, Martha, Lydia, William, Benjamin, and William II.
3. Joseph, b 3 June 1715; d.y.
4. Martha, b 29 Nov 1716; d 9 July 1794, 78 yr, wid; m Br 24 Oct 1736 John HOWLAND, b 27 Sept 1713, son Samuel and Abigail (Cary) Howland. Her ch have a Myflwr desc from John Howland. She had two kn ch b Br, surname Howland: John, b 29 Jan 1736/37 who d.y., and John II, b 9 Mar 1738/39 who m 25 Oct 1759 Elizabeth LEFAVOUR, and had thirteen ch b Br (6:28, 56, 83, 140).
5. Joseph II "Jr", b 6 Oct 1718; d 10 Sept 1746; m Br 23 Feb 1737/38 Jemima LINDSEY, b 20 May 1719, d 9 Sept 1796, 78 yr, dau John and Elizabeth (Munro) Lindsey Jr. He had four daus b Br (6:32, 56, 87, 110, 163, 170): Jemima, b 18 Dec 1738; Elizabeth, b 20 Aug 1741; Martha, b 14 Dec 1743; and Lydia, b 13 Dec 1745.
6. Son, b 6 Aug 1720; d 18 Aug 1720.
7. John, b 12 Oct 1720 (6:110) (sic, prob error for 1721); d betw 25 Jan 1770 and 7 Jan 1771; m 11 Oct 1741 Phebe HOWLAND, b 9 Mar 1720/21, d 30 Nov 1794, 74 yr, dau Samuel and Abigail (Cary) Howland. Their desc have a Myflwr desc from John Howland. He was a freeman of Br when he took the Oath of Bribery and Corruption there on 10 Feb 1746/47 (Munro, p 161), and he was a Lt when he was in one of the four Br companies which in 1754 went on the Expedition against Crown Point (Repre Men RI, 1:-372). John had eleven ch b Br (6:110), all of whom were mentioned in his will dtd 25 Jan 1770 and pvd 7 Jan 1771, he termed gentleman of Br. In it he named wife Phebe; sons John eldest, Nathaniel second son, Joseph, Samuel, Daniel, and Allen; daus Phebe and Susanna both m, and Mary, Elizabeth and Tabitha, some under age (RIGR, 6:-153). His dau, Phebe, m James SMITH, and dau Susannah m Daniel GLADDING (6:56, 110).
8. Stephen, b unrec but b 1722 per d rec; d 6 Aug 1799, 77 yr; m (1) Br 18 Dec 1746 Mehitabel HOWLAND, b 1 Feb 1724/25 and d 13 Feb 1764, dau Samuel and Abigail (Cary) Howland (6:56, 83, 170-171; Repre Men RI, 1:372-373). Their desc also have a Myflwr desc from John Howland. Stephen m (2) 16 Apr 1768 wid Jemima (OXX) BOURNE, bp 28 Feb 1732/33, d Br 19 Aug 1815, 83 yr (RIGR, 12:183), dau Capt Samuel and Mary (Lindsey) Oxx Sr of Br, and wid of Aaron Bourne Jr (Repre Men RI, 1:373). Stephen owned a tavern on Hope St in Br. He had six ch b Br by his first wife, Mehitabel (6:110): Elizabeth, Abigail, Stephen, Josiah, James and Hannah; and five ch by his second wife, Jemima (RIGR, 12:183): Benjamin, Priscilla, Jemima, John,

and Benjamin II.
9. Elizabeth, b unrec; d aft father's will of 6 Sept 1753; m (1) 2 Aug 1744 Nathaniel TOMKINS of LC, RI; and m (2) Br by Rev John Burt, as Mrs Elizabeth Tomkins, 28 Aug 1750 John PHILLIPS (6:44, 53, 56).
10. Susannah, b 1728; d 14 Dec 1806, 78 yr, wid; m 19 Oct 1752 William GLADDING, b 1 June 1730, d 7 Jan 1801, 71 yr, son William and Esther (Drowne) Gladding. No issue (6:23, 56, 78, 134-135).

Benjamin^3 (Uzell^2, William^1) Wardwell was b Br 9 Apr 1688 and d betw 29 Aug and 16 Oct 1739. He m (1) Mary____, who d 2 May 1733; and m (2) (int) 18 Jan 1734 wid Elizabeth HOLMES of Norton, Mass, who d 6 June 1737 (6:170; Repre Men RI, 1:373). He was a cooper. The will of Benjamin Wardwel of Br, dtd 29 Aug 1739 and pvd 16 Oct 1739, mentioned no wife, but named sons Usual, William, Jonathan, David and Isaac Wardwel; daus Mary and Olive (no surnames); son-in-law (stepson) Samuel Holmes, eldest son of his last wife; and his brother-in-law, Nathaniel Bosworth of Br, blockmaker (Rounds, 1:284).

CHILDREN, all by first wife, Mary (Repre Men RI, 1:373):
1. Mary^4, m (int) 27 May 1731 Nathaniel TURNER (6:54). No issue in VR Br or Newport.
2. Uzel, killed 17 Sept 1745 at Cape Breton, Canada; m 4 Nov 1739 Sarah LINDSEY, b 17 Sept 1719, d 2 Apr 1761 as wid, dau Samuel and Keziah (Joslin) Lindsey. He had two ch b Br: Mary, b 3 Sept 1740, and Sarah, b 10 Mar 1743/44 (6:56, 110, 170; 8:210).
3. Benjamin, d June 1739 at sea per Repre Men RI, or d Jan 1739 per VR Br 6:170. He must have d bef 17 Dec 1738 when his father, Benj Wardwel of Br, cooper, was appointed to admin his est (Rounds, 1:275).
4. William, b 1722; d 1760 at sea; m 26 Sept 1742 Mary HOWLAND, b 18 Mar 1722/23, dau Samuel and Abigail (Cary) Howland. His desc have a Myflwr line from John Howland. His ch were: Abigail, William, Major Benjamin, and two ch who d.y. (6:56, 83, 170).
5. Jonathan, killed May 1745 at Cape Breton, Canada (6:170-171).
6. David, killed 17 Sept 1745 at Cape Breton (Ibid).
7. Isaac, b 1730 per d rec; d 7 May 1810, 80 yr; m Br 9 Sept 1756 Sarah WALDRON, b 10 Feb 1734, d 5 July 1812, 79 yr, dau Cornelius and Ann(a) (Throope) Waldron of Br. He had five ch b Br and bp Congre Ch, Br (6:111; 8:291): Lydia who m Col Samuel Wardwell, Sarah, Jonathan, Anna, and Willoby. Isaac rem to Providence, RI (6:109, 111, 170-171).
8. Olive, m 19 June 1753 John GODDARD of Newport, RI. The VR Newport, 4:32 incorrectly call her Olive Wood.

79. RICHARD WHITE

It has so far been imposs to identify this man, who has no other entry in the VR Br than his attendance at the first town meeting on 1 Sept 1681. He never settled in Br as there are no b's, d's or m's for him or his family. Neither Sav nor Torrey gave a Richard White who was in Br.

80. JOHN WILSON

It is not kn when or where this John Wilson was b, or who his parents were. Sav did not identify him, and Torrey on p 825 said only that he m Esther___, had a ch b 1689, and lived in Br, RI. He signed the Oath of Fidelity in Br on 9 Aug 1686 (Munro, p 144). The 1689 Census of Br showed him as the only Wilson who was then head of a family there. His household included a wife, three ch, and no servants (Geneals RI Fames, 1989, 2:402). He was not taxed on the Br tax list of 1695, and he had d bef 4 June 1696 when Esther Willson, wid, had a horse described in Br (TAG, 65:-118).

KNOWN CHILDREN, b Br (6:112):
1. Benjamin^2, b 1 June 1689 (IGI RI lists this under both Br and Warren, RI); m (1) 9 Jan 1719/20 at Newport, RI Amy GREENMAN of Newport (VR Newport, 4:33) who d bef 4 Mar 1729 when Benjamin m (2) Newport by Samuel Vernon, JP, Elizabeth COGGESHALL (Ibid, 4:78). He had three kn ch by his first wife, b Newport (Ibid, 4:124; IGI RI): Mary, Benjamin and William.
2. Esther, b 20 Aug 1691 (IGI RI lists this under both Br and Warren); bp Congre Ch, Br 30 Sept 1695 as "Hester, dau John Wilson and his wife" (Geneals RI Fams, 1989, 2:372). The IGI RI says she m 1717 William GREENMAN of Newport, RI. One ch, Job of William and Esther Greenman, d 28 Sept 1738 in 16 yr and was bur in the Common Bur Ground of Newport (VR RI, Beaman, New Series, 11:-192).
3. Mary, b 17 Aug 1693 (IGI RI lists this in both Br and Warren).

81. HUGH WOODBURY

Hugh^2 Woodbury was the son of William Woodbury (1589-1677) who m 29 Jan 1616 or 1616/17 Elizabeth Patch in So Petherton, England, and had a grant of land in Salem, Ma in 1637 (Torrey, p 836-837). William's will was dtd 5 June 1663 and pvd 26 June 1677. The inv of his est said he was aged ca 88 and d 29 Jan 1677. In it he named wife

Elizabeth, one dau, and five sons, including Hugh. The date of Hugh's b is not kn, but Sav, 4:634, said that he was one of the founders of the Ch on the Beverly side of Salem, and m in Dec 1650 Mary DIXEY, perhaps dau of Thomas of Salem. Hugh was a mariner, and d in Br 17 Apr 1702 (6:-174) and Mary, his wife, d there as wid of Hugh in 1705 (Ibid). He took the Oath of Fidelity at Br on 20 June 1683 (Munro, p 114). The 1689 Census of Br showed him there with a fam of a wife, five ch, and no servants (Geneals RI Fams, 1989, 2:401). Hugh joined the Congre Ch, Br on 7 May 1687 and his wife, Mary, joined it on 12 June 1695 (8:268). On 28 June 1686 he was one of six men, "all leading men of the town" (Munro, p 128), who petitioned the Rev Increase Mather and Church in Boston, in a letter, concerning a controversy over Mr Benjamin Woodbridge, the then minister at Br.

The agreement re settling the est of Hugh Woodbery and Mary Woodbery, his wife, both dcd, was dtd 3 Oct 1706 and signed by: William Fulton of Br, attorney for Jonathan Woodbery of Br, mariner and guardian of Samuel and Sarah Woodbery, brother and sister of the said Jonathan, who are all ch of Capt Samuel Woodbery, mariner, dcd: Mary Woodbery of Br, wid of John Woodbery, mariner dcd, and guardian of Nathaniel Woodbery, son of the dcd John; Joseph Pratt of Br, sadler, and Elizabeth his wife; Edward Gross of Newport, mariner, and Mary his wife (Rounds, 1:36).

CHILDREN, b Salem, Mass, order unkn (Sav, 4:634):
1. Samuel^3, b 6 Dec 1651, bp 25 Jan 1652; d.y.
2. Capt Samuel II, bp 4 June 1654; m Br by 1684 Mary___ (Torrey, p 836). See #16, this book.
3. Hugh, b 12 Feb 1657, bp 9 Mar 1657.
4. John, b 5 Sept 1658, bp 6 Mar 1659; d 3 Mar 1698/99 (6:174); m 18 May 1694 Mary REYNOLDS of Br, who d 27 Sept 1718 (Ibid), dau Nathaniel^2 Reynolds (Torrey, p 836; 6:45, 60). He had one ch rec Br, Nathaniel, b 23 June 1697 (6:113), m (int) 13 Apr 1720 Abigail COFFIN of Mendon, Mass (6:60), and had three ch b Br (6:113): Mary, Abigail and Priscilla.
5. Priscilla, b 8 Apr 1666.
6. Mary, m Edward GROSS of Newport, RI, mariner, and had three ch b Br, surname Gross (6:81): Dixie, Benjamin, and Priscilla.
7. Elizabeth, m Joseph PRATT, "sadler", and had two ch b Br, surname Pratt (6:100): Elizabeth, and Elizabeth II.

BIBLIOGRAPHY

The American Genealogist, 65 Vols (hereafter TAG).
Ancient and Honorable Artillery Co of Mass 1638-1774, Women Descendants of (hereafter Anc and Hon Artill Co).
Arnold, James
  Vital Records of RI. Vol 2, Providence; Vol 4, Newport; Vol 6, Bristol, Barrington and Warren; Vol 8, Bristol (hereafter VR Prov, VR Newport; VR Br, Bar or War).
Austin, John O.
  The Genealogical Dictionary of RI (hereafter Austin).
  One Hundred and Sixty Allied Families (hereafter Austin, 160 Fams).
Bailey, Frederick W.
  Early Connecticut Marriages, 7 Books (hereafter Bailey).
Banks, Charles E.
  Topographical Dictionary of 2885 English Emigrants to New England 1620-1650 (hereafter Banks Topogr Dic Eng Emigrants).
  The History of Martha's Vineyard, Dukes Co, Mass, 3 Vols (hereafter Banks).
Bartlett, John R.
  RI Census Inhabitants of the Colony of RI and Providence Plantations in 1774 (hereafter Bartlett).
Beaman, Alden G.
  Vital Records of RI. New Series, 13 Vols (hereafter VR RI, Beaman, New Series).
Bicknell, T.W.
  History of Barrington, RI (hereafter Bicknell).
Bliss, Leonard Jr.
  History of Rehoboth (Mass) (hereafter Bliss).
Bodge, George M.
  Soldiers of King Philip's War (hereafter Bodge).
Boston Reports of Record Commissioners, Births, Marriages and Deaths 1630-1699, and Births 1700-1800. Edited by William S. Appleton (hereafter Appleton).
Boston Marriages. Vol 1, 1700-1751; Vol 2, 1752-1809. Compiled by E.W. McGlenen (hereafter Boston Mars).
Bowen, Richard L.
  Early Rehoboth (Mass), 4 Vols.
Bowman, Fred Q.
  10,000 Vital Records of Eastern New York 1777-1834 (hereafter F.Q. Bowman).
Bowman, George E.
  Mayflower Marriages. From his files at the Mass Society of Mayflower Descendants. Compiled by Susan E. Roser (hereafter Bowman).
Cary, Seth C.
  John Cary, the Plymouth Pilgrim (hereafter Seth C. Cary).

Caulkins, Frances
  History of New London, Conn (hereafter Caulkins).
Chamberlain, George W.
  Genealogies of Early Families of Weymouth, Mass (hereafter Chamberlain).
Chamberlain, Mildred M., transcriber
  1777 Military Census of RI.
Clark, Franklin C.
  Bristol Branch of the Finney Family. In Genealogies of RI Families, 1989, Vol 1, p 448-490.
Clark, Mary B.
  Bosworth Genealogy. Descendants of Edward Bosworth (hereafter Bosworth Gen).
Clemens, William M.
  Darling Family in America (hereafter Darling Fam).
Cole, Ernest B.
  Descendants of James Cole of Plymouth, 1633 (hereafter Cole).
Colket, Meredith B. Jr
  Founders of Early American Families 1607-1657 (hereafter Colket).
Colonial Revolutionary Lineages of America (hereafter Col Rev Lin Amer).
Connecticut DAR
  Connecticut Revolutionary Pensioners (hereafter Conn Rev Pens).
Connecticut Families, Genealogies of, 3 Vols (hereafter Gen Conn Fams).
The Connecticut Nutmegger, 23 Vols (hereafter Conn Nutmegger).
Cutter, William R.
  Genealogies of New England Families (hereafter Cutter).
Daughters of the American Revolution, National Society
  DAR Patriot Index, Vol 1, 1966 (hereafter Pat Index).
Davis, William T.
  Genealogical Register of Plymouth Families (hereafter Gen Reg Plym Fams).
Dimond, Edwin R.
  Diman or Dymont Family of E. Hampton, Long Island (hereafter Diman Fam).
Fales, DeCoursey
  Fales Family of Bristol, RI (hereafter Fales Fam).
Gallup, John D.
  Genealogical History of the Gallup Family in the US (hereafter Gallup Fam).
Giddings, Minot S.
  The Giddings Family; Descendants of George Giddings (hereafter Gidding Fam).
Gladding, Henry C.
  The Gladding Book (hereafter GB).
Guild, Georgiana and H.S. Gorham
  The Gorham Family in RI. In NEHGS Register, Vol 54, p

168-174.
Hammatt, Abraham
  Hammatt Papers (hereafter Hammatt).
Hazen, Henry A.
  History of Billerica, Mass (hereafter Hazen).
Heitman, Francis B.
  Historical Register of Officers of the Continental Army,
  Revolutionary War (hereafter Heitman).
Hurd, D. Hamilton
  History of New London County, Conn, 2 Vols (hereafter
  Hurd).
Jacobus, Donald L.
  Families of Ancient New Haven, 8 Vols (hereafter Fams
  Anc New Haven).
Jacobus, Donald L. and E.F. Waterman
  Hale, House and Related Families (hereafter Hale, House).
Lewis, Alonzo and J.R. Newhall
  History of Lynn, Mass (hereafter Lewis and Newhall).
MacGunnigle, Bruce C., compiler
  RI Freemen 1747-1755 (hereafter MacGunnigle).
The Mayflower Descendant (hereafter MD).
Mayflower Families, Genealogies of, 3 Vols. Articles from
  the NEHGS Register. (hereafter Geneals Myflwr Fams).
Mayflower Families in Progress through Five Generations,
  4 Vols plus brochures (hereafter Myflwr Fams thru Five
  Gens).
Mayflower Source Records. Articles from the NEHGS Register. (hereafter Myflwr Source Recs).
Mitchell, Nahum
  History of Bridgewater, Mass (hereafter Mitchell).
Munro, Wilbur
  History of Bristol, RI (hereafter Munro).
New England Families, English Origins of. 1st and 2nd Series, each 3 Vols (hereafter Eng Origins New Eng).
New England Historic and Genealogical Society's Register,
  144 Vols (hereafter NER).
Noyes, Sybil, C.T. Libby and W.G. Davis
  Genealogical Dictionary of Maine and New Hampshire
  (hereafter Gen Dict Me and NH).
Paige, Lucius R.
  History of Cambridge, Mass 1630-1877 (hereafter Paige).
Peck, Ira B.
  Descendants of Joseph Peck (hereafter Peck Gen).
Rattray, Jeannette E.
  History of East Hampton, Long Island (hereafter Rattray).
Reynolds, Marion H.
  History and One Line of Descendants of Robert and Mary
  Reynolds of Boston (hereafter Reyn Gen).
Rhode Island Families, Genealogies of, 1983, 2 Vols. From
  RI periodicals (hereafter Geneals RI Fams, 1983).
Rhode Island Families, Genealogies of, 1989, 2 Vols. From

NEHGS Register (hereafter Geneals RI Fams, 1989).
Rhode Island Genealogical Register, 13 Vols (hereafter RIGR).
Rhode Island, Representative Men and Old Families of (hereafter Repre Men RI).
Rhode Island Roots, 16 Vols (hereafter RI Roots).
Rounds, H.L. Peter, compiler
   Bristol County, Mass Probate Records Abstracts. Vol 1, 1687-1745; Vol 2, 1745-1762 (hereafter Rounds).
Savage, James
   New England Genealogical Dictionary, 4 Vols (hereafter Sav).
Steiner, Bernard C.
   History of Guilford and Madison, Conn (hereafter Steiner).
Stiles, Henry R.
   History of Ancient Windsor (Conn). Vol 2 (hereafter Stiles).
Tilden, William S.
   History of Medfield, Mass 1650-1886 (hereafter Tilden).
Torrey, Clarence A.
   New England Marriages Prior to 1700 (hereafter Torrey).
Virkus, Frederick O.
   Compendium of American Genealogy, 7 Vols (hereafter Virkus).
Vital Records of: Braintree, Mass; Branford, Conn; Freetown, Mass; Ipswich, Mass; Lynn, Mass; Rehoboth, Mass; Saybrook Colony, Conn. For Bristol, see under James Arnold.
Wait, Estelle W.
   Papillons of Boston and Bristol. In NEHGS Register, Vol 124, p 161-182.
Wheeler, Richard A.
   History of Town of Stonington, County of New London, Conn (hereafter Wheeler).
Whitaker, Rev Epher
   History of Southold, Long Island (hereafter Whitaker).
Wilbour, Benjamin F.
   Little Compton, RI Families (hereafter LC Fams).

INDEX

ADAMS Abigail 52 Bethia 52 Chloe 52 Christian 52 Ebenezer 52 53 Hannah (Allen) 52 53 Martha (Hunt) 52 Mary 52 53 Newdigate 52 Rachel 53 Sarah 52 Stephen 52
ADCOCKE Neele 22
ALDEN David 134 Elizabeth 2 119 134 135 John 2 3 19 36 119 134 135 150 Mary (Southworth) 134 Priscilla (Mullins) 36 134 135 150
ALGER Mr 90 Sarah 90
ALLEN/ALLIN Abigail 30 101 103 139 Benjamin 48 Elizabeth 4 9 152 Hannah 52 53 124 Hannah () 53 Hopestill () 48 James 124 Jemima 48 John 4 Joseph 53 Lydia 124 Lydia () 124 Mathew 152 Phebe (Wardwell) 166 Rachel () 101 103 Ruth (Stockbridge) 152 Samuel 124 Sarah 4 123 124 Sarah (Smith) 124 Thomas 63 166 Viall 63
ALMY Job 14
ANDROS Abigail 113 Gov Edmund 4 122 Elizabeth 113 Ephraim 109 113 Hannah 113 John 113 Nathaniel 113 Patience 113 Sarah (Morey) 109 113
ANTILL Antills 83 Edward 81 82 Mary 25 81 82 83 134 Sarah () 81 82
ARCHER John 14 Mary 14
ARNOLD Ruth 73
ATHERTON Elizabeth (Rigby) 53 Humphrey 53 Phillip 114 Samuel 53 Watching 53
ATWATER Abigail 114 Mary 93
ATWOOD Elizabeth 73
AYRAULT Daniel 57 Hart (Brenton) 57
AYRERS Hannah (Lovell) (Dutch) 69 Joseph 69
BABBITT Esther 62
BACKAWAY/BARKAWAY Mary (Brown) 57 58 65
BAILEY/BAYLEY Daniel 157 David 148 159 Elizabeth 69 74 76 Elizabeth () 159 John 54 81 Joshua 14 54 81 82 134 Lydia (Redfield) 54 Mary 26 27 54 Mary (Gallup) 54 81 134 Rachel () 54 81 Rebecca (Throope) 148 Rebecca (Waldron) (Howland) 157 159 Sarah (Church) 9 Thomas 54
BAKER Edward 109 Hannah 109 110 113 Rev Luther 74 Mary 6 Rachel 11 141 150 Sarah 101
BALCH Sarah (Bosworth) 50 Varen 50
BALDWIN Abigail (Wardwell) 166 John 166
BARKER Abigail 166 Anne 166 Edward 166 James 166 Jonathan 166 Joseph 166 Mary 166 Mary (Wardwell) 165 166 Patience (Howland) 103 Rebecca 166 Samuel 103 Sarah 166
BARNES Abigail 71 Amy 140 Charlotte 71 Corban 71 Deborah 71 Dorcas (Corban) 71 Elizabeth/Betsy 71 John 71 Mary 71 Mary (Finney) 71 Patty 71 Rebecca 71

BARNEY Ann (Witt) 96 138 139 Anna 138 Dorcas 138
  139 Elizabeth 138 Rev Jacob 96 138 139 John 138
  Mary 138 Mary (Throope) 138 Sarah 96 Susanna 145
  William 138
BARSTOW Ann (Hubbard) 12 Mary 12 William 12
BARTHOLOMEW Abigail 1
BARTON Elizabeth (Phinney) 75 Haile 75
BASSETT Jane 40 118
BASTER/BASTAR Joseph 53 Mary 53 Richard 53 Roger
  53
BATEMAN Mary 140
BATES Rachel 61 62
BATT Sarah (Wilson) 136
BAXTER Elizabeth (Gorham) (Downs) 91 Jane (Baxter) 91
  Rev Joseph 120 Mary/Molly (Coffin) 91 Rebecca (Lee)
  (Saffin) 120 Richard 91 Shubael 91 Temperance
  (Gorham) (Sturgis) 8 Thankful 91 Thomas 8
BECKWITH Sarah (Lewis) 55 Thomas 55
BEDFORD Stephen 53
BELCHER Edward 101 Lydia (Howland) 101
BELLAMY Bridget () 42 107 Jeremiah 42
BENNETT Frances 47 James 119 John 119 Mary (Cobham)
  119 Ruth (Rogers) 119
BILLINGS Mary 147 148 156 157 Rev Richard 147 148
  Sarah (Little) 148
BIRGE/BURGE Elizabeth 55 Hannah (Bragg) 54 55 John
  54 55 Mary 55 Patience 55 Rebecca () 54 Richard
  54 Samuel 54 55 Sarah () 54 55
BISHOP Abigail 74 Abigail (Keene) 3 Deborah (Throope)
  140 Eleanor (Burton) 3 Eliphalet 3 Hudson 3 Ira
  140 Nathaniel 3 Thomas 74
BISSELL Zerviah 140
BISSETT Anstis (Gold) 38 Thomas 38
BLACKMAN Susanna (Palmer) 135
BLAGROVE Elizabeth (Allen) (Oliver) 4 Nathaniel 4 5
  6
BLAGUE Joseph 135 Martha (Kirtland) 134 135 136
  Mary 135
BLANCH Anna 30
BLETSOE/BLESGO Thomas 55
BLIGH John 29 Sarah (Everton) 29 Sarah (Reynolds)
  29 Thomas 29
BLISS Mehitable 145
BONNEY Daniel 3 Elisha 3 Elizabeth (Burton) 3 El-
  izabeth (Lincoln) 3 Jonathan 3 Seth 3
BORDEN Elizabeth 50
BOREMAN Mary 165
BOSWORTH Abigail 49 Abigail (Potter) (Munroe) 47 Al-
  fred 47 Allen 49 Ann(e) 46 Anna/Hannah (Willard)
  (LeFavour) 48 Bathsheba 50 144 Bellamy 42 43
  44 45 46 Benjamin 32 44 45 46 47 48 49 55
  56 154 Bridget 42 43 44 46 49 Bridget () (Bell-

amy) (Lobdell) 42 107 Celinda/Selinda (Ingraham) 21 Daniel 46 47 50 Ebenezer 46 49 Edward 42 43 44 48 49 56 Elizabeth 43 44 47 48 49 50 60 105 132 Elizabeth () 144 Elizabeth (Chamberlain) 48 Elizabeth (Dorby) (Miller) 43 Elizabeth (Estabrook/Easterbrook) 43 44 Elizabeth (Layton?) Lindsey 45 46 47 Elizabeth (Mayhew) 46 Elizabeth (Morton) 43 Elizabeth (Peck) 45 130 Elizabeth (Peckham) 47 Ephraim 43 Esther/Hester 44 45 84 85 86 Esther (Maxfield) 46 Frances 33 47 154 Frances (Bennett) (Nichols) 47 Hannah 42 43 44 49 50 107 Hannah (Morton) 56 Henry 48 Hopestill 49 Jacob 48 50 James 49 166 Jemima 49 Jemima (Allen) 48 49 Jeremiah 42 43 48 50 Jeremy 42 Jerom 44 John 42 43 44 47 48 166 Jonathan 49 50 60 143 144 Joseph 21 42 43 49 85 Judith 49 85 Judith (Torrey) 48 49 Lemuel 43 Lydia 46 47 50 Lydia (Cornish) 45 46 Lydia (Jones) 50 Lydia (Kent) 85 Mary 25 42 43 44 45 49 138 143 144 166 Mary/Merry () 43 44 Mary Bradford 47 Mary (Church) 32 47 154 Mary (Fales) 23 24 45 Mary (Hayward) 48 Mary (Hicks) 49 Mary (Morton) 43 Mary (Smith) 43 44 Mehitable 49 Mehitable () 48 49 Mr 90 Nathaniel 42 43 44 45 46 47 48 49 50 56 107 165 166 169 Obadiah 45 46 47 Pearce 21 Peleg 47 Peter 49 Phebe (Eddy) 48 Polly Taylor 21 Priscilla 166 Rebecca 45 49 50 138 166 Ruth 10 22 45 50 124 130 132 153 Ruth (Lawton) 47 Ruth (Lowder) 45 Ruth (Squire) 50 Samuel 43 45 49 50 130 Sarah 44 48 49 50 166 Sarah () 43 47 48 166 Sarah (Wardwell) 49 165 166 Submit 50 Susan(nah) 49 Susannah (Field) 50 William 23 24 45
BOURNE Aaron 168 Allen 34 126 127 152 Elizabeth A. 126 Elizabeth/Betsey (Smith) 34 126 127 George J. 126 George S. 34 Hannah 131 152 Jemima (Oxx) 168 John Waldron 152 Martha 152 Mary 152 Rebecca S. 126 Ruth 45 153 Ruth (Bosworth) (Church) 10 45 153 Ruth Waldron 126 Ruth (Waldron) 127 131 152 Shearjashub 10 45 127 131 152 153
BOWEN Avis 73 Elizabeth 162 163 Elizabeth (Munroe) 99 Elizabeth (Walker) 162 163 Esther 162 163 Frances (Davis) (Throope) 141 James 73 John 162 163 Jonathan 99 Molly 98 99 Pardon 99 Pennel/Penuel 141 Ruth (Arnold) 73 Sarah 162 163 Thomas 162 163 ___ 163
BOWERMAN Ann (Hooper) 81 Edward 81 Elizabeth 81 Elizabeth (Gallup) 81 134 Samuel 81 134 Tristram 81
BRACKETT Elizabeth 60 94 101 123 132 Elizabeth (Bosworth) 60 Peter 28 60 Priscilla 28 29 Richard 60

BRADFORD Alice 146 Alice (Richards) 119 Allen Taylor Smith 128 Daniel 34 158 Edward James 128 Elizabeth 119 Elizabeth () 128 Elizabeth (Finney) 76 Elizabeth (Reynolds) 34 Gamaliel 119 Gershom 119 Hannah 119 Hannah (Rogers) 119 Jerusha 119 Mary 30 Mary L. 106 Mary/Polly (Smith) 128 Nancy Smith 128 Perez 119 Samuel 34 119 Sarah (Reynolds) 34 Welthea 119 William 119 128 146 William Parnell 128 ___ 76
BRADLEY Hannah (Gorham) (Lewis) 93 Stephen 93 Susannah (Brown?) 95 ___ 95
BRAGG Ann 82 Bethiah (Howland) 102 Elizabeth () 84 Elizabeth (Mackmollen) 55 102 Experience 84 Hannah 54 55 Henry 54 82 97 102 John 81 82 84 Mary (Gallup) 81 82 Nicholas 102 Susanna(h) 97 Susanna () 82 97 William 102
BRANSON Anna (Shapleigh) 29
BRATTLE Elizabeth 3 Elizabeth (Hayman) 5 Elizabeth (Tyng) 3 5 Katherine (Saltonstall) 5 Thomas 3 5 William 5
BRENTON Abigail 2 9 57 Ann 57 Benjamin 56 57 Ebenezer 11 56 57 Elizabeth 57 Frances 57 Frances (Cranston) 57 Hannah (Davis) 56 Hart/Heart 57 Janleel 56 57 Martha 2 57 Mary 57 Mary () 57 Mercy 57 Priscilla (Byfield) (Waldron) 11 57 Rachel (Cook) 57 Samuel 56 57 Sarah 57 Thomas 57 William 2 56 57
BREWSTER Elizabeth 146
BRIGGS Abigail 73 Hannah 11
BRISTOW/BRISTON/BRISTOL Elizabeth 70 110 Elizabeth () 70 Thomas 70
BROOKS Elizabeth 110
BROWN(E) Abigail 158 Abner 95 Bethia 58 Bethia (Gorham) 95 Chad 63 Deliverance 58 65 Eleazer 93 Hannah 57 58 65 Hannah (Hobart) 119 James 100 Jemima/Jennings/Jinnus? (Williams) 57 58 65 John 58 119 Lydia 137 149 Lydia (Parchment) 57 Mary 57 58 65 100 120 Mary () 100 Obadiah 63 Polly 100 Sarah 58 63 93 Sarah () 58 Sarah (Rowe) 93 Susanna(h) 58 65 95 William 57 58 65 95
BROWNING Joseph 119 Marah (Cobham) 119
BRUSHETT Christabell 79
BRUTTON see BRENTON
BUCKINGHAM Temperance 136
BUCKMASTER George 153 Martha (Waldron) 153
BUELL Deborah 140
BUNKER Martha 8
BURGESS Hannah (Reynolds) 34 James P. 34 Mary 140
BURR Nancy (Champlin) 143 Samuel 143 Sarah 68
BURRILL Dinah 59 Dinah (Nicholson) 58 59 Elizabeth 59 Elizabeth () 58 Francis 58 59 George 58 Hannah 59 James 58 59 Jane 59 Joseph 59 Mary

(Cooper) 58 Sarah 59
BURROUGHS Abigail 60 Abigail () 59 60 Amy 60 Anne () 59 60 Benjamin 60 Desire 60 Elizabeth 59 Ezekial 60 Freeborn 60 James 59 Mary 59 60 Peleg 60 Samuel 60 Sarah (Church) 59 Thomas 59 60 William 60
BURT Rev John 15 16 26 45 46 47 98 103 127 169
BURTON Abigail (Brenton) 2 9 Alice (Wadsworth) 3 Eleanor 3 Elizabeth 3 Elizabeth (Winslow) 2 Martha 2 3 9 Penelope 3 Stephen 2 4 9 Thomas 3
BUSH Ann (Waldron) 154 Arnold Howland 154
BUTLER Jemima (Daggett) 67 Malachi 67 Thankful (Daggett) 67 Zephaniah 67
BUTTERWORTH Hannah (Fry) 77 78 John 77 78 Joseph 78
BYFIELD Deborah 7 Deborah (Clark) 6 7 Nathaniel 4 6 7 22 Priscilla 5 11 57 Richard 6 Sarah (Leverett) 6
CALDWELL Elizabeth () 35 Mary 35 Robert 35
CAMPBELL Caleb 70 Jeremiah 70 Mary 70 110 Mary () 70 Ruth 70 Sylvanus 70
CANADA/KENNEDY Mary 61 62 63
CAR(E)Y Abigail 101 103 125 139 168 169 Abigail (Allen) 30 101 103 139 Abigail (Paul) 62 Abigail (Waldron) 158 Allen 70 71 98 Amey Brown 64 Angeline 64 Ann 139 Asa 63 Bashua/Beersheba/Bathsheba 61 101 Benjamin 60 140 158 Bethia 61 92 94 Caleb 64 Catherine 62 Chad 63 Chloe 62 David 60 61 62 63 64 84 92 94 101 123 132 Ebenezer 63 Ebenezer Garnsey 64 Edward 62 Eleazer 138 139 Elizabeth 61 62 123 132 139 Elizabeth (Brackett) 60 61 84 92 94 101 123 132 Elizabeth (Godfrey) 51 60 Ephraim 158 161 Esther 62 Hannah (Church) 9 70 71 98 Henry 61 62 Jemima 30 85 John 30 51 60 64 101 103 139 John Paul 62 Joseph 30 60 Josiah 30 85 104 Lydia 139 Lydia (Throop) 138 139 Martha 139 Martha (Garnsey/Guernsey) 63 64 Mary/Molly 61 62 63 70 71 139 Mary (Canada/Kennedy) 61 62 63 Mehitable 51 61 Michael/Micah/Micha 63 Molly (Garnsey/Guernsey) 63 Nancy (Waldron) (Gladding) 161 Nathan(iel) 30 63 64 104 Patty (Gunsey) 63 Peter 61 Phebe 98 Polly (Moore) 64 Priscilla 61 62 84 Rachel (Bates) 61 62 Ruth (Reynolds) 30 85 104 Sarah/Sally 61 62 63 84 Sarah (Brown) 63 Susannah 84 140 147 Susannah (Kent) 140 Tabitha (Howland) 104 Thomas 62 63
CARPENTER Abigail (Briggs) 73 Abigail (Newton) 152 Elisha 73 Hannah (Finney) 73 Joseph 152 Louisa/Loiza 73 Mary 73 Peter 73
CARR Elizabeth 143 Elizabeth (Hoar) 98 Priscilla

(Waldron) 155 Robert 155 William 98
CARTEE Benjamin 158 160 Betsey (Talbee) 157 158 160
CARTER Martha 75
CHAFFEE Dorothy 22
CHAMBERLAIN Elizabeth 48 Henry 48
CHAMPLAIN/CHAMPLIN Bridget 143 Elizabeth (Carr) 143
  James 143 John 99 143 Joshua 143 Martha 143
  Mary 99 Nancy 143 Phebe 141 143 155 Phebe Hall
  143 Phebe (Throop) 143 Thomas 143 William 143
CHANDLER Dorothy (Church) 10 22 25 Dorothy (Paine) 25
  Elizabeth 26 John 10 23 24 25 Mary (Church) 10
  23 Mary (Raymond) 24 Samuel 10 22 Sarah 25 Sarah
  () (Paine) 23 24 25 ___ 25
CHAPIN Josiah 137 Lydia 137 Lydia (Brown) 137 Mary
  () 137
CHAPMAN Ann 145 Bathshua 145 Elias 145 Joseph 145
  Lydia (Wills) 137 138 Martha 145 Mary 137 138
  139 145 Mary (Throope) 144 145 Ralph 137 Susanna
  (Barney) 145 Sybbel 145 Thomas 144 145 Throop
  145
CHASE/CHACE Hannah (Bosworth) 44 Henry Clay 88 John
  Gladding 88 Joshua 44 Lucretia Gladding 88 Lucre-
  tia (Gladding) 88 Otis 88 Samuel 88 Sylvia 73
CHAUNC(E)Y Charles 1 Isaac 1 Mary 1 Sarah (Walley)
  1 Walley 1
CHENERIE see GENERY
CHESEBROUGH Abigail (Ingraham) 13 Elizabeth 13 Samuel 13
CHICKERING Esther 43 44
CHILTON James 35 71
CHRISTOPHER Sarah (Paine) 26 William 26
CHURCH Abigail 2 9 103 Abigail (Howland) 34 103
  123 125 Alice 6 9 135 Alice (Southworth) 2 5 8
  9 22 41 134 Ann 10 Ann () 105 Benjamin 2 5 8
  9 10 22 41 54 81 100 134 Caleb 47 Charles 9
  10 22 24 31 32 Col 22 Constant 9 10 22 24
  31 32 47 Deborah 47 138 139 140 Deborah (Woodworth) 47 Dorothy 10 22 Edith 9 Edward 2 9 El-
  iza/Elizabeth 6 9 10 11 22 41 45 47 105 Elizabeth (Bosworth) 47 Elizabeth (Viall) 9 Elizabeth
  (Warren) 8 59 Elizabeth (Woodman) 9 Eunice (Peckham) 32 Grace (Shaw) 103 Hannah/Anne 9 10 22 24
  70 71 98 Hannah (Dyer) 9 Hannah (Gay) 32 Hannah/
  Anne (Paine) 10 22 31 Israel 103 125 Joseph 103
  139 Martha 9 Martha (Burton) 2 9 Mary 9 10 23
  24 31 32 47 149 153 154 Mary (Reynolds) 10 22
  31 47 Mary (Tucker) 139 Mercy 9 Nathaniel 9 10
  11 22 24 45 47 103 Patience (Cook) 9 Peter 10
  24 31 32 Priscilla 9 Richard 8 59 71 Ruth
  (Bosworth) 10 22 45 153 Samuel 105 Sarah 5 9
  10 22 59 103 129 Sarah (Fales) 32 Sarah (Hayman) 5 Sarah (Horsewell) 9 Susannah 129 Susan

(Hayman) 9 Thomas 5 6 9 47
CHURCHMAN Ann(a) 40 119
CLARK(E) Deborah 6 Edward 33 Elizabeth 12 70 Elizabeth (Clark) 12 Elizabeth (Watson) 33 Ezekial 73 George Gibbs 73 Hannah (Church) (Carey) 98 Hannah (Parker) 73 Henry Finney 73 Jeremiah 76 Joannah (Finney) 76 Jonas 12 Katharine 12 Latham 59 Margaret 12 Martha 88 Mary 73 Mary (Finney) 73 76 77 Parker 73 Samuel 12 Sarah 12 Sarah (Sprague) 12 Submit 139 Thomas 6 Timothy 12 ___ 76 77
CLOSE Hannah 28
COBBETT Elizabeth () 64 John 64 Samuel 64 Sarah 64 Sarah () 64 Thomas 64
COBHAM Josiah 119 Marah 119 Mary 119 Mary (Haffield) 119
COBLEIGH/COBLYE John 138 143 144 Martha 138 143 144 Mary (Bosworth) 138 143 144
COCKRAN Eliza (Paine) 25 John 25
COFFIN Abigail 171 Mary/Molly 91
COGGESHALL Anstis (Wilkins) 39 Charlotte 159 Eliza/Elizabeth 143 170 George 74 143 Hannah () 143 159 Henry 74 James 89 Josiah 71 74 Loring Finney 74 Martha 74 Mary Pearse (Finney) 71 74 Mehitable 89 Molly (Finney) 71 74 Nancy 89 Patience 143 164 Patty () 89 Sarah (Throop) 143 Thomas 39 William 71 74 143
COGGIN Abigail (Bishop) 74 Henry 74
COIT Eunice (Gladding) 88 Joseph 88
COLBURN Deborah 142
COLE Alvin 98 Eleanor (Nichols) 142 Elizabeth 142 143 Isaiah 142 Judith 88 Lucretia G. 89 Luther 142 Lydia Burr (Hoar) 98 Martha F. 161 Nehemiah 88 161 Patience 99 Sarah (Gladding) 88 Thomas 143
COLLIER Elizabeth 9 80 133 William 80 133
COLLINS Mary 103
COOK(E) Alice (Southworth) 136 Hannah (Finney) (Morton) 74 John 9 74 135 Mary (Havens) 9 Patience 9 Rachel 57 Ruth (Shaw) 136
COOPER Ann 74 Lydia 43 Mary 58
CORBAN Dorcas 71
CORBIN Joan 12
CORNISH James 45 46 Lydia 45 46
CORNWALL Ann 116
CORPE/CORPS Anna 58 65 Benajah 65 David 65 Deliverance (Brown) 58 65 Elizabeth 58 66 Elizabeth () 65 Hope 58 65 John 58 64 65 Mary 58 65 Rebecca 65 Sarah 58 66
CORY Abigail (Waldron) 157 Ephraim 157
COTTON Hopestill 77 Rev Nathaniel 14 15 24 25 79 92
COWELL Sarah 13 79 167
COX Sarah 33 34

COY   John   42   115   Jonathan Woodbury   42   Mary   70   72
   Samuel   42   70   72   Sarah   42   Sarah (Woodbury)   42
   115   William   42
CRAFTS   Abigail   51
CRANSTON   Frances   57   Samuel   57
CROMPTON/CRUMPTON   Francis   165   Hannah   165   Hannah (Wardwell)   165   Mary   165
CROSSMAN   John Andrews   131   Julia Augusta   131   Luther Andrews   131   Sarah/Sally (Smith)   130   131
CUMMINGS   Elizabeth   86
CUNNELL   Elizabeth (Bosworth)   50
CURTIS   Abigail   66   Abigail ()   66   Deodate/Diodatus   66
   Eleazer   66   Hannah (Porter)   66   Mary   66   Nathaniel   66   Prudence (Gatlive/Gatliffe)   66   Rebecca ()   66
   Samuel   66   Solomon   66   William   66   Zachary   66   Zechariah   66
CUTHBERT   Patience   55
CUTTER   Hannah   48
DAGGETT/DOGGETT   Brotherton   67   Elizabeth (Hawes)   67
   Hannah   67   Hannah (Mayhew)   67   Jemima   67   John   67
   Mary (Pearse)   67   Mary (Smith)   67   Samuel   67   Thankful   67   Thankful (Daggett) (Butler)   67   Thomas   66
   67   Timothy   67
DANA   Bethia   142   Frances   141
DANIEL   Deborah (Waldo) (Ford)   77   Samuel   77
DARLING   Denice/Dennis   111   Hannah   110   111   Hannah
   (Francis)   111   Priscilla (Ingraham)   16   William   16
DAVENPORT   Elizabeth   68   Elizabeth (Taylor)   68   Elizabeth (Wood)   68   Israel   68   Jeremiah   68   Noah   68
   Phebe   68   Phillis ()   68   Ruth   68   Samuel   68   Sarah
   (Burr)   68   William   68
DAVIS   Abigail   119   Amanda   73   Ann (Low)   141   Anthony
   73   Bethiah (Howland) (Bragg)   102   Charles   10   David
   73   Dolor   115   Elizabeth   82   83   Elizabeth (McIntosh)
   83   Frances   141   Hannah   10   56   Hannah/Anne (Church)
   10   22   Ichabod   73   Jesse   73   John Jeremiah Finney
   73   Lucinda   73   Mary/Polly   73   96   115   Mercy   41
   115   Rebecca (Finney)   73   Simon/Simeon   10   22   83
   102   115   141   Sylvia (Chase)   73
DAY   Abigail (Crafts) (Ruggles)   51   Ralph   51
DEAN   John   118   Samuel   118   Sarah (Edson)   118   Sarah
   (Robinson)   118
DEAUR   David   122   Elizabeth (Eddy)   122
DEIGHTON   Frances   40   118   Jane (Bassett)   40   118   John
   40   118
DENISON   Ann (Borodell)   8   George   8   Mercy (Gorham)   8
DE WOLF   Abigail   15   17   72   131   Abigail (Potter)   17
   22   131   Charlotte   72   Charlotte (Finney)   72   Elizabeth   125   Elizabeth (Martin)   104   105   107   Henry   72
   Levi   130   131   Lydia Potter   131   Lydia Potter (Smith)
   130   131   Maria   72   Mark Ant(h)ony   17   72   105   131

Mary 131 Sarah 131 William 72
DICKERMAN Abigail 93 Isaac 93 Mary 166 Mary (Atwater) 93
DIMAN Ann(a) (Gallup) 16 82 Daniel 69 Dolly (Fales) 161 Elizabeth (Waldron) 33 154 George Waters 162 Hannah 87 161 Hannah (Finney) 69 109 Hannah (James) 69 Hannah (Waldron) 161 162 James 69 Jeremiah 69 82 154 John 69 82 161 162 John Williams 162 Jonathan 69 161 Lucretia 69 86 87 124 128 129 Margaret 162 Mary 16 82 Nancy 82 Nancy (Munro) 162 Nancy Munro 162 Nathaniel 16 82 Phebe 69 Rebecca 69 Sarah (Giddings/Giddens) 82 154 Serephine 162 Thomas 33 69 109 129 154 William 82 162
DIXEY Mary 40 171 Thomas 171
DOLLIVER John 55 Mary (Birge) 55
DONELLY/DONNELS Catherine 62 Mary (Carey) 62 Terrance 62
DORBY Elizabeth 43
DORMAN Benjamin 93 Lydia 93 Sarah (Tuttle) 93
DOWNS Edward 91 Elizabeth (Gorham) 91 Samuel 91 William 91
DRING see DRURY
DROWN(E) Alathea 24 Elizabeth 94 123 124 Esther 84 169 Esther (Bosworth) 84 85 86 124 Irene 24 Martha 157 Mary 85 86 129 Mary (Paine) 22 24 Sarah (Paine) 24 25 Solomon 84 85 124 Thomas 24 25
DRURY/DURY Austin 131 Hannah (Smith) 130 131 Dr John 130 131 John People 131 Luke 131 Lydia Potter (Smith) 131
DURFEE Amy (Burroughs) 60 Mr 60
DURKEE Louise 16
DUTCH Ann (Lovell) 69 Benjamin 69 Ebenezer 69 Elizabeth 69 Hannah 69 Hannah (Lovell) 69 Mary (Kimball) 69 Osman 69 Robert 69 Thomas 69
DWIGHT Hannah (Close?) 28 John 28 Josiah 142 Sarah 28 29
DYER Abigail (Fitch) 146 Hannah 10 John 146 Sibel/Sybel 140 145 146
EATON Hannah 92 93
EDDY/ADY Elizabeth 122 Elizabeth (Waldron) 157 Hannah 17 Hannah (Smith) 122 Jeremiah 157 John 122 Joseph 122 Lydia 17 Phebe 48 Preserved 17 William 122
EDSON Sarah 118
ELLERY Abigail 39 Abigail (Wilkins) 38 39 Anstis 39 Benjamin 38 39 Hannah 39 John 39 Mehitable (Redwood) 39 Samuel 39 William 39
EMERSON Elizabeth 137 James 137 Sarah () 137
ESSEX/ESSIA Rebecca (Corpe) 65
ESTABROOK/EASTERBROOK Elizabeth 43 44 Sarah (Woodcock) 44 Thomas 44

EVELETH Bridget (Bosworth) (Papillion) (Pecker) 44 45
    Edward 44
EVERTON Sarah 29
FAIRBANKS Abigail 116 Benjamin 116 David 116 Deborah 116 Elizabeth 116 Hannah 116 Jeremiah 116 Jerusha 116 Jonathan 116 Mary 116 Mary (Penfield) 116 Nathaniel 116 Rebecca 116 Sarah 114
FALES/FAILES Abby F. 71 Alathea (Paine) 22 23 Alethea 23 149 Amarentia 125 127 128 Betsey P. 71 Charlotte 71 130 Deborah 23 24 Deborah (Fisher) 23 Dolly 161 Dorothy 34 35 Edward 130 Elizabeth Gardner (Thomas) 23 Fidelia 71 Hannah (Peck) 23 127 Hannah (Reynolds) 33 34 35 Henry DeWolf 71 James 23 71 James Gibbs 71 John 71 Jonathan 23 24 54 127 Joseph Jackson 71 Lydia Smith 130 Martha (Finney) 71 Martha G. 71 Mary 23 45 154 Mary (Smith) 130 Nancy C. 71 Nathaniel 23 35 71 130 149 Samuel 23 Sarah/Sally 32 34 35 Sarah (Little) 23 35 71 130 149 Stephen Smith 130 Timothy 22 23 35 71 103 William 130
FAUNCE Jane 77 Jane (Nelson) 77 Thomas 77
FIELD Abigail 95 Abigail (Waterman) 95 Jeremiah 95 Susanah 50
FINNEY/PHINNEY Abigail 70 72 110 Abigail (Bishop) (Coggin) 74 Allen 71 Ann/Nancy 72 75 Ann (Toogood) 75 Avis 73 Avis (Bowen) 73 Benjamin 75 Catherine 74 Charlotte 71 72 Christian(a) 74 Clark 70 David 75 Deborah 70 73 110 Deborah (Loring) 70 72 Ebenezer 77 Elisha 76 Eliza Atwood 74 Elizabeth 70 71 72 73 75 76 Elizabeth (Bailey) 69 74 76 109 Elizabeth (Bristow) 70 110 Elizabeth Clark 70 Elizabeth (Clark) 70 Elizabeth (Mann) 75 Elizabeth (Wood) (Tibbitts) 75 Esther 70 71 109 110 Esther (Lewis) 69 109 Experience (Pearse) (Hersey) 73 George 72 74 Hannah 69 73 74 76 77 109 Jabez 75 Jane (Faunce) 77 Jeremiah 69 70 71 72 73 74 75 109 110 Joanna 76 Joanna (Kennicut/Kinnicutt) 76 Joel 75 John 69 70 73 74 75 76 109 110 Jonathan 74 75 76 Joseph 71 Joshua 74 75 Josiah 70 71 75 Josiah Morton 70 Keziah 75 Levi Loring 74 Loring 71 72 73 Lydia 26 75 76 77 Martha 71 75 Martha (Carter) 75 Martha (Gibbs) 70 71 Mary/Molly 69 70 71 73 74 75 76 77 109 Mary (Campbell) 70 110 Mary/Molly (Carey) 70 71 Mary (Coy) 70 72 Mary Pearse 71 73 Mary (Rogers) 74 Mehitable 69 76 109 Mercy 75 76 Mercy (Read) 76 Mercy (Watts) 75 Nathaniel 75 Nelson 77 Oliver 75 Rebecca 70 73 109 Robert 74 Ruth 70 Ruth Thurston 72 Samuel 75 Sarah/Sally 72 Susanna 72 Thomas 70 72 73 74 Thomas Gibbs 72 William 75

FISHER Deborah 23
FITCH Abigail 146 Alice (Bradford) 146 James 146
  John 37 Mary () 72 Oliver 72 Richard 72 Susanna
  (Finney) 72
FLETCHER John 158 Nancy () 158
FO(R)BES Martha (Pabodie) 135 Mary 135 William 80
  133 135
FORD Andrew 77 Deborah 77 Deborah (Waldo) 77 Eleanor (Lovell) 77 Joseph 77
FOSDICK Anna (Shapleigh) (Branson) 29 John 29 Sarah
  (Reynolds) (Bligh) 29
FRANCIS Hannah 111
FREEBORN Alice (Talbee) 158 160 Isaac 158 160
FREEMAN Mercy (Southworth) 134 Samuel 134
FRENCH Abby Finney 72 Elkanah 72 Emily P. 72 Esther
  72 Hannah (Walker) 72 Lydia (Ingraham) 16 17 Ruth
  Thurston (Finney) 72 Timothy 16 17
FRISBIE Lois 166
FRY Abigail (Spink) 79 Anthony 77 78 79 116 Deliverance 14 15 Deliverance () 78 Hannah 116 Hannah () 77 78 79 116 James 78 John 14 15 78 79
  Martha 79 Mary 14 15 78 79 86 Mercy 78 Mercy
  (Taylor) 79 Nathaniel 78 79 Stephen 78 Thomas 78
  ___siar 78
FULLER Desire 113 Edward 113 Elizabeth 50 Naomi
  (Rowley) 113 Robert 117 Samuel 113 Sarah 117
FULTON Mary (Woodbury) 41 William 41 171
GAGER Mary 147
GALLUP/GALLOP Abigail 17 82 Ann(a) 6 82 83 Antill
  83 Benadam 79 80 Christabell (Brushett) 79 Edward
  83 Eliza(beth) 25 81 82 83 134 Eliza () 82 Elizabeth (Southworth) 54 80 81 133 134 Hannah (Lake)
  79 Joan 79 John 54 79 134 Mary 54 81 82 83
  134 Mary () 81 82 134 Mary (Antill) 25 81 82 83
  134 Nathaniel 79 81 134 Rebecca 83 Samuel 54 79
  80 81 82 83 133 134 Sarah 83 Susannah 145 William 25 79 80 81 82 83 134
GAMLYN Elizabeth 137
GARNSEY/GUERNSEY Ebenezer 63 Martha 63 64 Martha ()
  63 Molly 63 Patty 63
GATES Mary 67
GATLIVE/GATLIFFE Prudence 66 Prudence () 66 Thomas
  66
GATLINE Mary (Pearse?) 117
GAY Hannah 32
GENERY/CHENERIE Deborah 137 Elizabeth (Gamlyn) 137
  Isaac 137
GEORGE Elizabeth 53
GEREARDY Deliverance (Brown) (Corps/Corpe) 58 65 John
  58 65 Sweet 58 65
GIBBS Ann 15 Eliza(beth) 19 21 James 15 20 70 71

John 19 21 86 Martha 70 71 Martha (Giddings) 70 71 Mary 15 86 Mary (Ingraham) 15 Nathaniel 15 Sarah (Ingraham) 20 Sarah (Jones) 19 21 86 Thomas 15
GIDDINGS/GIDDENS Grace ()? (Wardwell) 165 166 Joseph 166 167 Martha 70 71 104 105 166 167 Mary 166 Sarah 82 154 166 Susannah 166 Susanna(h) (Rindge) 166 167
GILBERT David 93 Elizabeth (Gorham) 93 Experience (Perkins) 93
GILES/GILLS Mary 10 22 30 31 148 Susannah 36
GILLAM Anne 4
GILLETT Daniel Ordway 146 Ebenezer 146 Israel 146 Martha (Throope) 146
GILMAN Mary 43 107
GLADDING Abigail 87 Alice 62 85 165 Alice (Wardwell) 62 84 165 Allen Ingraham 20 88 Alzada 89 Amanda (Martin) 86 Anne 89 Anstress T. 90 Bathsheba 84 Benjamin 62 84 86 88 89 129 Benjamin S. 89 Car(e)y 62 84 85 Charles 85 86 Charlotte (Ingraham) 20 88 Daniel 86 87 89 90 107 160 168 Daniel S. 87 89 David 62 85 Ebenezer 62 84 165 Edmund 20 88 Edward 88 Edward Talbee 89 Elizabeth/Betsey 62 84 85 86 165 Elizabeth (Cummings) 86 Elizabeth (Rogers) 165 Ella Fales 89 Ella Frances 89 Elsa () 86 Esther 84 Esther (Drowne) 84 169 Eunice 20 88 Experience (Bragg) 84 Ezra 87 George 86 87 Gilbert Richmond 20 88 Hannah 87 88 129 158 160 161 Hannah (Short) 85 86 Hannah T. 89 Hannah V. (Harding) 89 Henry 62 85 James 85 James Cogeshall 90 James D. 88 James Nickerson 89 James S. 87 Jemima (Carey) 85 John 15 16 20 62 84 85 86 87 88 89 90 105 123 129 158 161 165 John G. 89 Jonathan 61 62 84 165 Jonathan Peck 90 Joseph 61 62 84 85 86 87 165 Joshua 87 161 Josiah 87 Judith 85 86 Judith (Boswell) 85 Julia Ann T. 89 Lefavour Howland 90 Lillis 85 Lucretia 87 88 129 158 Lucretia () 105 Lucretia G. (Cole) 89 Lucretia James 89 Lucretia (Smith) 20 86 87 105 106 129 158 161 Lydia 86 87 88 89 Martha/Patty 15 16 86 87 91 160 Martha () 123 Martha (Clarke) 88 Martha James 20 88 Martha (Smith?) 84 85 Martha T. 86 Martha Turner 90 Mary 15 16 86 87 105 165 Mary () 85 Mary (Drowne) 85 86 129 Mary (Gibbs) 86 Mary Ingraham 20 88 Mehitable (Coggeshall) 89 Molly/Polly 87 88 90 129 Nancy 90 Nancy Ann 90 Nancy (Coggeshall) 89 Nancy (Peck) 90 Nancy (Waldron) 87 161 Nathan/Nathaniel 62 84 85 86 90 165 Peter 62 87 91 Phebe 86 91 107 Philip 86 Priscilla 62 84 100 Priscilla (Carey) 61 62 84 85 Rachel 89 90 Rachel Talbee 89 Rachel (Talby/Talbee) 87 88 Rebecca

84 85 88 Rhoda 85 Richard 88 129 Richard Smith 20 88 Samuel 20 62 85 86 88 89 129 Samuel T. 89 Sarah/Sally 62 84 85 86 87 88 91 129 165 Sarah () 161 Sarah (Alger) 90 Sarah (Carey) 61 62 84 Sarah Cole 89 Sarah (Wardwell) 87 161 Solomon 84 87 161 Stephen 62 89 Stephen T(alby/Talbee) 88 Susan(nah) 87 90 Susannah (Carey) 84 Susannah W. 90 Susanna(h) (Wardwell) 84 87 90 107 160 167 168 169 Timothy 62 84 87 William 84 85 165 169
GODDARD John 169 Olive (Wardwell) 169
GODFREY Abigail 24 Caleb 24 Elizabeth 51 60
GOFF Esther (Smith) 124 Huldah 105 James 124 Jeremiah 99 Joseph 105 Lucy () 99 Mary (Gladding) 84 Mary (Ormsbee) 124 Patience () 105 Robert 84
GOLD Anstis 38
GORHAM Abigail (Dickerman) 93 Abigail (Field) 95 Althea 94 Benjamin 61 91 92 94 Bethia(h) 61 94 Deborah 93 Desire 7 67 Desire (Howland) 7 61 91 130 Elizabeth 8 61 91 92 93 94 95 Hannah 8 91 92 93 94 Hannah (Huckins) 8 Hannah (Miles) 92 93 Hannah (Sturgis) (Gray) 8 61 91 Hezekiah 93 Isaac 91 92 93 94 130 Jabez 8 61 91 94 95 James 8 Jemima 61 95 Jemima (Potter) 93 94 130 131 John 7 8 61 92 93 130 Joseph 8 91 92 Leah () 91 92 Lydia 8 94 Lydia (Dorman) 93 Margaret (Stephenson) 7 Mary 92 93 94 124 130 131 Mary () 92 93 Mary (Otis) 8 Mary (Punchard) 93 Mary (Wardwell) (Maxfield) 92 Mercy 8 Nathan(iel) 93 Priscilla/Puella (Hussey) 8 Ralph 7 Rebecca 93 Richard 94 Samuel 61 91 92 93 95 Sarah 61 94 95 Sarah (Brown) 93 Sarah (Sturgis) 8 Sarah (Thomas) 94 Shubael 8 92 Temperance 8 Timothy 93 Thomas 92 William 94 Bethia(h) (Carey) 61 92 94
GRA(I)NGER Ann(a) (Ingraham) 20 Elizabeth (Gorham) 94 95 John 20 Thomas 95
GRAY Abigail (Brown) 158 Deborah (Church) 138 139 140 Desire 134 Dorothy 139 Edward 134 Hannah (Sturgis) 8 61 91 John 8 91 Lydia M. 158 Mary (Winslow) 134 Pardon 158 Reliance () 158 Ruth 148 158 Samuel 139 Sarah 163 Thomas 148 158
GREEN(E) Abigail (Wardwell) 165 Andrew 165 Benjamin 10 Ebenezer 165 Elizabeth (Church) 10 22 Enfield 165 Hannah 10 165 James 165 Jane 165 John 165 Joseph Whipple 18 Mary 10 165 Nathaniel 10 Rebecca (Ingraham) 17 18 Robert 165 Thomas 10 22 Thomas Ingraham 18 Usal 165 William 165
GREENLAND J. 110
GREENMAN Amy 170 Esther/Hester (Wilson) 170 Job 170 William 170
GREENWOOD Rev John 32 33 85 103 Lydia 32 33 126 Lydia () 33
GREGORY Eliza Atwood (Finney) (Ladieu) 74 John 74

Matthew 163 Rebecca (Little) 163
GRISWOLD Rev Alexander V. 15
GROSS Benjamin 171 Dixie 171 Edward 171 Mary (Woodbury) 171 Priscilla 171
HADWIN Martha 161
HAFFIELD Mary 119
HALE/HAILE Coomer 19 Elizabeth (Strong) 147 Enoch 147 Margaret (Ingraham) 19 Nathan 147 Octavia 147 Octavia (Throope) 147 Richard 147 Sally 147 Sibilla 147
HALL Gideon 143 Hannah (Bosworth) 50 Phebe 142 Phebe (Champlin) 143 Submit (Bosworth) 50
HALLETT Elizabeth (Gorham) 8 Joseph 8
HAMMON(D) Deacon 86 Edward 58 95 Elizabeth () (Smith) 95 Margaret 58 95 Martha 58 95 Mary (Gladding) 86 Rebecca (Ormsbee) 95 Richard 95 Susannah (Brown) 58 65 95 Susanna (Brown) (Bradley) 95
HAMPTON Abigail 96 Henry 96 John 96 Katheren 96 Mary (Davis) 96 Sarah (Barney) 96
HAND Sarah 140
HANDY Abigail (Brenton) 57 Charles 57
HARDING Hannah V. 89 James 89
HARPER Alexander 30 Sarah (Reynolds) (Young) 30
HARRIS Joseph 147 Rebecca (Finney) 70 109 Samuel 70 109 Sybil (Throope) 147
HARRISON Jacob 166 Sarah (Wardwell) 166
HASKILL John 123 Mary (Smith) 122 123
HATHAWAY Rev George W. 17 James 160 Jemima (Waldron) 160
HAVENS Mary 9
HAWES Desire (Gorham) 7 67 Edmund 7 Elizabeth 67 John 7 67
HAYMAN Elizabeth 5 Elizabeth (Allen) 4 9 Grace 4 5 6 John 4 5 6 Mary 5 6 Nathan(iel) 4 5 9 Priscilla (Waldron) 5 Sarah 5 Susan 9
HAYWARD Mary 48 Samuel 48
HAZARD Abigail 40
HEAL(E)Y Mary 149
HEART Mercy () 43 Richard 43
HEATH Elizabeth Lefavour (Pitman) 106 Nathan B. 106
HEDGE Elizabeth 96 Elizabeth (Sturges) 96 John 96 William 96
HEFFERLAND John 58 Mary (Brown) (Backaway/Barkaway) 58
HERSEY Experience (Pearse) 73 Gideon 73
HICKS Elizabeth 125 Mary 49
HILL John 143 Martha (Champlin) 143
HINCKLEY Charles 146 Elizabeth 96 Elizabeth (Throope) 146
HOAR Abigail 98 Abner 100 Allen 98 99 Allen Carey 99 Ann 98 Benjamin 97 98 99 100 152 Betsey 99 David 99 Eliza(beth) 98 99 100 Elizabeth () 98

99 100 Elizabeth () 98 Frances () 99 George 99 Hannah 97 98 100 151? Hannah (Sanders) 98 99 Hannah (Wright) 96 97 151 Henry Irvine 99 Hope Sanders 99 John 99 John R. 99 John Waldron 100 Joseph 97 99 Joseph Sanders 99 Lewis 98 99 Lewis Thomas 99 Lucy () (Goff) 99 Lydia Burr 98 Maria Rogers 99 Mary 97 98 100 Mary Bowen 99 Mary/Polly (Brown) 100 Mary (Champlain) 99 Mary Rogers 99 Molly (Bowen) 98 99 Nancy 98 Nathan 99 Pardon Bowen 99 Paul 97 Phebe 98 99 Phebe (Carey) 98 Priscilla (Waldron) (Waldron) 98 99 100 152 Rebecca 97 Rebecca (Smith) 97 Samuel 97 98 99 Sarah 98 Sarah () 97 Sarah (B___) 99 Susannah 98 Susannah (Bragg) 97 William 96 97 98 99 100 151
HOBART Hannah 119 Rev Peter 119
HOBBS Martha 4
HODGES Ebenezer 114 Elizabeth 113 114 Esther () 114 Experience (Williams) 118 Hannah () 114 John 113 Marcy/Mary () 113 Mary 114 Mehitable 114 Nathan-(iel) 114 118
HOLMES Elizabeth () 166 169 Samuel 169
HOOPER Ann 81
HOPKINS Desire (Burroughs) 60 Mr 60 ___ 137
HORSEWELL Francis 9 Mary 9 Sarah 9
HOUSE Gideon 68 Hannah 68 Hannah (Davenport) 68 John 68 Jonathan 68 Nathaniel 68 Rebecca 68 Sarah 68 Simon 68
HOWARD Ann (Brenton) 57 Martin 57 Susanna 3
HOWE Abigail (DeWolf) 15 17 James 18 John 132 Louise (Smith) 132 Mark Anthony 17 Mark Antony DeWolf 132
HOWLAND Abigail 34 103 106 123 125 Abigail () 103 Abigail (Carey) 101 103 125 168 169 Allen 91 Ann Burt 106 Bashua/Beersheba/Bathsheba (Carey) 61 101 103 Bethiah 101 102 Bethia (Tha[t]cher) 61 100 Charles 106 Daniel 106 159 168 Daniel LeFavour 91 107 Desire 7 61 67 91 130 Dorothy (Hunt) 101 103 Eliza(beth) 17 61 100 101 102 103 106 158 Elizabeth (LeFavour) 104 105 158 159 168 Elizabeth (Martin) (DeWolf) 104 105 107 Elizabeth (Tilley) 7 91 100 Experience 101 Frederick 106 Hannah (Peck) 106 Jabez 58 61 100 101 102 103 John 7 17 34 61 67 90 91 100 101 103 104 105 106 125 126 130 158 159 168 169 Joseph 61 100 101 104 Josiah 100 101 105 106 107 Judah 101 LeFavour 91 105 107 Lydia 61 101 Major 89 Martha 105 106 Martha (Wardwell) 104 168 Mary/Mercy 102 103 104 169 Mary (Gladding) (Munro) 105 Mary L. (Bradford) 106 Mehitable 103 105 168 Molly (Miller) 104 Mr 88 Nancy Burt 106 Nathaniel 101 106 Parnel (Taylor) 104 Patience 102 103 Patience (Stafford) 101 102 Peleg 105 106 Phebe 87 90 103 104 125 126

168   Phebe (Gladding)   91   107   Polly/Molly (Gladding)
88   Rachel () (Allen)   101   103   Rebecca   106   Rebecca
(Munro)   105   Rebecca (Waldron)   106   159   Samuel   43
100   101   103   104   105   106   125   162   168   169   Sarah
17   102   105   106   Sarah (Baker)   101   Sarah (Smith)
103   Seth   101   104   Tabitha   103   104   Thomas   102
103   William Martin   105   107   Yetmercy   101   Yetmercy
(Howland) (Palmer)   101   Yetmercy (Shove)   101
HUBBARD   Ann   12   John   49   Lydia   93   94   Priscilla (Bosworth)   49
HUCKINS   Hannah   8   Rose   8   Thomas   8
HULL (error for HALL)   Hannah   1   Phebe (Champlin)   143   Sarah   123
HUMMERY   Elizabeth   78
HUMPHREY   Anna   21
HUNT   Dorothy   101   103   Martha   52
HUNTINGTON   Bethiah (Throope)   140   Dorothy (Paine) (Williams)   23   24   Hannah   23   24   William   140   ___   23
HUSSEY   Martha (Bunker)   8   Priscilla   8   Puella   8   Stephen   8
HYDE   Dorothy (Gray) (Throope)   139
INGALLS/INGELL   Benjamin   107   Waitstill ()   107
INGRAHAM   Abigail   13   15   79   Abigail (DeWolf) (Howe)   15   17   18   Abigail (Munro)   16   Allen   17   20   Ann(a)   16   20   21   Ann Hammond   16   Anna (Humphrey)   21   Benjamin   16   Betsey   16   Celinda/Selinda   21   Charlotte   20   88   Daniel   16   17   21   Edward   14   Eliza   14   21   Elizabeth   13   14   15   20   Elizabeth (Chesebrough)   13   Elizabeth (Gibbs)   19   21   Eliza(beth) (Lindsey)   14   15   Elizabeth (Smith)   17   Esther   13   George   18   George Gibbs   21   Hannah   20   Hannah (Eddy)   17   Hannah Luther   16   Henry   18   Hezekiah   13   Isaac   14   15   James   21   James Davis   16   17   Jarrett   13   Jeremiah   13   14   15   16   17   18   79   John   14   15   16   17   79   86   Joseph   15   79   Joshua   14   19   20   21   88   160   Lawton   19   21   Lois (Sanford)   16   Louise (Durkee)   16   Lydia   15   16   17   Lydia French   16   Lydia Pearce   16   Margaret   19   Martha   15   18   20   21   79   Martha (Lawton)   14   19   20   Mary/Molly   13   14   15   16   18   20   21   79   160   162   Mary (Barstow)   12   Mary (Diman)   16   Mary (Fry)   14   15   79   86   Mary (Gladding)   15   16   86   Mary (Richmond)   14   19   88   160   Mary (Vickery)   15   Melvin Diman   16   Mercy (Munro)   14   Molly   18   21   Nancy   21   Nathaniel   14   16   17   Peggy (Wardwell)   18   Phebe   21   Polly   17   18   Polly Taylor (Bosworth)   21   Priscilla   16   Rachel   15   79   Rebecca   17   18   Rebecca (Munro)   15   17   18   Richard   13   Ruth   19   Salome   14   Salome/Silence (Mason)   14   Samuel   13   15   16   79   Sarah   14   20   21   166   167   Sarah (Cowell)   13   79   167   Sarah (May)   18   Sarah (Munro)   20   Sarah (Peck)   18   Simeon   18   19   20   Thomas   15   18   21   79   Thomas Lawton   20   Timothy   13   14   15   20   79   167

IRISH Elizabeth () 135 John 134 135 Priscilla (Southworth) (Talbot/Talby) 134 135
JACOB(S) Benjamin 43 108 Hannah 108 Hannah (Bosworth) 42 43 107 Joseph 43 107 108 Mary 43 108 Mary (Gilman) 43 107 Mercy () 108 Nathaniel 43 107 108 Nicholas 43 107 Penelope 3 Penelope (Burton) 3 Samuel 3 Seth 3 Susanna (Howard) 3
JAMES Benjamin 133 Elizabeth (Smith) 132 133 Hannah 69 Leonard 10 22 Ruth 124 129 Samuel 133 Sarah (Church) 10 22 William 133
JARVIS Leonard 10 23 Sukey (Smith) 130 131 ___ 131
JENKINS Anstis 38 Martha (Brenton) 57 Mary (Wilkins) (Pepper) 38 Richard 38 Robert 57
JOHNSON Abigail 27 Isaac 48 Richard 4 Sarah (Oliver) 4
JOLLS/JOLES Mary 82 Robert 110
JONES Bathsheba/Bathshua (Bosworth) 50 144 Benjamin 42 50 51 144 Elizabeth 50 100 Elizabeth (Borden) 50 Harriet (Waldron) 159 Joseph 50 Lydia 50 Lydia (Neale) 50 Robert 50 51 Sarah 19 21 86 Thomas 159
JOSLIN Keziah 169
JOY Esther 70 Esther (Finney) 70 109 110 Joseph 70 110
KEENE Abigail 3
KELLEY Joseph 167 Sarah (Wardwell) (Salisbury?) 167
KEMPTON/KENTON Esther/Hester (Throope) 142 Thomas 142
KENNEDY see CANADA
KENT Joseph 59 Lydia 85 Susannah 140
KIDDER Elizabeth (Brackett) (Carey) 61 Ephraim 61
KIMBALL Mary 69
KING Lydia 40
KINGSLEY Barton 159 John H. 159 Lorana () 159 Lucy B. or C. (Waldron) (Phillips) 159
KINNICUT/KENNECUT Elizabeth 36 Elizabeth () 76 Elizabeth (Luther) 76 Hannah (Gorham) 92 Joanna 76 Joanna (Sheper[d]son) 76 John 76 92 Roger 76 Sarah (Bosworth) 44 Thomas 44
KINSMAN Mary 165 Mary (Boreman) 165 Robert 165
KIRTLAND John 136 Martha 134 135 136 Nathaniel 135 Parnell () 135 Temperance 136 Temperance (Buckingham) 136
LADIEU/LADUE Curtis 74 Eliza Atwood (Finney) 74 Rachel (Tew) 74 Samuel 74
LAKE Hannah 79 John 79 Margaret (Reade) 79
LAMBERT Samuel 91 Thankful (Baxter) (Thacher) 91
LAN(G)DON Ann(a) (Lobdell?) 108 Daniel 108 Deborah 108 Dorcas 37 James 108 Joshua 108 Martha 108 Mary (York) 108 Mercy 108 Samuel 108 William 108
LAWLESS John 84 Mary (Gladding) 84 Mary (Wardwell) 165 Sarah 90 Sarah () 90 ___ 165

LAWTON   Eliza   112   Isaac   102   John   102   Joshua   102
   Margaret ()   14   19   102   112   Martha   14   19   Ruth   47
   112   Sarah (Howland)   102   Susanna (Martin)   112   Thomas   14   19   102   112   William   102
LAYTON   Elizabeth?   45   46   47
LEE   Joseph   55   Rebecca   120   Rebeckah (Lewis)   55   Rev Samuel   120
LEFAVOUR   Anna   48   Anna/Hannah (Willard)   48   Daniel   48   Elizabeth   48   104   105   158   159   168   Elizabeth (Bosworth)   105   Timothy   48   105
LEONARD   Anne (Tisdale)   32   George   32   Phebe   30   32   152   153
LEVERETT   John   6   Sarah   6
LEWIS   Abigail   110   Deborah   55   Edmund   108   Edward   109   Elizabeth   55   Elizabeth (Birge)   55   Elizabeth (Brooks)   110   Esther   69   109   Hannah   55   109   113   Hannah (Baker)   109   110   113   Hannah (Gorham)   93   Hepzebath   109   110   John   55   109   Joseph   55   Leonard   93   Mary   110   116   Mary ()   69   109   Nathaniel   110   Rebeckah   55   Rebecca (Bosworth)   50   Sarah   55   Thomas   69   109   110   113
LIDGETT   Elizabeth (Scammon)   120   Peter   120
LINCOLN   Elizabeth   3
LINDSEY   Benjamin   9   168   Christopher   45   46   Eliza-(beth)   14   112   Elizabeth (Church)   9   Elizabeth (Layton?)   45   46   47   Elizabeth (Munro)   14   125   168   Hannah   106   Hannah T. (Gladding)   89   Jemima   125   168   John   14   125   168   Keziah (Joslin)   169   Lydia   168   Martha   168   Mary   168   Mary (Wardwell)   167   168   Mr   89   Rebecca   159   168   Samuel   169   Sarah   169   William   168
LINSFORD   Margaret   113
LISCOMB   Abby Cary (Waldron)   161   162   Ann   55   167   Benjamin   156   Catherine   162   Hannah Pearse   162   Isaac   156   162   John   156   157   Joseph Diman   161   162   Leah   156   Leah (Waldron)   90   155   156   Margaret D.   162   Margaret (Diman)   162   Nancy Ann (Gladding)   90   Nathaniel   90   156   Priscilla   156   Rebecca   156   Rebecca (Thurston)   156   157   Samuel   90   156   Sarah (Lawless)   90
LITTLE   Ann (Warren)   163   David   135   Edward   162   163   Elizabeth   162   163   Eliza(beth) (Howland)   102   Elizabeth (Southworth)   135   Ephraim   135   Isaac   102   Jane   102   Lemuel   163   Mary   32   162   163   Mary (Sturtevant)   135   Mary (Walker)   162   163   Nathaniel   163   Otis   102   Rebecca   163   Samuel   163   Sarah   23   35   71   130   148   149   162   163   Sarah (Gray)   163   Thomas   163
LLOYD   Rebecca   4
LOBDELL   Ann(a)?   108   Bridget () (Bellamy)   42   107   John   42   43   Mary   42   Nathaniel   42   Nicholas   42   Sarah   42   ___ (Bosworth)   43
LORING   Deborah   70   72   150   Elizabeth   6   Israel   6

John 6 Jonathan 6 Mary 6 Mary (Baker) 6 Mary (Hayman) 6 Nathan 6 Sarah 6
LOVELL Ann () 69 Eleanor 77 Hannah 69 Thomas 69
LOW Ann 141 John Wilson 85 Judith (Bosworth) (Gladding) 85
LOWDER Ruth 45
LOWELL John 29 Naomi (Torrey) 29 Ruth 29 30
LUCAS Bethia 121
LUDEN Elizabeth (Finney) (Bradford) 76 ___ 77
LUTHER Elizabeth 76 Elizabeth (Finney) 75 Huldah 75 Nathan(iel) 75 83 Sarah (Gallup) 83
LYDE Byfield 7 Deborah (Byfield) 7 Edward 7 Mary (Wheelwright) 7
LYMON Elizabeth 140
LYON Amos 142 Bethia (Dann) 142 Deborah (Colburn) 142 Ebenezer 142 Frances 142 Moses 142 Rebecca (Throope) 141 142 Wareham 142 William 142
MACEY Deborah 138 139
MACKMOLLEN Elizabeth 55 102
MACOMBER Elizabeth (Williams) 40 John 40
MANCHESTER Phebe 20 123
MANN Elizabeth 75 148 149 John 75 76 Mercy (Finney) 75 76 Ziporah 139 147
MANSFIELD Margaret (Prout) 145 Mercy 145 Moses 145
MARBLE Gershom 107 Waitstill () (Ingalls) 107
MARCY Esther 142 Hadlock 142 Ichabod 142 Joseph 142 Lidia 142 Mary (Throope) 142 Nathaniel 142 Rebeckah 142 Smith 142 Stephen 142 Thomas 142
MARION Edward 30 Mary (Reynolds) 30
MARSHALL Capt 37
MARSHFIELD Hannah (Brown) 57 58 65
MARTIN Abigail 110 Amanda 86 Anne () 156 Ann (Munro) 111 Benjamin 111 Charity 111 Christian (Pelton) 111 123 155 Cornelius 156 Ebenezer 111 Eliza(beth) 104 105 107 155 156 Elizabeth () 105 Eliza (Lindsey) 112 Experience (Rue) 111 Hannah () 156 Hannah (Darling) 110 111 156 Hannah (Smith) 112 123 John 110 111 Jonathan 110 Joseph 110 Martha 111 Martha (Newton) 112 Mary 110 111 Mary /Mercy () 110 111 Mary (Mudge) 110 111 May 111 Nathaniel 86 Rachel 155 Rachel (Waldron) 112 155 156 Rebecca () 110 Robert 110 Susan(na) 112 Susan () 86 Thomas 110 111 112 123 155 156 William 105 111 112 123 155
MARTINDALE Isaac 102 Mary/Mercy (Howland) (Pearse) 102 Sarah 33 154 Sarah (Park) 154 Sion 154
MASON Perez 160 Rebecca (Waldron) 160 Silence/Salome 14
MATHER Increase 4 171 Jerusha 4
MAXFIELD Christian 14 Daniel 92 Esther 46 Margaret 14 Mary (Wardwell) 92 Samuel 14 Timothy 14

MAY   Elizabeth   159   Sarah   18   124   125
MAYBERRY   Amelia   132
MAYHEW   Elizabeth   46   Hannah   67   Thomas   67
MAYNARD   Hannah   67   John   67   Mary (Gates)   67
McINTOSH   Elizabeth   83   Elizabeth ()   83   Henry   83   Mary   83
McSPARRAN   Rev James   81
MEAD   Ebenezer   112   Elizabeth   112   Elizabeth ()   112   John   113   Joseph   113   Katherine   112   Nicholas   112   Susanna   112
MILES   Hannah   92   93   Hannah (Eaton)   92   93   Richard   92   93
MILLER   Augustus N.   160   Barnard   125   Elizabeth (Dorby)   43   Elizabeth (Hicks)   125   Harriot (Waldron)   160   Molly   104   125   Nathan   72   Paul   43
MOORE   Polly   64   Susanna (Smith)   129   Thomas   129
MOREY/MOWRY   Abigail   109   114   Benjamin   109   114   Desire (Fuller) (Sawyer)   113   Elizabeth   114   Elizabeth (Hodges)   113   114   George   109   113   114   Hannah   109   113   Hannah (Lewis)   109   113   John   109   113   Linsford   113   Margaret (Linsford)   113   Martha   109   114   Mary   109   113   114   Mary (Hodges)   114   Mary (Throope)   141   Mehitable (Hodges)   114   Ruth   113   Sarah   109   113   Thomas   109   114
MORTON   Abigail (Pratt)   149   Ann (Cooper)   74   Ebenezer   74   Elizabeth   43   Ephraim   74   Hannah   56   74   149   Hannah (Finney)   74   John   43   74   Joseph   74   Lettice   43   Lydia (Cooper)   43   Mary   43   Nathaniel   43   Thomas   149
MUDGE   Mary   110   Thomas   110
MULLINS   Priscilla   36   134   135   150
MUMFORD   Ann   38   Edward   38   Elizabeth   38   Frances (Brenton)   57   John   38   Mary (Wilkins) (Pepper) (Jenkins) (Rogers)   38   39   Mr   57   Stephen   38   39
MUNRO(E)   Abigail   16   82   Abigail (Gallup)   17   82   Abigail (Gladding)   87   Abigail Howland   106   Abigail (Howland)   106   Abigail (Potter)   47   Abigail (Wardwell)   82   Allen   126   Amarentia (Fales)   125   127   128   Ann   111   Ann (Pitman)   106   Archibald   129   167   Benjamin   123   Bennet   49   91   Charles   123   Daniel   105   David   167   Dorcas   167   Edward   91   Eleanor   91   Eleanor (Smith)   128   Elizabeth   14   99   125   168   George   129   167   Hannah Carey   106   Henry   87   127   Jeremiah   129   John   128   Josiah   129   Lydia   19   82   Mary   129   162   167   Mary ()   123   167   Mary (Jolls)   82   Mercy   14   Nancy   162   Nathaniel   17   82   Phebe Howland   91   Polly/Molly (Gladding)   88   Priscilla (Smith)   123   Rebecca   15   17   105   129   167   Rebecca ()   105   Rebecca (Smith)   129   Rebecca (Wardwell)   17   20   129   167   Ruth (Smith)   126   Sally (Gladding)   91   Samuel   82   88   Samuel S.   106   Sarah   20   154   167   Sarah (Bosworth)   49   Simeon   17   20   106   129   167   William   83   ___   105

MURDOCK Samuel 140 Submit 140 Submit (Throope) 140
   William 140
NASH Elizabeth (Bosworth) (Smith) 132 Rev Sylvester
   132
NEALE Lydia 50
NEGROES Ceaser 164 Peleg 164
NELSON Jane 77
NEWGATE Sarah 3
NEWMAN Abigail Howland (Munro) 106 James 106
NEWTON Abigail 152 Elizabeth (Finney) 73 Isaac L.
   73 Lydia () 73 Martha 33 112 151 152 155 Richard 73 Thomas 151 152
NIBBS Ebenezer 151 Martha (Waldron) 151 Thomas 151
NICHOLS Benjamin 47 Eleanor 142 Frances (Bennett) 47
NICHOLSON Abigail 147 148 Dinah 58 59 Jane () 58
   John 148 Joseph 58 59 Mary 147 148 Mary (Throope)
   148
NOONING Hannah (Talbee) 158 160 Jonathan 158 160
OLDRIDGE John A. 151 Martha (Waldron) (Nibbs) 151
OLIVER Anne (Gillam) 4 Brattle 4 Elizabeth 4 Elizabeth (Brattle) 3 Hopestill (Wensley/Winsley) 4 James
   4 Jerusha (Mather) 4 Martha (Hobbs) 4 Mary 4 Nathaniel 3 4 Peter 3 4 Rebecca (Lloyd) 4 Sarah 4
   Sarah (Newgate) 3
OREM Rev James 102
ORMSBY/ORMSBEE Esther 123 Esther (Smith) (Goff) 124
   Ezra 124 Mary 124 Rebecca 95
OSBORN(E) Jeremiah 41 114 115 Jeremy 115 John 115
   Katherine 41 115 Margaret 41 42 115 Mary/Mercy
   115 Mary () 114 Mary (Gorham) 92 Mercy (Davis) 41
   115 Richard 114 Robert 115 Samuel 92 115 Sarah
   115 Sarah () 115 Thomas 114
OTIS Grace (Hayman) 6 Grace (Smith) 6 John 8 Mary
   8 Richard 6
OWEN(S) Caleb 146 Elizabeth (Brewster) 146 Esther
   146 Jemima (Gorham) 95 Jemima (York) 95 Joel 146
   Joseph 95 Martha 146 Priscilla (Throope) 146 Samuel 94
OXX Jemima 157 159 160 168 Mary (Lindsey) 168 Rebecca (Lindsey) 159 Samuel 159 168
PAINE Abigail (Johnson) 27 28 Alathea/Alethea 22 23
   Bethia () 27 28 Betsey Torrey 28 Dorothy 22 23
   24 25 Dorothy (Rainsford) 10 22 24 Edward 23 24
   25 26 49 Elizabeth 22 23 24 25 26 27 Eliza-
   (beth) Gallup 25 26 83 Elizabeth/Betsey (Torrey)
   27 28 Huldah (Vigil) 27 Hannah 10 22 23 24 26
   31 John 59 Jonathan 23 24 Mary 22 23 24 25
   26 27 28 Mary (Bailey) 26 27 Mary (Bosworth) 25
   26 49 Mary P. (Smith) 129 Nathaniel 10 21 22 23
   24 25 26 83 Nathaniel P. 129 Nathaniel Terrey
   (Torrey?) 28 Neele (Adcocke) 22 Olive () 27 28

Peter Torrey 28 Priscilla 28 Priscilla (Royall) 23 26 29 30 Royall 26 27 30 Royal Luther 28 Samuel Clark 25 Samuel Royall 27 28 Samuel Smith 28 Sarah 22 23 25 26 Sarah () 24 83 Stephen 22 23 24 26 27 28 29 30 Stephen Royal 23 24 26 Thomas 26 27 Timothy 25 William Henry Richmond 28
PALMER Elizabeth 135 Elizabeth (Richmond) 135 Isaac 101 John 135 Sarah 136 Susanna 135 Yetmercy (Howland) 101
PAPILLION/PAMPILLON Bridget (Bosworth) 44 45 Ebenezer 45 Hester/Esther 45 Hester/Esther (Bosworth) 44 45 Joan () 44 45 John 44 45 Mary 45 Obadiah 44 45 Peter 44 45 115 Rebecca (Bosworth) 45 49 Samuel 44 45 49
PARCHMENT Lydia 57 William 57
PARK Sarah 154
PARKER Hannah 73
PARRIS Elizabeth 162 163
PATCH Elizabeth 170 171
PAUL Abigail 62 Edward 62 Esther (Babbitt) 62
PEABODY/PABODIE Abigail 49 Abigail (Bosworth) 49 Elizabeth 36 119 Elizabeth (Alden) 119 134 135 Ephraim 49 Martha 135 Mary 134 Rebecca 134 135 William 119 134 135
PEARSE Polly (Gladding) 90 William 90
PEARSE Eliza 149 Elizabeth (Atwood) 73 Experience 73 George 102 Jeremiah 129 162 Lydia (Brown) 149 Mary? 117 Mary/Mercy (Howland) 102 Mary (Munro) 162 Phebe 126 Rebecca (Waldron) 161 162 Samuel 73 Sanford Munro 161 162 Sarah (Smith) 129 William 129 149
PEASE Martha (Gladding) 86 Mary 67 Zephaniah 86
PECK Abigail 34 149 Abigail (Atwater) 144 Ann (Reynolds) 34 Elizabeth 45 131 138 144 Elizabeth (Smith) 130 131 Elizabeth (Throope) 138 144 Frances 131 Hannah 23 106 127 Hannah (Waldron) 152 Hannah (Wood) 149 152 153 Isaac 138 John 34 130 131 149 Jonathan 18 24 34 35 90 106 130 138 144 149 152 153 Martha 106 144 Martha (Howland) 106 Mary 35 131 138 144 149 Mary (Richmond) 106 Mary (Throop) 18 34 35 90 106 131 148 149 Mercy 138 Nancy 90 149 Nicholas 130 131 138 144 149 Rebecca 152 153 Rebecca (Bosworth) 138 Samuel Viall (not Samuel S., an error) 106 138 Sarah 18 149 Thomas 106 138 William 138 144
PECKER Bridget (Bosworth) (Papillion) 44 James 44
PECKHAM Abigail 104 Elizabeth 47 68 Eunice 32 John 104 Robert 104 Samuel 104 Tabitha (Howland) (Carey) 104
PELHAM Penelope 2
PELTON Christian 111 123 155

PENFIELD Abigail 78 116 117 Anne () 116 117 Ann
   (Cornwall) 116 Benjamin 117 Hannah 117 Hannah (Fry)
   78 116 Isaac 116 John 116 Jonathan 117 Mary 116
   Mary () 116 117 Mary (Lewis) 116 Nathaniel 78 116
   Peter 78 116 Rebecca 117 Samuel 78 116 Sarah 116
PENNIMAN James 118 Joseph 118 Lydia 51 Lydia ()
   118 Sarah 118 Waiting (Robinson) 118
PEPPER Mary (Wilkins) 38 ___ 38
PERKINS Edward 57 Elizabeth (Brenton) 57 Experience
   93 Mehitabel 93
PHILLIPS Benjamin 44 Bridget 46 Bridget (Bosworth) 44
   45 46 Elizabeth (Wardwell) (Tomkins) 167 169 John
   169 Joseph 43 44 46 Lucy B. or C. (Waldron) 159
   Michael 46 Nathaniel 44 Susannah () 43 46 ___ 159
PHIPS William 80
PHINNEY see FINNEY
PIERCE see PEARCE
PITMAN Abigail 106 Ann 106 Eliza F. (Slade) 106 El-
   izabeth Lefavour 106 George 106 Hannah (Lindsey) 106
   James Davis 17 Rev John 68 98 99 John Howland 106
   Josiah Howland 106 Mary 17 67 68 Mary (Ingraham)
   17 Mary (Saunders) 68 Mary (Wardwell) 106 Peleg 17
   106 Polly (Ingraham) 17 Samuel 17 106 Sarah (How-
   land) 17 106
PITTS Bethiah (Robinson) 118 Mercy 32 Peter 118
POPE John 117
PORTER Hannah 66
POTTER Abigail 17 47 72 131 Hannah (Paine) 26 Hope-
   still 26 76 77 93 94 Jemima 93 94 130 131 Lydia
   (Finney) 26 76 77 Lydia (Hubbard) 93 94 Simeon 26
PRATT Abigail 149 Elizabeth 171 Elizabeth (Woodbury)
   171 Joseph 171
PRICE Francis 24 Mary 24
PRINCE Elizabeth (Paine) 24 ___ 24
PROSSMAN see CROSSMAN
PROUT Margaret 145
PUNCHARD Mary 93 Mary (Gorham) 93 Mehitabel (Perkins)
   93 William 93
RAINSFORD Dorothy 10 22 Jonathan 22 Mary (Sutherland)
   22
RANGER Amos 117 Anna (Smith) 117 Edmund 117 Elizabeth
   (Wylls) 117 John 117 Mary 117 Mary (Pearse?) (Gat-
   line) 117 Prudence 117 Samuel 117 Sarah 117
   Sarah (Fuller) 117 Stephen 117
RANNEY Mary (Little) 163 Thomas 163
RAWSON Ann(e) (Waldron) 155 Eliza(beth) (Walker) 164
   George 164 Grindall 30 35 36 Mary (Reynolds) 36
   Stephen 164 Susanna(h) 30 35 Susanna (Wilson) 30
   35 Thomas 35 155 William 155 Wilson 35 155
RAYMOND Mary 24
READ/REED Mercy 76 Margaret 79
REDFIELD James 54 Lydia 54

REDWOOD   Abraham   39   Mehitable   39
REXFORD   Rev Jordan   161
REYNOLDS   Abigail   35   Abigail (Peck)   34   Ann(a)   29   34   36   Anna (Blanch)   30   Benjamin   29   30   33   35   36   37   154   155   Betsey Peck   35   Constant   37   Dorcas (Landon)   37   Dorothy ()   36   154   Ebenezer   30   Eleazer   31   148   Elizabeth   32   33   34   37   125   126   127   George   32   33   34   35   Greenwood   34   35   Grindall   36   37   Grinnel   37   Hannah   23   26   29   30   33   34   35   Hannah ()   35   John   26   29   30   31   33   36   147   148   154   John Greenwood   35   Jonathan   33   34   35   Joseph   29   30   32   33   34   35   36   126   152   153   Joshua   153   Lydia   33   34   35   Lydia (Greenwood)   32   33   126   Mary   10   22   28   29   30   31   33   34   35   36   147   148   154   171   Mary (Caldwell)   35   Mary (Giles/Gills)   10   22   30   31   148   Mary (Little)   32   Mary (Peck)   35   Mary (Snell)   30   Mercy   34   Mercy (Pitts)   32   Mercy/Marcy (Throope)   31   147   148   Molly (Waldron)   33   36   154   Naomi   30   Nathaniel   28   29   30   31   32   37   85   171   Peter   10   22   29   30   31   148   Phebe   32   34   152   153   154   Phebe (Leonard)   30   32   152   153   Philip   30   Priscilla   36   Priscilla (Brackett)   28   29   Robert   28   Robert Caldwell   35   Ruth   29   30   85   104   Ruth (Lowell)   29   30   Samuel   32   33   34   35   36   Samuel Godfrey   35   Sarah   29   30   34   36   37   Sarah ()   36   Sarah (Cox)   33   34   Sarah (Dwight)   28   29   Sarah (Searles)   36   Susannah (Giles)   36   Susannah (Rawson)   30   35   Thomas   31   147   148   William   34
RHODES   Deborah (Finney)   73   Lucius   73
RICE   Bridget   11   150   Joseph   48   Phinehas   48   Sarah (Bosworth)   48
RICH   Susan (Gladding) (Waldron)   90   William   90
RICHARDS   Alice   119
RICHARDSON   Ruth (Bosworth)   50   Sarah   39   40
RICHMOND   Abigail (Davis)   119   Althea (Gorham)   94   Deborah (Loring)   150   Edward   119   150   Elizabeth   119   135   Elizabeth (Rogers)   19   119   160   Eliza(beth) (Throope)   148   150   Gilbert   94   Hannah   119   Hannah (Fry)   79   Ichabod   94   119   Mary   14   19   88   106   160   Mary ()   94   Peleg   119   Perez   119   150   Rogers   19   119   160   Ruth   119   Sarah   119   Sylvester   119   Thomas   79   William   119
RIDGEWAY   Naomi (Reynolds)   30   Samuel   30
RIGBY   Elizabeth   53   Elizabeth (George)   53   Samuel   53
RINDGE/RING   Daniel   165   Mary (Kinsman)   165   Susanna(h)   166   167
ROBINSON   Abigail   118   Bethia   118   Ebenezer   118   Hannah   40   118   Increase   118   Josiah   118   Mehitable (Williams)   118   Sarah   118   Sarah (Penniman)   118   Waiting   118   William   118
ROCKWOOD   Lydia (Penniman)   51
ROGERS   Ann(a) (Churchman)   40   119   Daniel   33   Eliza-

beth   19   40   118   119   160   165   Elizabeth (Pabodie)
36   119   Hannah   119   Hannah (Hobart) (Browne)   119
John   19   36   40   118   119   160   Marah (Cobham) (Browning)   119   Mary   74   Mary (Wilkins) (Pepper) (Jenkins)
38   Rev Robert   18   Ruth   119   Sarah   33   36   119
Thomas   32   36   40   118   ___   38
ROSBOTHAM   Alice   11   156   Benjamin   11   Elizabeth   11
Elizabeth (Church)   10   11   41   Hannah   11   Joseph   10
41
ROSS   Rev Arthur A.   89
ROWE   Sarah   93
ROWLEY   Naomi   113
ROYALL   Elizabeth (McIntosh)   83   Hannah (Reynolds)   23
26   29   30   Isaac   83   Priscilla   23   26   30   Samuel
23   24   26   29   30   55
RUE   Experience   111
RUGGLES   Abigail (Crafts)   51   John   51
RUSSELL   Anna   23   24   Betsey Bourne   128   Elizabeth ()
128   John   128   John Willard   128   Jonathan   24   Joseph
10   23   24   46   163   Nancy Smith   128   Nancy (Smith)
128   Nathaniel   24   128   Parnel Taylor   128   Pastor
138   139   147   Rev Samuel   166   Sarah   23   24   Sarah
(Paine)   23   24
SABIN   Lucretia   129
SAFFIN   Benjamin   121   Elizabeth (Scammon) (Lidgett)   120
John   5   120   121   Joseph   121   Josiah   121   Martha
(Willet)   120   121   Rebecca (Lee)   120   Simon   121
Thomas   120   121
SALISBURY   Archibald   167   Caleb   148   157   Lydia   148
157   160   Sarah   167   Sarah (Wardwell)   167
SALTER   Deborah   119
SALTONSTALL   Katherine   5
SAMMANA/SAMMENATTER/SEMANATT   Abby/Abigail (Waldron)   159
John   159
SAMPSON   Elizabeth   115   Eliza(beth) (Church)   9   41   Elizabeth (Church) (Rosbotham)   10   11   James   11   John
9   10   11   41   Mary   11
SA(U)NDERS   Capt   37   Christian   37   Christopher   37
Daniel   37   Elizabeth   37   Elizabeth ()   37   George   37
Hannah   98   99   Henry   37   Lovett   37   Mary   68   Susanna(h)   37
SANDY(S)/SANDS   Benjamin   121   Bethia   121   Bethia (Lucas)
121   Elizabeth   121   John   121   Joseph   121   Mary   121
Sarah   121
SANFORD   Elizabeth   16   Esbon/Esban   123   George   16   Hannah   167   Hannah (Wardwell)   167   Honora   39   Lois   16
Martha (Smith)   123   Samuel   167
SANGER   Mary (Reynolds)   29
SATLEY   Elnathan   108   Martha (Landon)   108
SAWYER   Desire (Fuller)   113
SCAMMON   Elizabeth   120   Humphrey   120
SEARLE(S)   Deborah   120   Deborah (Salter)   119   Elizabeth

(Kinnicut) 36 John 120 Nathaniel 36 119 120 Robert 119 Sarah 36 120 Sarah (Rogers) 119 120
SEWALL Elizabeth (Walley) 1 Hannah (Hull) 1 Joseph 1 Samuel 1
SHAILEY/SHARLEY Elizabeth (Lewis) 55 Hezekiah 55
SHAPLEIGH Anna 29
SHAW Grace 103 Ruth 136
SHEPER(D)SON Joanna 76
SHERMAN Hope Sanders (Hoar) 99 Levi 99 S. 90 Susan (Glading) (Waldron) (Rich) 90
SHORT Hannah 85 86 Philip 85 86
SHOVE George 101 Hannah (Walley?) 101 Yetmercy 101
SIMMONS Eliza Atwood (Finney) (Ladieu) (Gregory) 74 Isaiah 74
SIMMS/SYMS Bathsheba (Throope) 144 John 144 Lydia 144 Martha 144 Mary 144
SLADE Eliza F. 106
SMITH Abigail 123 126 127 Abigail () 112 122 Abigail (Howland) (Church) 34 103 123 125 Allen Taylor 127 128 Amarentia (Fales) (Munro) 125 127 128 Amelia (Mayberry) 132 Ann(a) 117 132 Anthony 125 Barnabus Taylor 127 Barnard 125 Bathsheba 132 Benjamin 34 103 123 125 126 127 Benjamin Bosworth 130 132 Betsey 34 Daniel 43 44 61 122 132 David 61 132 133 Eleanor 34 127 128 Eleanor (Taylor) 103 125 126 Eliza(beth) 17 34 61 123 124 125 126 127 130 131 132 133 Elizabeth () 95 Elizabeth Bosworth 130 132 Elizabeth (Bosworth) 132 Elizabeth (Bourne) 127 Elizabeth (Carey) 61 123 132 Elizabeth (DeWolf) 125 Elizabeth (Drowne) 94 123 124 Elizabeth (Reynolds) 33 34 125 126 127 Esther 124 Esther (Chickering) 43 44 Ezra 49 George Reynolds 34 127 Grace 6 Hannah 112 122 123 124 130 Hannah (Bourne) 131 152 Harriot 130 131 Henry 130 132 James 95 123 124 125 126 168 Jemima (Lindsey) (Wardwell) 103 125 Job 125 John 5 61 121 122 132 John Munro 128 Jonathan 34 127 Joseph 34 125 127 132 Josiah 34 103 125 126 127 128 Joyce 61 132 133 Joyce () 61 122 Judith (Bosworth) 49 Louisa 130 132 Lucretia 20 86 87 105 106 129 158 Lucretia (Diman) 86 87 124 128 129 Lydia 123 130 Lydia Potter 131 Martha 84 85 123 125 128 Martha (Gladding) 123 Mary 34 43 44 67 122 123 124 127 130 132 Mary () 132 Mary (Bateman) 140 Mary (Collins) 103 Mary (Gorham) 94 124 130 Mary (Wardwell) 125 Mary (Wardwell) (Maxfield) (Gorham?) 92 Mercy () 122 Molly/Polly 125 128 Molly (Miller) 125 Mr 82 Nancy 128 Nathan(iel) 61 103 112 122 123 125 127 128 132 133 Nathaniel Wardwell 125 Parnel (Taylor) 125 127 128 Phebe 125 Phebe (Man-

chester) 123 Phebe (Pearse) 126 Phebe (Wardwell)
124 125 168 Priscilla 123 Rebecca 97 121 122
126 127 128 129 138 141 151 155 Richard 54 61
85 86 87 105 122 123 124 128 129 Ruth 126 130
132 Ruth (Bosworth) 124 130 132 Ruth (James) 124
129 Samuel 55 85 94 103 122 123 124 125 126
129 131 132 Sameul C. 17 Sarah/Sally 103 105 123
124 125 126 129 130 131 144 Sarah () 103 123
Sarah (Antill) 82 Sarah (May) 124 125 Stephen 92
94 123 124 130 131 132 Sumner 132 Susannah/Sussan/Sukey 127 129 130 131 Susanna () 121 Susanna
(Treby) 129 130 Thomas 122 129 Turpin 131 132
William 61 103 123 125 132 133
SNELL Mary 30 46
SNELLING Rev John 89
SOUTHWORTH/SOUTHARD Abigail () 136 Alice 2 5 8 22
134 135 Alice (Church) 135 Andrew 136 Benjamin 135
Constant 9 80 133 134 Desire (Gray) 134 Edward
134 135 Elizabeth 54 80 81 133 134 135 Elizabeth (Collier) 9 80 133 134 Elizabeth (Palmer) 135
Elizabeth (Woodworth) 135 Gideon 136 Joseph 135
Martha (Kirtland) (Blague) 134 135 136 Mary 134
Mary (Blague) 135 Mary (Fobes) 135 Mary (Pabodie)
134 Mary (Torrey) 136 Mary (Wilbore) 136 Mercy 134
Nathaniel 134 136 Patience (Thurston) 136 Priscilla
80 133 134 135 Rebecca (Pabody) 134 135 Samuel
134 136 Stephen 136 Susanna (Palmer) (Blackman) 135
Temperance (Kirtland) 136 Thomas 134 136 William
80 133 134 135
SPARHAWK Rev John 10 19 22 24 26 92 101 111
SPARK(E)S Amanda 89 Hannah T. (Gladding) (Lindsey) 89
Joseph 89 Rachel (Gladding) 89 Samuel 89
SPAULDING Audr(e)y (Stafford) 131 Edward 131 Sukey
(Smith) (Jarvis) 130 131
SPINK Abigail 79
SPOONER Abigail () 158 Wing 158
SPRAGUE Joan (Corbin) 12 Ralph 12 Richard 12 Sarah
12
SPRINGER John 15 Joseph 15 Martha (Ingraham) 15 18
SQUIRE Elizabeth (Fuller) 50 Luke 50 Philip 50 Ruth
50
STAFFORD Audr(e)y 131 Mercy (Westcott) 101 102 Patience 101 102 Samuel 101 102
STANBURY Elizabeth 144 145
STANDISH Mehitable (Cary) (Adams) 51 Miles 51 52
STANHOPE Abigail (Smith) 123 Ralph 123
STEPHENSON Margaret 7
STOCKBRIDGE Ruth 152
STRONG Elizabeth 147
STURGIS/STURGES Edward 8 91 96 Elizabeth 96 Elizabeth (Hinckley) 96 Hannah 8 61 91 Sarah 8 Temperance (Gorham) 8

STURTEVANT   Mary   135
SUTHERLAND   Mary   22
SWAN   Hannah   18   Hannah (Gladding)   87   Margaret (Woodbury)   115   Samuel   87   ___   115
TABER   Benjamin   114   Constant   101   Elizabeth (Howland)   101   Martha (Moorey/Morey)   109   114   Thomas   109   114   Timothy   114
TAFT/TAFFE   Aaron   137   Abigail   137   Alice   137   Benjamin   136   137   Caleb   137   Daniel   137   Deborah   137   Deborah (Genery/Chenerie)   137   Ebenezer   137   Eleazer   137   Elizabeth   137   Elizabeth (Emerson)   137   Elizabeth (Woodward)   137   Ephraim   137   Eunice   137   Gideon   137   Hannah   137   Hannah ()   137   Isaac   137   Israel   137   Jane   137   Japhat   137   Jemima   137   John   137   Joseph   137   Josiah   137   Lucy   137   Lydia   137   Lydia (Chapin)   137   Margaret   137   Martha   137   Mary   137   Mijamin?   137   Moses   137   Paul   137   Peter   137   Rachel   137   Rebecca   137   Robert   136   137   Samuel   137   Sarah   137   Sarah ()   136   Sarah (Thomas)   137   Silas   137   Stephen   137   Susannah   137   Tabareh   137   Thomas   137
TALBY/TALBEE/TALBOT?   Alice   160   Alice ()   135   Alice (Rosbotham)   156   Anstis   141   155   Anstis (Waldron)   87   88   155   156   160   Betsey   157   160   Edmund   156   Edward   87   88   156   160   Hannah   135   156   160   Hannah ()   135   Lydia   156   Polly/Molly (Waldron)   157   158   160   Priscilla   156   Priscilla (Southworth)   80   133   134   135   Rachel   87   88   156   158   160   Samuel   80   133   134   135   Stephen   135   156   157   160
TAYLOR   Rev Barnabus   23   25   104   127   Eleanor   103   125   126   Elizabeth   68   Elizabeth (Peckham)   68   Mercy   79   Parnel   104   125   127   128   Peter   68   Rowland   95   Sarah (Gorham)   95   Susannah   138   141
TERRY   Dorcas   140   Rachel   140
TEW   Rachel   74
THA(T)CHER   Anthony   8   100   Bethiah   100   Elizabeth (Jones)   100   John   8   Lydia (Gorham)   8   Thankful (Baxter)   91   Thomas   91
THINGLEY   see KINGSLEY
THOMAS   Amos   94   Elizabeth Gardner   23   Jemima ()   94   Sarah   94   137
THOM(P)SON   Rev Charles   75   143   Robert   137   ___   (Hopkins)   137
THORNTON   Daniel   15   Rachel (Ingraham)   15
THROOP(E)   Abigail   147   148   149   Abigail ()   131   138   149   Alathea (Fales)   149   Amos   141   142   Amy (Barnes)   140   Ann(e,a)   141   148   151   155   169   Bathsheba/Bathshua   144   Benjamin   140   144   145   146   147   148   150   Bethia   140   Betsey   149   157   Billings   148   149   Carey   140   Chloe   146   Clarissa   147   Dan/Daniel   138   139   140   146   147   Deborah   139   140   Deborah (Buell)   140   Deborah (Church) (Gray)   138   139   140   Deborah

(Macey) 138 139 Dorcas 139 Dorcas (Barney) 138 139 Dorcas (Terry) 140 Dorothy (Gray) 139 Dyer 146 147 Ebenezer 142 Eliza(beth) 138 140 144 145 146 148 150 Eliza (Coggeshall) 43 Eliza (Pearse) 149 Elizabeth (Cole) (Cole) 142 143 Elizabeth (Lymon) 140 Elizabeth (Mann) 148 149 Elizabeth (Stanbury) 144 145 Esther/Hester 142 148 150 Frances 141 Frances (Dana) 141 Frances (Davis) 141 George 145 148 149 150 Hannah 87 88 106 148 149 156 157 159 Hannah (Morton) 149 Hannah (Walker) 149 Isabella 146 Jerusha 150 John 138 141 142 143 145 146 147 151 155 John Rutherford 145 Joseph 140 144 145 Josiah 145 Lidiah/Lydia 138 139 142 144 145 147 148 150 Macey 140 Martha 141 144 146 Martha (Cobleigh/Coblye) 138 143 144 Mary 18 34 35 90 106 131 138 139 140 141 142 144 145 146 148 149 Mary (Bateman) (Smith) 140 Mary (Billings) 147 148 156 157 Mary (Burgess) 140 Mary (Chapman) 137 138 139 Mary (Gager) 147 Mary (Heal[e]y) 149 Mehitable (Bliss) 145 Mercy 31 138 139 147 148 Mercy (Mansfield) 145 Molly 149 Nathaniel 141 Octavia 147 Pamella 149 Peggy 149 Phebe 143 Phebe (Hall) 142 Priscilla 146 Rachel (Terry) 140 Rebecca 141 142 Rebecca (Smith) 138 141 151 155 Rhoda 141 Samuel 139 141 148 149 Sarah 143 144 147 148 149 Sarah () 142 Sarah (Hand) 140 Sarah (Smith) 144 Submit 140 Submit (Clarke) 139 Susannah 140 146 147 148 150 Susannah (Carey) 140 147 Susannah (Gallop) 145 Susannah (Taylor) 138 141 Sybil/Sybel 147 Sybel (Dyer) 140 145 146 Thomas 31 138 139 146 147 148 149 150 156 157 William 34 71 137 138 139 140 143 144 145 147 148 149 157 Zerviah (Bissell) 140 Ziporah (Mann) 139 147
THURSTON David 150 Elizabeth 68 John 150 Jonathan 136 Patience 136 Rebecca 156 167 Sarah () 136
TIBBITTS Elizabeth (Wood) 75 Thomas 75
TIFFANY Hezekiah 52 Sarah 52 Sarah (Adams) 52 ___ 52
TILLEY Elizabeth 7 91 100
TIMBERLAKE Hannah 9
TISDALE Anne 32
TOMAN Martha 152 Martha (Newton) 33 151 152 155 Stephen 151 152 Thomas 152
TOMKINS Elizabeth (Wardwell) 169 Nathaniel 169
TOOGOOD Ann 75
TOPPIN Abigail () (Burroughs) 60
TORREY Angel 48 Elizabeth/Betsey 27 Hannah () 48 Josiah 136 Judith 48 Mary 136 Naomi 29 Sarah (Wilson) (Batt) 136
TOWNSEND Elizabeth (Howland) 100 101 Nathan 100 101

Rev Solomon   21   103
TREBY/TREEBE   Abigail (Hazard)   40   Elizabeth ()   39   Honora (Sanford)   39   John   39   Mehitable   39   Mehitable (Shepard)   39   Mehitable (Wilkins)   39   Peter   39   129   Ruth   39   Samuel   39   Sarah (Richardson)   39   40   Susanna   129   130   Susannah ()   39   Susannah (Church)   129   Wilkins   39
TROOP   see THROOP(E)
TUCKER   Mary   139
TURNER   Rev David   68   Mary (Wardwell)   169   Nathaniel   169
TUTTLE   Sarah   93
TWING   John   43   Mercy ()   43
TYLER   Hannah (Wardwell)   166   Joseph   166
UNIS   Alice (Church)   6   9   Paul   6   9
USHER   Ann ()   72   Anne Francis   72   George F.   34   George Finney   72   Hezekiah   72   Rev John   25   72   97   Rebecca S. B.   34   Sarah/Sally (Finney)   72
VAN DOORN   Anthony   19   Hannah   20   Lydia (Munro)   19   Mark Anthony   19   Martha   19   Moses   19   Phebe (Manchester)   20   Ruth (Ingraham)   19
VAUGHAN   Daniel   144   Elizabeth   144   John   144   Martha   144   Martha (Throope)   144   Mary   144
VERNON   Elizabeth (Paine) (Prince)   22   23   24   25   Samuel   22   24   170
VIALL   Elizabeth   10   Samuel   152
VICKERY   Joseph   15   Mary   15   Susannah   15
VIGIL   Hulda   27
VINAL   Rev William   47
WADSWORTH   Alice   3   Elisha   3   Elizabeth (Wiswall)   3
WALDO   Deborah   77
WALDRON   Abby Cary   87   162   Abigail/Abby   11   148   153   157   158   159   161   Abigail (West)   156   Abraham   11   Alexander   11   Allen   91   152   160   Ambrose   21   87   129   148   157   159   160   161   Ann(e)   141   154   155   157   Ann (a,e) (Throope)   141   148   151   155   169   Anstis   87   88   141   155   156   160   Benjamin   11   98   100   148   151   157   159   Benjamin B(osworth)   154   Betsey   157   160   Billings   21   87   148   157   158   159   160   161   Bridget (Rice)   11   150   Charlotte (Coggeshall)   159   Cornelius   141   148   151   155   156   169   D.   90   Daniel   32   33   36   152   153   154   157   160   David   21   157   160   Edward   11   Eliza(beth)   21   33   100   153   154   157   160   162   Elizabeth ()   98   100   157   161   Eliza (Martin)   156   Elizabeth (Allin)   152   Elizabeth (Howland)   158   Elizabeth Jackson   161   Ellen Smith   159   Eveline   157   160   Frances   154   Frances (Bosworth)   33   154   Frederick   157   160   George   11   141   150   153   154   157   Hannah   87   88   151   152   153   158   159   161   162   Hannah (Briggs)   11   Hannah (Diman)   87   161   Hannah (Gladding)   87   158   160   161   Hannah (Hoar?)   151   Hannah (Throope)

21 87 88 106 148 156 157 159 Harriet/Harriot
159 160 Harriet Newell 161 Henry 157 160 Isaac
5 11 57 141 150 151 155 156 157 Jacob 151
Jemima 160 Jemima (Oxx) 157 159 160 John 87 98
100 141 148 151 152 153 155 156 157 158 160
161 John H. 161 John Wardwell 159 Jonathan 153
Jonathan Diman 161 Joseph 33 141 148 151 152 153
155 157 159 Leah 90 141 155 156 Leonard 33 87
153 154 161 Levi 160 Lucretia (Gladding) 87 88
158 Lucy B. or C. 159 Lydia 161 Lydia M. (Gray)
158 Lydia (Salisbury) 148 157 160 Marshall 87 161
162 Martha 151 153 Martha (Drowne) 157 Martha F.
(Cole) 161 Martha/Patty (Gladding) 91 160 Martha
(Hadwin) 161 Martha (Newton) (Toman) 33 141 151
155 Mary/Maria 11 159 160 161 Mary Billings 21
160 Mary (Fales) 154 Mercy/Nancy 33 87 155 161
Molly 33 36 153 154 Molly/Mary (Ingraham) 21 160
162 Nancy see Mercy Nancy Roth 152 Nathaniel 21 87
88 106 141 148 149 152 153 155 156 157 158
159 160 161 Newton 33 153 154 Phebe 154 Phebe
(Reynolds) 32 33 36 152 153 154 Polly 87 157
160 161 Polly () 158 Priscilla 5 98 99 100 141
152 155 Priscilla (Byfield) 5 11 57 Rachel 112
141 155 156 Rachel (Baker) 11 141 150 Rebecca 87
106 148 153 157 159 160 161 162 Rebecca (Peck)
152 153 Richard 129 Richard S(mith) 87 88 158
161 162 Ruth 127 131 152 Ruth (Bourne) 153 Ruth
(Gray) 148 158 Samuel 11 21 33 148 150 151 154
157 159 160 162 Sarah 87 141 155 156 169 Sarah
(Martindale) 33 154 Sarah (Munro) 154 Sarah (Wardwell) 159 Susan (Gladding) 90 Susanna () 157 Thomas 88 148 151 152 157 158 William 11 157 William Coggeshall 159 William T./William Throop 148 157
159 160 Willoby/Willoughby 141 155 156
WALKER Abigail 164 David 149 Eliza(beth) 163 164
  Elizabeth (Parris) 162 163 Hannah 49 72 149 Hannah () 163 164 Hannah (Bosworth) 49 Jane 162 163
  John 163 164 Mary 162 163 164 Patience (Coggeshall) 164 Rachel 164 Rebecca 164 Sarah () 149
  Thomas 162 163 William 162 163 164 ___ 49
WALLACE Elizabeth (Little) 163 ___ 163
WALLEY Elizabeth 1 51 Hannah? 101 John 1 2 4 5
  Lydia 1 2 Sarah 1 Thomas 1
WANTON Abigail (Church) 9 Abigail (Wilkins) 39 George
  9 39
WARD sister of James Burrill 59
WARDWELL Abigail 82 105 165 166 168 169 Abigail
  (Smith) 126 127 Alice 84 165 Alice () 165 Allen
  104 126 127 168 Anna/Nancy 156 169 Ann (Liscomb)
  167 Benjamin 104 105 165 166 168 169 Daniel 104
  168 David 169 Dolly/Dorothy (Fales) 34 35 Eleanor

Taylor 126 Elizabeth 104 105 167 168 169 Elizabeth (Church) 105 Elizabeth () (Holmes) 166 169 Elizabeth (May) 159 George S. 126 Grace 165 166 Grace () 49 165 166 Hannah 105 165 166 167 168 Hannah Carey (Munro) 106 Hannah (Swan) 18 Huldah (Goff) 105 Isaac 87 156 169 James 105 165 166 167 168 Jemima 103 167 168 Jemima (Lindsey) 125 168 Jemima (Oxx) (Bourne) 168 John 18 87 90 104 125 126 128 167 168 Jonathan 156 169 Joseph 104 105 125 159 165 166 167 168 Josiah 105 168 Josiah Smith 126 Lois (Frisbie) 166 Lydia 156 167 168 169 Martha 104 167 168 Martha (Giddings/Giddens) 104 105 166 167 Martin 105 Mary 92 104 105 106 125 126 165 166 167 168 169 Mary () 104 166 169 Mary (Howland) 103 104 169 Mary (Kinsman) (Rindge/Ring) 165 Mary S. 126 Mehitabel (Carey) 61 Mehitabel (Howland) 103 105 168 Mr 61 Nancy R. 126 Nathaniel 34 35 104 168 Olive 169 Peggy 18 Phebe 104 124 125 166 168 Phebe (Bassett) 166 Phebe (Howland) 87 90 103 104 125 126 168 Priscilla 168 Rebecca 17 20 129 166 167 Samuel 104 105 106 168 169 Col S(amuel?) 90 169 Sarah 49 87 105 156 159 161 165 166 167 169 Sarah (Ingraham) 166 167 Sarah (Lindsey) 169 Sarah (Smith) 105 Sarah (Waldron) 87 155 156 169 Stephen 105 167 168 Susanna(h) 84 87 90 104 107 160 167 168 169 Tabitha 104 168 Uzell/Uzal 49 164 165 166 169 William 104 105 165 166 169 William T. 126 Willoby 156 169
WARREN Ann 163 Elizabeth 8 59 Nathan 158 Priscilla () 158 Richard 8 22 32 47 59 102 103 125 139 140 148 149 153 156 163
WATERMAN Abigail 95 Richard 95
WATSON Daniel 33 Elizabeth 32 33 118 Elizabeth (Reynolds) 32 John 32 33 Lucia (Marston) 33 Sarah (Rogers) 33
WATTS Mercy 75
WAUGH Alexander 140 Elizabeth (Throope) 140
WEAVER Elisha 164 John 164 Mary (Walker) 164 William 164
WELD Edmund 37 Sarah (Reynolds) 36 37
WENSLEY/WINSLEY Hopestill 4
WEST Abigail 156 Benjamin 124 Elizabeth 123 Elizabeth (Smith) 124
WESTCOTT Mercy 101 102
WHEATON John 85
WHEELDING Hannah (Gorham) 8 Joseph 8
WHEELER Eliza (Pearse) (Throope) 149 Jeremiah 149
WHEELWRIGHT Jeremiah 45 46 John 46 Mary 7 Mary (Bosworth) 45 46 Mary (Snell) 46
WHIPPLE Sarah (Gorham) (Taylor) 94 95 ___ 95

WHITE   Richard   170
WIGHT   Rev Henry   21   35   128   153
WILB(O)UR/WILBORE   John   136   Mary   136   Mary (Carey)   63   Mr   63   Sarah (Palmer)   136
WILCOX   David Sands   162   Serephine (Diman)   162
WILKINS   Abigail   38   39   Anstis (Gold) (Bissett)   38   John   38   40   Mary   38   Mehitabel   38   39   Samuel   38   39
WILLARD   Anna/Hannah   48   David   48   Hannah (Cutter)   48   Simon   2
WILLET   Martha   120   Mary (Brown)   120   Thomas   120
WILLIAMS   Bathsheba   140   Deborah   140   Deborah (Throope)   140   Dorothy (Paine)   22   23   24   Elizabeth   24   40   Elizabeth (Rogers)   40   118   Elizabeth (Watson)   118   Experience   118   Frances (Deighton)   40   118   George   140   Hannah (Robinson)   40   118   Jemima/Jinnus   57   58   65   Joanna   140   John   22   23   24   40   118   Joseph   118   Lydia (King)   40   Mary   140   Mehitable   118   Nathaniel   40   118   140   Priscilla   140   Rebecca   140   Richard   40   118   Sarah (Dean)   118   Silas   118   Simeon   118   Submit   140   Theody   140   Timothy   118
WILLOUGHBY   Abigail (Bartholomew)   1   Francis   1   Nehemiah   1   Sarah (Walley) (Chauncey)   1
WILLS/WYLLS   Elizabeth   117   Lydia   137
WILSON   Amy (Greenman)   170   Benjamin   170   Elizabeth (Coggeshall)   170   Esther/Hester   170   Esther ()   170   John   170   Mary   170   Sarah   136   Susanna   30   35   William   170
WINSLOW   Edward   3   Elizabeth   2   John   88   89   Josiah   2   Lydia (Gladding)   88   89   Mary   134   Penelope (Pelham)   2
WISWALL   Elizabeth   3
WITT   Ann   96   138   139
WOLCOTT   Simon   37
WOOD   Elizabeth   68   75   Elizabeth (Thurston)   68   Hannah   149   152   153   John   75   153   Jonathan   68   Mary (Church)   149   153   Olive   169
WOODBRIDGE   Rev Benjamin   6   171
WOODBURY   Abigail   171   Abigail (Coffin)   171   Benjamin   11   Elizabeth   171   Elizabeth (Church) (Rosbotham) (Sampson)   11   41   Elizabeth (Patch)   170   171   Elizabeth (Sampson)   115   Hugh   40   41   170   171   John   29   171   Jonathan   41   42   115   171   Katherine   42   Katherine (Osborne)   41   115   Lydia ()   42   Margaret   42   115   Margaret (Osborne)   41   42   115   Mary   171   Mary ()   11   40   41   115   171   Mary (Dixey)   40   171   Mary (Reynolds)   29   171   Nathaniel   171   Priscilla   171   Samuel   11   40   41   42   115   171   Sarah   41   42   115   171   William   40   41   170
WOODCOCK   Sarah   44
WOODMAN   Edith   9   Hannah (Timberlake)   9   John   9

WOODWARD Elizabeth 137
WOODWORTH Catharine 68 Deborah 47 Elizabeth 135
  Walter 68
WRIGHT Hannah 96 97 Robert 96 97
YORK Jemima 95 Mary 108
YOUNG David 133 Elizabeth 133 George 133 Isaac
  133 Joyce (Smith) 133 Robert 30 Sarah 133 Sarah
  (Reynolds) 30 William 133

www.ingramcontent.com/pod-product-compliance
Lightning Source LLC
Chambersburg PA
CBHW050146170426
43197CB00011B/1986